FIONN DAVENPORT

D0967236

DUBLIN

C I T Y   G U I D E

Crossing distinctive Ha'penny Bridge (p126) would once have cost you said ha'penny.

Definition of a great city: a place that makes virtue out of vice and knows exactly where to find fun. Welcome to Dublin, the greatest city in Europe.

At first glance, it's kind of difficult to see why. Dublin isn't as sexy or as sultry as other Europea capitals, the architecture is a bit of a jumble and it seems *everyone* has something to compla about. Dubs can be brutally unsentimental about their city, but their warts-and-all attachme is born out of a genuine love of a place that oozes personality, a city whose soul and sociabili makes it the most charismatic of capitals.

Sure, the almost mythical economic growth of the last 15 years and the explosion of multicu turalism, which has seen people settle in the city from fields as far flung as Nairobi and Nagoy have given the city a cosmopolitan strut and swagger it never had before – not to mention whole new world of distractions and delights to rival those of any other city of comparable siz But Dublin's greatest draw remains Dubliners themselves, both native-born and blown in.

You should visit the excellent museums, amble through the landscaped parks and enga; with Dublin's myriad cultural offerings, but make enough time for socialising, the beating hea that makes this city thrive. Garrulous, amiable and witty, Dubliners at their ease are the greate hosts of all, providing a life-affirming experience that will restore your faith in human natur How many other places can you say that about?

CITY LIFE

The designer gear hangs neatly in the wardrobe, the golf clubs sit tidily in the boot of the car and Jarek the Polish tiler and his crew are coming to do up the bathroom first thing Monday morning. Next week, let's celebrate the new house in that trendy Thai place the *Irish Times* gave such a great review to – I just hope we can get a table.

This yuppie idyll is just one element of the new Dublin, but the themes are vaguely universal to a city that is just now getting used to the most radical transformation in its thousand-plus year history, where for most of it the majority of Dubliners didn't have a pot to piss in and weren't in the least bit concerned with spray-on tans and Versace bling.

Despite common belief to the contrary, your average Dubliner isn't a smiling optimist but a fatalist who knows the immeasurable value of black humour in getting through the tough times – and in this climate, 'tough' means a crappy health service, venal politicians who just can't help doing it for themselves and a near-permanent gridlock that would try the patience of Job.

Everyone loves the prosperity, but many Dubliners are suspicious of the crass commercialism that accompanies it, and the Celtic cubs are dismissed as a bunch of D4 dickheads. What the hell is D4? Only the most sought-after postal district in town, comprising the southern suburbs of Donnybrook, Sandymount and Ballsbridge. Disdain and envy are often comic bedfellows.

> 'visit excellent museums, amble through landscaped parks and engage with Dublin's myriad cultural offerings, but make enough time for socialising, the beating heart that makes this city thrive'

Feel the merriment on an Irish-music pub crawl (p240) at the Auld Dubliner (p168), Temple Bar.

HIGHLIGHTS

ARTY FACTS

Dublin's collection of canvases and other arty bits are signed by some of the world's most famous names, both classic and contemporary, and can be found in galleries and museums on both sides of the Liffey.

❶ National Gallery
The home of the Great Masters and Ireland's own Jack B Yeats. (p79)

❷ Dublin City Gallery – The Hugh Lane
A priceless collection including Francis Bacon's actual studio. (p101)

❸ Irish Museum of Modern Art
Outstanding examples of the best of contemporary art. (p96)

❹ Russborough House
A collection so stunning they tried to steal it – four times. (p224)

❺ Douglas Hyde Gallery
Trinity College gets a dose of cutting-edge contemporary art. (p70)

1 St Stephen's Green
Office workers, strollers and lovers all flock to this landscaped square. (p71)

2 Hill of Howth
Climb through the gorse and bracken for stunning views. (p214)

3 Malahide Demesne
Watch cricket in the expansive grounds surrounding the old castle. (p216)

4 Phoenix Park
A huge park twice the size of London's major city parks put together. (p114)

5 Merrion Square
Elegant, graceful and surrounded by Georgian beauty. (p77)

RUB OF THE GREEN

Not that made-up nonsense about good Irish luck, but the green lungs that help Dubliners breathe, relax and take a break from the grey concrete that surrounds them: Dublin's beautiful green spaces.

1 Croke Park
The home of Gaelic games and – for now – rugby and football. (p117)

2 Fairyhouse Racecourse
Come for the Grand National on Easter Monday. (p193)

3 Shelbourne Park
A night at the dogs is one of the best experiences in town. (p193)

4 Dalymount Park
Home of the Bohemians Football Club, aka the Gypsies, pride of the northside. (p190)

5 Donnybrook Rugby Ground
Provincial side Leinster plays at this handsome ground in Dublin 4. (p194)

A SPORTING CHANCE

Dubliners are passionate about their sport, whether it's supporting the Blues playing Gaelic Football or watching the dog in trap four take your betting dreams and crush them against the rail.

RETAIL THERAPY

Did you know that Europe's busiest shopping street is in Dublin? At first we were surprised too, but take a walk down Grafton or Henry Sts and you'll see why.

❶ Moore St Market
Where the genuine Molly Malones sell their flowery, meaty and fishy wares. (p139)

❷ George's St Arcade
Beautiful covered Victorian arcade for the hipsters and younger spirits. (p135)

❸ Costume
Elegant, cutting-edge designs for women with their own style. (p133)

❹ Fallon & Byrne
This gourmet New York–style deli is all the rage. (p133)

❺ Meeting House Square Market
Organic foods and tastes from everywhere at this weekend fair. (p139)

DUBLIN DESIGNS

Dublin's beautiful architecture is not just about the Georgian city – there are buildings both old and new that will make you stop in your tracks and pull out the camera.

① National Museum of Ireland – Decorative Arts & History
The army was loath to leave this extraordinary former barracks. (p105)

② Berkeley Library
Brilliant, brutalist building in a thoroughly modern style. (p70)

③ St Patrick's Cathedral
Ireland's longest church is also the city's most impressive. (p90)

④ Royal Hospital Kilmainham
A stunning example of the pre-Georgian Anglo-Dutch style. (p96)

⑤ Leinster House
Ireland's parliament is a suitably magnificent Palladian mansion. (p82)

1 JJ Smyth's
Nod your head approvingly at the best jazz sessions in town. Nice. (p181)

2 Cobblestone
Superb nightly music sessions performed by traditional musicians. (p183)

3 Grafton Street
Brilliant buskers guarantee top-class music...for free. (p181)

4 Boom Boom Room
Experimental noises in all genres at this super-hip venue. (p182)

5 Vicar Street
Soul, jazz, blues and other sultry sounds for discerning audiences. (p183)

A MUSICAL NOTE

Whether it's jazz or rock, traditional or totally experimental, Dublin's musical scene is one of the unavoidable highlights of any trip to the city – you'll hear music everywhere.

1 Kehoe's
Atmospheric, beautiful Kehoe's is popular with Dubliners and visitors alike. (p165)

2 Mulligan's
Tourists aside, it's what a traditional pub should look and sound like. (p167)

3 Long Hall
A Victorian classic that has retained its integrity. (p165)

4 Grogan's
The favourite pub of Dublin's artists and writers. (p165)

5 Gravediggers
This unreconstructed treasure is worth the trip to the suburbs. (p172)

A PINT OF PLAIN

As the world discovers the exported Irish pub, the traditional boozer is becoming something of an endangered species in Dublin, but there are still enough of the real deal to quench your thirst for a genuine experience.

JUST FOR KICKS

'Dublin can be heaven/with coffee at 11/and a stroll down Grafton St.' Or so goes the old song. Test the theory with some aimless ambles that will prove to be not so aimless after all.

1 Temple Bar
Look for the zaniest hen party or the largest group of visiting students. (p84)

2 South Wall
Great views along the south wall to Poolbeg Lighthouse. (p100)

3 Grand Canal
Be inspired: follow in the footsteps of poet Patrick Kavanagh. (p98)

4 Phoenix Park
Winter football at the Fifteen Acres: at least it's not you. (p116)

5 Killiney
Be on Bono Watch in the neighbourhood of the stars. (p218)

PSST. TELL NO-ONE

Some of the city's most memorable attractions have escaped the tourist hordes and the marketing hype – for now.

1 Marsh's Library
A magnificently preserved scholars' library next to St Patrick's Cathedral. (p93)

2 James Joyce Museum
Martello tower, where James Joyce's *Ulysses* kicks off. (p218)

3 Iveagh Gardens
The 'forgotten' gardens of the city's Georgian parks. (p75)

4 Shaw Birthplace
The restored birthplace of one of Dublin's Nobel Prize winners. (p76)

5 War Memorial Gardens
Hardly anyone visits these Lutyens-designed gardens to the west. (p97)

CONTENTS

Continued from previous page.

THE AUTHOR

Fionn Davenport

Half-Italian and a lifelong supporter of Liverpool Football Club, Fionn is the ideal Dubliner, a native son in love with the city of his birth but with one eye forever on somewhere else. He's left the city many times – usually looking for warmer weather or a job – but always he returns, because too much sun is bad for you and all jobs get boring. But the reason he loves Dublin so much is that it treats gallows humour as high art: why look for a straight answer when a funny one is far more satisfying. Lonely Planet has kept him busy for the last 12 years or so, but in recent times Fionn has branched out, hosting his own radio show on Newstalk 106–108 (you can listen to *Culture Shock* online at www.newstalk.ie) and making the occasional foray into television.

FIONN'S TOP DUBLIN DAY

My best Dublin day begins with a copy of the *Irish Times* and a caffeine Big Gulp, followed by a stroll through St Stephen's Green (p71). It's one of those warm, sunny autumn days Dublin regularly gets as recompense for a wet summer, so everyone is in a good mood and I don't have to work – the perfect recipe for idleness. I nurture my retail chi around Grafton St (p130) and assuage my material guilt with a silent visit to my favourite museum of all, the Chester Beatty Library (p70), home to some of the most beautiful objets d'art and books I've ever seen. A freshly made sandwich in Fallon & Byrne (p146) is all I need for lunch, after which I meet a friend visiting from out of town and I show off my knowledge of the lesser-known attractions of the city by taking her to Marsh's Library (p93) and the magnificent Memorial Gardens (p97) down by Islandbridge. A quick skip across the Liffey and we're on the way to the Strawberry Beds (p115) and a drink at the Wren's Nest before heading back across the city towards the south wall. I time our walk out to the lighthouse with the setting of the sun – there's surely no more romantic spot in Dublin (that's right: my friend is very friendly!). We follow dinner in Town Bar & Grill (p145) with a show: perhaps a gig at Vicar Street (p183) or a play at the Gate (p186), followed by late drinks at the Long Hall (p165) on South Great George's St or, if we're on the north side, at the small but splendid Sackville Lounge (p172). And then it's off home, and for my perfect day, it's a room in the main house of the Merrion Hotel (p201)!

Dublin is a cinch in virtually every respect but budget, where it's often a pinch. The city is small, easy to get around and offers no greater challenge than struggling to be cultural the morning after the night before. That is, of course, if you don't care about the gridlock or the fact that nightclubs are calling chucking out time when their equivalents in southern climes are just getting going. Otherwise, just get stuck in.

WHEN TO GO

You don't like the weather? Wait 15 minutes. So goes the old refrain about a city where it's virtually impossible to predict the climate other than to make vague generalisations about it being warmer in summer than in winter – which are true, at least most of the time. From June to August, the days are reasonably warm and – most importantly – very long. At the height of summer you won't need to turn on lights until after 10pm. It is also peak tourist season, which means there are far more people pretty much everywhere and prices are at their highest.

Not surprisingly, most of the yearly festivals occur during these times so as to take advantage of the crowds and the more favourable weather. But then there was the 'summer' of 2007, when the thermometer barely rose above 15°C and it rained for 59 days in a row: the wettest since records began.

Spring and autumn are usually good times for a peek, although the city's popularity as a tourist destination can often blur the lines between mid- and high-season tourism. Still, you have a better chance of some peace and quiet and the weather can be surprisingly better in April and September than in mid-July – again, it's all part of the uncertainty principle.

Winters are dark, wet and cold, with December the wettest of all (an average 76mm of rainfall), but hey, it's Christmas and everyone is high-spirited; plus, you can enjoy indoor pleasures and you won't feel as guilty lounging in the pub. January is the only time the city's not really itself, when it's a little quiet and cranky after the festivities, and the days seem interminably gloomy.

FESTIVALS

Dubliners need to justify their propensity for celebrating stuff – 'it's Wednesday!' just doesn't work for some – so the city's party planners have conveniently laid on an ever-changing menu of festivals and events for everyone to feel better about their hangovers.

January
NEW YEAR'S CELEBRATIONS
Experience the birth of another new year with a cheer among thousands of revellers at Dublin's iconic Christ Church Cathedral (p94).

ADVANCE PLANNING

From Easter to September, queues can be horrendous at popular attractions; arrive early. Most fee-paying sights offer discounts to students, the elderly, children and families. If you're serious about sightseeing, buy the Dublin Pass (p234) as soon as you set foot in the airport – it'll give you a free ride on the Aircoach.

Two Weeks Before You Go

Advance purchase is a must if you want to take in a hit play at the Abbey (www.abbeytheatre.ie; see also p184) or the Gate (www.gate-theatre.ie; see also p186). A couple of weeks ahead should be plenty of time. Ditto if you want to watch a game at Croke Park (p117), especially for the latter stages of the championship, which runs from April to September.

Three Days Before You Go

The very best and newest of Dublin's restaurants can be pretty tough to get a booking in for the first few months of business, but you shouldn't have any problems a couple of days in advance.

ONLY IN DUBLIN

All-Ireland Finals (☎ 836 3222; www.gaa.ie) The climax of the year for fans of Gaelic games when the season's most successful county teams battle it out for the All-Ireland championships in hurling and football, on the second and fourth Sundays in September, respectively. The capital is swamped with fans from the competing counties, draped in their colours and swept along by their good-natured, family-oriented exuberance.

Bloomsday (☎ 878 8547; www.jamesjoyce.ie) Every 16 June a bunch of weirdos wander around the city dressed in Edwardian gear, talking nonsense in dramatic tones. They're not mad – at least not clinically – they're only Blooms-dayers committed to commemorating James Joyce's epic *Ulysses* through readings, performances and re-created meals, including Leopold Bloom's famous breakfast of 'kidneys with the faint scent of urine'. Yummy.

Christmas Dip at the Forty-Foot Possibly the most hardcore hangover cure known to man, this event takes place at 11am on Christmas Day at a famous swimming spot below the Martello tower – made famous by James Joyce in *Ulysses* – in Sandycove, 9km from the centre of Dublin. A group of the very brave, and certifiably insane, plunge into the icy water and swim 20m to the rocks and back. With heads cleared after their frozen frolics, each heads home for Christmas lunch.

Handel's Messiah (Map p85; ☎ 677 2255; Neal's Music Hall, Fishamble St) *Messiah,* Handel's most highly esteemed composition and one of the most renowned works in English sacred music, was performed for the first time at this site in today's Temple Bar on 13 April 1742, an event commemorated with a special gala-style performance each April.

Liffey Swim (☎ 833 2434) Since 1924, at summer's end (late August/early September), hundreds of swimmers – or lunatics, as they're colloquially known – traditionally dive into the Sniffy Liffey for a swim through 2km of mud and murk in the centre of Dublin, from Rory O'More Bridge to the Custom House. There are separate handicap races for men and women and it's fun to line the bank and watch the competitors trying not to swallow a drop. You can see it depicted in Jack B Yeats' famous *Liffey Swim* painting in the National Gallery (p79).

February

JAMESON DUBLIN INTERNATIONAL FILM FESTIVAL

☎ 872 1122; www.dubliniff.com

Local flicks, arty international films and advance releases of mainstream movies make up the menu of the city's film festival, which runs over two weeks in late February (see the boxed text, p178).

SIX NATIONS RUGBY

☎ 647 3800; www.irishrugby.ie

Pending the reconstruction of the Lansdowne Road stadium, Ireland will play its home games at Croke Park, in the northern suburb of Drumcondra (see p117). The season runs from February to April.

March

ST PATRICK'S FESTIVAL

☎ 676 3205; www.stpatricksfestival.ie

The mother of all Irish festivals. Hundreds of thousands gather to 'honour' St Patrick over four days around 17 March on city streets and in venues throughout the centre. Events include the three-day Guinness Fleadh music festival in Temple Bar.

May

DUBLIN GAY THEATRE FESTIVAL

www.gaytheatre.ie

A fortnight devoted exclusively to gay theatre – plays by gay writers past and present that have a gay or gay-related theme.

HEINEKEN GREEN ENERGY FESTIVAL

☎ 0818 719 300; www.heinekenmusic.ie

A four-day festival that takes place in different venues around the city, with an open-air concert in the grounds of Dublin Castle as a highlight.

June

BUD RISING

☎ 0818 719 300; www.budweiser.ie

What began as a movable feast of music a few years ago at venues all over the city is now just a series of big gigs at Marlay Park from June to September.

CONVERGENCE FESTIVAL

☎ 674 6415; www.sustainable.ie; 15-19 Essex St

A 10-day green festival on sustainable living, with a diverse programme of workshops, exhibitions and children's activities in Temple Bar.

DIVERSIONS

☎ 677 2255; www.temple-bar.ie
Free outdoor music, children's and film events occur during weekends from June to September in Temple Bar's Meeting House Sq.

DUBLIN WRITERS FESTIVAL

www.dublinwritersfestival.com
Four-day literature festival attracting Irish and international writers to its readings, performances and talks.

MARDI GRAS

☎ 873 4932; www.dublinpride.org
Dublin's Gay Pride event has turned into a week-long festival of parties, workshops, readings and more parties at gay venues around town, although these are just to warm up for the parade that takes place – and takes over – on the last Saturday of June or the first Saturday of July.

WOMEN'S MINI-MARATHON

☎ 670 9461; www.womensminimarathon.ie
This 10km road race for charity (on the second Sunday in June) is the largest of its kind in the world and attracts around 40,000 runners each year.

July

OXEGEN

☎ 0818 719 300; www.oxegen.ie; Punchestown Racecourse, County Kildare
This fabulous music festival takes place over the July weekend closest to 12 July and manages to pack a few dozen heavy-weight acts into its two-day line-up.

August

DUBLIN HORSE SHOW

Royal Dublin Society (RDS); ☎ 668 0866; www.dublinhorseshow.com
The first week of August is when Ireland's horsey set trot down to the capital for the social highlight of the year. Particularly popular is the Aga Khan Cup, an international-class competition packed with often heart-stopping excitement in which eight nations participate.

DUN LAOGHAIRE FESTIVAL OF WORLD CULTURES

☎ 230 1035; www.festivalofworldcultures.com
A colourful multicultural music, art and theatre festival featuring up to 200 different acts is held on the last weekend of August in the southern suburb of Dun Laoghaire.

ELECTRIC PICNIC

☎ 478 9093; www.electricpicnic.ie; Stradbally Castle, County Laois
Our favourite festival of all is in the grounds of Stradbally Castle, County Laois, about 80km southwest of Dublin; this two-day experience in August combines top class acts with organic food and a mind-body-soul area. Let your good vibes flow.

SLANE FESTIVAL

☎ 041-982 4207; www.heinekenmusic.ie
Traditionally the biggest gig of the year, this August festival takes place in the grounds of Slane Castle, County Meath, about 45km northwest of Dublin, and usu-ally features the biggest stars of the musi-cal firmament: REM, Bruce Springsteen, the Stones and U2 have all played here.

September–October

DUBLIN FRINGE FESTIVAL

☎ 1850 374 643; www.fringefest.com
Our favourite theatre showcase precedes the main theatre festival (following) with 700 performers and 100 events – ranging from cutting edge to crap – taking place over three weeks. It's held in The Famous Spiegeltent, which has been erected in different positions in recent years; for more, see the boxed text, p185.

DUBLIN THEATRE FESTIVAL

☎ 677 8439; www.dublintheatrefestival.com
This two-week festival is Europe's largest and showcases the best of Irish and inter-national productions at various locations around town. In tandem with the theatre festival is a children's season at the Ark (p86).

BULMER'S COMEDY FESTIVAL

☎ 679 3323; www.bulmerscomedy.ie
Big laughs over three weeks from an ever-widening choice of comic talents, both known and unknown. It takes place at more than 20 venues throughout the city.

DUBLIN CITY MARATHON

☎ 677 8439; www.dublincitymarathon.ie
If you fancy a 42km (and a bit) running tour through the streets of the city on the last Monday of October, you'll have to register at least three weeks in advance. Otherwise, you can have a lie-in and watch the winner cross the finishing line on O'Connell St at around 10.30am.

DUBLIN ELECTRONIC ARTS FESTIVAL

DEAF; ☎ 872 8933; www.deafireland.com
A must for anyone into the cutting edge of music, DEAF showcases the work of some truly innovative musical – and visual – talents, both home-grown and international. From moog to movies, this is the future, now. Venues vary; check the website for details.

GREEN SYNERGY

☎ 0818 719 300; www.heinekenmusic.ie
A small five-day live music festival centred on the venues on Wexford and Camden Sts – Anseo, Crawdaddy, Tripod and the Village, among others.

SAMHAIN/HALLOWE'EN

Tens of thousands take to the city streets on 31 October for a night-time parade, fireworks, street theatre, drinking and music in this traditional pagan festival celebrating the dead, end of the harvest and Celtic new year.

December

LEOPARDSTOWN RACES

☎ 289 3607; www.leopardstown.com
Blow your dough and your post-Christmas crankiness at this historic and hugely popular racing festival at one of Europe's loveliest courses. Races run from 26 to 30 December.

FUNDERLAND

Royal Dublin Society (RDS); ☎ 668 0866; www.rds.ie
Dublin's traditional funfair (from 26 December to 9 January) features all kinds of stomach-turning rides and arcade games, as well as hundreds of thousands of light bulbs and millions of reasons why the kids needn't be cooped up indoors.

COSTS & MONEY

Wondering if Dublin is expensive is a bit like asking if Elizabeth Taylor owns a wedding dress. Dublin's pricey tag is obvious, but if you think it's bad for you, imagine what it's like for those who live here. According to Mercer (the folks who do those cost-of-living indices), Dublin ranks 16th in the list of the world's most expensive cities and comes eighth on the European list after London, Paris, Milan, Oslo, Copenhagen and every big town in Switzerland. You won't find nearly as many rip-off merchants as you do in some of the major tourist destinations of continental Europe (well, apart from in the Temple Bar area and taxi drivers from the airport) but Dublin *is* very expensive these days and you don't generally get value for money. Accommodation, meals, taxis, entertainment and shopping will all make your wallet sag and your purse pout.

Let's start with the big expense: accommodation. Dublin's got some pretty pricey pillows, and you won't get much change out of €200 for the better bedrooms in the city centre; a midrange room will cost upwards of €100 in the low season, while those on a tight budget will have to settle for a hostel (where dorm beds cost at least €13) or those fleapits around

NO SMOKE WITHOUT IRE

It was unenforceable. The irascible, irrepressible Irish just wouldn't be coddled by a nanny state. It would be a disaster; the police would be pulled this way and that, trying to enforce a law that went against the independent Irish spirit of iconoclasm and rebellion. It would kill tourism and put publicans out of business. Basically, it was the end of the world.

Such was the frenzy of doubt that greeted the announcement that the government was banning smoking in the workplace – which meant pretty much everywhere indoors except for one's own home. When it eventually came into effect in March 2004 after a couple of months' delay, the whole country took a deep breath…and that was it. Incredibly, Ireland went smoke-free and the withdrawal was as gentle as a spring breeze. It's true, some pubs have seen a slowdown in trade, but for the most part the only difference now is the gaggle of smokers clustered outside pubs and the different air within them, an air now scented with the dubious fragrance of beer farts.

HOW MUCH?

Admission to a big-name club on a Friday €20

CD €18.99

City-centre bus ticket up to €1.80

Cup of coffee €2.80

Petrol per litre €1.36

Pint of Guinness Temple Bar/city/suburbs €4.80/€4.10/€3.50

The Irish Times €1.70

Theatre ticket €13-25

Three-course meal with wine/beer from €40

Ticket to a Gaelic match €25-45

the northern end of Gardiner St. If you're willing to endure a little bit of taxi trauma or the tolerance test of public transport, hotels on the north side of the city or in the salubrious suburbs south of the Grand Canal will give you far more bang for your buck.

Then there's food, that other great bugbear of the value-conscious Dubliner: memorable meals don't even begin to register for less than €16 a main dish, while if you're looking to spend no more than €10 on lunch, you'd better like sandwiches. Lunch and early bird specials – those three-course things that inevitably only ever include the menu's less inviting choices – are ubiquitous and a good way to save a few euro.

So, between a place to crash and daily sustenance, you should factor in anything between €50 (at the truly budget end of the scale) and, well, the sky's limit (ok, let's say a minimum of €250) daily. Anything less than that and you're performing miracles; anything more and we want *you* to take *us* on holiday.

But Dublin is about a hell of a lot more than sleeping and eating – let's not forget the all-important nights out. The price of a pint hovers around the €4.70 mark, so you can calculate how drunk you can actually afford to get from there. And if you're really popular, there's the round system to contend with – whereby you take turns buying a round of drinks for the group. But that roughly works out even in the end, unless of course you're only in for one or two and your 10 new friends are all looking thirsty.

Phew. And that's the bad news. The good news is that you can also have a great time in Dublin without your plastic going into meltdown. Parks are all free, as are the

National Gallery (p79), National Museum (p80), Museum of Natural History (p81), Dublin City Gallery – The Hugh Lane (p101) and pretty much all of the city's other gallery spaces – not to mention our favourite collection of all: the Chester Beatty Library (p70). Cinemas all have an early-bird price for shows up to 2pm of about €5, while there's absolutely no charge for strolling along the beach in Killiney (p218), climbing Howth Head (p214) or enjoying the musical entertainment along Grafton St!

INTERNET RESOURCES

www.balconytv.com Interviews and music from a balcony in central Dublin.

www.beaut.ie A superb blog ostensibly about beauty tips but really a great commentary on the Irish and their wants.

www.blogorrah.com Brilliantly funny blog on what's really going on in Ireland.

www.dublincity.ie Dublin Corporation's own website has a great link to live traffic cams.

www.ireland.ie Official website of Discover Ireland, the public face of the Irish Tourist Board.

www.nixers.ie A good place to check if you're looking for casual work over summer.

www.overheardindublin.com Proof that the general public are better than any scriptwriter.

www.philippankov.com Great black-and-white photos of the city by a great photographer.

www.thedubliner.com Gossip, features and other Dublin-related titbits.

www.visitdublin.com Official website of Dublin Tourism.

SUSTAINABLE DUBLIN

Dublin ain't that green, but it's trying. It's been tough trying to get a city that just got rich a wet week ago *not* to buy that new car

ECOCABS

In 2007 a new fleet of ecocabs – basically modern-looking rickshaws – were introduced, offering a clean and green solution to public transport in the city centre. Ecocabs (Map pp66–7; www.ecocabs.ie) are available for up to two passengers each between 10am and 8pm daily, and are free of charge for short distances within the city centre – a gratuity for your hard-pedalling driver is always appreciated. Pick one up at the top of Grafton St, by the St Stephen's Green Shopping Centre.

or go on three foreign holidays a year, especially in a city that for generations got around in a clapped-out Ford its uncle used to own and holidayed down the road in County Wexford.

The saving grace for Dublin's small-but-growing band of eco-responsible agitators has been the queue, which has done more than any Al Gore movie to remind Dubliners that life needs to get a little more sustainable. Endless traffic jams, snaking queues at overburdened airports and just general waiting in line to get stuff drives most Dubliners crazy, so when they're informed that becoming eco-responsible will go some way towards restoring a sense of sanity, they will react positively.

Which is how they reacted when the government passed a total ban on smoking in the workplace (see the boxed text, p19) and introduced a €0.15 levy on plastic bags – which was increased to €0.22 in 2007. Within a few months of its introduction it had reduced the use of plastic bags by 90%. We urge you to use as few of them as possible; most shops sell cloth bags that can be stashed away when not in use. Also in 2007, Environment Minister John Gormley (of the Green Party) announced that on-the-spot fines for littering would be raised to €150, although we suspect he's gotten tough on litterbugs because in order to get into the coalition in the first place the Greens had to forego most of their green-friendly platform.

The best resource in town is Cultivate (Map p85; ☎ 674 5773; www.cultivate.ie; 15-19 West Essex St) in Temple Bar, Ireland's only sustainability-focused living and learning centre. It has an eco-shop and lots of information stands, and hosts workshops and classes on everything from composting to green building.

Fly Less

There are numerous boat services to Dublin from Britain and often some return fares don't cost that much more than one-way tickets, not

to mention the plethora of special offers designed to challenge the cheap flight hegemony. Boats arrive in Dublin Port or Dun Laoghaire; for details, see p229.

Stay Longer

An extended visit – as opposed to the rush-in, rush-out limitations of city break travel – is preferable because it allows for 'slow travel', the kind of exploratory travel that allows you to take your time and get to know a place without needing to rush. And it's the only way to get to know Dubliners properly!

Offsetting

Paying someone else to offset your greenhouse gas emissions isn't the perfect solution to the major issue of global warming, but it is a step in the right direction. The most popular offsetting programme involves tree-planting, but there are other schemes such as methane collection and combustion. Carbon Neutral Ireland (www.carbonneutralireland.ie) can help you calculate your emissions and work out how to offset them.

HISTORY

More than just about any other city we know, Dublin wears its history on its sleeve. Dubliners themselves are highly passionate scholars of their own history – and we mean their *own* history. Perhaps because it continues to have such a strong bearing on modern life, it's near impossible for any two Irish people to agree on the details of any one historical episode.

The general facts of the city's history are outlined in the timeline that runs at the bottom of these pages, but in order to contribute to the general debate we have included four relatively compact examinations of some facet of Dublin history that has played an important role in shaping the city's identity. On your travels, you will surely hear different spins on the same subjects and bear in mind that *everybody* has a bias – some are just cleverer at hiding it than others. See if you can spot ours.

IRELAND RISING: A GLORIOUS FAILURE

Irishmen and Irishwomen: In the name of God and of the dead generations from which she receives her old tradition of nationhood, Ireland, through us, summons her children to her flag and strikes for her freedom.

As Pádraig Pearse read out these words on the steps of the General Post Office (GPO; see p107) on Easter Monday, 24 April 1916, the shoppers and passers-by listened with bemusement and then, in typical Dublin fashion, began making snide remarks about what must have appeared a pretty ridiculous scene. What they didn't know, however, was that Pearse and his band of conspirators were in deadly earnest, and that within a week *everyone* in Ireland and England would know it too, as the most important revolt against British rule since the rebellion of 1798 was played out in bloody, dramatic fashion. See the boxed text (opposite) for more on Pádraig Pearse.

To Fight or Not to Fight

The rebellion was beset by major problems from the outset, not least a substantial debate over the use of physical force. Britain was comprehensively engaged in the Great War, and while a small group of Irish Volunteers (who were also members of the secret and revolutionary Irish Republican Brotherhood, founded in 1867) had adopted the dictum that 'England's difficulty is Ireland's opportunity', the chief-of-staff and founder of the Volunteers, Eoin MacNeill, opposed any rebellion unless Britain imposed conscription on Ireland. Consequently, the organisers, made up of Pearse, Eamonn Ceannt, Joseph Plunkett, Tom Clarke and Seán MacDiarmada, proceeded to plot in secrecy. They were later joined by socialist revolutionary James Connolly, founder of the Irish Citizens' Army (a militia that grew out of the devastating experience of the Great Lockout of 1913), and nationalist poet and playwright Thomas MacDonagh.

The Rising was planned for Easter Sunday 1916, which fell on 23 April. As cover, Pearse arranged for three days of 'parades and manoeuvres' by the Volunteers: the plan was that the

10,000–8000 BC	AD 431–432	837
Human beings arrive in Ireland during the Mesolithic era, originally crossing a land bridge between Scotland and Ireland and later the sea in hide-covered boats.	Pope Celestine I sends Bishop Palladius to Ireland to minister to those 'already believing in Christ'; St Patrick arrives the following year to continue the mission.	Plundering Vikings take a break from attacking monasteries, raping and pillaging to establish a new settlement at the mouth of the harbour and call it 'Dyfflin', which soon becomes a centre of economic power. They begin making alliances with some Irish kings.

PÁDRAIG PEARSE & THE BLOOD SACRIFICE

It is doubtful that the leaders of the Rising thought they could achieve anything more than a symbolic victory. One of its ringleaders, the poet and passionate patriot Pádraig Pearse, was convinced of the need for 'blood sacrifice'. During his oration at the funeral of another Irish rebel, O'Donovan Rossa, he said, 'Life springs from death, and from the graves of patriotic men and women spring living nations.' Pearse was a visionary with his head in the clouds, not a military man, and the ragtag brigade that turned up for the Rising couldn't have had much of an idea of what he was banging on about. Each of the signatories of the proclamation, however, would have known that by putting their name to that document they were virtually condemning themselves to certain death when the insurrection failed.

true republicans within the organisation would know what was really meant, while others like O'Neill would take it at face value. But O'Neill got wind of the rebels' plans and threatened to do everything to thwart them 'short of phoning Dublin Castle'. He was temporarily mollified when informed that a shipment of German weapons was about to land in Kerry, but when that landing was scuttled O'Neill ordered that all actions be cancelled for Sunday.

Chaos Reigns

It merely put off the rebels for one day, but it drastically reduced the number of men involved – no-one outside the capital would participate, leaving only a force of about 1250. The original plan had been to seize key buildings in Dublin, including Trinity College and Dublin Castle, but the lack of troops was to prove fatal, especially in their failure to take Dublin Castle – Connolly's men made a half-hearted effort, not realising that the castle was poorly defended, but were repulsed. As a result, the various Volunteer brigades were left to occupy other locations around the city but had no way of joining up with each other.

The British reacted slowly at first. Unsure of how many rebels there were, the British commander, Brigadier-General Lowe, had only 1200 men at his disposal. Martial law was established, and they sought to consolidate the castle and isolate the leaders within the GPO. The gunboat *Helga* was used to shell the rebels from the Liffey, but the firing was initially so inaccurate that British troops thought it was the rebels who were shelling them, and so returned fire!

In the meantime, the rebel leaders weren't having such a great time of it. Connolly had been badly injured in the fighting, and was forced to command his troops from a bed in the GPO. The continuous shelling of the GPO made it impossible for the leaders to fight any more than a holding action, whereas other rebels were ensconced within the likes of the Four Courts, Boland's Mills and St Stephen's Green, and were held there under heavy British fire (British numbers by now reinforced by the arrival of 16,000 extra troops). The only real success for the rebels was in the Mount St area around the Grand Canal, where a mere 17 armed volunteers led by Cathal Brugha inflicted heavy losses on troops trying to enter the city over the canal bridge.

Not surprisingly, Dublin was in chaos. Widespread looting was common, as the city's slum population took advantage of the breakdown of law and order to break into the shops on and around O'Connell St. Ever the socialist, Connolly reacted furiously to countermand a volunteer order that the looters be shot.

988	1169	1170
High King Mael Seachlainn II leads the initial Irish conquest of Dyfflin, giving the settlement its modern name in Irish – Baile Átha Cliath, meaning 'Town at the Hurdle Ford'.	Henry II's Welsh and Norman barons quickly capture Waterford and Wexford with the help of Dermot MacMurrough (King of Leinster). Although no one knew it at the time, this was the beginning of an 800-year occupation of Ireland by Britain.	Strongbow captures Dublin and then takes Aoife, MacMurrough's daughter, as his wife before being crowned King of Leinster. The marriage is the subject of a famous painting by Daniel Maclise that can be viewed in the National Gallery (p79).

By 29 April the rebels could no longer hold their positions. The leaders had been forced to abandon the GPO, and from their new position on Moore St, Pearse ordered a cessation of all hostilities. In six days, 318 Irish were dead and 2217 wounded, of which 64 were volunteers. The British reported casualties of 116 dead, 368 wounded and nine missing. The Rising was over, and all the resultant rage of most of the population.

It got even worse for the rebels. The new British commander, General John Maxwell, was hardly in a conciliatory mood and ordered the arrest of all Sinn Féiners (members of the political wing of the Irish Republican Army, IRA), including 'those who have taken an active part in the movement although not in the present rebellion'. Sinn Féin was neither militant nor republican, and had not taken part in the rebellion, but the British failure to differentiate between the various strands of Irish nationalism was hardly new. It was to seriously backfire this time.

As Britain was engaged in the Great War, the rebels were treated as traitors and a series of court martials resulted in the sentencing to death of 90 men. Although only 15 of them were actually carried out in the grounds of Kilmainham Gaol (p95), they included 18-year-old Willie Pearse, whose main crime was being the brother of Pádraig. James Connolly, the hero of the working man, was severely injured during the Rising and then detained at the military hospital in Dublin Castle. At dawn on 12 May, he was taken by ambulance to Kilmainham Gaol, carried on a stretcher into the prison yard, strapped into a chair and executed by firing squad. More than 3500 others were arrested, and many were deported to internment camps in Britain.

Conscription & Rebellion

Although it is commonly accepted that the cold-blooded execution of the rebels was the thing that turned popular opinion in favour of the rebels, the radicalisation of Irish political aspirations – from a limited form of home rule to total independence from Britain – was brought about largely by the conscription crisis of 1918, whereby the British government forced through conscription despite the total opposition of all Irish parties.

The British had won few Irish friends with the executions and the heavy artillery shelling that had left much of the city centre a smouldering wreck. But the conscription crisis hardened opinion to such a degree that the rebel leaders were now seen as visionaries and martyrs rather than misguided romantics, and returning internees from the British camps were given a hero's welcome. The general election of 14 December 1918 resulted in the obliteration of the moderate Irish Parliamentary Party and their home rule agenda, and the almost total victory

WOMEN OF THE REVOLUTION

The 1916 Proclamation was a radical document for its day, and called for equal rights between men and women (Britain only gave women full suffrage in 1928). Two key reasons for this were Countess Markievicz (1868–1927) and Maud Gonne (1865–1953), two English women who inspired a generation of revolutionaries. A committed republican and socialist, Countess Markievicz was a military leader of the 1916 Easter Rising and went on to become a minister in the first government. Before independence she'd been the first woman ever elected to the British Parliament, although as a member of Sinn Féin (who didn't recognise British governance in Ireland), she never took her seat. Maud Gonne, also a staunch republican, is perhaps better known as WB Yeats' gorgeous muse (and desperately unrequited love).

1172	1350–1530	1534
King Henry II of England invades Ireland, using the 1155 Bull Laudabiliter issued to him by Pope Adrian IV to claim sovereignty over the island, and forces the Cambro-Norman warlords and some of the Gaelic Irish kings to accept him as their overlord.	The Anglo-Norman barons establish power bases independent of the English crown. Over the following two centuries, English control gradually recedes to an area around Dublin known as 'the Pale'.	'Silken' Thomas Fitzgerald, son of the reigning earl of Kildare, storms Dublin and its English garrisons. The rebellion is squashed, and Thomas and his followers are subsequently executed.

of Sinn Féin, which had been reorganised the previous year as the vanguard of the Irish independence movement.

On 21 January 1919, the newly elected Sinn Féin deputies, who had pointedly refused to take their seats in Westminster, gathered in the Mansion House to form Dáil Éireann and adopt the Declaration of Independence.

Although the Rising was by any stretch a total disaster, not even the leaders could have predicted that their doomed rebellion would be seen as the touch-paper that would ignite the independence movement and inspire the final push towards Irish freedom. British ignorance of and insensitivity towards Irish moods were a longstanding fact of occupation. But the events of 1916–18, which occurred against a backdrop of a war ostensibly in defence of small nations, proved to the Irish once and for all that Britain didn't care about the needs of this small nation, and that the only recourse was for the Irish to strike out on their own.

BACKGROUND HISTORY

top picks

BOOKS ON DUBLIN HISTORY

- A Short History of Dublin (2000) Pat Boran
- Dublin – A Celebration (2000) Pat Liddy
- Dublin: A Cultural & Literary History (2005) Siobhán Kilfeather
- Cities of the Imagination: Dublin (2007) Siobhán Kilfeather
- Encyclopaedia of Dublin (2005) Douglas Bennett

A MATTER OF FAITH

Although officially the vast majority of Dubliners are Roman Catholic (around 90%), a majority of them could be considered á la carte Catholics, with faith for some amounting to having a quiet snooze at the back of the church during their very infrequent attendances at mass.

In 2007, a joint survey by a Catholic and a Protestant organisation revealed that only 52% of young people in the capital knew the names of the four Evangelists…and that only 38% knew that there were four of them (Matthew, Mark, Luke and John, just so you know). Only 10% knew that the Immaculate Conception referred to Mary and less than half could name the Father, Son and the Holy Spirit (or Ghost) as the three persons of the Trinity.

A sharp decline in religious practice is a Europe-wide phenomenon, particularly among Christians, but Ireland is a special case, for religion is a central feature of Irish history and the centuries-old struggle for identity and independence has been intimately intertwined with the struggle for recognition and supremacy between the Roman Catholic and Protestant churches. There are few European countries where religion has played such a key role and continues to exert huge influence – not least in the fact that the island remains roughly divided along religious lines. For many outside observers Ireland is akin to a Christian Middle East, a complex and confusing muddle that lends itself to over-simplified generalisations by those who don't have two lifetimes to figure it all out. Like us, for instance, in this short essay.

Early Days

Dublin's relationship with Christianity began with St Patrick, who founded the See of Dublin sometime in the mid-5th century and went about the business of conversion in present-day Wicklow and Malahide before laying hands on Leoghaire, the King of Ireland, using water from a well next to St Patrick's Cathedral. Or so the story goes. Irrespective of the details, Patrick

1592	1640s–1682	1680
Trinity College is founded on the grounds of a former monastery just outside the city walls, on the basis of a charter granted by Elizabeth I to 'stop Ireland being infected by popery'.	Dublin's resurgence begins as the city's population grows from 10,000 in the mid-1640s to nearly 60,000 in 1682.	The architectural style known as Anglo-Dutch results in the construction of notable buildings such as the Royal Hospital, Kilmainham (p96), now the Irish Museum of Modern Art.

and his monk buddies were successful because they managed to fuse the strong tradition of druidism and pagan ritual with the new Christian teaching, which created an exciting hybrid known as Celtic, or Insular Christianity.

Compared to new hotspots like Clonmacnois in County Offaly and Glendalough in County Wicklow, Dublin was a rural backwater and so didn't really figure in the Golden Age, when Irish Christian scholars excelled in the study of Latin and Greek learning and Christian theology. They studied in the monasteries that were, in essence, Europe's most important universities, producing brilliant students, magnificent illuminated books like the Book of Kells (now housed in Trinity College, p69), ornate jewellery and the many carved stone crosses that dot the island 'of saints and scholars'.

The nature of Christianity in Ireland was one of marked independence from Rome, especially in the areas of monastic rule and penitential practice, which emphasised private confession to a priest followed by penances levied by the priest in reparation – which is the spirit and letter of the practice of confession that exists to this day. The Irish were also exporting these teachings abroad, setting up monasteries across Europe, such as the ones in Luxeuil in France and Bobbio in Italy, both founded by St Columbanus (AD 543–615).

Papal Intervention & Protestantism

The Golden Age ended with the invasion of Ireland by Henry II in 1170, for which Henry had the blessing of Pope Adrian IV and his papal laudabiliter, a document that granted the English king dominion over Ireland under the overlordship of the pope. Ireland's monastic independence was unacceptable in the new political climate brought on by the Gregorian reform movement of 1050–80, which sought to consolidate the ultimate authority of the papacy in all ecclesiastical, moral and social matters at the expense of the widespread monastic network.

The long-standing (St) Laurence O'Toole, Archbishop of Dublin, tried his best to hold off the Norman onslaught – going so far as to implore an army of Danes to intercede – but it was to no avail. In 1179, Pope Alexander III softened the blow of Laurence's loss of ecclesiastical freedom by appointing him papal legate in Ireland. The influence of the monasteries began to wane in favour of the Norman archbishops who succeeded Laurence – an unbroken line of 25 English-born archbishops that would last for 400 years. The first couple of these oversaw the construction of the great cathedrals, most notably Dublin's two outstanding churches, St Patrick's (p90) and Christ Church (p94).

The second and more damaging reform of the Irish Church occurred in the middle of the 16th century, and once again an English monarch was at the heart of it. The break with the Roman Catholic Church that followed Henry VIII's inability to secure papal blessing for his divorce of Catherine of Aragon in 1534 saw the establishment in Ireland (as in England) of a new Protestant church, with Henry as its supreme head. In 1536 Henry appointed George Brown to the Dublin see, and he set about breaking the resistance of the city's clergy by gathering up all of their relics, including St Patrick's crozier (known as the 'staff of Jesus'), into a heap and setting them on fire. It wasn't quite enough, however: the Irish resisted the new religion and remained largely loyal to Rome, setting the religious wars that would dominate Irish affairs for the next 200 years and cast a huge shadow over the country that has not quite faded yet. The new religion gained its strongest foothold in Dublin, where the clerical and lay authorities were soon overhauled by newly constituted Protestants.

1695	1757	1759
Penal laws – aka the 'popery code' – prohibit Catholics from owning a horse (a military tactic), marrying outside their religion and, most importantly, from buying or inheriting property; within 100 years Catholics will own only 5% of Irish land.	The Wide Street Commission is set up to design new civic spaces and the framework of a modern city: new parks are laid out, streets widened and new public buildings commissioned, rendering Dublin a magnificent example of Georgian town planning.	Arthur Guinness buys a disused brewery on a plot of land opposite St James' Gate, once part of the city's western defences. Initially he brews only ale, but in the 1770s turns his expertise to a new beer called porter.

Dublin's role in the wars of pacification, initiated by Henry but really kicked into high gear by his daughter Elizabeth I, was at odds with the rest of the country. Dublin was the power-base of the English occupation, the heart of the Pale – the area of Ireland completely controlled by the Crown. Beyond it was the wild countryside, full of Irish rebel chieftains who would sooner die than abandon their freedom, which included the all-important right to refer to the pope as God's number one emissary.

Anti-Catholic Laws

The resistance had its most glorious moment in the Nine Years' War (1594–1603), when a combined alliance of Irish chieftains led by Hugh O'Neill fought the English armies to a standstill before eventually surrendering in 1603. The 'Flight of the Earls' in 1607, which saw O'Neill and his allies leave Ireland forever, marked the end of organised Irish rebellion and the full implementation of the policy of Plantation, whereby the confiscated lands of Catholic nobles was redistributed to 'planted' settlers of exclusively Protestant stock. This policy was most effective in Ulster, which was seen by the English as the hotbed of Irish resistance to English rule.

Alongside the policy of Plantation, the English also passed a series of Penal Laws in Ireland, which had the effect of almost totally disenfranchising all Catholics and, later, Presbyterians. The Jacobite Wars of the late 17th century, which pitted the Catholic James II against his son-in-law, the Protestant William of Orange, saw the Irish take sides along strictly religious lines. The disenfranchised Catholic majority – which included the poor of Dublin – supported James while the recently planted Protestant landowning minority lent their considerable support to William. It was William who won the day, and 12 July 1690 – when James was defeated at the Battle of the Boyne – has been celebrated ever since by Ulster Protestants with marches throughout the province.

Until the Catholic Emancipation Act of 1829, Irish Roman Catholics were almost totally impeded from worshipping freely. Clerics and bishops couldn't preach, with only lay priests allowed to operate, and even then only so long as they were registered with the government. The construction of churches was heavily regulated, and when allowed, they could only be built in barely durable wood. The most effective of the anti-Catholic laws, however, was the Popery Act of 1703, which sought to 'prevent the further growth of Popery' by requiring that all Catholics divide their lands equally among their sons, in effect diminishing Catholic land holdings. When the Emancipation Act was passed, it only granted limited rights to Catholics who owned a set amount of land; the land separation that preceded it ensured that they were few in number.

Influence of the Church

It was hardly surprising then that the Catholic Church was heavily involved in the struggle for Irish freedom, although the traditionally conservative church was careful to only lend its support to lawful means of protest, such as Daniel O'Connell's Repeal Movement and, later, Parnell's Home Rule fight. When Parnell became embroiled in a divorce scandal in 1890, the church condemned him with all its might, thereby ending his career. It also condemned any rebel notion that smacked of illegality or socialism – the Easter Rising was roundly denounced from the pulpit for its bloodletting and its vaguely leftist proclamation.

1801	1845–51	1905
The Act of Union unites Ireland politically with Britain. The Irish Parliament votes itself out of existence following an intensive campaign of bribery. Dublin's role as 'second city of the Empire' comes to a swift end.	A mould called phytophthora ravages the potato harvest. The Great Famine is the single greatest catastrophe in Irish history, with the deaths of between 500,000 and one million people, and the emigration of up to two million others.	Journalist Arthur Griffiths founds a new movement whose aim is independence under a dual monarchy, similar to that of the Austro-Hungarian empire. Making a case for national self-reliance, he names the movement Sinn Féin, meaning 'ourselves alone'.

If the Roman Catholic Church was shackled for much of the English occupation, it more than made up for it when the Free State came into being in 1922. The church's overwhelmingly conservative influence on the new state was felt everywhere, not least in the state's schools and hospitals and over virtually every aspect of social policy. Divorce, contraception, abortion and all manner of 'scurrilous literature' were obvious no-nos, but the church even managed to say no to a variety of welfare plans that would provide government assistance to young mothers in need, for instance.

The Free State – and the Republic of Ireland that followed it in 1948 – was 96% Catholic. Although 7.5% of the Free State population in 1922 was Protestant, their numbers had halved by the 1960s, with a disproportionately high rate of emigration among Protestants who felt threatened or unwelcome in the new Catholic state. The Catholic Church compounded the matter by emphasising the 1907 Ne Temere decree, which insisted that the children of mixed marriage be raised as Catholic under penalty of excommunication.

The dramatic decline in the influence of the church over the last two decades is primarily the result of global trends and greater prosperity in Ireland. But the terrible revelations of widespread abuse of children by parish priests, and the untidy efforts of the church authorities to sweep the truth under the carpet – including the shuffling of guilty priests from parish to parish – have provoked a seething rage among many Dubliners at the church's gross insensitivity to the care of their flock. Many older believers feel an acute sense of betrayal that has led them to question a lifetime's devotion to their local parishes. A belated apology on the part of church authorities has assuaged some, but is considered far too little, far too late by many others.

One group to buck this trend is the largely Catholic Polish community in Dublin, which has increased dramatically in recent years and continues to keep the faith, as do large numbers of the African community, although they tend to affiliate with smaller Reformist churches like the Baptists.

PRAISIN' IN HARMONY

Until very recently, Sunday Mass – that regular fixture of so many a Dubliner's week – was seen as something between a duty and a penance, a ritual that many young people endured rather than enjoyed. No wonder Mass attendances have dwindled. What Mass needed, according to St Francis Xavier Church on the north side's Gardiner St, was an injection of song – so enter the Gardiner Street Gospel Choir (🎵 services 7.30pm Sun mid-Sep–Jun), who remind us that a little music in your soul hardly means that the devil has come to stay. Oh, happy day.

A CITY OF OUTSIDERS

One of Dublin's most popular contemporary buzzwords is 'multiculturalism', used with pride and, in some quarters, concern to describe the city's new culture, which is being transformed by new arrivals from Africa, Asia and – since the accession of 10 new states into the EU in 2004 – from Eastern Europe. Here's a number for you: Dublin apparently has around 50,000 new arrivals from Poland alone – in a city that barely tops 1.5 million, that's a lot of people. Take a walk around the north city centre and you'll see the multicultural melting pot in all its cosmopolitan glory, where Russians shop for tinned caviar and *prianik* cookies while Nigerian teenagers discuss the merits of hair extensions and Koreans hawk phone cards from their hatches.

1916	1919–21	1921–22
The Easter Rising: dedicated republicans take the GPO in Dublin and announce the formation of an Irish Republic. After less than a week of fighting, the rebels surrender to the superior British forces and are summarily executed.	The Irish War of Independence begins in January 1919. Two years (and 1400 casualties) later, the war ends in a truce on 11 July 1921, leading to peace talks.	An Irish delegation signs the Anglo-Irish Treaty on 6 December. It gives 26 counties of Ireland independence and six largely Protestant Ulster counties the choice of opting out, with a Boundary Commission to decide on the final frontiers between north and south. The Irish Free State is founded in 1922.

Dubliners are, for the most part, tickled pink by the new cultures on display – it lends weight to their assertion to living in a truly international capital. And it makes going out for dinner a hell of a lot more interesting, given the new range of authentic choices.

The Vikings & Strongbow

Labour shortages, a buoyant economy and a relatively generous social welfare system might be enticing this generation of immigrants, but this is hardly the first time that Dublin has opened its doors to accommodate outsiders. Lost in the overwhelming statistics of Ireland as a nation of emigrants is a history of immigration – beginning with the origins of the capital itself.

Raids by marauding Vikings had been a fact of Irish life for quite some time before a group of them decided to take some R-and-R from their hell-raising and built a harbour (or *longphort*) on the banks of the Liffey in 837. Although a Celtic army forced them out some 65 years later, they returned in 917 with a massive fleet, established a stronghold (or *dun*) by the black pool at Wood Quay (Map pp90–1), just behind Christ Church Cathedral, and dug their heels in. They went back to plundering the countryside but also laid down guidelines on plot sizes and town boundaries for their town of 'Dyflinn', which became the most prominent trading centre in the Viking world. But their good times came to an end in 1014 when an alliance of Irish clans led by Brian Ború decisively whupped them at the Battle of Clontarf, forever breaking the Scandinavian grip on the eastern seaboard. Rather than abandoning the place in defeat, however, the Vikings liked Dublin so much that they decided to stay and integrate.

When the Anglo-Normans arrived in 1169, led by Richard de Clare (better known as Strongbow), they were so taken with the place that they decided to stay. They took Dublin the following year, and essentially kept it for the following 750 years. Strongbow inherited the kingship of Leinster – of which modern Dublin is capital – and made himself at home. The English king, Henry II, soon sent his own army over to keep an eye on Strongbow and his consorts who, he reckoned, were becoming 'more Irish than the Irish themselves'.

The Huguenots

One of the most important immigrant groups to settle in Dublin was the Huguenots, mostly French Calvinist Protestants who began arriving in Dublin from about 1630 onwards. They were fleeing religious persecution in Europe – the worst example was in France, where 20,000 were murdered during the infamous St Bartholomew's Day Massacre of 1572. The trickle of arrivals became a flood after Louis XIV revoked the Edict of Nantes in 1685, which ended the little legal protection they had. Most of the Huguenot immigrants settled in the Coombe, which is part of the Liberties, where they immediately set about adding to the commercial and artistic life of the city with their skills in weaving, textile design and working with gold and silver. They were also involved in sugar baking, setting up no fewer than 30 sugar bakeries in the city.

The Huguenots knew how to make money, and they spent it on a city that was immensely grateful for their presence: Huguenot wealth went a long way towards financing the major urban redesign that was to transform Dublin from medieval misery pit into a Georgian masterpiece. One prominent Huguenot was goldsmith Jeremiah D'Olier, originally from Toulouse, who became a City Sheriff, a founder of the Bank of Ireland and a member of the Wide Streets Commission.

1948	1969	1972
Fine Gael, in coalition with the new republican Clann an Poblachta, wins the 1948 general election and declares the Free State to be a republic at last. Ireland leaves the British Commonwealth (1949), and the south cut its final links to the north.	Marches in Derry by the Northern Ireland Civil Rights Association (NICRA) are disrupted by Loyalist attacks and heavy-handed police action, culminating in the 'Battle of the Bogside' (August 12–14). It is the beginning of the Troubles.	On Bloody Sunday, 30 January, 13 civilians are killed by British troops in Derry. Westminster suspends the Stormont government and introduces direct rule; a crowd of 20,000 protest outside the British Embassy in Dublin, which is burnt to the ground.

Other prominent Huguenot names include Georgian architects James Gandon and Richard Cassels (see p49); Gothic horror novelists Joseph Sheridan LeFanu and Charles Robert Maturin (authors of, respectively, the lesbian vampire classic *Carmilla* and *Melmoth the Wanderer*); and a certain Monsieur Becquet, who was not famous in his own right but whose descendant was none other than Samuel Beckett. His ancestor's grave is in the small but centrally located Huguenot Cemetery, at the northeastern corner of St Stephen's Green (Map pp66–7). Finally, the Huguenots had another important influence on the city: their extensive international trade links lent credence to the city's Anglo-Irish gentry's cosmopolitan pretensions, altogether necessary if Dublin was indeed to be thought of as the second city of the empire. And who says that history doesn't repeat itself?

The Jews

The other important group to arrive in Dublin as a result of religious persecution were Jews, the first wave arriving here in the mid-18th century from Spain and Portugal. They established a synagogue on Crane Lane, just off Dame St, which has long since disappeared (the most prominent building there now is a gay sauna) along with most of the original settlement, which had dispersed by 1790. Another small group arrived in 1820, opening synagogues in Wolfe Tone St and Mary's Abbey on the northside, but it wasn't until 1880 when Jewish settlers really established a foothold in Dublin. Fleeing the pogroms of Russia, they had intended to make their way to America, but many ended up staying here, settling around the South Circular Rd in an area that by the beginning of the 20th century was known as 'Little Jerusalem'. By the mid-1940s there were about 4000 Jews living in Ireland, but post-war emigration to the US and Israel has diminished their number to around 1500.

Nevertheless, their Dublin legacy is a notable one: two former Lord Mayors of Dublin were Jewish, Robert Briscoe (1956–57) and his son Ben (1988–89). The Jewish Museum on Walworth Rd (p76), in two adjoining houses that once served as the city's most important synagogue, was opened in 1985 by the then President of Israel, Chaim Herzog (1918–97). He grew up just around the corner at 33 Bloomfield Ave and was educated at one of Dublin's top schools, Wesley College. His son Isaac is currently the Israeli Minister for Social Affairs.

And who could forget the most famous Dublin Jew of them all, the man 'who ate with relish the inner organs of beast and fowl', James Joyce's greatest creation, Leopold Bloom? Born and raised at 13 Clanbrassil St, he married Molly and moved to 7 Eccles St, from where he embarked on his famous adventure of one very long day.

NURSE OF THE PEOPLE, CURSE OF THE PEOPLE

A wet, cold and inclement climate, a tendency towards self-reflection and the oppressive presence of a foreign occupier who just won't go away are three pretty good reasons to justify a spot of escapism, and the capital has plenty of experts in 'the cure', as taking a drink to beat the blues is euphemistically known. And as demand will often generate supply, Dublin has a particularly rich history in the twin arts of brewing and distilling – providing, in the words of Arthur Guinness, the 'nurse of the people' (beer) and the 'curse of the people' (whiskey). Arthur's bias notwithstanding, Dublin's drinkers could at least console themselves that they were contributing to the cyclical wealth of the local economy by maintaining brand loyalty, which really meant they were drinking some of the best beer and whiskey in the world.

1974	1988	1990
A series of simultaneous bombings in Monaghan and Dublin on 17 May leave 33 dead and 300 injured, the biggest loss of life in any single day in the history of the Troubles.	Dublin celebrates its millennium, even though the town was established long before 988.	Barrister and human rights campaigner Mary Robinson becomes Ireland's first female president. She wields considerable informal influence over social policies, shifting away from traditionally conservative attitudes on divorce, abortion and gay rights.

Wine, Mead & Whiskey

There's been booze in Dublin since Celtic times. The first settlers round these parts weren't especially picky, displaying a love of malt liquor, imported wine (thanks to Roman traders) and other kinds of fermented drinks, including mead. The Vikings were especially partial to mead, a simple enough drink made of boiled honey and water, which was considered the drink of the Gods and the heroes living in Valhalla.

Wine and mead were good enough, but the Irish were looking for something with a little more punch, and by the 12th or 13th century (the early history is unclear – maybe the historians were a little too addled to note these things down?) they had it. And it was all thanks to monks who had picked up a couple of tricks from Middle Eastern perfume-making techniques and Roman texts about the distillation of *aqua vitae* – the 'water of life'. The Irish, who were more inclined to feeling good than smelling well, translated the name directly and called their new potion *uisce beatha* (ish-ke ba-ha); the first word sounds suspiciously like…whiskey. And considering that the Irish and the Scots have been engaged in a longstanding rivalry as to who exactly invented the stuff, we'll point out that the first recorded mention of whiskey in Ireland was in 1405, 91 years before the word (shorn of the 'e') was written down in Scotland. So there.

Until 1608, distilling was largely a clandestine affair, with pot stills all over the country producing whiskey of widely diverging quality. King James I's ministers then recognised the taxable potential of this popular pastime and granted the governor of Ulster, Sir Thomas Phillips, the very first licence to distil *uisce beatha*.

In Dublin, the first commercial distillery was set up in 1757 when Peter Roe bought a small distillery on Thomas St and powered it with the largest smock windmill in Europe of the time – you can still see the blue-capped copper top of St Patrick's Tower in the grounds of the Guinness Brewery (see p88).

Guinness: A Brand was Born

Two years later, another entrepreneur of booze got in on the act. Arthur Guinness, who had learnt the brewer's trade from his father Richard, took out a long-term lease on a small, disused brewery across the street from Roe's distillery and began producing ale. Then, in the mid-1770s, he got wind of a new, dark-coloured ale (due to the roasting of hops), which was the favourite of the porters of Covent Garden and Billingsgate in London. Arthur decided this was the way to go, so he refined and strengthened the dark ale, calling it extra stout porter, which soon became known simply as 'stout'. When he died in 1803 he could hardly have realised that he had laid the foundations for not just one of the world's most famous breweries, but arguably the world's most beloved beer and the single most defining symbol of the city he lived in.

As an employer, the company reached its apogee in the 1930s, when there were more than 5000 people working here, making it the largest employer in the city. For nearly two centuries it was also one of the best places to work, paying 20% more than the market rate and offering a comprehensive package of subsidised housing, health benefits, pension plans, longer holidays and life insurance. In the 19th century, young women of marrying age in Dublin were advised by their mothers to get their hands on a Guinness man, as he'd be worth more than most alive or dead!

1990s	2005	2007
Thanks to low corporate tax, decades of investment in domestic higher education, transfer payments from the EU and a low-cost labour market, the 'Celtic Tiger' booms, transforming Ireland from one of Europe's poorer countries into one of its wealthiest.	On 28 July the IRA issues a statement formally ending its campaign of violence and orders all of its units to dump arms and to assist 'the development of purely political and democratic programmes through exclusively peaceful means'.	A general election sees Fianna Fáil and Taoiseach Bertie Ahern re-elected for a third term, albeit as majority partners in a coalition that includes, for the first time, the Greens.

The Whiskey Trade

The Guinness gang were so successful, so utterly dominant, that no other brewer could really survive in Dublin. Not so with whiskey, and for a time, the capital had a number of important distilleries whose aim, presumably, was to keep as many of the citizenry as possible in a state of sozzle. In 1780, John Jameson bought an interest in a small distillery in Bow St, creating one of the great whiskey dynasties. His son, grandson and great-grandson – all called John – steered the firm of John Jameson & Son towards huge success, eventually replacing the original distillery with a much bigger building in 1880, now a whiskey museum (p106). Nine years later, Jameson's united with Roe's to form the Dublin Distilling Company, although each continued to sell under their own name. Roe's distillery alone covered 17 acres – the largest in Europe – and was producing two million gallons of whiskey annually, with a chunk of it being exported to the US, Canada and Australia.

The whiskey trade might have been immensely popular, but its sale was riddled with problems, largely because all distillers sold their product through bonders – merchants who aged whiskey in a bonded warehouse for at least four years before bottling. Common practice, however, was to mix the good stuff with inferior provincial distillates and sell the lot under the bonder's name. Then along came James Power, whose father James had founded a distillery on the grounds of what is now the National College of Art & Design on Thomas St in 1791.

In an early example of brand awareness, James devised a method whereby whiskey sold through merchant bonders could only carry a special 'John Power & Son' white label that also proclaimed it as a 'Dublin Whiskey'. His innovations earned him a knighthood, an appointment as High Sheriff of Dublin and the friendship of no less than the Liberator himself, Daniel O'Connell. The company continued its groundbreaking tradition in 1866 by making the move towards glass bottles (whiskey was always sold in wooden casks), offsetting the expense by labelling the bottled whiskey as 'Gold Label' and selling it as a really special reserve. Finally, Powers was the first distiller to produce miniature bottles, the famous 'Baby Powers', which required an act of parliament before they were allowed. Airline travel and hotel overnights just wouldn't have been the same.

The city's brewers and distillers were unquestionably an entrepreneurial lot, but their particular business meant that they were directly contributing to the social ills of society – not everyone was content with a snifter of whiskey or a quick half of beer after a hard day at the grindstone. Consequently, some of the major names were quick to engage in acts of munificence, in part inspired by the 19th-century spirit of philanthropy but equally to ensure that they didn't get labelled as purveyors of moral corruption. And what better way to avoid it than, say, to spend the modern-day equivalent of €30 million to fix up the city's most famous cathedral (the Roe's), or build a load of housing for low-income families and sponsor the clean-up of the city's favourite green space (the Guinness family)?

End of an Era

The whiskey industry has long since disappeared in Dublin – nearly all of it is now produced in a purpose-built factory in Midleton, County Cork, but Guinness still rules supreme, for the moment. The once mighty brewery, which had grown even bigger with the 1949 acquisition of the old Roe Distillery (which had folded in 1945), was, as of 2007, examining its long-term options. Sadly this could mean selling up St James's Gate (for a simply astronomical profit, we assume) and relocating to a new and smaller factory outside Dublin. If it does happen – and we pray fervently that it doesn't – it'll mean the end of a long and important tradition that has helped define and shape the city in ways few other enterprises ever could.

ARTS

Dublin has always operated an enormous cultural surplus, filling the world's artistic coffers with far greater wealth than should ever have been expected from so small a city. There's hardly been any let-up in the last couple of centuries and the city is still racing further and further into the black. Even by Ireland's standards, the capital is especially creative these days, with more poetry readings, book launches, live gigs, contemporary dance shows, operas, plays, films, comedy acts and club nights than you could shake a decent listings guide at, while Dubliners continue to regale the world with books, films and albums.

LITERATURE

Dubliners know a thing or two about the written word. No other city of comparable size can claim four Nobel Prize winners for literature, but the city's impact on the English-reading world extends far beyond the fab four of Shaw, Yeats, Beckett and Heaney…one name folks: James Joyce.

Before Dublin was even a glint in a Viking's eye, Ireland was the land of saints and scholars, thanks to the monastic universities that sprung up around the country to foster the spread of Christianity and the education of Europe's privileged elite (the nearest to Dublin was Glendalough). But for our purposes, we need to fast-forward 1000 years to the 18th century and the glory days of Georgian Dublin, when the Irish and English languages began to cross-fertilise. Experimenting with English, using turns of phrase and expressions translated directly from Gaeilge, and combining these with a uniquely Irish perspective on life, Irish writers have dazzled and delighted readers for centuries. British theatre critic Kenneth Tynan summed it up thus: 'The English hoard words like misers: the Irish spend them like sailors.'

Dublin has as many would-be sailors as Hollywood has frustrated waitresses, and it often seems like a bottomless well of creativity. The section given over to Irish writers is often the largest and busiest in any local bookstore, reflecting not only a rich literary tradition and thriving contemporary scene, but also an appreciative, knowledgeable and hungry local audience that attends readings and poetry recitals like rock fans at a gig.

Indeed, Dublin has produced so many writers, and has been written about so much, that you could easily plan a Dublin literary holiday. *A Literary Guide to Dublin,* by Vivien Igoe, includes detailed route maps, a guide to cemeteries and an eight-page section on literary and historical pubs. A Norman Jeffares' *Irish Writers: From Swift to Heaney* also has detailed and accessible summaries of writers and their work.

See p121 for our Literary Dublin walking tour.

Old Literary Dublin

Modern Irish literature begins with Jonathan Swift (1667–1745), the master satirist, social commentator and dean of St Patrick's Cathedral. He was the greatest Dublin writer of the early Georgian period and is most famous for *Gulliver's Travels,* a savage social satire that has morphed into a children's favourite. He was an 'earnest and dedicated champion of liberty', as he insisted on writing in his own epitaph.

He was followed by Oliver Goldsmith (1728–74), author of *The Vicar of Wakefield,* and Thomas Moore (1779–1852), whose poems formed the repertoire of generations of Irish tenors. Dublin-born Oscar Wilde (1854–1900) is renowned for his legendary wit, immense talent and striking sensitivity (also see Theatre, p41). Bram Stoker (1847–1912) is another well-known literary figure and is most celebrated for his gothic novel *Dracula,* one of the world's most popular books. The name of the count may have come from the Irish *droch fhola* (bad blood).

Playwright and essayist George Bernard Shaw (1856–1950), author of *Pygmalion* (which was later turned into *My Fair Lady*), hailed from Synge St near the Grand Canal, while James Joyce (1882–1941), the city's most famous son and one of the greatest writers of all time, was born not far away in Rathgar.

William Butler (WB) Yeats (1865–1939) is best remembered as a poet, though he also wrote plays and spearheaded the late-19th-century Irish Literary Revival, which culminated in the founding of the Abbey Theatre in 1904. *Sailing to Byzantium* and *Easter 1916* are two of his finest poems – the latter, about the Easter Rising, ends with the famous line 'A terrible beauty is born'. His poetry is mostly tied up with his sense of Irish heroism, esoteric mysticism and the unrequited love he had for Maud Gonne (see p24).

JAMES JOYCE

Uppermost among Dublin writers is James Joyce, author of *Ulysses*, the greatest book of the 20th century – although we've yet to meet five people who've actually finished it. Still, Dubliners are immensely proud of the writer once castigated as a literary pornographer by locals and luminaries alike – even George Bernard Shaw dismissed him as vulgar. Joyce was so unappreciated that he left the city, never to reside in it again, though he continued to live here through his imagination and literature.

Born in Rathgar in 1882, the young Joyce had three short stories published in an Irish farmers' magazine under the pen name Stephen Dedalus in 1904. The same year he fled town with the love of his life, Nora Barnacle (when James' father heard her name he commented that she would surely stick to him). He spent most of the next 10 years in Trieste, now part of Italy, where he wrote prolifically but struggled to get published. His career was further hampered by recurrent eye problems and he had 25 operations for glaucoma, cataracts and other conditions.

The first major prose he finally had published was *Dubliners* (1914), a collection of short stories set in the city, including the three stories he had written in Ireland. Publishers began to take notice and his autobiographical *A Portrait of the Artist as a Young Man* (1916) followed. In 1918 the US magazine *Little Review* started to publish extracts from *Ulysses* but notoriety was already pursuing his epic work and the censors prevented publication of further episodes after 1920.

Passing through Paris on a rare visit to Dublin, he was persuaded by Ezra Pound to stay a while in the French capital, and later said he 'came to Paris for a week and stayed 20 years'. It was a good move for the struggling writer for, in 1922, he met Sylvia Beach of the Paris bookshop Shakespeare & Co, who finally managed to put *Ulysses* (1922) into print. The publicity of its earlier censorship ensured instant success.

Buoyed by the success of the inventive *Ulysses*, Joyce went for broke with *Finnegans Wake* (1939), 'set' in the dreamscape of a Dublin publican. Perhaps not one to read at the airport, the book is a daunting and often obscure tome about eternal recurrence. It is even more complex than *Ulysses* and took the author 17 years to write.

In 1940 WWII drove the Joyce family back to Zürich, where the author died the following year.

Ulysses

Ulysses is the ultimate chronicle of the city in which, Joyce once said, he intended to 'give a picture of Dublin so complete that if the city suddenly one day disappeared from the earth it could be reconstructed out of my book'. It is set here on 16 June 1904 – the day of Joyce's first date with Nora Barnacle – and follows its characters as their journeys around town parallel the voyage of Homer's *Odyssey*.

The experimental literary style makes it difficult to read, but there's much for even the slightly bemused reader to relish. It ends with Molly Bloom's famous stream of consciousness discourse, a chapter of eight huge, unpunctuated paragraphs. Because of its sexual explicitness, the book was banned in the US and the UK until 1933 and 1937, respectively.

In testament to the book's enduring relevance and extraordinary innovation, it has inspired writers of every generation since. Joyce admirers from around the world descend on Dublin every year on 16 June to celebrate Bloomsday and retrace the steps of its central character, Leopold Bloom. It is a slightly gimmicky and touristy phenomenon that appeals almost exclusively to Joyce fanatics and tourists, but it's plenty of fun and a great way to lay the groundwork for actually reading the book.

Oliver St John Gogarty (1878–1957) is said to have borne a lifelong grudge against his one-time friend James Joyce because of his appearance as Buck Mulligan in the latter's *Ulysses*. He was a character in his own right and his views are presented in his memoirs *As I Was Going Down Sackville Street* (1937). He had a mean streak though, and took exception to a throwaway remark written by Patrick Kavanagh (1904–67) alluding to him having a mistress; he successfully sued the poet, whom he described as 'that Monaghan boy'.

Kavanagh, from farming stock in Monaghan, walked to Dublin (a very long way) in 1934 and made the capital his home. His later poetry explored Ireland's city versus country dynamic. He was fond of the Grand Canal, along the banks of which he is commemorated, with 'just a canal-bank seat for the passer-by', as he had wished.

You can't imagine the brooding Samuel Beckett (1906–89) hanging around in this company and, while his greatest literary contributions were as a dramatist in self-imposed exile (also see Theatre, p41), he did write a collection of short stories in Dublin, *More Pricks Than Kicks* (1934), about an eccentric local character. The book so irked the new Free State government that it was banned, no doubt hastening Beckett's permanent move to Paris.

One-time civil servant Brian O'Nolan (1911–66), also known as Flann O'Brien and Myles na Gopaleen, was a celebrated comic writer and career drinker. He wrote several books, most notably *At Swim-Two-Birds* (1939) and *The Third Policeman* (1940), but was most fondly remembered for the newspaper columns he penned for nearly three decades before his death.

DUBLIN'S NOBEL LAUREATES

- George Bernard Shaw (1925)
- William Butler Yeats (1938)
- Samuel Beckett (1969)
- Seamus Heaney (1995; born in Derry but lives in Dublin)

He was eclipsed – at least in the drinking stakes – by novelist, playwright, journalist and quintessential Dublin hell-raiser, Brendan Behan (1923–64), who led a short and frantic life. In 1953, Behan began work as a columnist with the now-defunct *Irish Press*, and over the next decade wrote about his beloved Dublin, using wonderful, earthy satire and a keen sense of political commentary that set him apart from other journalists. A collection of his newspaper columns was published under the title *Hold Your Hour and Have Another*.

The Contemporary Scene

For close to two decades, Dublin's literary scene has been partly in the shadow of the massive commercial success of Roddy Doyle (1958–), the one-time secondary school teacher who turned his observations of the capital's suburban working classes into literary gold with the Barrytown trilogy – *The Commitments* (1987), *The Snapper* (1990) and *The Van* (1991) – which were all turned into successful movies. He won the prestigious Booker Prize in 1993 for his semi-autobiographical *Paddy Clarke Ha Ha Ha*, and his output since then has gotten more and more serious. He tackled domestic violence in *The Woman Who Walked into Doors* (1997), social and political history in *A Star Called Henry* (2000) and nonfiction with *Rory & Ita* (2002) – essentially an interview with his parent. In *Paula Spencer* (2006), we revisit the forlorn alcoholic character first introduced in *The Woman Who Walked into Doors*, now nine years older, newly sober and facing the challenges of life one day at a time.

The critics' favourite and a genuine contender for top literary heavyweight is the sometimes impenetrable but always brilliant John Banville (1945–), who was shortlisted for the Booker Prize with *The Book of Evidence* (1989), before actually winning it in 2005 with *The Sea*. Our favourite, however, is *The Untouchable* (1998), a superb *roman á clef* based loosely on the secret-agent life of art historian Anthony Blunt. The other big hitter in Irish literary circles was John McGahern (1934–2006), although his appeal is a little more local. Besides his Booker-nominated *Amongst Women* (1990), McGahern has a string of superb books to his credit, including his last book, the non-fiction *Memoir* (2005), published in the US as *All Will be Well*.

A noteworthy name is Colm Tóibín (1955–), born in County Wexford but resident in Dublin (his birthplace is almost part of the capital these days anyway). He took four years to find a publisher for his first novel *The South* (1990) but has gone on to become a hugely successful

LIVING POET'S SOCIETY

Seamus Heaney (1939–) was born in Derry but now lives mostly in Dublin. He is the bard of all Ireland and evokes the spirit and character of the country in his poetry. He won the Nobel Prize for Literature in 1995, and the humble wordsmith compared all the attention to someone mentioning sex in front of their mammy. *Opened Ground – Poems 1966–1996* (1998) is our favourite of his books.

Dubliner Paul Durcan (1944–) is one of the most reliable chroniclers of changing Dublin. He won the prestigious Whitbread Prize for Poetry in 1990 for *'Daddy, Daddy'* and is a funny, engaging, tender and savage writer. Poet, playwright and Kerryman Brendan Kennelly (1936–) is an immensely popular character around town. He lectures at Trinity College and writes a unique brand of poetry that is marked by its playfulness, as well as historical and intellectual impact. Eavan Boland (1944–) is a prolific and much-admired writer, best known for her poetry, who combines Irish politics with outspoken feminism; *In a Time of Violence* (1995) and *The Lost Land* (1998) are two of her most celebrated collections.

If you're interested in finding out more about poetry in Ireland in general, visit the website of the excellent Poetry Ireland (www.poetryireland.ie), which showcases the work of new and established poets.

RECOMMENDED READING

At Swim-Two-Birds (1939; Flann O'Brien) By the late satirical columnist and regarded by many as the great Dublin novel. It's funny and absurd, and uses inventive wordplay in telling the story within a story of a student novelist.

Dubliners (1914; James Joyce) In our humble opinion, one of the most perfectly written collections of short stories ever; 15 poignant and powerful tales of Dubliners and the moments that define their lives. Even if you never visit, read this book.

Amongst Women (1990; John McGahern) Focuses on a rough old republican whose story is told through his three daughters. It's essentially a study of the faults and comforts of humanity and an exploration of family ties, told by an exceptionally skilled author who combines a gentle tone with an unfailing eye for the human condition.

At Swim, Two Boys (2001; Jamie O'Neill) A beautifully crafted masterpiece that has drawn comparisons to Joyce and Beckett for its language and characterisation. Essentially it's a coming-of-age tale of gay youth set against the backdrop of revolutionary Dublin circa 1916. It's ambitious, absorbing and absolutely brilliant.

The Book of Evidence (1989; John Banville) Written by the former literary editor of the Irish Times, this consists of the prison memoir of Freddie Montgomery, on trial for the brutal murder of a female servant. It's a terrific and elaborate piece of literary, philosophical and political fiction.

Death in Summer (1998; William Trevor) Ireland's master of the short story shows his skills with this novel, which is a riveting and sympathetic portrait of the sadness and distress of ordinary people.

The Ginger Man (1955; JP Donleavy) A high-energy foray around Dublin from the perspective of an Irish-American scoundrel. It received the Catholic Church's 'seal of approval' by being banned in Ireland for many years.

The Informer (1925; Liam O'Flaherty) The classic book about the divided sympathies that plagued Ireland during its independence struggle and the ensuing Civil War. Set in the Dublin underworld, this enthralling revolutionary drama was successfully brought to the big screen by the legendary John Ford.

My Left Foot (1954; Christy Brown) The story of the author's life growing up with cerebral palsy, which he overcame to become an accomplished painter and writer. This autobiography was later expanded into the novel Down all the Days (1970), which formed the basis of the acclaimed film My Left Foot.

New Dubliners (2005; edited by Oona Frawley) The likes of Maeve Binchy, Dermot Bolger, Roddy Doyle, Colum McCann and Joseph O'Connor lend their respective talents to creating short stories about modern-day Dublin.

Paula Spencer (2006; Roddy Doyle) A terrifically well-observed and sensitive novel about the everyday struggles of a suburban alcoholic looking to piece her life back together after finally quitting the booze.

The Journey Home (1990; Dermot Bolger) Depicts the underside of modern Irish society with a pacy, absorbing narrative and beautifully crafted characters and scenarios. The tourist board would probably have it banned if it had its way.

The Speckled People (2003; Hugo Hamilton) A brilliant – and pertinent to today's immigrants – novel-memoir of the author's German-Irish upbringing in 1950s Dublin; a boy tells of a family's homesickness for a culture to call their own.

Tatty (2003; Christine Dwyer Hickey) A beautiful and brutal portrayal of an alcoholic Dublin family and its slow and terrible disintegration as seen through the eyes of a child.

novelist and scholar – his latest work, *The Master* (2004), about Henry James, won the Los Angeles Times' Novel of the Year award.

Joseph O'Connor (1963–), Sinéad's older brother, burst onto the scene with *Cowboys and Indians* (1991) and has delivered a string of popular novels, none better than *The Star of the Sea* (2002), a murder mystery set on board a 19th-century famine ship. Another contemporary notable is Jamie O'Neill (1962–), whose *At Swim, Two Boys* (2001) is the great Irish gay novel (attentive readers will have recognised the pun on Flann O'Brien's book).

Walk into any bookstore in town and you will undoubtedly notice the preponderance of so-called chick lit titles penned by Irish authors. The doyenne of the style is unquestionably Maeve Binchy (1940–) whose mastery of the 'come here and I'll tell you a story' approach has seen her outsell many of the greats of Irish literature, including Beckett and Behan, and her long list of bestsellers includes *Light a Penny Candle* (1982) and *Circle of Friends* (1990); both have been made into successful films. Following on her heels is Marion Keyes (1963–), who has written 10 incredibly successful novels (*Rachel's Holiday* – 1998 – is our sneaky favourite), and former agony aunt Cathy Kelly, whose latest book, *Lessons in Heartbreak* (2008), *can* be judged by its cover. Even Taoiseach (Prime Minister) Bertie Ahern's daughter Cecilia (1981–) has cashed in on the chick lit phenomenon. Her first book, *P.S., I Love You* (2004), was a huge hit (and is currently being made into a movie with Hilary Swank in the lead role) and we expect nothing less from her equally saccharine follow-up, *Where Rainbows End* (2005).

For more serious fare, Jennifer Johnston's (1930–) latest novel is *Grace and Truth* (2005), while the excellent Anne Enright (1962–) has seen her new novel *The Gathering* (2007) win the 2007 Booker Prize. Another young writer worth keeping an eye on is Claire Kilroy, whose novels *All Summer* (2003) and *Tenderwire* (2006) have been turning more than pages.

MUSIC

Dublin's literary tradition may have the intellectuals nodding sagely, but it's the city's musical credentials that has the rest of us bopping, for it's no cliché to say that music is as intrinsic to the local lifestyle as a good night out. Feelings are all right, Dubs will tell you, but don't you dare express them outside a song. Which goes some way towards explaining the city's love affair with the singer-songwriter, the guy or gal with a guitar who unpeels the layers of their heart through the tortured choruses of song. But even if the slovenly sentiment of the miserable minstrel doesn't draw you in, there's plenty else that will: rock gigs, DJ nights and traditional sessions take place in venues throughout the city every night of the week and, if someone isn't actually making the music, you can be sure there's a fancy stereo filling in the background so that you hear something else besides the sound of your own voice. Oh, for an occasional bit of *whist* (silence): does every new bar have to test our eardrums? Even the streets – well, OK, Grafton St – are alive with the sounds of music, and you can hardly get around without stubbing your toe on the next international superstar busking their way to a record contract. One thing's for certain, you'll have the music of Dublin ringing in your ears long after your gig here is done.

Traditional & Folk

Dublin's not the best place in Ireland to savour a traditional session although, thanks to the tourist demand, it's a lot better than it was 10 years ago. There are some lively sessions in pubs throughout the city, and some of them are as good as you'll hear anywhere in the country.

Irish music has retained a vibrancy not found in other traditional European forms, which have lost out to the overbearing influence of pop music. This is probably because,

top picks

DUBLIN SONGS

- Raglan Road (1972) Luke Kelly & the Dubliners
- Lay Me Down (2001) The Frames
- One (1990) U2
- Still in Love With You (1978) Thin Lizzy
- I Don't Like Mondays (1979) Boomtown Rats

although Irish music has retained many of its traditional aspects, it has itself influenced many forms of music, most notably US country and western – a fusion of Mississippi Delta blues and Irish traditional tunes that, combined with other influences like Gospel, is at the root of

THE NUTS & BOLTS OF TRADITIONAL MUSIC

Despite popular perception, the harp isn't widely used in traditional music (it *is* the national emblem, but that probably has more to do with the country traditionally being run by people pulling strings). The *bodhrán* (bow-rawn) goat-skin drum is much more prevalent, although it makes for a lousy symbol. The uillean pipes, played by squeezing bellows under the elbow, provide another distinctive sound although you're not likely to see them in a pub. The fiddle isn't unique to Ireland but it is one of the main instruments in the country's indigenous music, along with the flute, tin whistle, accordion and bouzouki (a version of the mandolin). Music fits into five main categories (jigs, reels, hornpipes, polkas and slow airs) while the old style of singing unaccompanied versions of traditional ballads and airs is called *sean-nós*.

top picks

TRADITIONAL PLAYLIST

- The Quiet Glen (1998) Tommy Peoples
- Paddy Keenan (1975) Paddy Keenan
- Compendium: The Best of Patrick Street (2000) Patrick Street
- The Chieftains 6: Bonaparte's Retreat (1976) The Chieftains
- Old Hag You Have Killed Me (1976) The Bothy Band

rock and roll. Other reasons for its current success include the willingness of its exponents to update the way it's played (in ensembles rather than the customary *céilidh* – communal dance – bands), the habit of pub sessions (introduced by returning migrants) and the economic good times that encouraged the Irish to celebrate their culture rather than trying to replicate international trends. And then, of course, there's *Riverdance*, which made Irish dancing sexy and became a worldwide phenomenon, despite the fact that most aficionados of traditional music are seriously underwhelmed by its musical worth. Good stage show, crap music.

If you want to hear musical skill that will both tear out your heart and restore your faith in humanity, go no further than the fiddle-playing of Tommy Peoples on *The Quiet Glen* (1998), the beauty of Paddy Keenan's uillean pipes on his eponymous 1975 album, or the stunning guitar playing of Andy Irvine on albums like *Compendium: The Best of Patrick Street* (2000).

The most famous traditional band – arguably the original 'band' – is The Chieftains, formed in 1963 and still going strong after four decades. The most loved band in the capital, although more folksy than traditional, is the Dubliners, fronted by the distinctive gravel voice and grey beard of Ronnie Drew, whose photograph should appear above the word Dublin whenever it's printed. Luke Kelly (1940–84) was the most talented and beloved member of the band and his solo version of *Scorn Not His Simplicity* is one of the saddest, most beautiful songs ever recorded. Another band whose career has been stitched into the fabric of Dublin life is the Fureys, comprising four brothers originally from the travelling community (no, not like the Wilburys) along with guitarist Davey Arthur. And if it's rousing renditions of Irish rebel songs you're after, you can't go past the Wolfe Tones. Ireland is packed with traditional talent and we strongly recommend that you spend some time in a specialised traditional shop like Claddagh Records (p137).

Since the 1970s, various bands have tried to blend traditional with more progressive genres with mixed success. The first band to pull it off was Moving Hearts, led by Christy Moore, who went on to become the greatest Irish folk musician ever (see the boxed text, below).

While traditional music continues to be popular in its own right both in Ireland and abroad, it also continues to provide the base for successful new genres. Think of ambient music with a slightly mystical tinge and invariably Enya will come to mind, while a wonderful product of contemporary Ireland has been the Afro-Celt Foundation, which fuses African rhythms and electronic beats with traditional Irish sounds to great effect.

CHRISTY MOORE: THE TRADITION MOVES ON Stuart Cooper

Kildare-born Christy Moore (1945–) is one of Ireland's best-loved singers in the traditional mode. Combining a ready wit and puckish charm with his undoubted talent, he has produced more than 20 solo albums of breathtaking diversity and scope.

The causes he has championed – travellers, anti-nuclear protests, South Africa, Northern Ireland – might give one the wrong impression: Christy is equally at home singing tender love songs *(Nancy Spain)*, haunting ballads *(Ride On)*, comic ditties *(Lisdoonvarna)* and bizarre flights of lyrical fancy *(Reel in the Flickering Light)*. He was also influential as a member of Planxty and Moving Hearts, as Ireland experimented during the 1970s and 1980s with its traditional musical forms to combine folk, rock and jazz in a heady and vibrant fusion.

Moore's first big break came with *Prosperous*, on which he teamed up with the legendary Donal Lunny, Andy Irvine and Liam O'Flynn. They went on to form Planxty and record three ground-breaking albums.

Among all the phoney Oirishness, Moore stands out as the genuine article: passionate, provocative and distinctive. He has built an international reputation as a writer and interpreter of a living tradition, and sits at the head of the table of Irish traditional music. For tour dates, see www.christymoore.com.

Recommended listening: *The Christy Moore Collection, 81–91*.

Popular Music

Dublin may rely on the rest of the country to buck up its traditional rep, but no such help is required with rock music, save maybe the huge and overwhelming influence of London, which has inspired, attracted, rejected and made many a Dublin rock band.

Fuelled by the Pop Explosion and the 1960s London scene, Dublin bands began to believe that they had a future beyond the stages of their local dance hall. The most important of these was Thin Lizzy, formed in 1969 and led by the simply fantastic Phil Lynott (see the boxed text, p182); they finally got their breakthrough with *Jailbreak* (1975). Their finest hour, literally, was *Live & Dangerous* (1978), one of the greatest live albums ever recorded. Thin Lizzy's music aged better than its charismatic and hard-living lead singer, whose life and creativity were blighted by drug use and physical deterioration – he died in 1986.

During the punk explosion of the mid-1970s, Bob 'for fuck's sake' Geldof and the Boomtown Rats carried the mantle for Dublin, strutting their way to centre stage with hit singles *Rat Trap* and *I Don't Like Mondays*. By the time the band had begun to wane, Geldof had moved onto more important matters and for the last 20 years he has been mixing moral outrage and annoying condescension in his lecture to the world on the terrible crisis that afflicts Africa. To be fair, without him we would never have had Live Aid, Live Eight or those Make Poverty History wristbands.

Just as the Rats were celebrating the virtues of sex, drugs and rock 'n' roll, a young drummer pinned a note on his school notice board looking for fellow pupils who were interested in forming a band. Over the next four years, Larry Mullen and his new-found band learned that they were rubbish at playing covers and so devoted themselves to writing their own songs. The release of their debut, *Boy* (1980), proved that they were absolutely brilliant at it. And so U2 was born.

Bono and the boys went on to produce a string of brilliant albums before becoming the World's Biggest Rock Act in the aftermath of the truly wonderful *The Joshua Tree* (1987). They've remained supernovas in the pop firmament through thick and thicker: their musical creativity may have slowed somewhat, Bono's impressive and diverse range of interests may keep him out of the studio more than ever, but the U2 boys haven't quite draped the shawl of sad rockers around their 40-something shoulders. Their last album, *U218* (2006), was a long-awaited singles collection that barely does justice to their high-quality output and in 2007 they were back in the recording studio working on material for a new album.

U2's success cast a long shadow over the city's musical scene in the 1980s – despite the valiant and wonderful efforts of Sinead O'Connor to bask in her own sunlight and the singular genius of My Bloody Valentine, who were the true pioneers of the shoegazer alt-rock movement of the late 1980s – but their global megastardom and the explosion of dance music in the 1990s lessened their day-to-day relevance to Dublin. U2 became

top picks

DUBLIN ALBUMS

Five albums by Dublin artists to provide a decent soundtrack for your city visit:

- Loveless (My Bloody Valentine) Utterly intoxicating indie classic that just piles on the layers of sound and melody.
- Boy (U2) Best debut album of all time? We think so.
- The End of History (Fionn Regan) Too early to say if it's a classic, but it's bloody good.
- Live & Dangerous (Thin Lizzy) Released in 1978, it remains one of the greatest live albums ever recorded.
- I Do Not Want What I Haven't Got (Sinead O'Connor) Try listening to the Prince-penned 'Nothing Compares to U' and not feel her pain – or your own!

yet another example of the city producing artistic genius for the world to savour and for Dubliners, in their own, inimitable begrudgery, to shrug their shoulders and give out about Bono being a pretentious arsehole.

The late 1990s saw a thriving economy, and the feel-good vibes of a city anaesthetised by pleasure was hardly a healthy breeding ground for great rock. Enter the too-horrible-for-words phenomenon of the boy band, masterfully manipulated by impresario Louis Walsh, who created Boyzone, Ronan Keating and Westlife, and got very rich in the process. And that's enough type wasted on them.

Infinitely more memorable – although not necessarily for the biggest participants – was the emergence of the dance music scene, a five-year party fuelled by ecstasy, bottled water and the pounding beat of techno. International DJs and producers led the way, but a couple of local names managed to find a place in the starting line-up, none more so than Billy Scurry (see the boxed text, below) whose skills on the decks were a match for any overpaid superstar DJ from across the water.

top picks

DUBLIN DJS

- **Billy Scurry** Simply the best techno DJ in the city. Back in the early '90s he set the tone for the e-fuelled revolution in the city's dancing habits and has never looked back. A true Dub, totally unaffected by fame and reputation, he plays his records in a seamless, perfect way, pulling the crowd this way and that for hours on end.

- **DJ Mek** The best hip-hop DJ this country has ever produced. A scratch and mix genius, he has the unique ability (in Ireland anyway) not to get lost in his technical prowess (which is virtually infinite) and keep the party going. He once ate a can of beans on stage and then proceeded to scratch like he was farting. Sensational.

- **Johnny Moy** Another superb techno DJ. Back in the 1990s he was invited to play the legendary Hacienda Club in Manchester. He started well, got the crowd going and then, halfway through his set, let the track fade out. Silence for nearly 20 seconds as everyone looked around going 'what the hell?' Then came the explosive sound of the Jam's *Going Underground*. The crowd went absolutely mental; a moment of pure genius that took balls of brass (or lots of drugs) to pull off.

- **DJ Tu-Ki** Straight out of Mek's inner circle, Tu-Ki was the very first Irish DJ to make it to the finals of the World DMC Championships (2003), the *crème de la crème* for hip-hop DJs throughout the world (Beck's DJ is a former winner). Needless to say, he's a wizard on the wheels of steel.

- **DJ Arveene** A freestyle DJ who packs his record bag with techno, house, hip-hop, hardcore rock, punk, soul and pop, which he mixes, scratches and cuts to keep the party going. Great fun, great skill and perfect to dance to.

The Contemporary Scene

Dance music hasn't quite disappeared, but it's got awful quieter in the last few years. Instead, Dublin has witnessed the return of the rock band – although most of them would argue with great irritation that rock never went away. The biggest noise of all is being made by Snow Patrol, whose blend of indie-lite guitar and soaring melody has made them the favourite darlings of the mortgage rock brigade: their 2006 offering, *Eyes Open* (2006), was one of the biggest hits of the year both in Ireland and the UK. Other successful debut albums of recent years include *Future Kings of Spain* by the indie rock band of the same name, and the also-eponymous *Hal*, a feast of cheerful and melodic pop that's guaranteed to put a smile on anyone's face.

Dublin has always had a terrific tradition of singer-songwriters, and the current crop is plentiful, if not always brilliant. The best-known names include Paddy Casey, who followed up his multi-platinum album *Living* (2004) with *Addicted to Company* (2007), and Damien Rice (he followed up his multi-million selling *O* with the disappointing *9*). A pair of new arrivals are the supremely talented Fionn Regan (his 2006 debut *The End of History* was pipped at the line for the 2007 Mercury Award) and the Belfast-born Duke Special, whose left-of-centre *Songs from the Deep Forest* (2006) has also earned plenty of critical acclaim. Other performers to look out for are Julie Feeney – her debut, *13 Songs* (2005), scooped the top prize at the 2006 Choice Music Prize, Ireland's answer to Britain's Mercury Award – and soul-folk-rockers The Frames, who have a phenomenally loyal following earned over more than 15 years of releasing albums and touring. Finally, a word about the northside's favourite son, Damien

Dempsey, who wears his street cred very much on his sleeve and has earned himself a lot of fans for his in-your-face style and hard-hitting phrasing, but we thought his lyrics were silly and pedestrian. Judge for yourself with his latest release, *To Hell or Barbados* (2007).

THEATRE

Dubliners have a unique affinity with theatre; it seems to course through their veins. Perhaps this explains why dramatists Oliver Goldsmith, Oscar Wilde and George Bernard Shaw conquered the theatre world in London even before there was such an entity as Irish drama. While Dublin has a long association with the stage – the first theatre was founded here in 1637 – it wasn't until the late-19th-century Celtic Revival Movement and the establishment of the Abbey Theatre that Irish drama really took off.

Perhaps the first renowned Dublin playwright was Oliver Goldsmith (1730–74) who enjoyed much success with *The Good Natur'd Man* (1768) and *She Stoops to Conquer* (1773) before his early death. Language enthusiasts might like to know that another Dublin-born London favourite, Richard Brinsley Sheridan (1751–1816), gave us the word 'malapropism' after the misguided character Mrs Malaprop from his play *The Rivals* (1775).

The infinitely quotable Oscar Wilde (1854–1900) left Dublin for London after studying at Trinity and caused a sensation with his uproarious, challenging plays such as *The Importance of Being Earnest* (1895) and *An Ideal Husband* (1895). However, his most important and vigorous work is *The Ballad of Reading Gaol* (1898), which he wrote while serving a prison sentence for being a progressive homosexual in a backward time. Wilde paid a heavy toll for the harsh prison conditions and the ignorance of Victorian society, dying bankrupt not long after his release.

Fellow Trinity alumnus John Millington Synge (1871–1909) was one of the first to create headlines at Dublin's Abbey Theatre, established in 1904 by WB Yeats and Lady Gregory to stage Irish productions and stimulate the local scene. In stark contrast to Wilde, Synge's plays focused on the Irish peasantry, whose wonderful language, bawdy witticisms and eloquent invective he transposed into his plays. His honest portrayal of the brutality of rural life in his most famous drama, *The Playboy of the Western World* (1907), resulted in rioting when it first opened at the Abbey. Sadly for Irish drama, Synge died of Hodgkin's disease within two years, aged just 38.

Sean O'Casey (1880–1964), from the working-class north inner city, didn't even become a full-time writer until his 40s but made up for the slow start with a brilliant burst in which he wrote the powerful trilogy on patriotism and life in Dublin's slums, *Shadow of a Gunman* (1923), *Juno and the Paycock* (1924) and *The Plough and the Stars* (1926). The latter also caused riots in the Abbey Theatre when it was first staged and it's a wonder WB Yeats and co could afford the insurance to carry on.

Brendan Behan (1923–64) was another immensely talented Dublin playwright whose creative fire was quenched much too early. A die-hard republican, he shot to prominence with his autobiographical accounts of his time in prison in Dublin and England, in the play *The Quare Fellow* (1954) and the tale *Borstal Boy* (1958). His masterpiece was *The Hostage* (1958), a devastatingly satirical play about an English soldier being ransomed by the IRA. He struggled to cope with the fame his talent brought, and his alcoholism – and the image of celebrity hell-raiser that he tried to live up to – delivered his early demise.

It hardly seems possible that he could have shared the same era as Dublin-born Samuel Beckett (1906–89). Beckett spent most of his adult life in Paris and wrote much of his work in French, but is still thought of as an Irish playwright, perhaps because it was as much his rejection of Irish culture that drove him as a longing for anything else. His greatest works are associated with the bleakness and self-examination that occurred in continental Europe following WWII, from which he himself spent a good time on the run. Many consider his *Waiting for Godot* (1953) to be the modernist theatrical masterpiece. Beckett got the nod from the Nobel committee in 1969 and literary Dublin got another feather in its well-plumed cap.

The Contemporary Scene

Irish theatre is still sincerely and refreshingly self-absorbed, which means it offers visitors a direct short cut into the heart of Irish culture – at least in theory. After a mid-century descent into the doldrums – when lack of funds and resources, coupled with a tired theatrical vision, missed an important artistic opportunity to offer an insight into a sick and stagnant society – the theatre bounced back in the early 1990s, thanks largely to a reinvigorated establishment and a host of new companies geed up by the boundless possibilities of the new economy. Inspired by the ground-breaking work being explored in other countries, Irish companies began their own forays into experimentation, creating a buzz of activity not seen on the city's stages since the days of Yeats and Lady Gregory.

Yet a buoyant economy has had a negative effect too: rising property prices and the developers' bottom line has meant that no new stages have opened up in the city centre, forcing companies onto the streets – literally. Open-air performances are an increasing part of the theatrical landscape. So are the purpose-built performance centres in the suburbs, which are themselves a wonderful addition to the local cultural landscape but hardly speak loudly of a city committed to its theatrical identity. Basically, Dublin wants its theatres, but it wants them out of the way of the ongoing development of every inch of centre space.

Under pressure to justify itself as a going concern, Dublin theatres have subconsciously turned more and more towards the fizz bang wallop of spectacle, often at the expense of quality. Some of the most successful plays of recent years seem obsessed with re-creating the high-paced neurotic energy of the action thriller on the stage, as though the audience isn't patient enough to be engrossed by the slow build-up usually associated with theatrical drama. The introduction of more noise, more guns and sharp dialogue out of an American pulp novel might keep the audience laughing on the edge of their seats, but it doesn't make for lasting, quality theatre.

Theatre's tattered flag is still kept flying, however, by the efforts of some excellent writers and companies. Brian Friel and Tom Murphy are the country's leading established playwrights; neither is from Dublin although most of their work premieres here, often in the Gate Theatre. Rough Magic, one of the most successful independent companies of recent years, specialises in bringing new works to Ireland and new Irish writers to the stage, so the future may be very bright indeed for a bunch of new writers like Michael Collins, John Comiskey, Oonagh Kearney, Gina Moxley and Arthur Riordan. The present is also pretty shiny for the likes of Enda Walsh, author of *Disco Pigs* (1996) and *Bedbound* (2000), with the former made into a film starring Cillian Murphy. Mark O'Rowe, who presented an electrifying picture of gangland Dublin in his award-winning *Howie the Rookie* (1999) and followed it with *Made in China* (2001) and *Crestfall* (2003), is one of the very hot names in the contemporary scene, but he too has made the move into film writing, co-scripting the awful *Intermission* (2003); his latest play, *Terminus* (2007), was very well-received. Eugene O'Brien's excellent *Eden* (2001) was followed by the disappointing *Savoy* (2004), which reminded us a bit of *Cinema Paradiso*, only set in a provincial Irish town. O'Brien has since moved on to some questionable TV work.

The really exciting period for Dublin theatre is festival time, usually late September/early October. The main Dublin Theatre Festival attracts some worthy plays, but the superb fringe festival is also worth attending: it runs just before the bigger event and features some of the best work you'll see all year. For more information, see p185.

CINEMA & TV
Cinema

Ireland's film-making tradition is pretty poor, largely because the British cinema industry drained much of its talent and creative energies and the Irish government pleaded poverty anytime a film-maker came looking for some development cash. Then, in 1993, the re-establishment of the Irish Film Board (after an abortive run from 1981) saw the government attempt to revive the dead with a two-pronged plan: inviting international film crews to make their movies here through generous tax incentives, the proceeds of which would hopefully stimulate local production.

Part one worked just fine: international crews came, took the cash and used the landscapes and towns of Ireland as film sets. Among others, the beaches of Wexford doubled as Normandy for *Saving Private Ryan* and Kilmainham Gaol starred as an English prison for *In the Name of the Father*…but part two of the plan has been a little more problematic.

RECOMMENDED VIEWING

About Adam (2000; Gerry Stembridge) Set in contemporary Dublin, a watchable tale that focuses on one man's ability to woo three sisters by appealing to what each woman wants in a man (apparently, sometimes more than a Dublin accent). It features local actor Stuart Townsend and US sensation Kate Hudson.

Adam and Paul (2004; Lenny Abrahamson) Mark O'Hallorahan and Tom Murphy put in compelling and convincing performances as two junkies from the inner-city projects desperate for a fix. It's funny, pithy and occasionally silly, but a great debut for Abrahamson nonetheless.

Dead Bodies (2003; Robert Quinn) A dark and stylish thriller set in contemporary Dublin against the backdrop of a general election. It's a terrific debut from the first-time director and features serial Irish bad guy Gerard McSorley among a terrific cast.

The Dead (1987; John Huston) Based on a short story from James Joyce's *Dubliners, The Dead* focuses on a dinner party in Dublin at the end of the 19th century and specifically the thoughts of one of the party goers. A difficult task for Huston in his last film, and he pulls it off with aplomb.

I Went Down (1997; Paddy Breathnach) A quirky comedy caper with two characters borrowed from Quentin Tarantino's rogues gallery, which works particularly well with the Irish humour and sensibility. It stars one of our favourite actors, Brendan Gleeson, and is Ireland's all-time highest grossing film.

The Snapper (1993; Stephen Frears) A made-for-TV movie about how a Dublin family copes when their daughter gets 'up the pole' and won't tell anyone who the father is. Our choice of the Barrytown trilogy, which also included *The Commitments* and *The Van*. Full of slang, humour and pathos, it is Dublin to the core and absolutely brilliant. Colm Meaney is outstanding as the father.

A Man of No Importance (1994; Suri Krishnamma) Stars the brilliant Albert Finney as a repressed bus conductor trying to come to terms with his own homosexuality in 1960s Dublin while at the same time staging an amateur production of Oscar Wilde's *Salome*. Melancholy and beautiful, it feels like a poem.

Inside I'm Dancing (2004; Damien O'Donnell) One of our favourite Irish films of the last decade is an uplifting yarn about a young man with cerebral palsy (played by Steven Robertson) whose institutionalised life is transformed by the arrival of the fast-talking, rebellious and fatally ill Rory (James McAvoy). Brenda Fricker is excellent as the formidable Eileen, a Nurse Ratchett–type character.

The Magdalene Sisters (2002; Peter Mullan) A confronting and uncompromising film based on the true story of four young 'sinners' who were sent to one of the infamous Magdalene asylums in Dublin in the 1960s, where they suffered abuse by the nuns who ran the place (instances of inhumanity still being investigated by the state). It's as moving as it is bleak.

The General (1998; John Boorman) A portrayal of Ireland's most notorious and enigmatic crime boss who, during the early 1990s when he was the pinnacle of gangland Dublin, was seen as much as a folk hero as a thug. Brendan Gleeson turns in a terrific performance, but the film tries far too hard to be funny.

Michael Collins (1996; Neil Jordan) This biopic of the man who delivered Irish independence and was assassinated during the 1922 civil war is an epic tale and a great film with pride and passion. The only downside is Jordan's shameful revision of history, specifically his portrayal of Eamon de Valera as a weak and pathetic collaborator in Collins' murder.

My Left Foot (1989; Jim Sheridan) The best film made in and about Dublin in modern history. Based on the life story of Christy Brown, an Irish writer/artist with cerebral palsy, this stirring and triumphant film is made by the astonishing performance of Daniel Day-Lewis, who didn't leave his character on set for the duration of the shoot, even forcing crew to carry him around.

When Brendan Met Trudy (2001; Kieron Walsh) A likable, light-hearted romance based in Dublin that apes scenes from old movies (there's a clue in the title) to add an extra layer for anyone who feels stiffed by the superficiality of a feel-good flick.

Ireland has worked hard to cast off that ridiculous 'Oirland' identity so beloved of Hollywood's plastic paddies – watch *The Quiet Man* (1952) and you'll get the picture – but the local film industry is under huge pressure to come up with the goods, and in film, the 'goods' means a commercial success. Exit the creative space to make really insightful films about a host of Irish subjects, enter the themed film designed to make a commercial splash in Britain and the US.

THINGS YOU DIDN'T KNOW ABOUT DUBLIN

That little Oscar statuette that reduces spoiled millionaire actors to floods of tears was actually designed by a Dublin-born art director, Cedric Gibbons, who took up a job as supervising art director for MGM in 1924. Over the next 32 years he worked on 1500 films and was nominated for his own statuette 37 times, winning it on 11 occasions.

Favourite themes include Mad 'n' Quirky – *The Butcher Boy* (1997) and *Disco Pigs* (2001); Smart-arse Gangsters – *I Went Down* (1997) and *Intermission* (2003); and Cutsy Formulaic Love Story – *When Brendan Met Trudy* (2001). Never mind the Irish Welles or Fellini, where's the local equivalent of Loach, Leigh or Winterbottom?

The film board may wince and then point us in the direction of Neil Jordan and Jim Sheridan. Jim Sheridan has reeled off a series of well-made hits, including *The Field* (1989), *In the Name of the Father* (1993) and *The Boxer* (1997), but he followed up with his tepid and far too 'oirish' *In America* (2002), a semi-autobiographical film that was strictly for plastic paddy consumption. Neil Jordan, however, is unquestionably a major talent, having thrilled us with a diverse selection of films that began with the excellent *Angel* (1982), continued with the weird and wonderful *The Company of Wolves* (1983), the just brilliant *Mona Lisa* (1986) and *The Crying Game* (1992), the blockbuster biopic *Michael Collins* (1996), the already mentioned *Butcher Boy* and, more recently, *The End of the Affair* (1999) and the vastly under-rated *The Good Thief* (2002). In 2007 he brought us the thriller *The Brave One* starring Jodie Foster and was working on a film version of the horror novel *Heart-Shaped Box*.

New directors include the impossibly-young-but-well-connected Kristen Sheridan (born 1977), daughter of Jim and director of *Disco Pigs*. Another bright talent is Damien O'Donnell, who debuted with *East is East* (1999) and went from strength to strength with *Heartlands* (2002) and the outstanding Irish film of 2004, *Inside I'm Dancing*. That same year saw the release of *Adam and Paul*, written by Mark O'Hallorahan and directed by Lenny Abrahamson, a half-decent portrayal of two Dublin junkies and their quixotic quest for a fix. It was a roaring success at the Irish box office.

As far as actors are concerned, Ireland – and Dublin – have been pouring them out for years. Hot on the heels of such luminaries as Liam Neeson (*Schindler's List, Star Wars* etc), Gabriel Byrne *(Miller's Crossing, The Usual Suspects)*, Stephen Rea *(The Crying Game, The End of the Affair)* and the Oscar-winning Daniel Day-Lewis and Brenda Fricker (both for *My Left Foot*) are the late-arriving but always excellent Brendan Gleeson, the very handsome Cillian Murphy and the bad boy himself, Colin Farrell, whose lifestyle and bad movie choices has seriously threatened to derail a movie career that once promised so much.

On an up note, director John Carney turned Hollywood heads with the awfully lovely *Once* (2006), starring The Frames front man Glen Hansard (in his first film role since *The Commitments*) and Czech newcomer Markéta Irglová. Set in Dublin, it's a love story between a busker and a young immigrant. The soundtrack, performed by Hansard and Irglová, is excellent.

TV

Irish TV is small fry, it always has been. It lacks the funding and the audience available to behemoths like the BBC. But – and this is a huge but – compared to that of most other European countries it is actually good. Critics lambast it for being parochial and conservative, but most Irish are pretty pleased that their national station hasn't gone down the road of endless variety shows featuring semi-clad wannabe starlets and really crap humour.

Instead, RTE plods along with a homemade drama, a farming programme or a series exploring the importance of faith in the modern world. Ireland is a small country with a culture in flux, and while RTE may not be leading the charge into the world of tomorrow it is careful not to throw the baby out with the bathwater. Hold on a minute, say the critics, what about the Angelus? Turn on the TV at 6pm (or the radio at noon or 6pm) and you will hear Ireland's very own call to prayer, 18 sombre hits of a church bell. The Angelus has been broadcast every day since radio and TV began in Ireland. It is undoubtedly out of step with the fast-paced change overcoming Irish society, but what's so wrong with stopping for a minute to ponder something deeper than the price of petrol or whether the light blue goes well with the off-white?

RTE's strength is in its news and current affairs programming – it's thorough, insightful and often hard-hitting. Programmes like *Today Tonight, Questions and Answers* and *Prime Time* are as good as, or better than, anything you'll see elsewhere in the world; the reporting treats the audience like mature responsible adults who don't need issues dumbed down or simplified.

Where RTE falls way short is in drama. Its most popular programme is the long-running soap *Fair City*, which depicts working-class life in Dublin and is known locally as 'Fairly Shitty'. The national broadcaster is also home to the world's longest-running chat show, the *Late Late Show* (Friday 9.30pm), which began in 1962 and is still going meekly along under the terribly wooden guidance of its host Pat Kenny, who replaced the inimitable Gay Byrne in 1999. If you're watching it during your visit to Dublin you've made a mistake in planning your Friday night.

Anyhow, Dublin viewers have seen their viewing choices multiply in recent years; not only have all the major English TV stations turned up on their dials, but the arrival of digital TV in many homes and most hotels has meant that you can watch old reruns of crap 1970s American sitcoms at any time of the day or night.

The following are the four main Irish channels:

RTE 1 Ireland's main station, with a pretty standard mix of programmes, from news, current affairs and sports programmes to variety shows, soap operas and movies.

RTE 2 The second state-controlled channel generally has lighter programmes.

TG4 A mostly Irish-language station (most programmes have English subtitles) that also offers a terrific selection of English-language movies and sport (try watching a Spanish league match with an Irish commentary).

TV3 An independent channel with a strictly lightweight programming philosophy; it does show the odd good film though.

PAINTING & VISUAL ARTS

Although they started off brilliantly – think of the gold and bronze works in the National Museum and the *Book of Kells* – Irish artists never really delivered on their early promise, and in recent decades, the country has been more famous for its art heists than artists. Russborough House in County Wicklow has been robbed four times since 1974, with Vermeer, Goya and Gainsborough all among the targets.

Beyond one impressionist who settled and died in Dublin, Jack B Yeats, and the surrealist Francis Bacon, who wanted nothing to do with the city after he left it aged 16, Dublin has contributed little to the world of art. Or perhaps it just seems little compared to its other artistic endeavours.

But even this apparent cultural fallibility has been revised in recent years with 20th-century Irish art more than tripling in value since 1990. While it was probably underrated beforehand, this revaluation no doubt has more to do with the wealth of Irish collectors, their rediscovery of indigenous art and their hunger for a piece of heritage.

FRANCIS BACON

Dubliners like to tell you that Francis Bacon, the foremost British painter of his generation, was actually Irish, although it's a pretty tenuous claim to call him one of their own.

Born in Dublin – of English parentage – in 1909, Bacon was thrown out of home at the age of 16 when his parents discovered he was actively homosexual. In the great Irish artistic tradition, Bacon split as soon as he could and turned his back on his narrow-minded home town forever, pointedly denying his roots thereafter. He flitted about Berlin and Paris before settling in London in 1928, where he developed his distinctive, distorted, violent and utterly captivating style.

Critics dismissed him as a warped caricaturist, and it is true that his best-known works are distortions of other painters' creations – Velázquez' *Portrait of Innocent X* became Bacon's most celebrated series *The Screaming Popes* (1949–55) – but there is no denying his extraordinary ability to paint isolation, pain and suffering, major themes of post-WWII iconography and of homosexuality in repressed times.

His notoriously debauched lifestyle was nearly as well publicised as his genius. Although remarkably productive, he destroyed many of his canvases and relatively little of his work survives. Precious little is on display in Dublin – no doubt the way he would have wanted it – although the Hugh Lane Gallery (p101) did acquire the contents of the London studio where Bacon worked for three decades until his death in 1992. It has been faithfully reconstructed here in perhaps the most oddly compelling art exhibit in Dublin.

top picks

GALLERIES

- National Gallery (p79)
- Dublin City Gallery – The Hugh Lane (p101)
- RHA Gallagher Gallery (p83)
- Douglas Hyde Gallery (p70)
- Temple Bar Gallery & Studios (p86)

The National Gallery (p79) has an extensive Irish School collection, much of it chronicling the personages and pursuits of the Anglo-Irish aristocracy. Garrett Murphy (1680–1716) and James Latham (1696–1747) were respected portrait painters of their day. Nathaniel Hone (1831–1917), an important 19th-century landscape artist, was born in Ireland and returned to Dublin after a lengthy stint working in France.

Roderic O'Conor (1861–1940) was the first Irish painter to make a splash. He was dubbed the Irish Van Gogh because he grasped the Dutch genius's revolution and matched his vibrant, exuberant and extraordinary strokes. He too was drawn to France, but never returned to his homeland. Dublin-born William Orpen (1878–1931) became well known for his depictions of Irish life – his *Portrait of Gardenia St George with Riding Crop* (1912) once held the distinction of being the most expensive Irish painting ever sold at auction, fetching £1.8 million. That was until 2005, when he was posthumously beaten into second place by *The Bridge at Grez* (1883) by Belfast-born John Lavery (1856–1941), which sold for £2.18 million.

The most original and famous of the Irish painters was Jack B Yeats (1871–1957), the first impressionist painter from the British Isles. Like his big brother, poet WB, Jack was a champion of the Celtic Revival Movement. He mastered a range of painting techniques but is best known for setting down thick and broad strokes of pigment in a bold and gutsy spin on impressionism. This style provided a self-confident art form for the newly independent Ireland, created after the formation of the Irish Free State in 1922. The characters he drew were often strong, isolated and solitary – and every stroke seems to reveal his deep love for all things Irish. The National Gallery has a specific gallery devoted to his work, and a visit here should be one of the highlights of your trip to Dublin. Among our favourites are *The Liffey Swim* (1923), *Returning to the Shore* (1948) and *The Singing Horseman* (1949).

Most modern Irish artists turned their backs on the nationalism that so defined the work of Yeats. The abstract painters Mainie Jellett (1896–1943) and Evie Hone (1894–1955) are considered two of the greatest innovators of modern Irish art. The self-taught Louis le Brocquy (1916–) is one of the foremost Irish painters of the 20th century and, while his works aren't necessarily innovative (they borrow heavily from Picasso, Manet and others), they are unique in their Irishness. He is most famous for his depictions of the travelling community in the 1940s in a series known as the *Tinker Paintings*.

Today Dublin is at the forefront of a new Irish artistic revolution that has seen a fundamental transformation in the infrastructure and culture of visual arts. There is now a thriving network of part-funded and fully commercial galleries in the city, and a buoyant, dynamic local scene. Local artists to look out for include the Corkonian Dorothy Cross, whose work is exhibited in both the Irish Museum of Modern Art (p96) and the Dublin City Gallery (p101); video artist James Coleman; Shane Cullen, who carved the 11,500 words of the 1998 Anglo-Irish Good Friday Agreement in his vast sculptural work *The Agreement* (2002); and Grace Weir, whose multimedia work is both beautiful and challenging.

However, despite the submissions of both Cross and Weir, the biggest commission in recent years has gone to English artist Antony Gormley (of Angel of the North fame), who won a competition for a new piece of art to adorn the Docklands area. At some point in the next couple of years, the Dublin skyline will include a 48m metal frame depicting a standing figure. The sketches suggest a powerful piece in keeping with Gormley's deeply humanistic work; critics have already lambasted the piece as being outrageously out of scale.

THE LAST SUPPER

One of our favourite works of art is John Byrne's *Last Supper* (2004), on public display along a wall in the Quartier Bloom, by Caffè Cagliostro. This visually striking piece is a re-interpretation of Da Vinci's masterpiece – with a contemporary Irish twist. In an effort to reflect the changing face and growing cultural mix of Irish society, Byrne has cast two women: an East African and, in the role of Jesus, a Sikh studying at Trinity College.

COMEDY

The Irish are renowned for being funny, which is hardly surprising considering that this is a nation that has regularly dealt with its difficulties and crippled emotions with the greatest defence mechanism of them all: humour. Self-deprecating but always brilliantly observed wit is a strong suit of the great Irish comic; crap, I-drank-so-much-last-night-I-complimented-my-mother-in-law jokes are the choice of every other halfwit who thinks being Irish automatically entitles them to a sense of humour. Sadly, there are far too many of the latter.

The former are fewer in number and, mostly, living in England, as Ireland is sadly too small to support their talents. Of the recent greats, our highly subjective list of the capital's comedy talents include the greatest storyteller of them all, Dave Allen, who sadly left us in 2005; the pioneering stand-up of Sean Hughes; and the greatest Irish satirist of the modern age, Dermot Morgan, who followed his brilliant political radio sketch show *Scrap Saturday* with his unforgettable role as *Father Ted*.

The contemporary crop includes Dylan Moran and his one-time school classmate Tommy Tiernan, who have both gone on to great international success. Deirdre O'Kane has been making audiences laugh for years, while the recently arrived Maeve Higgins is another in a new brood of comics worth paying the admission price to see. Irish-American Des Bishop, PJ Gallagher and Jason Byrne, who has sold more tickets at the Edinburgh Festival in recent years than any other comedian, are all popular names, but our favourite of all is unquestionably Dara O'Briain, Ireland's very own Jerry Seinfeld and now a mainstay of British TV comedy panel shows like *Have I Got News For You*.

DANCE

There's good and bad news. Yes, *Riverdance* and its various mutations like Lord of the Tight Pants are still going strong, stomping their way around the world, but the *good* news is that you're far less likely to be bombarded with the hand-by-the-sides phenomenon in Dublin than just about anywhere else in the world. Now don't get us wrong. We've got nothing against the sexing up of Irish dancing – there's nowt wrong with a little quick-step pizzazz – but *Riverdance* and its spin-offs are the dancing equivalent of boy bands. Take a bite, have a chew and move on.

Broadway hits and multiple international touring companies are a far cry from the dusty halls of rural Ireland where the tradition of Irish dancing was preserved on life support throughout the last century. Formerly the dancing was only performed at *céilidhs* and accompanied by traditional bands with musicians in green waistcoats. The etiquette was rigidly strict, fun was discouraged, and it seemed like most of the dancers were there under duress rather than to celebrate a tradition that has been around in some form since at least the 16th century. But not any more. Since *Riverdance*, the roots of Irish dancing have been given a good soaking and the tradition is blossoming once again. While still true to the jigs and reels of its past, the dancing has evolved into something more tribal, vital and – we can still hardly believe it – sexy.

Up until fairly recently, Irish dancing was virtually the only dancing in Ireland, although this is no longer the case: Dublin has become a destination for touring companies, while city venues are putting on their own shows and local companies creating their own.

ARCHITECTURE

Dublin raced into the third millennium with most of its finest architecture intact and with a rate of development not seen since the height of its Georgian heyday, when the city was regarded as one of the finest in Europe. Most of the public architecture to rise out of the booming town has generated a wonderful sense of energy and adventure about renaissance Dublin. Of course some mistakes have been made in the mad recent rush to build, but Dubliners have learned from them and are more architecturally savvy these days. They demand higher standards of design for their most deserving city and local authorities haven't let them down.

Although there's been a lull in activity in the last couple of years, it's a good opportunity for planners to take stock and refocus on the old problems, such as housing and transport.

MEDIEVAL DUBLIN

For architectural evidence of the pre-Norman settlers you will have to look further afield than the capital, which has been rebuilt far too many times, often in spite of the wealth of historical residue below ground. Treatment of the remains of Viking Dublin found at Wood Quay during the laying of the foundations for two massive modern buildings for the Dublin Corporation was one of the biggest crimes against culture and heritage perpetrated by the Irish State (see the boxed text, p50). Dublin's tangled history has left very few survivors, even from Norman days, and what is left is either fragmentary or has been heavily reconstructed. The imposing Dublin Castle (p74) – or the complex of buildings that are known as Dublin Castle – bears little resemblance to the fortress that was erected by the Anglo-Normans at the beginning of the 13th century and more to the neoclassical style of the 17th century. However, there are some fascinating glimpses of the lower reaches of the original, which you can visit on a tour.

Although the 12th-century cathedrals of Christ Church (p94) and St Patrick's (p90) were heavily rebuilt in Victorian times, there are some original features, including the crypt in Christ Church, which has a 12th-century Romanesque door. The older of the two St Audoen's Churches (p97) dates from 1190 and it too has a few Norman odds and ends, including a late-12th-century doorway.

ANGLO-DUTCH PERIOD

After the restoration of Charles II in 1660, Dublin embarked upon almost a century and a half of unparalleled growth as the city raced to become the second most important in the British empire. The grandest example of 17th-century architecture, and indeed Dublin's first classical building, is the hugely impressive Royal Hospital Kilmainham (1680; p96), which was designed by William Robinson as a home for invalid soldiers. Comprising a vast, cobbled courtyard in the centre of a quadrangular building with arcades, it was given a stunning makeover in the 1980s and now houses the Irish Museum of Modern Art (IMMA).

Similar in stature – and now also in shape, size and function – the Royal Barracks (Collins Barracks; 1701; p105) was built by Thomas Burgh as the first purpose-designed military barracks in Europe. The awesome square could accommodate six regiments, and the barracks was the oldest to remain in use until the National Museum commandeered the premises to stock its decorative arts.

Robinson moved from the mammoth to the miniature when he built the enchanting Marsh's Library (1701; p93), which was the first public library in Ireland and has remained virtually untouched.

GEORGIAN DUBLIN

Dublin's architectural apogee can roughly be placed in the period spanning the rule of the four English Georges, between the accession of George I in 1714 and the death of George IV in 1830. The greatest influence on the shape of modern Dublin throughout this period was the Wide Street Commissioners, appointed in 1757 and responsible for designing civic spaces and the framework of the modern city. Their efforts were complemented by Dublin's Anglo-Irish Protestant gentry who, flush with unprecedented wealth, dedicated themselves wholeheartedly towards improving their city.

Their inspiration was the work of the Italian architect Andrea Palladio (1508–80), who revived the symmetry and harmony of classical architecture. When the Palladian style

GEORGIAN PLASTERERS

The handsome exteriors of Dublin's finest Georgian houses are often matched by superbly crafted plasterwork within. The fine work of Michael Stapleton (1770–1803) can be seen in Trinity College (p64), Ely House (Map pp78–9) near St Stephen's Green, and Belvedere House (p111) in north Dublin. The LaFranchini brothers, Paolo (1693–1770) and Filippo (1702–79), are responsible for the outstanding decoration in Newman House on St Stephen's Green (p73). But perhaps Dublin's most famous plastered surfaces are in the chapel at the heart of the Rotunda Hospital (p111). Although hospitals are never the most pleasant places to visit, it's worth it for the German stuccodore, Bartholomew Cramillion's fantastic rococo plasterwork.

reached these shores in the 1720s, the architects of the time tweaked it and introduced a number of, let's call them, 'refinements'. Most obvious were the elegant brick exteriors and decorative touches, such as coloured doors, fanlights and ironwork, which broke the sometimes austere uniformity of the fashion. Consequently, Dublin came to be known for its 'Georgian style'.

The architect credited with the introduction of this style to Dublin's cityscape was Sir Edward Lovett Pearce (1699–1733), who first arrived in Dublin in 1725 and turned heads with the building of Parliament House (Bank of Ireland; 1728–39; p73). It was the first two-chamber debating house in the world and the main chamber, the House of Commons, is topped by a massive pantheon-style dome.

DESIGNS ON DUBLIN

There are two terrific websites that enable you to keep an eye on Dublin's development. Reflecting City (www.reflectingcity.com) offers virtual tours of all the major urban renewal areas, while Archéire (www.irish-architecture.com) is a comprehensive site covering all things to do with Irish architecture and design. If you want something in book form, look no further than Christine Casey's superb *The Buildings of Ireland: Dublin* (2005; Yale University Press), which goes through the city literally street by street.

Pearce also created the blueprint for the city's Georgian town houses, the most distinguishing architectural feature of Dublin. The local version typically consists of four storeys, including the basement, with symmetrically arranged windows and an imposing, often brightly painted front door. Granite steps lead up to the door, which is often further embellished with a delicate leaded fanlight. The most celebrated examples are on the south side of the city, particularly around Merrion and Fitzwilliam Sqs (Map pp78–9), but the north side also has some magnificent streets, including North Great George's and Henrietta Sts (Map pp102–3). The latter features two of Pearce's originals (at Nos 9 and 10) and is still Dublin's most unified Georgian street. Mountjoy Sq (Map pp102–3), the most elegant address in 18th-century Dublin, is currently being renewed after a century of neglect.

German architect Richard Cassels (Richard Castle; 1690–1751) hit town in 1728. While his most impressive country houses are outside Dublin, he did design Nos 85 and 86 St Stephen's Green (1738), which were combined in the 19th century and renamed Newman House (p73), and No 80 (1736), which was later joined with No 81 to create Iveagh House, now the Department of Foreign Affairs; you can visit the peaceful gardens (p75) there still. The Rotunda Hospital (1748; p111), which closes off the top of O'Connell St, is also one of Cassels' works. As splendid as these buildings are, it seems he was only warming up for Leinster House (1745–48; p82), the magnificent country residence built on what was then the countryside, now the centre of government.

Dublin's boom attracted such notable architects as the Swedish-born Sir William Chambers (1723–96), who designed some of Dublin's most impressive buildings, though he never actually bothered to visit the city. It was the north side of the Liffey that benefited most from Chambers' genius: the chaste and elegant Charlemont House (Hugh Lane Gallery; 1763; p101) lords over Parnell Sq, while the Casino at Marino (1755–79; p119) is his most stunning and bewitching work.

Across the river, Chambers designed the Examination Hall (1779–91; p70) and the Chapel (1798; p68), which flank the elegant 18th-century quadrangle of Trinity College, known as Parliament Sq. However, Trinity College's most magnificent feature, the old Library Building, with its breathtaking Long Room (1712; p69), had already been designed by Thomas Burgh.

It was towards the end of the 18th century that Dublin's developers really kicked into gear, when the power and confidence of the Anglo-Irish Ascendancy seemed boundless. Of several great architects of the time, James Gandon (1743–1823) stood out, and he built two of Dublin's most enduring and elegant neoclassical landmarks, Custom House (1781–91; p107) and the Four Courts (1786–1802; p106). They were both built on the quays to afford plenty of space in which to admire them.

Gandon's greatest rival was Thomas Cooley (1740–84), who died too young to reach his full potential. His greatest building, the Royal Exchange (City Hall; 1779; p76), was butchered to provide office space in the mid-19th century, but returned to its breathtaking splendour in a stunning 2000 restoration.

REGENCY & VICTORIAN

There is precious little 19th-century Dublin architecture, which is a reflection of the city's sharp decline during the period. Francis Johnston (1760–1829) was unfortunate to miss out on the boom, which ended with the Act of Union in 1801. His most famous building is the General Post Office (GPO; 1814; p107) on O'Connell St, although he's also well known for something he didn't do. When Parliament House was sold in 1803, on the proviso that it could never again be used for political assembly, Johnston was hired to adapt the building and he managed to surreptitiously maintain the architectural integrity of the House of Lords, a piece of history which you can now tour (p74). Cheers, Frank.

A rare Victorian highlight is the stunning series of curvilinear glasshouses in the National Botanic Gardens (p119), which were designed mid-century by the Dublin iron-master Richard Turner (1798–1881) and restored in 1995.

After Catholic Emancipation in 1829, there was a wave of church building, and later the two great Protestant cathedrals of Christ Church (p94) and St Patrick's (p90) were reconstructed. In a space between two Georgian houses on St Stephen's Green, Cardinal Newman commissioned his professor of fine arts at Newman University, John Hungerford Pollen (1820–1902), to create the splendidly ornate and incongruous Newman University Church (1856; p73), which was done in a Byzantine style simply because the cardinal was none too keen on the Gothic that was all the rage at the time.

Most public funds from the mid-18th to late 20th century were spent on providing sanitation and housing, and for the most part Dublin's architecture and infrastructure deteriorated. Perhaps a reflection on where priorities lay during this time, one of the best examples of high-Victorian architecture – and the one we've seen most of – is the magnificent Stag's Head pub (1895; p166) on Dame Ct, which has a dazzling interior of panelling, arcading, mirrors and stained glass.

MODERN ARCHITECTURE

The beginning of the 20th century was more about destroying notable buildings than erecting them; the GPO, Custom House and Four Courts all became collateral damage in Ireland's rocky road to independence.

As an exception, one of Dublin's most majestic constructions, and the last great British building here, the Royal College of Science (1904–22, p82) was actually completed after independence. It was massively and lavishly refurbished in the late 1980s to become the Government Buildings, and was dubbed 'Taj MaHaughey' after the controversial Taoiseach of the time.

The Dublin Airport terminal (1940; p228) was built by a consortium of architects and comprises a curved, Art Deco building that embraces incoming passengers. But it wasn't until the bus sta-

SAMPLING SAM STEPHENSON

One of the architects who designed the Electrical Supply Board (ESB) offices that broke up Dublin's 'Georgian Mile' – and a name synonymous with the 'rape of the city' in the 1970s and '80s – was Sam Stephenson. To be fair, he owes much of his notoriety to being in the right place (in with the government) at the wrong time (a government that happened to be more than a little dodgy). His two most infamous buildings are the Central Bank of Ireland (1975; Map p85) and the Dublin Corporation Offices (Phase I, 1976; Map pp90–1) at Wood Quay, neither of which he was allowed to complete for various reasons.

The Central Bank of Ireland is a bold geometric presence towering over today's Temple Bar. Although innovatively designed, its brutal bulkiness was controversially at odds with the low-rise old city it occupied. Furthermore, the building was left incomplete because brazen project managers exceeded the height limit and the roof had to be removed.

Even more vilified were the Dublin Corporation Offices he designed for Wood Quay. His original plan was for four squat towers descending towards the river and linked by a glass atrium but, not long after construction began, the remains of the Viking city were discovered, and so began several years of hurried excavations, court cases and much palaver. The corporation eventually went ahead with its plans – the archaeological treasure was sealed and the bunkers built – but bottled out halfway through and, compounding the damage, only completed half the plan. In the mid-1990s an extension was added to the original building, which proved popular among the public and critics alike. It's certainly easier on the eye, although we think it looks a bit like a camel.

tion, Busáras (1953; Map pp102–3), that modernity really began to express itself in Dublin – amid howls of protest from a population unimpressed with its expense and stark appearance. It was designed by the influential Michael Scott, and is noteworthy for its pioneering glass façades and wave canopy roof. Locals still love it and loathe it in equal measure, but you have to admire its vigour and personality. A major revamp, mostly internal, was completed in 2004.

The tallest most denigrated structure – for now, at least – is the shamefully shabby Liberty Hall (1965; Map pp102–3) on the quays; *this* is probably why the city has dragged its heels on sky-scrapers. Paul Koralek's bold and brazen Berkeley Library (1967; p70), in the grounds of Trinity College, is the most interesting construct to come out of 1960s Dublin.

The poorly regulated building boom of succeeding decades paid no attention to the country's architectural heritage and destroyed more than it created. There were no noble causes to blame this time around, just sheer stupidity. The most notorious case of cultural vandalism occurred in 1970 when the state-owned Electricity Supply Board (ESB) demolished 16 Georgian houses on Lower Fitzwilliam St to build its headquarters, breaking a unique, mile-long Georgian streetscape. Adding insult to injury, after just 30-odd years, the company is in the process of selling the building and shifting out to the suburbs.

The 1980s were a miserable time to be in Dublin; the city was in the jaws of a depression and seemed to be disintegrating into 100 shades of grey. The Temple Bar area was being left to waste away and, according to Frank McDonald, environment correspondent of the *Irish Times,* there wasn't a single private apartment available for sale in the centre of Dublin. In 2004 there were some 15,000 apartments and the city is *still* one of the lowest density capitals in Europe, although there is currently a commitment to more high density housing such as sky-rises and larger apartment blocks.

BOOM TOWN

Ireland's explosive growth during the 1990s was mostly focused on its capital, where the tower cranes punched the sky triumphantly. Naturally enough, considering the breakneck speed of the developments, some opportunities were wasted. Near Custom House, the International Financial Services Centre (IFSC; Map pp102–3), while mostly completed around the turn of the century, was conceived back in the late 1980s when Dublin was still desperate to appear modern. It is huge, sparkles and is remarkably unremarkable. The most interesting feature of the complex known as 'Canary Dwarf' – a cylindrical timber-clad apartment block – is hidden away in the heart of the behemoth.

More successful developments around Dublin include the Waterways Visitor Centre (1994; p100), which is colloquially known as the 'box in the docks' because the steel-framed, white-panelled structure appears to float. The Millennium Wing (2001; p79) of the National Gallery is a superb example of civic architecture and has a compelling, sculpted Portland stone façade and a tall, light-filled atrium.

Another terrific civic development is the Boardwalk (2001; Map p85), a 650m promenade along the Liffey, which complements the new bridges, makes a feature of the river, and provides a pleasant, occasionally even sunny, stroll away from the noise and traffic fumes of the northern quays.

Entire areas have been earmarked for redevelopment, creating different centres around the city. One of the most ambitious is taking place around the previously dilapidated Smithfield market area, which now has a stunning plaza (2000) and an old chimney converted into an observation tower (p110), offering fabulous views of historic Dublin. Flanking the square are a series of lofty lighting masts topped by gas braziers, which evoke a sense of the area's medieval past.

Another area being given a major makeover is the Grand Canal Docks (Map pp78–9), where historic warehouses are being restored and massive new residential and recreational development is underway. It is already the site of the striking 16-floor Charlotte Quay Apartments (1998), the tallest residential building in the country. The U2 Tower (Map pp78–9) – so-called because the band's recording studio will occupy the top two floors – is a wild-looking, 60m, twisted high-rise block that was slated for completion in 2007; planning snafus have meant that the plan is still wrapped up in red tape.

And the Grand Canal Docks is going to get fancier. Although it's still at the design stage, the centrepiece of the whole area will be a 2000-seat Performing Arts Centre designed by the world's hottest architect, Daniel Libeskind. The centre will be complemented by a new five-star

NIAMH KIERNAN, ARCHITECT

The development of Dublin continues at a pace unknown since Georgian times, and not surprisingly the city's future appearance is of major concern to most people, not least the capital's very own architects. Niamh Kiernan understands the concerns of the critics who feel that the developers are exclusively about turning a profit rather than doing what is best for the city's long-term future.

'Development has two major problems. It has been so incredibly fast that transport development has lagged seriously behind land-use development; and large sites in the city are often developed at the expense of the nature and the grain of the traditional urban block.'

But it isn't all development gloom. 'Developers and planners have become increasingly aware of the merits of the traditional European planning model of "living over the shop", using the grain, scale and nature of the urban block to instigate development. Some of the most successful urban development schemes using this model have been Quartier Bloom, Clarion Quay in the IFSC and the apartments along Cowes Lane in Temple Bar, where walking along these "inhabited" pedestrian routes is both interesting and a pleasure.'

We asked Niamh for her top five buildings or spaces in town:

- **Berkeley Library** (p70) I often try to walk through the internal courtyards of Trinity College: in wet weather there is an amazing light that bounces off the cobblestones, and this superb building by Paul Koralek is a timeless piece of architecture. I love the texture of the boarded concrete and the considered attention that the architects have given to detail.
- **George's St Arcade** (p135) They speak for themselves really. These are a collection of beautifully busy, richly decorated market buildings that have retained a wonderful sense of character and liveliness that is hard to equal elsewhere in the city.
- **Utility Building** (off Map pp62–3) This wonderful, award-winning building on Vernon Ave in Clontarf by Tom de Paor stops me in my tracks every time I pass it. The diamond shaped green copper cladding is so eye-catching.
- **Printworks** (Map p85) I love the depth of the building façade of this building in Temple Bar, designed by Group 91/Derek Tynan. It is a lovely element to the building as often we think of façades as two-dimensional elements only.
- **Wooden Building** (Map p85) The materiality of this building by de Blacam and Meaghar is wonderful. It is a very soft and interesting building set among the grey limestones and granites. It looks as though the entire timber façade wants to fold down to the ground.

hotel, the brand new Grand Canal Sq and an array of shops, bars, restaurants and cafés. Work has already been completed on the installation of imaginative streetscape features including lighting, cobbling, seating and trees along the restored quayside at Grand Canal Dock and Sir John Rogerson's Quay.

At last, all of the work on O'Connell St (Map pp102–3) has finally borne some fruit. Although not quite completed – the upper end of the street is still under wraps – the pavements are cleaner and wider, a pedestrianised plaza beneath the Spire (p109) has given Spanish students and junkies a whole new spot to hang out in, and traffic has been severely limited up and down the thoroughfare. Now if they could just get rid of those poxy fast-food joints…

Some of the most impressive works of recent times have been the superb restorations and redevelopments of wonderful buildings, such as the Royal Hospital Kilmainham (p96), Collins Barracks (p105), City Hall (p76) and Dublin Castle (p74).

The Guinness Brewery also commissioned a spectacular refit of its original Fermentation House (1904; p88), reputedly the first steel-framed, multistorey building in the British Isles – an undertaking that some years ago would instead have seen the building torn down but for the prohibitive costs of demolition. It now houses the Guinness Storehouse (visitor centre; 2001), which is designed around a pint-shaped atrium and topped with the circular, glass-panelled Gravity Bar where you have awesome panoramic views of the city (which you can see through the bottom of the glass when you've finished your complimentary pint).

And finally, the long-running debate about high-rises has been won…in favour of those who would build up rather than extend the low-rise urban sprawl that is eating its way into the countryside around the city. Besides the two towers already slated for construction in the Docklands area, permission has been given for a new tower block to go up next to Heuston Station, on the edge of Kilmainham (Map pp90–1). Paradoxically, the city's only older residential high-rises, the notorious 'seven towers' of U2's *Running to Stand Still* (from *The Joshua Tree*) in the Ballymun neighbourhood of north Dublin, were finally demolished in 2004 and are being replaced by more modern, low-rise blocks of flats.

The slowdown in the growth of the economy has probably come at a good time for Dublin to take a breather, and for Dubliners to have another long, hard look at how their city is shaping up. Architectural integrity is a watchword these days, but only time will tell how well aesthetics and the needs of the burgeoning city are reconciled.

ENVIRONMENT & PLANNING

Though the city doesn't suffer the air pollution that chokes some other European capitals, James Joyce's 'dear, dirty Dublin' does have its fair share of environmental concerns. Chief among these are the woeful traffic congestion and urban sprawl that have emerged in the last decade – in fact, you can combine the two because it's the car-oriented sprawl into the countryside that is concerning planners most these days.

THE LAND

Dublin used to spread conveniently around the arc of Dublin Bay, but these days it's all over the place and the commuter belt has well and truly spilled over into neighbouring counties, poorly equipped to cope. Dubliners have been fleeing the exorbitant house prices and bursting through the former city boundaries. Ireland is one of the most car-dependent societies in the world and the vast majority of these commuters drive in and out of the city daily.

GREEN DUBLIN

The Green Party may be the junior coalition partners in the recently elected government, but the negotiations that brought them to the big table left much of their agenda outside the door. Dublin is becoming more environmentally responsible, but it is hardly leading the European charge – the European Environment Agency has rated the country's carbon footprint as 5.0 global hectares per person, more than double the global average.

The unparalleled construction boom of the last decade has resulted in a city that has sacrificed much of the green space it used to have to make way for myriad new housing developments that now crowd the city's suburban spaces. The resultant stress on the city's inadequate road system has created a major traffic crisis, with most of the city's arteries choked with pollution-emitting cars during most daylight hours.

Recycling is another major issue of concern, but the various local authorities have instituted a waste management plan that aims to achieve 59% recycling by 2010, with the remainder being disposed of by incineration (29%) and landfill (16%). By the end of 2006, there were 321 waste banks around the city – only 58 more than in 2003 – but most of these are small bring banks, still a far cry from the larger bring banks that allow you to dump all of your glassware, for instance, in one go.

One real plus has been the high-tech waste-water treatment centre that opened in 2003 and has already improved the water quality in Dublin Bay. But Dublin residents are still perplexed as to why their tap water, once as drinkable and tasty as any sporting a fancy French label, still tastes like a metallic mixture.

Check out the Sustainable Dublin section (p20) for how green policies and issues affect you; for other city-related waste info, you can go online to www.dublinwaste.ie.

URBAN PLANNING & DEVELOPMENT

After what seemed like a decade of talking and coming up with excuses, efforts have now been made to alleviate congestion and coax commuters onto public transport. The Luas light-rail system is a major step in the right direction, but plenty more are needed, not least a massive expansion of the system so that far more commuters can take advantage of it. In the meantime, the problems it was supposed to solve have already broadened along with the size of the metropolitan area – it's not uncommon for people to commute up to 80km to and from work these days.

But there are fears that the planners are never going to catch up with the problems. Ireland is far and away the fastest expanding country in the EU and the population grew by a staggering 8% from 1996 to 2002. At this rate, Dublin will be home to 2.2 million and half the country's population by 2020.

GOVERNMENT & POLITICS

The Irish political system is a parliamentary democracy, and virtually all national political sway rests with a government comprising of a cabinet of 14 all-powerful ministers. Whatever the government decides is approved by the Dáil (Irish parliament), which is dominated by the government. An appointed 'whip' ensures that everyone in the ruling party toes the party line when it comes to voting. The current Taoiseach (prime minister) and Tanaiste (vice prime minister) are Bertie Ahern and Mary Harney, leaders of the ruling Fianna Fáil and junior Progressive Democrats (PDs) parties, respectively.

The Republic's electoral system is proportional representation (PR), where voters mark the candidates in order of preference. Elections must take place at least once every five years. Bertie went to the polls in May 2007 and came away a winner yet again, making him the longest-serving taoiseach in the history of the state, albeit in a coalition.

Irish politics, and society at large, is largely homogenous and voters are mostly influenced by local issues and personalities rather than ideologies or national policies. You can hardly see light between the positions of the major parties and it's not unusual for supposedly left- and right-leaning parties to cosy up together to form government.

The centre-right Fianna Fáil party has a solid base of around 40% of the electorate and has dominated politics for most of the last 75 years. The second-biggest party is Fine Gael. These two parties are direct descendants, respectively, of the anti-Treaty and pro-Treaty sides in the Civil War.

The most important socialist party is centre-left Labour, which didn't fare too well in the smash-and-grab boom of the 1990s. Next up is the staunchly capitalist – further-than-centre-right – Progressive Democrats, who were decimated in the 2007 elections, losing six of eight seats, but still managed to stay in government. Next up is Fianna Fáil's newest coalition partner, the Green Party, which shed its socks-and-sandals image – along with most of its agenda – in an effort to win power. Sinn Féin, the political wing of the now-decommissioned IRA, promotes itself as the party for all the disenfranchised and currently has five TDs (deputies) – each of its TDs donates two-thirds of their parliamentary salary (€96,650) to the party.

The constitutional head of state is the president (An tUachtarán), elected by popular vote for a seven-year term. While this position has little real power, the largely apolitical (at least in an Irish party sense) Mary Robinson wielded considerable informal influence over social policies when she was elected in 1990. She was succeeded by the more low-key, although equally ballsy, Mary McAleese, a Belfast-born Catholic nationalist who was re-elected unopposed in 2004.

At local level, Dublin is mainly governed by two elected bodies: Dublin City Council and Dublin County Council. The city version used to be known as Dublin Corporation (the Corpo), a name synonymous with inefficiency and incompetence, but the new incarnation is a progressive and admired local government. Each year, it elects a Lord Mayor who shifts into the Mansion House, speaks out on matters to do with the city and is lucky if half of Dublin knows his or her name by the time they have to hand back the chains.

IN TERMS OF IRISH POLITICS

An tUachtarán (awn *uk*-ta-rawn) – president

Dáil (dawl) – Lower House

Oireachtas na Éireann (ow-rawk*tus* na *hair*-in) – Irish parliament

Tanaiste (*taw*-nashta) – vice prime minister

Taoiseach (*tea*-shok) – prime minister

Teachta Dalai (tee-ochta dawl-*lee*) – deputies, members of parliament; also known as TDs

MEDIA

Five national dailies, six national Sundays, stacks of Irish editions of British publications, hundreds of magazines, more than a dozen radio stations, four terrestrial TV stations and more digital channels than you could shake the remote control at… No, not New York, we're talking about Dublin, a city with a reach of just 1.5 million people.

The dominant local player is Independent News & Media, owned by Ireland's primo businessman, Tony O'Reilly. Its newspapers – the *Irish Independent, Sunday Independent* and *Evening Herald* – are by far the biggest sellers in each market. See p238 for details of Dublin-based newspapers and magazines.

The massive overspill of British media here, particularly in relation to the saturated Sunday market, is the biggest challenge facing the Irish media. Rupert Murdoch's News International recognised the importance of the Irish market early, established an office in Dublin and set about an assault of the newspaper racks with its main titles, the *Irish Sun, News of the World* and *Sunday Times.* An Irish edition of its flagship daily, the *Times,* is rumoured to be on the way.

What this means, of course, is that local papers lacking Murdoch's mammoth resources will struggle even more than they already do. The country's best newspaper, the *Irish Times,* nearly went under in 2002 and is constantly worried about circulation.

Magazine publishing has boomed with the economy in recent years and the biggest new development has been the English craving for celebrity rubbing off on the local market.

top picks

BLOGS

Some of the best and most fearless – not to mention funniest – reporting is done by bloggers, the best of which will reveal what is *really* going on in this city.

- **Blurred Keys** (www.blurredkeys.com) A superb blog that focuses on the media and how it covers current affairs – a watchdog for the watchdogs.
- **Dublin Blog** (www.dublinblog.ie) A great forum for all kinds of debate, from student housing to the weather.
- **Half-Arsed Blog** (www.ricksbreakfastblog.blogspot.com) Radio presenter Rick O'Shea on whatever irks/pleases/interests Rick and his audience on any particular day.
- **Irish Election** (www.irishelection.ie) The best political blog, featuring comprehensive analysis of all the major issues.
- **Sinead Gleeson** (www.sineadgleeson.com) An excellent cultural blog.
- **Twenty Major** (www.twentymajor.net) An award-winning blog regularly considered the best in the country for its in-your-face, hilarious commentary.

There are four terrestrial TV channels in Ireland (see p44). The best thing about the state broadcaster, RTE, is its news programming and its sports coverage, particularly of Gaelic games. Meanwhile, Dublin's gone digital and the two big players are the home-grown NTL – who may not even be in business by the time you read this – and the behemoth that is Sky, which continues to make solid progress in bringing the multichannel revolution into Dublin homes.

The state of local radio is much healthier. There is a huge choice incorporating talk radio, current affairs, pirate stations, progressive music channels and lots of commercial dross. If you want to take the pulse of the city, check out the housewives' favourite, talk-show host Joe Duffy on *Liveline* (RTE 1, from 1.45pm Monday to Friday), the favourite place for Ireland to have a moan. If you like sport, listen no further than *Off the Ball* (Newstalk 106-108, 7pm to 10pm Monday to Friday).

LANGUAGE

Although Gaeilge (Irish) is the official language – and all official documents, street signs and official titles are either in Gaeilge or bilingual – it's only spoken in isolated pockets of rural Ireland known as Gaeltacht areas.

While all Dubliners must learn it at school, the teaching of Gaeilge has traditionally been thoroughly academic and unimaginative, leading most kids to resent it as a waste of time. Ask Dubliners if they can speak Irish and nine out of 10 of them will probably reply, 'ahhh cupla focal' (literally 'a couple of words') and they generally mean it. It's a pity that the treatment of Irish in schools has been so heavy-handed because many adults say they regret not having a greater grasp of it. A new curriculum has been in place for the last few years that aims to redress this shortcoming by cutting the hours devoted to the subject, and making the lessons more fun, practical and celebratory.

Here are a few useful phrases *os Gaeilge* (in Irish) to help you impress the locals:

Fool.	ohm-a-*dawn*	Amadáin.
Hi.	dee-a gwit	Dia dhuit.
How are you?	kunas aw *taw* two	Conas a tá tú?
I don't like Big Brother.	*knee* moh lum Big Brother	Ní maith liom Big Brother.
I'm good.	thawm go*moh*	Táim go maith.
I'm never ever drinking again.	knee ohl-*hee* mey gu brawkh u-reesh	Ní ólfaidh mé go brách arís.
Kiss my arse.	*pogue* ma hone	Póg ma thóin.
My name is Amanda.	iss *mi*sha Amanda	Is mise Amanda.
One hundred thousand welcomes.	kade meela fallcha	Céad míle fáilte.
Shut your mouth.	doon daw klob	Dún do chlab.
Thanks.	gur rev moh ag*ut*	Go raibh maith agat.
What is your name?	cawd iss an*im* dit	Cad is ainm duit?
Your health/Cheers.	*slawn*-cha	Slainte.

While most Dubliners overlooked Gaeilge, their command of English and their inventive use of vocabulary is second to none. Huge numbers of foreign-language students, particularly from continental Europe, flock to the city for study because the average Dubliner's elocution is so clear. When travelling in Italy or Spain, it's gas (funny) to hear locals speaking English with Dublin accents. Dubliners love the sound of their own voices and they are genuinely interested in the way words sound as much as in their meaning. They're very articulate, generally confident orators, and like nothing more than a good debate (preferably over a pint).

DUBLIN SLANG

Dubliners are like the mad scientists of linguistics, and have an enormous lexicon of slang words from which to choose. For example, there is said to be more than 50 alternative words for 'penis', while it's quite possible they have more words to describe 'drunkenness' than the Eskimos have for 'snow'. Here are just a few doozies:

banjaxed – broken down

chiseller – a young child

couldn't be arsed – couldn't be bothered

fair play/fucks to you – well done

header – mentally unstable person

I will in me bollix – I won't

jax – toilet

make a bags of something – mess it up

me belly tinks me trote's been cut – I'm rather hungry

rag order – bad condition

ride – have sex with

scarlet (*scar*leh) – blushing

shite – rubbish

shorts – spirits

slagging – teasing

trow a wobbler – have a temper tantrum

work away – go ahead, after you

yer man – that guy

yer one – that girl

yer wha'? – excuse me?!?

yoke – inserted to describe a noun when the actual word has slipped the speaker's mind

Dublin accents – there are several – have all the traits of the typical Irish brogue, including softened, shortened vowels, hardened consonants and discarded 'h's in the 'th' sound (as in the old 't'irty t'ree and a t'ird' joke). The average, or neutral, Dublin accent is possibly one of the most eloquent and easily understandable in the English-speaking world while the extremes are barely comprehensible at all. The 'real Dublin' accent is clipped, drawn out and slack-jawed. It discards consonants disdainfully, particularly the letter 't' (all right becomes origh) and is peppered with so many instances of 'feck', 'jaysus' and 'yer wha'?' that you think the speaker might be dumbstruck without them.

Yet this Dublin accent is infinitely preferable to the plummy accent of affluent southsiders, who contort and squeeze vowels at will. Formerly known as the Dublin 4 accent, this diction has since come to be known as the 'DART accent' (or 'dort' as its speakers would pronounce it) because it has spread out south along the coastal railway line.

The spread of this pseudo-received accent is so alarming that Frank McNally of the *Irish Times* has suggested the only way to eradicate the DART accent would be to make it compulsory in schools – it damn nearly worked for Gaeilge!

BLUELIST[1] (blu,list) *v.*
to recommend a travel experience.
What's your recommendation? www.lonelyplanet.com/bluelist

NEIGHBOURHOODS

top picks

- **Chester Beatty Library** (p70)
  A stunning collection of books and *objets d'art*.
- **Trinity College** (p64)
  Ireland's foremost university and most beautiful campus.
- **Dublin City Gallery – The Hugh Lane** (p101)
  Modern art at its finest, including Francis Bacon's studio.
- **Kilmainham Gaol** (p95)
  Irish history in all its bloody gore and horror.
- **Irish Museum of Modern Art (IMMA;** p96)
  The country's foremost collection of contemporary art.
- **Marsh's Library** (p93)
  Ireland's oldest library is a well-kept secret wonder.
- **St Patrick's Cathedral** (p90)
  Elegance, piety and a tempestuous history.
- **National Museum** (p80)
  Cultural identity in thousands of artefacts.
- **National Gallery** (p79)
  Renaissance masters, Irish masterpieces and more.
- **Old Jameson Distillery** (p106)
  The nuts and bolts of Irish whiskey, plus a taster.

Dublin may be bulging round its ever-expanding edges, but the city centre – defined by the bits within the two canals that create an almost perfect ring around it – remains very compact, lending it the atmosphere of a busy provincial town rather than an alienating metropolis. Not that you can't get confused here though: the geographic area of the city centre may be small but it's a somewhat haphazard mix of medieval street arrangements and 18th-century town planning, which sought to make some sense of the spider's web of streets and alleys that spread their way on both sides of the river.

The River Liffey – that pea-brown stretch of barely moving water that bisects the city into neat halves – serves as the handiest way of determining your whereabouts: you're either north or south of it, presented simply as north-side and southside. The river also serves as the traditional social divide of Dublin: working class and poor north of the Liffey, posh and wealthy south of it. Spend enough time in Dublin and you'll hear the jokes.

> 'at the heart of it all is the pedestrianised shopping mecca that is Grafton St, bookended by the beautiful expanses of Elizabethan Trinity College and Georgian St Stephen's Green'

Although most of the city centre is in the grip of an overwhelming process of gentrification, the southside remains the most salubrious part of the city and probably the focus of most of your visit here. At the heart of it all is the pedestrianised shopping mecca that is Grafton St, bookended by the beautiful expanses of Elizabethan Trinity College to the north and Georgian St Stephen's Green to the south, as pretty a city square as you're likely to see anywhere in Europe. This is where you'll find the bulk of the city's main attractions, the best bars and most of the nightlife.

To the east, the equally elegant Merrion Sq provides the link between the Georgian heart of the older city and the exciting new developments that are transforming the area around the southern docks into Dublin's very own Docklands development. To the west, past the oldest bits of the city (the medieval Liberties) and the two Norman cathedrals, is the world-famous Guinness factory and museum, as well as Kilmainham Gaol and the Irish Museum of Modern Art, two outstanding attractions that should be a part of every itinerary.

North of the river, the graceful avenue that is O'Connell St introduces visitors to what many Dubliners believe is the 'real' Dublin, where salt-of-the-earth locals traditionally suspicious of their southside counterparts are now mixing it with whole new communities of non-nationals, creating genuinely multicultural neighbourhoods where old-style fish-and-fowl vendors of the Molly Malone variety and entrepreneurs from Nigeria, Korea, Poland and elsewhere are all looking to make a buck.

West of here is the old market section of Smithfield, which has a couple of interesting night-time distractions, and beyond it, the pride of all Dubliners, Phoenix Park – the city's gigantic green lung, which is twice the size of New York's Central Park.

Beyond the canals – the Royal to the north, the Grand to the south – are the suburbs, where you'll find a handful of interesting attractions, including a botanic garden, a superb sports museum and some lovely little seaside villages privileged Dubliners expensively call 'home'.

BEYOND THE ROYAL CANAL (pp117–20)

Drumcondra

East Wall

North Wall

Ringsend

Irishtown

Sandymount

Ballsbridge

BEYOND THE GRAND CANAL (pp98–100)

Donnybrook

Milltown

Phibsboro

NORTH OF THE LIFFEY (pp10–13)

TEMPLE BAR (pp84–7)

Trinity College

MERRION SQUARE & AROUND (p77–83)

GRAFTON STREET & AROUND (pp64–76)

Ranelagh

Rathmines

The Liberties

Dolphin's Barn

Harold's Cross

Cabra

KILMAINHAM & THE LIBERTIES (pp88–97)

PHOENIX PARK (pp14–16)

Islandbridge

Kilmainham

Goldenbridge

Inchicore

Drimnagh

Crumlin

1 km
0.6 miles

0
0

ITINERARY BUILDER

Dublin is small, but it's not that small, so you'll need to plan your days somewhat lest you end up lost with sore feet and shopping bags that are just getting heavier. The south central neighbourhoods all run into one another, but the northside is an expanse that runs the width of the city itself. The two neighbourhoods beyond the canal are best reached by public transport or taxi.

AREA	ACTIVITIES	Sights	Eating
	Grafton Street & Around	Trinity College (p64) Chester Beatty Library (p70) St Stephen's Green (p71)	L'Gueuleton (p147) Lock's (p147) Bottega Toffoli (p150)
	Merrion Square & Around	National Gallery (p79) Natural History Museum (p81) National Museum (p80)	L'Ecrivain (p152) Bang Café (p152)
	Temple Bar	Gallery of Photography (p86) Temple Bar Gallery (p86) Ark Children's Cultural Centre (p86)	Gruel (p154) Eden (p153) Mermaid Café (p153)
	Kilmainham & the Liberties	Guinness Storehouse (p88) Kilmainham Gaol (p95) Irish Museum of Modern Art (p96)	Leo Burdock's (p155)
	Beyond the Grand Canal	National Print Museum (p98)	Mash (p156) La Peniche (p155) Jo'Burger (p156)
	North of the Liffey & Phoenix Park	Dublin City Gallery – The Hugh Lane (p101) National Museum of Ireland (p105) Phoenix Park (p114)	Chapter One (p156) Winding Stair (p157) Alilang (p157)
	Beyond the Royal Canal	Croke Park & GAA Museum (p117) National Botanic Gardens (p119) Casino at Marino (p119)	Wongs (p158)

HOW TO USE THIS TABLE

The table below allows you to plan a day's worth of activities in any area of the city. Simply select which area you wish to explore, and then mix and match from the corresponding listings to build your day. The first item in each cell represents a well-known highlight of the area, while the other items are more off-the-beaten-track gems.

Drinking	Shopping	Nightlife, Arts & Activities
Anseo (p163) South William (p164) Kehoe's (p165)	Costume (p133) Barry Doyle Design Jewellers (p134) Avoca Handweavers (p132)	Tripod (p177 & p183)
Hartigan's (p167) Doheny & Nesbitt's (p167) James Toner's (p167)		National Concert Hall (p180) Sugar Club (p183)
Porterhouse Brewing Company (p168) Kennedy's (p167) Mulligan's (p167)	5 Scarlett Row (p137) Smock (p137) Urban Outfitters (p137)	Irish Film Institute (p179) Button Factory (p175 & p182)
Fallon's (p169)	Oxfam Home (p138) Fleury Antiques (p138)	Vicar Street (p183)
Kiely's (p170)	Havana (p138)	Civic Theatre (p185) Marlay Park (p182)
Shakespeare (p171) Dice Bar (p171) Sin É (p171)	Winding Stair (p139)	Abbey Theatre (p184) Gate Theatre (p186) Cobblestone (p183)
Gravediggers (p172)		Croke Park (p192)

DUBLIN

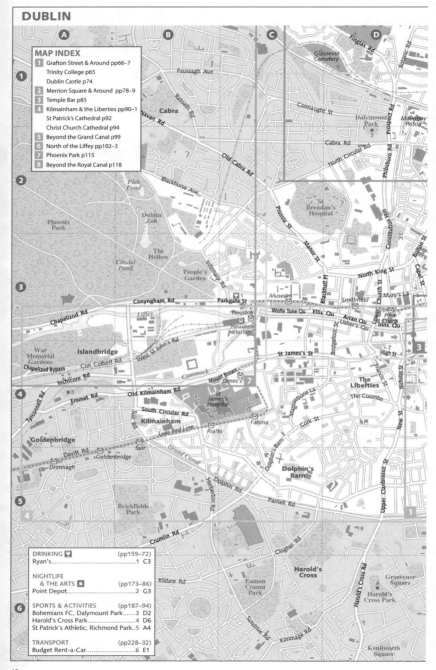

DRINKING 🍷 (pp159–72)
Ryan's..1 C3

NIGHTLIFE
& THE ARTS ✦ (pp173–86)
Point Depot....................................2 G3

SPORTS & ACTIVITIES (pp187–94)
Bohemians FC, Dalymount Park.......3 D2
Harold's Cross Park...........................4 D6
St Patrick's Athletic, Richmond Park..5 A4

TRANSPORT (pp228–32)
Budget Rent-a-Car...........................6 E1

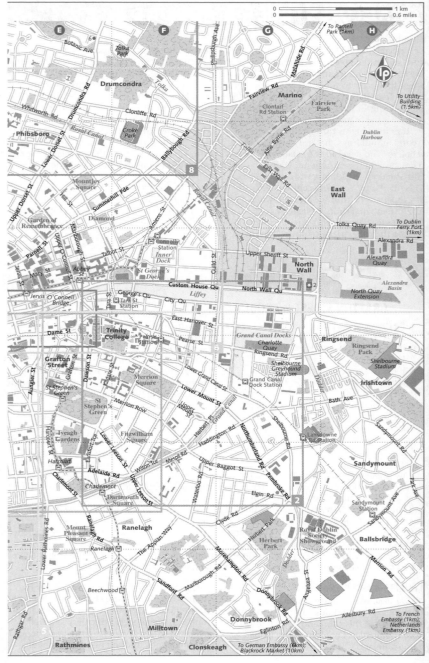

Eating p145; Drinking p162; Shopping p130; Sleeping p198

Less neighbourhood and more pulsating heart of the city, the swathe of supremely elegant streets and landscaped green spaces that fill out the area around Grafton St, directly south of the river, is what most visitors and not an insignificant number of Dubliners themselves are talking about when they refer to the 'city centre'. Bordered to the north by the Johnny-come-lately upstart that is Temple Bar, to the west by the medieval boundaries of the Liberties, to the south by the meandering Grand Canal, and to the east by the green edge of St Stephen's Green, this compact district is the focus of most visits to the city.

Running roughly through the middle of it is pedestrianised Grafton St, lined with four-storey Georgian buildings that are home to a mix of familiar international stores and chi-chi local retailers. The jewel in the retail crown remains Brown Thomas (p132), the swankiest department store in town. Its window displays in December are as important to a Dubliner's idea of Christmas as an old man with a white beard.

Named after the 17th-century Duke of Grafton, who owned much of these parts, Grafton St proper starts from the area known as College Green, directly in front of the elegant façades of Elizabethan Trinity College (Map pp66–7) and the Bank of Ireland (Map pp66–7; built to house Ireland's first parliament). An unremarkable statue of Molly Malone (Map pp66–7) leads us, bosoms first, to the pedestrianised street that is Grafton St.

top picks

GRAFTON STREET & AROUND

- The elaborate and expansive collection at Chester Beatty Library (p70)
- The magnificent, book-lined Long Room (p69) at Trinity College
- Trinity College (below), great for a wander
- Retail madness on and around Grafton Street (p130)
- Pub Life (p162), in the streets west and east of Grafton St
- A touch of graceful greenery in St Stephen's Green (p71), presenting work from around the world

The street has been a fashionable precinct for more than 200 years but only really took off in 1982 when the cars were driven out and the pedestrians paraded in on a newly cobbled surface. The Grafton St amble has been *de rigueur* ever since, for shoppers, walkers and people-watchers alike. Along its length an assortment of street performers set the mood, providing the soundtrack for a memorable stroll. On any given day, you can listen to a guitarist knock out some electrifying bluegrass, applaud young conservatory students putting Mozart through his paces or laugh your ass off at the brilliant comedian working an audience with his well-timed routine.

But to really get the most of the neighbourhood, you'll need to get off Grafton St and into the warren of narrow lanes and streets to the west of it – here you'll find a great mix of funky shops and boutiques, some of our favourite eateries and a handful of the best bars in the city.

Just south of Grafton St is the centrepiece of Georgian Dublin, St Stephen's Green, beautifully landscaped and dotted with statuary that provides a veritable who's who of Irish history.

Thankfully, Dublin's compact size doesn't mean you have to stay here to have it all at your doorstep, but if you do, you *absolutely* must be aware that most of the lodgings are pretty pricey – with the outstanding exception of the neighbourhood's western edge, home to one of the better hostels in town and one of our favourite B&Bs, Grafton House (Map pp66–7).

All cross-city buses make their way to - or through, at least - this part of the city; the Luas Green Line has its terminus at the top of Grafton St, on St Stephen's Green.

TRINITY COLLEGE Map p65

☎ 896 1000; admission free; ☽ 8am-10pm

Don your gown and dust off that tome on elocution, for this calm and cordial retreat from the bustle of contemporary Dublin is not just Ireland's most prestigious university (and the home of the blockbuster hit that is the *Book of Kells*) but a throwback to those far-off days when a university education was the preserve of a very small elite who spoke passionately of the importance of philosophy and the need for empire.

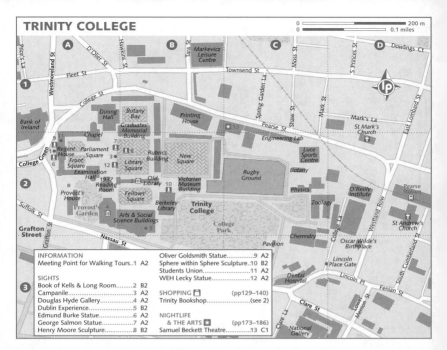

TRINITY COLLEGE

0 — 200 m
0 — 0.1 miles

Today's alumni are an altogether different bunch, but Trinity still *looks* the part, and on a summer's evening, when the crowds thin and the chatter subsides, there are few more delightful places in the world to be.

A great way to see Trinity's grounds is on a walking tour (☎ 896 1827; admission incl Book of Kells €10; ☼ tours every 40min 10.15am-3.40pm Mon-Sat, 10.15am-3pm Sun mid-May–Sep), which depart from the College Green entrance.

The college was established by Elizabeth I in 1592 on land confiscated from an Augustinian priory in an effort to stop the brain drain of young Protestant Dubliners, who were skipping across to continental Europe for an education and were becoming 'infected with popery'. With bigotry as a base, Trinity went on to become one of Europe's outstanding universities, producing a host of notable graduates – how about Jonathan Swift, Oscar Wilde and Samuel Beckett at the same alumni dinner?

It remained completely Protestant until 1793, but even when the university relented and began to admit Catholics, the Church forbade it; until 1970, any Catholic who enrolled here could consider themselves excommunicated. Although hardly the bastion of British Protestantism that it once was – most of its 15,000 students are Catholic – it is still a popular choice for British students. Women were first admitted to the college in 1903, earlier than at most British universities.

The 16-hectare site is now in the centre of the city, but when founded, it was described as being 'near Dublin' and was bordered on two sides by the estuary of the Liffey. Nothing now remains of the original Elizabethan college, which was replaced in the Georgian building frenzy of the 18th century. The elegant Regent House entrance on College Green was built between 1752 and 1759, and is guarded by statues of the writer Oliver Goldsmith (1730–74) and the orator Edmund Burke (1729–97). The railings outside the entrance are a popular meeting spot.

Through the entrance, past the Students Union, are Front Sq and Parliament Sq, the latter dominated by the 30m-high Campanile, designed by Edward Lanyon and erected from 1852 to 1853 on what was believed to be the centre of the monastery that preceded the college. Students who pass beneath it when the bells toll will fail

GRAFTON STREET & AROUND

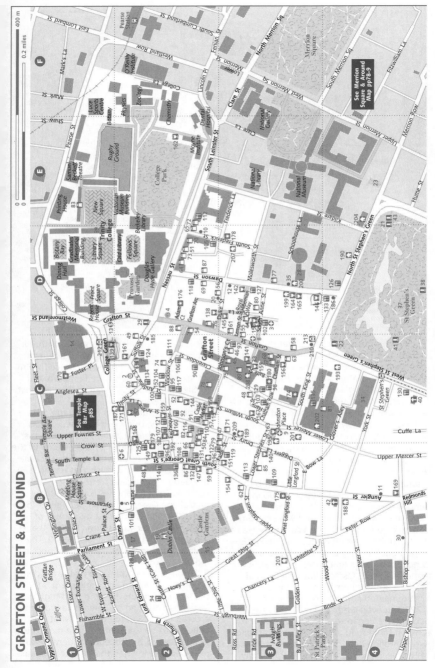

See Temple Bar Map pp95

See Merrion Square & Around Map pp78-9

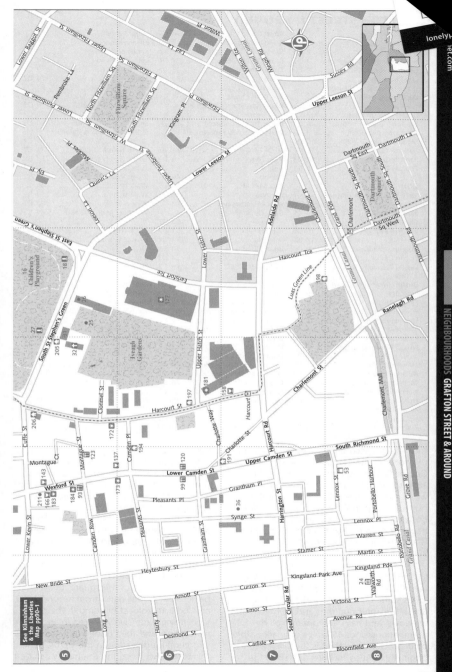

GRAFTON STREET & AROUND

their exams, according to superstition. To the north of the *Campanile* is a statue of George Salmon, the college provost from 1886 to 1904, who fought bitterly to keep women out of the college. He carried out his threat to permit them in 'over his dead body' by dropping dead when the worst happened. To the south of the *Campanile* is a statue of historian WEH Lecky (1838–1903).

North of Parliament Sq is the Chapel (☎ 896 1260; admission free), designed by William Chambers and completed in 1799. It has some fine plasterwork by Michael Stapleton, Ionic columns and painted glass windows, and has been open to all denominations since 1972. It's only accessible by organised tour. Next is the Dining Hall, originally built by Richard Cassels in the

mid-18th century. The great architect must have had an off day because the vault collapsed twice and the entire structure was dismantled 15 years later. The replacement was completed in 1761, but extensively restored after a fire in 1984.

On the grassy expanse of Library Sq is a 1969 sculpture by British sculptor Henry Moore (1898–1986), and two large Oregon maples. On the north side is the 1892 Graduates' Memorial Building, and an area known as Botany Bay.

On the far east of the square, the red-brick Rubrics Building dates from around 1690, making it the oldest building in the college. It was extensively altered in an 1894 restoration, and then underwent serious structural modification in the 1970s. Behind this is New Sq, featuring the highly ornate

Victorian Museum Building (☎ 608 1477; admission free), which houses a Geological Museum. It's open by prior arrangement only. The Doric-fronted Printing House, on the other side of the square, was also designed by Richard Cassels.

If you are following the less studious-looking throng, however, you'll find yourself magnetically drawn south of Library Sq to the Old Library (☎ 896 2320; East Pavilion, Library Colonnades; adult/student/child €8/7/free; 🕑 9.30am-5pm Mon-Sat year round, noon-4.30pm Sun Oct-Apr, 9.30am-4.30pm Sun May-Sep), home to Trinity's prize possession and biggest crowd-puller, the astonishingly beautiful Book of Kells (see the boxed text, p71).

Upstairs from the star attraction is the highlight of Thomas Burgh's building, the magnificent 65m Long Room with its barrel-vaulted ceiling. It's lined with shelves containing 200,000 of the library's oldest books and manuscripts, along with busts of eminent scholars, a 14th-century harp and an original copy of the *Proclamation of the Irish Republic*, read out by Pádraig Pearse at the beginning of the 1916 Easter Rising.

THE CLONING OF THE LONG ROOM

The Long Room has a few screen credits to its name (*Educating Rita* for instance) but its unlikeliest appearance was in *Star Wars Episode II: The Attack of the Clones*, when it showed up in CGI form as the Jedi Archive, complete with the same barrel-vaulted ceiling and similar statuary down the length of it. If nothing else, it makes for a good trivia question.

Despite Ireland's independence, the 1801 Library Act entitles Trinity College Library to a free copy of every book published in Britain. Housing this bounty requires nearly 1km of extra shelving every year and the collection amounts to about five million titles, which are stored at various facilities around town.

In Fellows' Sq is the brutalist and brilliant Berkeley Library, designed by Paul Koralek in 1967. It has been hailed by the Architectural Association of Ireland as the best example of modern architecture in the country. It's fronted by Arnaldo Pomodoro's sculpture *Sphere Within Sphere* (1982–83). George Berkeley (1685–1753), the distinguished Irish philosopher, studied at Trinity when he was only 15 years old. His influence spread to North America, where Berkeley (California) and its university are named after him.

Next around the square is the Arts & Social Science Building, which houses the underwhelming Dublin Experience (☎ 608 1688; adult/student €4.20/3.50; ☯ shows hourly 10am-5pm mid-May–Oct), a 45-minute audiovisual introduction to the city that is saccharine, clichéd, historically skewed, amateurish, takes itself too seriously and features exceedingly annoying actors trying to sound like Dublin taxi drivers.

West of this is another of Trinity's top treats for the discerning tourist, the Douglas Hyde Gallery (☎ 608 1116; Arts & Social Sciences Bldg, Trinity College; admission free; ☯ 11am-6pm Mon-Wed & Fri, 11am-7pm Thu, 11am-4.45pm Sat); its entrance is on Nassau St. This is one of the country's leading contemporary galleries, and hosts regularly rotating shows presenting the works of top-class Irish and international artists across a wide range of media. It's well worth checking out.

On the way back towards the main entrance, past the Reading Room, is the late-18th-century Palladian Examination Hall, which closely resembles the chapel opposite because it too was the work of William Chambers, and also features plasterwork by Michael Stapleton. It contains an oak chandelier rescued from the Irish parliament (now the Bank of Ireland – see p73).

Towards the eastern end of the complex, College Park is a lovely place to lounge around on a sunny day and occasionally you'll catch a game of cricket, a bizarre sight in Ireland. Keep in mind that Lincoln Place Gate is located in the southeast corner of the grounds, providing a handy shortcut to Merrion Sq (p77).

CHESTER BEATTY LIBRARY Map pp66–7

☎ 407 0750; www.cbl.ie; Dublin Castle; admission free; ☯ 10am-5pm Mon-Fri, 11am-5pm Sat, 1-5pm Sun, tours 1pm Wed, 3pm & 4pm Sun May-Sep, closed Sat-Mon Oct-Apr

Book of Kells, shmells...the world-famous Chester Beatty Library, housed in the Clock Tower at the back of Dublin Castle, is not just the best museum in Ireland but one of the best in Europe. This extraordinary collection, so lovingly and expertly gathered by New York mining magnate Alfred Chester Beatty (1875–1968) – a man of exceedingly good taste – is breathtakingly beautiful and virtually guaranteed to impress. How's that for a build-up?

An avid traveller and collector, Beatty was fascinated by different cultures, and amassed more than 20,000 manuscripts, rare books, miniature paintings, clay tablets, costumes and any other *objets d'art* that caught his fancy and could tell him something about the world. Fortunately for Dublin, he also happened to take quite a shine to the city and made it his adopted home. In return, the Irish made him their first honorary citizen in 1957.

The collection is spread over two levels. On the ground floor you'll find a compact but stunning collection of artworks from the Western, Islamic and East Asian worlds. Highlights include the finest collection of Chinese jade books in the world and illuminated European texts featuring exquisite calligraphy that stand up in comparison with the *Book of Kells*. Audiovisual displays explain the process of bookbinding, papermaking and printing.

The 2nd floor is a wonderful exploration of the world's major religions through decorative and religious art, enlightening text and a cool cultural-pastiche video at the entrance. The collection of Korans dating from the 9th to the 19th centuries (the library has more than 270 of them) is considered by experts to be the best example of illuminated Islamic texts in the world. There are also outstanding examples of ancient papyri, including renowned Egyptian love poems from the 12th century, and some of the earliest illuminated gospels in the world, dating from around AD 200.

THE PAGE OF KELLS

More than half a million yearly visitors queue up to see Trinity's top show-stopper, the world-famous *Book of Kells*. This illuminated manuscript, dating from around AD 800 and thus one of the oldest books in the world, was probably produced by monks at St Colmcille's Monastery on the remote island of Iona, off the western coast of Scotland. It contains the four gospels of the New Testament, written in Latin, as well as prefaces, summaries and other text. If it were merely words, the *Book of Kells* would simply be a very old book – it's the extensive and amazingly complex illustrations (the illuminations) that make it so wonderful. The superbly decorated opening initials are only part of the story, for the book has smaller illustrations between the lines.

Repeated looting by marauding Vikings forced the monks to flee to the temporary safety of Kells, County Meath, in Ireland in AD 806, along with their masterpiece. It was stolen in 1007, then rediscovered three months later buried underground. Some time before the dissolution of the monastery, the *cumdach* (metal shrine) was lost, possibly taken by looting Vikings who wouldn't have valued the text itself. About 30 of the beginning and ending folios (double-page spreads) are also missing. It was brought to the college for safekeeping in 1654. The 680-page (340-folio) book was rebound in four calfskin volumes in 1953.

And here the problems begin. Of the 680 pages, only two are on display – one showing an illumination, the other showing text – which has led to it being dubbed the *page* of Kells. No getting around that one, though: you can hardly expect the right to thumb through a priceless treasure at random. No, the real problem is its immense popularity, which makes viewing it a rather unsatisfactory pleasure. Punters are herded through the specially constructed viewing room at near lightning pace, making for a there-you-see-it, there-you-don't kind of experience.

To really appreciate the book, you can get your own reproduction copy for a mere €22,000. Failing that, the library bookshop stocks a plethora of souvenirs and other memorabilia, including Otto Simm's excellent *Exploring the Book of Kells* (€10.95), a thorough guide with attractive colour plates, and a popular DVD showing all 800 pages for €29.95.

The collection is rounded off with some exquisite scrolls and artwork from China, Japan, Tibet and Southeast Asia, including the two-volume Japanese *Chogonka Scroll*, painted in the 17th century by Kano Sansetu.

As if all of this wasn't enough for one visit, the library also hosts temporary exhibits that are usually too good to be missed. Not only are the contents of the museum outstanding, but the layout, design and location are also unparalleled, from the ubiquitous café and gift shop to the Zen rooftop terrace and the beautiful landscaped garden out the front. These features alone would make this an absolute Dublin must-do. Tours of the museum take place at 1pm Wednesday and 3pm and 4pm Sunday.

ST STEPHEN'S GREEN Map pp66–7

As you watch the assorted groups of friends, lovers and individuals escaping the confines of the office, splaying themselves across the nine elegantly landscaped hectares of St Stephen's Green and looking to catch a few rays of precious sun, consider that those same hectares once formed a common for public whippings, burnings and hanging. These days, the harshest treatment you'll get at Dublin's favourite lunchtime escape is the warden chucking you off the green for playing football or Frisbee.

The buildings around the square date mainly from the mid-18th century, when the green was landscaped and became the centrepiece of Georgian Dublin. The northern side was known as the Beaux Walk and it's still one of Dublin's most esteemed stretches, home to Dublin's original society hotel, the Shelbourne (p198). Nearby is the tiny Huguenot Cemetery (Map pp66–7), established in 1693 by French Protestant refugees.

Railings and locked gates were erected in 1814 when an annual fee of one guinea was charged to use the green. This private use continued until 1877 when Sir Arthur Edward Guinness pushed an act through parliament opening the green to the public once again. He also financed the central park's gardens and ponds, which date from 1880.

The main entrance to the green today is beneath Fusiliers' Arch (Map pp66–7), at the top of Grafton St. Modelled to look like a smaller version of the Arch of Titus in Rome, the arch commemorates the 212 soldiers of the Royal Dublin Fusiliers who were killed fighting for the British in the Boer War (1899–1902).

Across the road from the western side of the green is the 1863 Unitarian Church

GEORGE HOOK, BROADCASTER

We love Dublin – warts and all – but is it possible that the dramatic transformation of Dublin hasn't been an unqualified success for everyone? Absolutely, says radio host and TV rugby pundit George Hook, who doesn't like the new Dublin at all and declares ruefully that his view of Dublin 'is quite depressing'. The Cork native has made Dublin his home since 1960 but despairs that this one-time friendliest of cities, which had all the attributes of a capital and the intrinsic feel of small-town Ireland, has now become too frenetic and unfriendly.

Hook's reputation as a straight talker, who is unafraid of expressing his deeply held views even if they fly in the face of conventional opinion, has made him one of the country's most outspoken personalities and no stranger to a bit of controversy. His views of the capital are no different.

'We've lost the spirit of the old song "Dublin Saunter", whose lyrics were "For Dublin can be heaven with coffee at eleven and a stroll in Stephen's Green. There's no need to hurry, there's no need to worry,"' says Hook with a sigh. 'When I first came to Dublin and for a long time thereafter you didn't need money to have a good time. Now Dublin worships at the altar of Mammon and it seems that its primary role is to relieve you of your cash in the least amount of time for as little return as possible.'

Hook isn't at all impressed with the developers' imprint on his adopted city. He thinks the city is a monument to money and avarice, where everything is fair game. The houses, shops, streets and even the people have a plastic quality that makes them indistinguishable from any other city in the world, and that extends to the unique core of great Dublin institutions: the pub.

'Once upon a time,' he says, 'in the days of Kavanagh and Behan, virtually every pub had its own genuine characters, but they've been subsumed and the pub has been turned into a plastic commodity that is exported throughout the world. Twenty years ago, the Irish pub abroad wasn't anything like the real thing, but nowadays they're exactly the same because the local version has changed and become just like the ones you find abroad.'

And with that sobering thought he was on his way to the studio to prepare for yet another edition of *The Right Hook*, his immensely popular drive-time radio programme, which doles out the same kind of frank opinions to a nation of avid listeners every weekday from 4.30pm to 7pm on Newstalk 106–108FM.

(Map pp66–7; ☎ 478 0638; admission free; ⏱ 12.30-2.30pm Mon-Fri) and the early-19th-century Royal College of Surgeons (Map pp66–7), which has one of the finest façades on St Stephen's Green. During the 1916 Easter Rising, the building was occupied by rebel forces led by Countess Markievicz (1868–1927; see the boxed text, p24). The columns are scarred from the bullet holes.

Among the statues and memorials dotting the green, there's one of the Countess in the southeast corner. Since it was Guinness money that created the park you see today, it's only right that Sir Arthur should be present, and there's an 1892 statue of him on the western side of the park. Just north of here, outside the railings, is a statue of Irish patriot Robert Emmet (1778–1803), who was born across the road where Nos 124 and 125 stand; his actual birthplace has been demolished. The statue was placed here in 1966 and is a replica of an Emmet statue in Washington, DC. There is also a bust of poet James Clarence Mangan (1803–49) and a curious 1967 statue of WB Yeats by Henry Moore. The centre of the park has a garden for the blind, complete with signs in Braille and plants that can be handled. There is also a statue

of the Three Fates, presented to Dublin in 1956 by West Germany in gratitude for Irish aid after WWII. In the corner closest to the Shelbourne Hotel is a monument to Wolfe Tone, the leader of the abortive 1798 invasion; the vertical slabs serving as a backdrop to Wolfe Tone's statue have been dubbed 'Tonehenge'. At this entrance is a memorial to all those who died in the Famine.

On the eastern side of the green is a children's playground and to the south there's a fine old bandstand, erected to celebrate Queen Victoria's jubilee in 1887. Musical performances often take place here in summer. Near the bandstand is a bust of James Joyce, facing Newman House (opposite), part of University College Dublin, where Joyce was once a student. Also on this side is Iveagh House (Map pp66–7). Originally designed by Richard Cassels in 1730 as two separate houses, they were bought by Benjamin Guinness in 1862 and combined to create the family's city residence. After independence the house was donated to the Irish State and is now home to the Department of Foreign Affairs.

Of the many illustrious streets fanning from the green, the elegant Georgian

Harcourt St has the most notable addresses. Edward Carson was born at No 4 in 1854. As the architect of Northern Irish unionism, he was never going to be the most popular figure in Dublin but he did himself no favours acting as the prosecuting attorney during Oscar Wilde's trial for homosexuality. George Bernard Shaw lived at No 61.

NEWMAN HOUSE Map pp66–7
☎ 716 7422; 85-86 St Stephen's Green
Cardinal Newman established the Catholic University of Ireland here in 1865. To see one of the finest examples of Georgian architecture currently open to the public, you'll need to take one of the guided tours (adult/concession €5/4), which leave at noon, 2pm, 3pm and 4pm Tuesday to Friday from June to August (the house isn't open to general admission). The school provided education to the likes of James Joyce, Pádraig Pearse and Eamon de Valera, who would otherwise have had to submit to the Protestant hegemony of Trinity College if they wanted to receive higher education in Ireland. Newman House is still part of the college, which later decamped to the suburb of Belfield and changed its name to University College Dublin (UCD).

The house comprises two exquisitely restored town houses; No 85, the granite-faced original, was designed by Richard Cassels in 1738 for parliamentarian Hugh Montgomery, who sold it to Richard Chapel Whaley, MP, in 1765. Whaley wanted a grander home, so he commissioned another house next door at No 86.

Aside from Cassels' wonderful design, the highlight of the building is the plasterwork, perhaps the finest in the city. For No 85, the artists were the Italian stuccodores Paolo and Filipo LaFranchini, whose work is best appreciated in the wonderfully detailed Apollo Room on the ground floor. The plasterwork in No 86 was done by Robert West, but it is not quite up to the high standard of next door.

When the newly founded, Jesuit-run Catholic University of Ireland took possession of the house in 1865, alterations were made to some of the more graphic plasterwork, supplying the nude figures with 'modesty vests'.

During Whaley's residency, the house developed certain notoriety, largely due to the activities of his son, Buck, a notorious gambler and hell-raiser who once walked all the way to Jerusalem for a bet and somehow connived to have himself elected to parliament at the tender age of 17. During the university's tenure, however, the residents were a far more temperate lot. The Jesuit priest and wonderful poet Gerard Manley Hopkins lived here during his time as professor of classics, from 1884 until his death in 1889. Hopkins' bedroom is preserved as it would have been during his residence, as is the classroom where the young James Joyce studied while obtaining his Bachelor of Arts degree between 1899 and 1902.

NEWMAN UNIVERSITY CHURCH
Map pp66–7
☎ 478 0616; 83 St Stephen's Green; admission free; ⏰ 8am-6pm
Next to Newman House, this neo-Byzantine charmer was built in the mid-18th century (Cardinal Newman didn't care too much for the Gothic style of the day). Its richly decorated interior was mocked at first but has since become the preferred surroundings for Dublin's most fashionable weddings.

BANK OF IRELAND Map pp66–7
☎ 671 1488; College Green; ⏰ 10am-4pm Mon-Fri, 10am-5pm Thu
Facing Trinity College across College Green, this sweeping Palladian pile was built to house the Irish parliament and was the first purpose-built Parliament House in the world. The original building, the central colonnaded section that distinguishes the present-day structure, was designed by Sir

Edward Lovett Pearce in the first half of the 18th century.

When the parliament voted itself out of existence through the 1801 Act of Union, the building was sold under the condition that the interior would be altered to prevent it ever again being used as a debating chamber. It was a spiteful strike at Irish parliamentary aspirations, but while the central House of Commons was remodelled and offers little hint of its former role, the smaller House of Lords (admission free) chamber survived and is much more interesting (see p50). It has Irish oak woodwork, a mahogany longcase parliament clock and a late-18th-century Dublin crystal chandelier. The tapestries date from the 1730s and depict the Siege of Derry (1689) and the Battle of the Boyne (1690), the two Protestant victories over Catholic Ireland. In the niches are busts of George III, George IV, Lord Nelson and the Duke of Wellington. There are tours of the House of Lords (10.30am, 11.30am and 1.45pm Tuesday), which include a talk, as much about Ireland and life in general as the building itself.

Also part of the complex, and reached via the sedate Foster Place, is the Bank of Ireland Arts Centre (p180), which hosts a variety of cultural events, including classical concerts and regular free lunchtime recitals and poetry readings. It also screens an eight-minute film about banking and Irish history, called the Story of Banking (☎ 671 2261; adult/concession €1.50/1; ☯ screenings hourly 10am-3pm Tue-Fri). An exhibition features a 10kg silver-gilt mace that was made for the House of Commons and retained by the Speaker of the House when the parliament was dissolved. It was later sold by his descendants and bought back from Christies in London by the Bank of Ireland in 1937.

DUBLIN CASTLE Map p74
☎ 677 7129; www.dublincastle.ie; Cork Hill; adult/concession €4/3; ☯ 10am-5pm Mon-Fri, 2-5pm Sat & Sun

If you're looking for a medieval castle straight out of central casting you'll be disappointed; the stronghold of British power here for 700 years is principally an 18th-century creation that is more hotch-potch palace than turreted castle. Only the Record Tower survives from the original Anglo-Norman fortress built in the early 13th century. It was subject to a siege by 'Silken' Thomas Fitzgerald in 1534, virtually destroyed by a fire in 1684 and provided the setting for some momentous scenes during Ireland's battle for independence. It was officially handed over to Michael Collins on behalf of the Irish Free State in 1922, when the British viceroy is reported to have rebuked Collins on being seven minutes late. Collins replied, 'We've been waiting 700 years, you can wait seven minutes.' The castle is now used by the Irish government for meetings and functions, and can only be visited on a guided tour of the State Apartments and excavations of the former Powder Tower.

As you walk in to the grounds from the main Dame St entrance, there's a good ex-

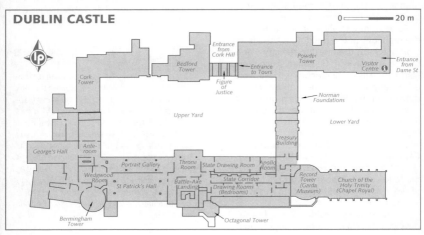

ample of the evolution of Irish architecture. On your left is the Victorian Chapel Royal (occasionally part of the Dublin Castle tours), decorated with more than 90 heads of various Irish personages and saints carved out of Tullamore limestone. The interior is wildly exuberant, with fan vaulting alongside quadripartite vaulting, wooden galleries, stained glass and lots of lively looking sculpted angels. Beside this is the Norman Record Tower, which has 5m-thick walls and now houses the Garda Museum (☎ 668 9998; admission free), which follows the history of the Irish police force. It doesn't have all that much worth protecting, but the views are fab (ring the bell for entry). On your right is the Georgian Treasury Building, the oldest office block in Dublin, and behind you, yikes, is the uglier-than-sin Revenue Commissioners Building of 1960.

Heading away from that eyesore, you ascend to the Upper Yard. On your right is a figure of Justice with her back turned to the city, an appropriate symbol for British justice, reckoned Dubliners. Next to it is the 18th-century Bedford Tower, from which the Irish Crown Jewels were stolen in 1907 and never recovered. Opposite is the entrance to the tours.

The 45-minute guided tours (departing every 20 to 30 minutes, depending on numbers) are pretty dry, seemingly pitched at tourists more likely to ooh and aah over period furniture than historical anecdotes, but they're included in the entry fee. You get to visit the State Apartments, many of which are decorated in dubious taste. There are beautiful chandeliers (ooh!), plush Irish carpets (aah!), splendid rococo ceilings, a Van Dyck portrait and the throne of King George V. You also get to see St Patrick's Hall, where Irish presidents are inaugurated and foreign dignitaries toasted, and the room in which the wounded James Connolly was tied to a chair while convalescing after the 1916 Easter Rising – brought back to health to be executed by firing squad.

The highlight is a visit to the subterranean excavations of the old castle, discovered by accident in 1986. They include foundations built by the Vikings (whose long-lasting mortar was made of ox blood, egg shells and horse hair), the handpolished exterior of the castle walls that prevented attackers from climbing them, the steps leading down to the moat and

top picks

IT'S FREE

- Chester Beatty Library (p70)
- National Museum – Archaeology & History (p80) & National Museum – Decorative Arts & History (p105)
- National Gallery (p79)
- Natural History Museum (p81)
- Glasnevin Cemetery tour (p118)

the trickle of the historic River Poddle, which once filled the moat on its way to join the Liffey.

IVEAGH GARDENS Map pp66–7

🕑 8.15am-6pm Mon-Sat, 10am-6pm Sun May-Sep, 8.15am-dusk Oct-Apr

Our favourite gardens in Dublin may not have the sculpted elegance of the other city parks, but they never get too crowded and the warden won't bark at you if you walk on the grass. They were designed by Ninian Niven in 1863 as the private grounds of Iveagh House, and include a rustic grotto, cascade, fountain, maze and rosarium.

MANSION HOUSE Map pp66–7

Dawson St

Built in 1710 by Joshua Dawson – after whom the street is named – this has been the official residence of Dublin's mayor since 1715, and was the site of the 1919 Declaration of Independence and the meeting of the first parliament. The building's original brick Queen-Anne style has all but disappeared behind a stucco façade added in the Victorian era.

ROYAL IRISH ACADEMY Map pp66–7

☎ 676 2570; 19 Dawson St; admission free; 🕑 10am-5.30pm Mon-Thu, 10am-5pm Fri

Next door to Mansion House is the seat of Ireland's pre-eminent society of letters, whose 18th-century library houses many important documents, including an extensive collection of ancient manuscripts such as the *Book of Dun Cow*, the oldest surviving Irish manuscript; the *Cathach of St Columba*; and the entire collection of 19th-century poet Thomas Moore (1779–1852).

POWERSCOURT TOWNHOUSE SHOPPING CENTRE Map pp66–7

☎ 679 4144; 59 South William St

This elegant Richard Cassels–designed town house was built between 1771 and 1774, and boasts some fine plasterwork by Michael Stapleton among its features. These days it struts its stuff as Dublin's most stylish shopping centre as well as one of the more pleasant spots to get a bite of lunch. See Eating (p145) and Shopping (p136) for more.

CITY HALL Map pp66–7

☎ 672 2204; www.dublincorp.ie/cityhall; Cork Hill; building admission free, exhibition adult/concession €4/2; ⏰ 10am-5.15pm Mon-Sat, 2-5pm Sun

One of the architectural triumphs of the Dublin boom was the magnificent restoration of City Hall, originally built by Thomas Cooley as the Royal Exchange between 1769 and 1779, and botched in the mid-19th century when it became the offices of the local government. In the 2000 restoration, the internal walls were cleared and the building was returned to all its gleaming Georgian glory. The rotunda and its ambulatory form a breathtaking interior, bathed in natural light from enormous windows to the east. A vast marble statue of former mayor and Catholic emancipator Daniel O'Connell stands here as a reminder of the building's links with Irish nationalism (the funerals of both Charles Stewart Parnell and Michael Collins were held here). Dublin City Council still meets here on the first Monday of the month, gathering to discuss the city's business in the Council Chamber, which was the original building's coffee room.

There was a sordid precursor to City Hall in the shape of the Lucas Coffee House and the adjoining Eagle Tavern, in which the notorious Hellfire Club was founded by Richard Parsons, Earl of Rosse, in 1735. Although the city abounded with gentlemen's clubs, this particular one gained a reputation for messing about in the arenas of sex and Satan, two topics that were guaranteed to fire the lurid imaginings of the city's gossipmongers.

The striking vaulted basement hosts a multimedia exhibition The Story of the Capital, which traces the history of the city from its earliest beginnings to its rosy future – with ne'er a mention of sex, Satan or sex with Satan. There's more info here than even the most nostalgic expat could take in, and exhibits are a little text heavy, but it's all slickly presented and the audiovisual displays are informative and easy to absorb.

IRISH-JEWISH MUSEUM Map pp66–7

☎ 453 1797; 4 Walworth Rd; admission free; ⏰ 11am-3.30pm Tue, Thu & Sun May-Sep, 10.30am-2.30pm Sun Oct-Apr; 🚌 16, 19 or 122 from Trinity College

Housed in an old synagogue, this museum recounts the history and cultural heritage of Ireland's small but prolific Jewish community. It was opened in 1985 by the Belfast-born, then-Israeli president, Chaim Herzog. The various memorabilia includes photographs, paintings, certificates, books and other artefacts.

SHAW BIRTHPLACE Map pp66–7

☎ 475 0854; 33 Synge St; adult/child/student €7/4.40/5.95; ⏰ 10am-1pm & 2-5pm Mon-Sat, from 11am Sun Easter-Oct; 🚌 16, 19 or 122 from Trinity College

Close to the Grand Canal, the birthplace of playwright George Bernard Shaw is now a restored Victorian home that is interesting even to nonliterary buffs because it provides an insight into the domestic life of the 19th century's middle classes. Shaw's mother held musical evenings in the drawing room, and it is likely that her son's store of fabulous characters was inspired by those who attended.

WHITEFRIARS STREET CARMELITE CHURCH Map pp66–7

☎ 475 8821; 56 Aungier St; admission free; ⏰ 8am-6.30pm Mon & Wed-Fri, 8am-9.30pm Tue, 8am-7pm Sat, 8am-7.30pm Sun

If you find yourself mulling over the timing of a certain proposal – or know someone who needs some prompting – walk through the automated glass doors of this church and head for the remains of none other than St Valentine, donated by Pope Gregory XVI in 1835. The Carmelites returned to this site in 1827, when they re-established their former church, which had been seized from them by Henry VIII in the 16th century. In the northeastern corner is a 16th-century Flemish oak statue of the Virgin and Child, which is believed to be the only wooden statue in Ireland to have escaped destruction during the Reformation.

MERRION SQUARE & AROUND

Eating p151; Drinking p167; Shopping p136; Sleeping p201

Genteel, sophisticated and elegant, the exquisite Georgian architecture spread around handsome Merrion Sq is a near-perfect mix of imposing public buildings, museums, and private offices and residences. It is round these parts that much of moneyed Dublin works and plays, amid the neoclassical beauties thrown up during Dublin's 18th-century prime. When James Fitzgerald, the earl of Kildare, built his mansion south of the Liffey, he was mocked for his foolhardy move into the wilds. But Jimmy Fitz had a nose for real estate: 'Where I go society will follow,' he confidently predicted and he was soon proved right. Today, Leinster House is used as the Irish parliament and is in the epicentre of Georgian Dublin.

The area around Kildare St is the administrative core of the country as well as a repository for its treasures, housed in places like the National Museum, National Gallery and Natural History Museum. The most celebrated emblems of the time are the magnificent Merrion and Fitzwilliam Sqs, surrounded by buildings that still retain their period features. This was the original stomping ground of Ireland's Protestant ascendancy, and the many plaques on the buildings remind us that it was behind these brightly coloured doors that the likes of Oscar Wilde and William Butler Yeats hung their hats.

The streets running off these squares house the offices of some of the country's most important businesses. When there's even a hint of sunshine, workers pour out into the various parks, or follow the lead of poet Patrick Kavanagh and lounge along the banks of the Grand Canal. When they clock off, these same workers head to the wonderfully atmospheric and historical pubs of Baggot St and Merrion Row for a couple of scoops of chips and some unwinding banter. There are also plenty of smart restaurants, including several of Dublin's best.

Most cross-city buses will get you here (or near enough); the most convenient DART stop is Pearse St, with the station entrance on Westland Row.

MERRION SQUARE Map pp78–9

St Stephen's Green may win the popularity contest, but elegant Merrion Sq snubs its nose at such easy praise and remains the most prestigious of Dublin's squares. Its well-kept lawns and beautifully tended flower beds are flanked on three sides by gorgeous Georgian houses with colourful doors, peacock fanlights, ornate door knockers and, occasionally, foot-scrapers, used to remove mud from shoes before venturing indoors. The square, laid out in 1762, is bordered on its remaining side by the National Gallery (p79) and Leinster House (p82) – all of which, apparently, isn't enough for some. One former resident, WB Yeats (1865–1939), was less than impressed and described the architecture as 'grey 18th century'; there's just no pleasing some people.

Despite the air of affluent calm, life around here hasn't always been a well-pruned bed of roses. During the Famine, the lawns of the square teemed with destitute rural refugees who lived off the soup kitchen organised here. The British Embassy was at 39 Merrion Sq East until 1972, when it was burnt out in protest against the killing of 13 innocent civilians on Bloody Sunday in Derry.

Damage to fine Dublin buildings hasn't always been the prerogative of vandals, terrorists or protesters. East Merrion Sq once continued into Lower Fitzwilliam St in the longest unbroken series of Georgian houses in Europe. Despite this, in 1961 the Electricity Supply Board (ESB) knocked down 26 of them to build an office block (see p82) – just another in a long list of crimes against architectural aesthetics that plagued the city in the latter half of the 20th century. The Royal Institute of the Architects of Ireland

top picks

MERRION SQUARE & AROUND

- Merrion Square (left), an oasis of calm steeped in Irish history
- The impressive collection at the National Gallery (p79)
- Antiquated Natural History Museum (p81), which will captivate young and old
- National Museum (p80), full of fascinating treasures
- Serene and inviting Iveagh Gardens (p75)

MERRION SQUARE & AROUND

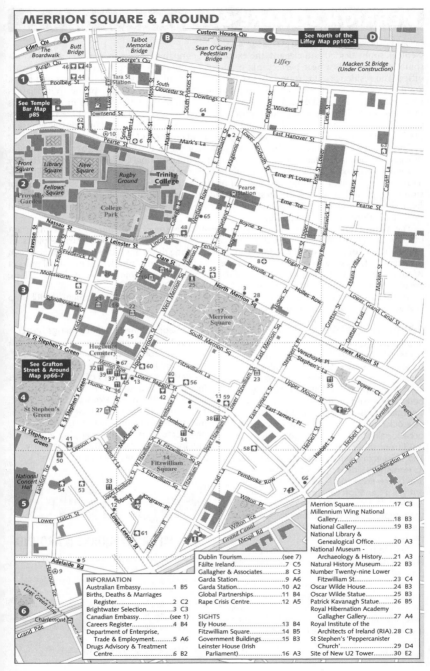

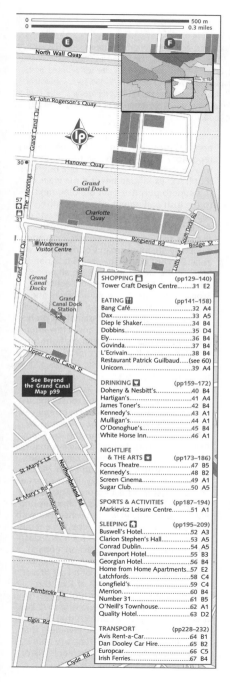

(☎ 676 1703; www.riai.ie; 8 North Merrion Sq; admission free; ⏰ 9am-5pm Mon-Fri) is rather more respectful of its Georgian address and hosts regular exhibitions.

NATIONAL GALLERY Map pp78–9

☎ 661 5133; www.nationalgallery.ie; West Merrion Sq; admission free; ⏰ 9.30am-5.30pm Mon-Wed, Fri & Sat, 9.30am-8.30pm Thu, noon-5.30pm Sun, free tours 3pm Sat, 2pm, 3pm & 4pm Sun

A stunning Caravaggio and a whole room full of Ireland's pre-eminent artist, Jack B Yeats, are just a couple of stand-out highlights from this fine collection, amassed by the State since 1854. Its original collection of 125 paintings has grown, mainly through bequests, to over 12,500 artworks, including oils, watercolours, sketches, prints and sculptures.

The building itself was designed by Francis Fowke (1823–65), whose architectural credits also include London's Victoria & Albert Museum. On the lawn in front of the main entrance is a statue of the Irish railways magnate William Dargan, who organised the 1853 Dublin Industrial Exhibition on this spot; the profits from the exhibition were used to found the gallery. Next to him is George Bernard Shaw, another great benefactor of the gallery.

The entire building comprises 54 galleries; works are divided by history, school, geography and theme. There are four wings: the original Dargan Wing, the Milltown Wing (1899–1903), the Beit Wing (1964–68) and the spectacular Millennium Wing, added in 2002. The new section – also accessible via a second entrance on Clare St – provides two floors of galleries for visiting exhibitions, a centre for the study of Irish art and a multimedia room that lets you track down any painting in the gallery.

The collection spans works from the 14th to the 20th centuries and includes all the major continental schools. Obviously there is an emphasis on Irish art, and among the works to look out for are William Orpen's *Sunlight*, Roderic O'Conor's *Reclining Nude* and *Young Breton Girl*, and Paul Henry's *The Potato Diggers*. But the highlight, and one you should definitely take time to explore, is the Yeats Museum, devoted to and containing more than 30 paintings by Jack B Yeats, a uniquely Irish impressionist and arguably the country's greatest artist (see p46). Some of his finest

LITERARY ADDRESSES

Merrion Sq has long been the favoured address of Dublin's affluent intelligentsia. Oscar Wilde spent much of his youth at 1 North Merrion Sq, and his house is now a museum (p82). Grumpy WB Yeats (1865–1939) lived at 52 East Merrion Sq and later, from 1922 to 1928, at 82 South Merrion Sq. George (AE) Russell (1867–1935), the self-described 'poet, mystic, painter and cooperator', worked at No 84. The great Liberator, Daniel O'Connell (1775–1847) was a resident of No 58 in his later years. Austrian Erwin Schrödinger (1887–1961), cowinner of the 1933 Nobel Prize for physics, lived at No 65 from 1940 to 1956. Dublin seems to attract writers of horror stories and Joseph Sheridan Le Fanu (1814–73), who penned the vampire classic Camilla, was a resident of No 70.

moments are *The Liffey Swim, Men of Destiny* and *Above the Fair.*

The absolute star exhibit from a pupil of the European schools is Caravaggio's sublime *The Taking of Christ,* in which the troubled Italian genius attempts to light the scene figuratively and metaphorically (the artist himself is portrayed holding the lantern on the far right). The masterpiece lay undiscovered for more than 60 years in a Jesuit house in nearby Leeson St, and was found accidentally by the chief curator of the gallery, Sergio Benedetti, in 1992. Fra Angelico, Titian and Tintoretto are all in this neighbourhood. Facing Caravaggio, way down the opposite end of the gallery, is *A Genovese Boy Standing on a Terrace* by Van Dyck. Old Dutch and Flemish masters line up in between, but all defer to Vermeer's *Lady Writing a Letter,* which is lucky to be here at all, having been stolen by Dublin gangster Martin Cahill in 1992, as featured in the film *The General* (see p43).

The French section contains Jules Breton's famous 19th-century *The Gleaners,* along with works by Monet, Degas, Pisarro and Delacroix, while Spain chips in with an unusually scruffy *Still Life with Mandolin* by Picasso, as well as paintings by El Greco and Goya, and an early Velázquez. There is a small British collection with works by Reynolds, Hogarth, Gainsborough and Turner. One of the most popular exhibitions occurs only in January, when the gallery hosts its annual display of watercolours by Joseph Turner. The 35 works in the collection are best viewed at this time due to the particular quality of the winter light.

NATIONAL MUSEUM – ARCHAEOLOGY & HISTORY Map pp78–9

☎ 677 7444; www.museum.ie; Kildare St; admission free; ☺ 10am-5pm Tue-Sat, 2-5pm Sun
The mother of Irish museums and the country's most important cultural institu-

tion was established in 1977 as the primary repository of the nation's archaeological treasures. The collection is so big, however, that it has expanded beyond the walls of this superb purpose-built building next to the Irish parliament into three other separate museums – the stuffed beasts of the Natural History Museum (opposite), the decorative arts section at Collins Barracks (p105) and a country life museum in County Mayo, on Ireland's west coast. They're all fascinating, but the star attractions are all here, mixed up in Europe's finest collection of Bronze- and Iron-Age gold artefacts, the most complete collection of medieval Celtic metalwork in the world, fascinating prehistoric and Viking artefacts, and a few interesting items relating to Ireland's fight for independence. If you don't mind groups, the themed guided tours (€1.50; ☺ 11am, 12.30pm, 2pm & 3pm Tue-Sat, 2pm & 3pm Sun) will help you wade through the myriad exhibits.

The Treasury is perhaps the most famous part of the collection, and its centrepieces are Ireland's two most famous crafted artefacts, the Ardagh Chalice and the Tara Brooch. The 12th-century Ardagh Chalice is made of gold, silver, bronze, brass, copper and lead; it measures 17.8cm high and 24.2cm in diameter, and, put simply, is the finest example of Celtic art ever found. The equally renowned Tara Brooch was crafted around AD 700, primarily in white bronze, but with traces of gold, silver, glass, copper, enamel and wire beading, and was used as a clasp for a cloak. It was discovered on a beach in Bettystown, County Meath, in 1850, but later came into the hands of an art dealer who named it after the hill of Tara, the historic seat of the ancient high kings. It doesn't have quite the same ring to it, but it was the Bettystown Brooch that sparked a revival of interest in Celtic jewellery that hasn't let up to this day. There are many other pieces that testify to Ireland's history as the land of saints and scholars.

Virtually all of the treasures are named after the location in which they were found. It's interesting to note that most of them were discovered not by archaeologists' trowels but by bemused farmers out ploughing their fields, cutting peat or, in the case of the Ardagh Chalice, digging for spuds.

Elsewhere in the Treasury is the exhibition Ór-Ireland's Gold, featuring stunning jewellery and decorative objects created by Celtic artisans in the Bronze and Iron Ages. Among them are the Broighter Hoard, which includes a 1st-century-BC large gold collar, unsurpassed anywhere in Europe, and an extraordinarily delicate gold boat. There's also the wonderful Loughnasade bronze war trumpet, which dates from the 1st century BC. It is 1.86m long and made of sheets of bronze, riveted together, with an intricately designed disc at the mouth. It produces a sound similar to the Australian didgeridoo, though you'll have to take our word for it. Running alongside the wall is a 15m log boat, which was dropped into the water to soften, abandoned and then pulled out 4000 years later, almost perfectly preserved in the peat bog.

On the same level is the Road to Independence exhibition, which features the army coat worn by Michael Collins on the day he was assassinated (there's still mud on the sleeve). In the same case is the cap purportedly also worn by Collins on that fateful day, complete with a bullet hole in its side – somehow, however, we think if the authorities had any confidence in this claim, the exhibit wouldn't be on the floor of the cabinet without even a note.

If you can cope with any more history, upstairs are Medieval Ireland 1150–1550, Viking Age Ireland – which features exhibits from the excavations at Wood Quay, the area between Christ Church Cathedral and the river (Map pp90–1) – and our own favourite, the aptly named Clothes from Bogs in Ireland, a collection of 16th- and 17th-century woollen garments recovered from the bog. Enthralling stuff!

NATURAL HISTORY MUSEUM Map pp78–9

☎ 677 7444; www.museum.ie; Merrion St; admission free; ☺ 10am-5pm Tue-Sat, 2-5pm Sun

Dusty, weird and utterly compelling, this window into Victorian times has barely changed since Scottish explorer Dr David Livingstone opened it in 1857 – before disappearing off into the African jungle for a meeting with Henry Stanley. The creaking interior is crammed with some two million stuffed animals, skeletons and other specimens from around the world, ranging from West African apes to pickled insects in jars. Some are freestanding, others behind glass, but everywhere you turn the animals of the 'dead zoo' are still and staring.

Compared to the multimedia, interactive this and that of virtually every modern museum, this is a beautifully preserved example of Victorian charm. It is usually full of fascinated kids, but it's the adults who seem to make most noise as they ricochet like pinballs between displays. The Irish Room on the ground floor is filled with mammals, sea creatures, birds and butterflies all found in Ireland at some

TRACING YOUR ANCESTORS

Go on, you're dying to see if you've got a bit of Irish in you, and maybe tracking down your roots is the main reason for your visit. It will have made things much easier if you did some preliminary research in your home country – particularly finding out the precise date and point of entry of your ancestors – but you might still be able to plot your family tree even if you're acting on impulse.

The Genealogical Office (p83) will advise you on how to trace your ancestry, which is a good way to begin your research if you have no other experience. For information on commercial agencies that will do the research for you, contact the Association of Professional Genealogists in Ireland (APGI, c/o the Genealogical Office, Kildare St). The Births, Deaths & Marriages Register (Map pp78–9; ☎ 671 1863; Joyce House, East Lombard St; ☺ 9.30am-12.30pm & 2.15-4.30pm Mon-Fri) and the files of the National Library and the National Archives (Map pp66–7; ☎ 407 2300; Bishop St, Dublin 8; ☺ 10am-5pm Mon-Fri) are all potential sources of genealogical information.

There are also lots of books on the subject, with Irish Roots Guide, by Tony McCarthy, serving as a useful introduction. Other publications include Tracing Your Irish Roots by Christine Kineally and Tracing Your Irish Ancestors: A Comprehensive Guide by John Grenham. All these, and other items of genealogical concern, can be obtained from the Genealogy Bookshop (Map pp66–7; 3 Nassau St).

point, including the skeletons of three 10,000-year-old Irish elk that greet you as you enter. The World Animals Collection, spread across three levels, has the skeleton of a 20m-long fin whale found beached in County Sligo as its centrepiece. Evolutionists will love the line-up of orang-utan, chimpanzee, gorilla and human skeletons on the 1st floor. Other notables include the extinct Australian marsupial the Tasmanian tiger (mislabelled as a Tasmanian wolf), a giant panda from China, and several African and Asian rhinoceroses. The wonderful Blaschka Collection comprises finely detailed glass models of marine creatures whose zoological accuracy is incomparable.

LEINSTER HOUSE – IRISH PARLIAMENT Map pp78–9

☎ 618 3000; www.oireachtas.ie; Kildare St

All the big decisions are made – or rubber-stamped – at Oireachtas na Éireann (Irish parliament). It was built by Richard Cassels in the Palladian style between 1745 and 1748, and was considered the forerunner of the Georgian fashion that became the norm for Dublin's finer residences. Its Kildare St façade looks like a town house (which inspired Irish architect James Hoban's designs for the US White House), whereas the Merrion Sq frontage was made to resemble a country mansion.

The first government of the Irish Free State moved in from 1922, and both the Dáil (lower house) and Seanad (senate) still meet here to discuss the affairs of the nation and gossip at the exclusive members bar. The 60-member Seanad meets for fairly low-key sessions in the north-wing saloon, while there are usually more sparks and tantrums when the 166-member Dáil bangs heads in a less-interesting room, formerly a lecture theatre, which was added to the original building in 1897. Parliament sits for 90 days a year. You get an entry ticket to the lower- or upper-house observation galleries (2.30-8.30pm Tue, 10.30am-8.30pm Wed, 10.30am-5.30pm Thu Nov-May) from the Kildare St entrance on production of photo identification. Free, pre-arranged guided tours (☎ 618 3271) are available weekdays when parliament is in session.

The obelisk in front of the building is dedicated to Arthur Griffith, Michael Collins and Kevin O'Higgins, the architects of independent Ireland.

NUMBER TWENTY-NINE Map pp78–9

☎ 702 6165; www.esb.ie/numbertwentynine; 29 Lwr Fitzwilliam St; adult/child/student €5/free/2.50; 10am-5pm Tue-Sat, 1-5pm Sun, closed 2 weeks at Christmas

In an effort to atone at least partly for its sins against Dublin's Georgian heritage – it broke up Europe's most perfect Georgian row to build its headquarters (see p77) – the ESB restored this home to give an impression of genteel family life at the beginning of the 18th century. From rat-traps in the kitchen basement to handmade wallpaper and Georgian cabinets, the attention to detail is impressive, but the regular tours (dependent on numbers) are disappointingly dry.

OSCAR WILDE HOUSE Map pp78–9

☎ 662 0281; www.amcd.ie/oscarwildehouse; 1 North Merrion Sq; admission €5; tours 10.15am & 11.15am Mon, Wed & Thu

In 1855 the surgeon William Wilde and his wife 'Speranza' Wilde moved into 1 North Merrion Sq – the first residence built on the square (1762) – with their one-year-old son Oscar. They lived here until 1878 and we imagine that the young Oscar's genius was stimulated by the famous literary salon hosted here by his mother. The family lived here right through Oscar's education at Trinity. In 1994 the house was taken over by the American College Dublin. The first two floors have been restored to an approximate version of their appearance in Oscar's day and can only be visited on a guided tour.

Across the road, just inside the railings of Merrion Sq, is a flamboyant statue of the man himself. Crafted from a variety of precious stones, it is an aptly colourful depiction of Wilde wearing his customary smoking jacket and reclining on a rock. Wilde may well be sneering at Dublin and his old home, although the expression may have more to do with the artist's attempt to depict the deeply divided nature of the man: from one side he looks to be smiling and happy; from the other, gloomy and preoccupied. Atop one of the plinths, daubed with witty one-liners and Wildean throwaways, is a small green statue of Oscar's pregnant mother.

GOVERNMENT BUILDINGS Map pp78–9

☎ 662 4888, ticket office ☎ 661 5133; www .taoiseach.gov.ie; Upper Merrion St

This gleaming Edwardian pile was the last building (almost) completed by the British before they were booted out; it opened as the Royal College of Science in 1911. When the college vacated in 1989, Taoiseach Charlie Haughey and his government moved in and spent a fortune refurbishing the complex. Among Haughey's needs, apparently, was a private lift from his office that went up to a rooftop helipad and down to a limo in the basement.

Free 40-minute guided tours (10.30am to 3.30pm Saturday only, tickets from National Gallery ticket office) take you through the Taoiseach's office, the Cabinet Room, the ceremonial staircase with a stunning stained-glass window – designed by Evie Hone (1894–1955) for the 1939 New York Trade Fair – and many fine examples of modern Irish arts and crafts.

Directly across the road from here, and now part of the Merrion Hotel, 24 Upper Merrion St is thought to be the birthplace of Arthur Wellesley (1769–1852), the first Duke of Wellington, who downplayed his Irish origins and once said 'being born in a stable does not make one a horse'. It is also possible that the cheeky bugger was born in Trim, County Meath.

FITZWILLIAM SQUARE Map pp78–9
South of St Merrion Sq, the smallest and the last of Dublin's great Georgian squares was completed in 1825. It's also the only one where the central garden is still the private domain of the square's residents. William Dargan (1799–1867), the railway pioneer and founder of the National Gallery, lived at No 2, and the artist Jack B Yeats (1871–1957; see p46) lived at No 18. Look out for the attractive 18th- and 19th-century metal coal-hole covers. The square is now a centre for the medical profession by day and a notorious beat for prostitutes at night.

ROYAL HIBERNIAN ACADEMY (RHA) GALLAGHER GALLERY Map pp78–9
☎ 661 2558; www.royalhibernianacademy.com; 25 Ely Pl; admission free; ⏰ 11am-5pm Mon-Wed, Fri & Sat, 11am-9pm Thu, 2-5pm Sun
This large, well-lit gallery at the end of a serene Georgian street has a grand name to fit its exalted reputation as one of the most prestigious exhibition spaces for modern and contemporary art in Ireland. Indeed, if your name is affixed to any of the works on ever-changing display you must be doing something right in the artistic world, especially as the gallery is working hard to shrug off its reputation for having conservative tastes and these days plays host to an increasingly challenging array of work. The big event is the RHA Annual Exhibition, held in May, which shows the work of those artists deemed worthy enough by the selection committee, made up of members of the academy (easily identified amid the huge throng that attends the opening by the scholar's gowns). The show is a mix of technically proficient artists, Sunday painters and the odd outstanding talent.

NATIONAL LIBRARY & GENEALOGICAL OFFICE Map pp78–9
☎ 603 0200; www.nli.ie; Kildare St; admission free; ⏰ 10am-9pm Mon-Wed, 10am-5pm Thu & Fri, 10am-1pm Sat
Next door to Leinster House, the suitably sedate National Library was built from 1884 to 1890, at the same time and to a similar design as the National Museum, by Sir Thomas Newenham Deane. Its extensive collection has many valuable early manuscripts, first editions, maps and other items of interest. Parts of the library are open to the public, including the domed reading room where Stephen Dedalus expounded his views on Shakespeare in *Ulysses*. Check in your bags at security for a look-see, although *you* won't expound anything at all in the stiflingly hushed atmosphere.

There's a Genealogical Office (☎ 603 0200; ⏰ 10am-4.45pm Mon-Fri, 10am-12.30pm Sat) on the 2nd floor, where you can obtain information on how best to trace your Irish roots (see the boxed text, p81).

ST STEPHEN'S 'PEPPER-CANISTER' CHURCH Map pp78–9
☎ 288 0663; Upper Mount St; admission free
Built in 1825 in Greek Revival style and commonly known as the 'pepper-canister' on account of its appearance, St Stephen's is one of Dublin's most attractive and distinctive churches, and looks particularly fetching at twilight when its exterior lights have just come on. It occasionally hosts classical concerts, but don't go out of your way to see the interior. It's only open during services, usually held at 11am Sunday and 11.30am Wednesday, with an extra one at 11am Friday July and August.

TEMPLE BAR

Eating p153; Drinking p168; Shopping p136; Sleeping p203

It is the city's party district, packed with brash bars and pubs that stand cheek to jowl with restaurants, cutesy little boutiques, funky shops…and more bars. For the legions of revellers who don their themed T-shirts and reveal-all outfits ready for a night of drinking, laughing and scoring, Temple Bar is the best part of the Dublin experience; for those looking for a more cultural, authentic insight into the capital, Temple Bar is a high-octane cheesefest, artificially manufactured to clean out unsuspecting wallets. It's all a far cry from the high-falutin' hyperbole spun by developers in the early 1990s about Dublin's cultural renaissance being centred on this maze of cobbled streets slotted between Dame St and the river, running roughly from Trinity College to the shadow of Christ Church Cathedral.

Fishamble St, the oldest street in Dublin, dates back to Viking times and marks the western boundary of Temple Bar. Brass symbols in the pavement direct you towards a mosaic, just southwest of the overpass between Christ Church Cathedral and Dvblinia, laid out to show the ground plan of the sort of Viking dwelling excavated here in the early 1980s. The land was acquired by William Temple (1554–1628) sometime after Henry VIII dissolved the monasteries in 1537 and turfed out the Augustinian friars. The narrow lanes and alleys date from the early 18th century, when Temple Bar became a disreputable area of pubs and prostitution.

In 1742 Handel conducted the first performance of his *Messiah* in Neal's Music Hall on Fishamble St (see the boxed text, p17), now part of a hotel that bears the composer's name – it's behind Kinlay House (on Lord Edward St). In the 19th century the area developed a commercial character, attracting small craft and trade businesses. On Parliament St, which runs down to the quays from Dublin Castle (p74), the Sunlight Chambers (named after a brand of soap; Map p85) has a beautiful frieze showing the Lever Brothers' view of the world and soap: men make clothes dirty, women wash them.

Despite the history, there's no denying that Temple Bar's attempts to create a sophisticated Left Bank atmosphere have not been altogether successful. It is an overly commercialised quarter, full of overpriced restaurants serving indifferent food, tacky souvenir shops and – with one or two exceptions – characterless bars that are more like meat markets than decent Dublin hostelries. Weekend nights are alcopop- and lager-fuelled mayhem; the whole area overflows with drunks doing their level best to justify the nickname 'Temple Barf'. Although there are plenty of hotels, they're generally cramped, packed and noisy as hell.

All of which sounds just right for anyone looking for a party, but Temple Bar *does* have more going on than stag parties from Nottingham begging a group of girls on a hen weekend to get their kit off for the lads – or the same hens daring the same lads to show them what they're made of.

OK, so the area isn't quite the new stomping ground for the radical philosophy crowd, but there are a host of slightly more brain-friendly offerings that don't make an abject mockery of the cultural quarter moniker. A handful of art galleries, a museum or two, some interesting shops and an entertaining daytime streetscape of young and old wandering about, stopping perhaps to listen to a busker or a comic, make Temple Bar well worth the effort, even if you make a point of escaping by sundown.

And it nearly didn't happen at all. It spent most of the 20th century languishing in dereliction (along with much of the city centre) and in the 1960s the government earmarked it as the perfect spot to build a gigantic bus depot. While it went about the slow business of acquiring the remaining properties, many of the condemned buildings were leased on short-term contracts to artists, artisans and community groups. Then, just as the 1990s and the Celtic Tiger first began to growl, a group of enlightened developers with close ties to the government had a brainwave and set about transforming the area into Dublin's very own cultural quarter. Its rundown buildings and streets were revitalised, derelict buildings demolished and new squares built. Among the cultural gems of the quarter are the progressive Project Arts Centre (p186), Temple Bar Gallery & Studios (p86) and the Irish Film Institute (IFI; p179). The Millennium Bridge opens up a fetching vista of Eustace St, to match Crown Alley and the atmospheric Merchant's Arch, which opens splendidly onto the Ha'penny Bridge.

As Temple Bar is right in the heart of the city, all cross-city buses will deposit you by the cobbled streets, making access – and escape – that bit easier.

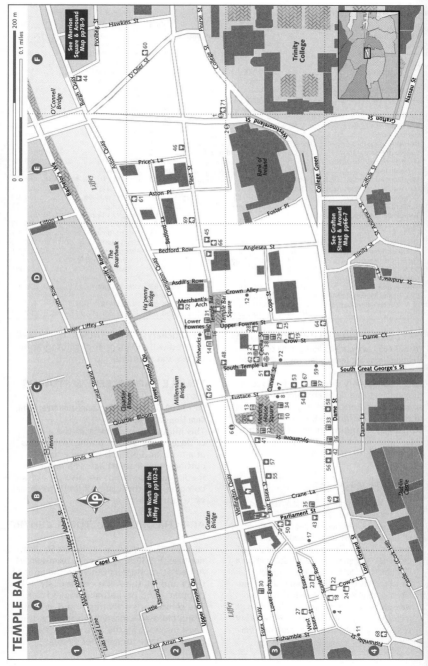

TEMPLE BAR

See Merrion Square & Around Map pp78-9

See Grafton Street & Around Map pp66-7

See North of the Liffey Map pp102-3

Trinity College

Bank of Ireland

Dublin Castle

Quartier Bloom

85

TEMPLE BAR

GALLERY OF PHOTOGRAPHY Map p85
☎ 671 4653; www.irish-photography.com;
Meeting House Sq, Temple Bar; admission free;
🕒 11am-6pm Mon-Sat
This small gallery devoted to the photograph is set in a light and airy three-level
space overlooking Meeting House Sq
in the heart of Temple Bar. It features a
constantly changing menu of local and
international work, and while it's a little too small to be considered a really
good gallery, the downstairs shop is well
stocked with all manner of photographic
tomes and manuals.

TEMPLE BAR GALLERY & STUDIOS
Map p85
☎ 671 0073; 5 Temple Bar; admission free; 10am-
6pm Mon-Sat, 2-6pm Sun
This huge gallery showcases the works
of dozens of up-and-coming Irish artists
at a time, and is the best place to see
cutting-edge Irish art across a range of
media. Artist's studios are also part of the
complex, but these are off limits to casual
visitors.

ARK CHILDREN'S CULTURAL CENTRE
Map p85
☎ 670 7788; www.ark.ie; 11a Eustace St; admission free; 🕒 9.30am-4pm Tue-Fri, 10am-4pm Sat
Aimed at youngsters between the ages of
three and 14, the Ark is enormously
popular – and perpetually booked out.
The centre runs activities aimed at stimu-
lating children's interests in science, the
environment and the arts, and has an
open-air stage for summer events.

HANDEL WITH CARE

In 1742 the nearly broke GF Handel conducted the
very first performance of his epic work *Messiah* in
the since-demolished Neal's Music Hall, on the city's
oldest street, Fishamble St. Ironically, Dean Swift –
author of *Gulliver's Travels* and dean of St Patrick's
Cathedral – suggested the choirs of St Patrick's and
Christchurch participate, but then he revoked his
invitation, vowing to 'punish such vicars for their
rebellion, disobedience and perfidy'. The concert
went ahead nonetheless, and the celebrated work
is now performed in Dublin annually at the original
spot – now a hotel that bears the composer's name
(Map p85).

HEY DOODLE, DOODLE Map p85

☎ 672 7382; 14 Crown Alley; admission €8; ☺ 11am-6pm Tue-Sat, 1-6pm Sun

Budding young ceramicists get their chance to display their talents at one of the city's more interesting kids' venues. Children pick a piece of pottery, paint it whatever way they like, and collect it a week later after it's been fired and glazed. The odd adult has been spotted with a paintbrush in hand too. It gets busy at weekends, and group bookings must be made in advance.

ORIGINAL PRINT GALLERY Map p85

☎ 677 3657; www.originalprint.ie; Black Church Studio, 4 Temple Bar; admission free; ☺ 10.30am-5.30pm Mon-Sat, 2-5pm Sun

This gallery specialises in original, limited-edition prints, including etchings, lithographs and silk-screens, mostly by Irish artists.

NATIONAL PHOTOGRAPHIC ARCHIVES Map p85

☎ 671 0073; Meeting House Sq, Temple Bar; admission free; ☺ 11am-6pm Mon-Sat, 2-6pm Sun

What should be a wonderful resource putting a face on all facets of Irish history is actually a sadly disappointing archive of photographs taken from the 19th century onwards. Its visitor-friendly catalogue is computer accessible and the eager staff are always willing to help with queries, but the available material is not nearly as extensive as we'd hoped.

KILMAINHAM & THE LIBERTIES

Eating p155; Drinking p169; Shopping p138

West of most of the action, Dublin's most traditional neighbourhoods are a little light on entertainment but they offer an insight into a bygone era and are home to three outstanding sights, including the most visited attraction in the whole city.

Coming from the heart of the city centre, you'll first stumble into the Liberties, so-called because in medieval times, when Dublin was but a mere twinkle in a developer's eye, this sprawling area outside the city walls was self-governing and free of many of the tithes and taxes of Dublin proper.

That the two major cathedrals of Christ Church and St Patrick's were built here is testament to its medieval importance. In some ways it became the engine room for Dublin's growth, a centre of industry, into which migrants flocked looking for employment. Around 10,000 Huguenot refugees from France flooded into the area from the mid-17th century, introducing silk and linen weaving, which transformed the place and had a profound effect on the city as a whole. The Liberties prospered, standards of living increased and a fierce community pride emerged. The boom busted when Britain imposed high levies on Irish produce from the late 18th century and Irish manufacturers lost out to cheaper imports. Tens of thousands of weavers were put out of work, gangs went about attacking people wearing foreign fabrics and the Liberties descended into squalor.

The Liberties has never really recovered and is still one of the inner city's most deprived areas, racked by unemployment and drug abuse. Yet it retains the passionate pride of a community that has been knitted together over many centuries, and many Dubliners are increasingly looking nostalgically towards the area as an example of their city 'in the rare auld times'.

Their nostalgia is usually expressed over a few pints, and the western border of the Liberties is where you'll find the source of their favourite nectar, the Guinness brewery at St James' Gate, where an old storehouse has been converted into the city's most visited museum (thanks in part to the promise of the best Guinness on the planet at the end of the visit). Further west again, just as the Liffey becomes more of a pastoral river in the riverside burg of Kilmainham, you'll come across the country's greatest modern art museum and Kilmainham Gaol, which has played a key role in the tormented history of a country's slow struggle to gain its freedom. Both are well worth the westward trek (which can be made easier by bus). This is strictly day-trip territory – there's almost nothing in the way of accommodation and decent eating options.

GUINNESS STOREHOUSE & ST JAMES'S GATE BREWERY Map pp90–1

☎ 408 4800; www.guinness-storehouse.com; St James's Gate Brewery; adult/child/student under 18/student over 18 & senior €14/5/7.50/9.50; ⏱ 9.30am-5pm; 🚌 21A, 78 or 78A from Fleet St, 🚊 Luas Green Line to James's Gate

More than any beer produced anywhere in the world, Guinness has transcended its own brand and is not just the best-known symbol of the city but a substance with near spiritual qualities, according to its legions of devotees the world over. The mythology of Guinness is remarkably durable: it doesn't travel well; its distinctive flavour comes from Liffey water; it is good for you – not to mention the generally held belief that you will never understand the Irish until you develop a taste for the black stuff. All absolutely true, of course, so it should be no surprise that the Guinness Storehouse, in the heart of the St James's

Gate Brewery, is the city's most visited tourist attraction, an all-singing, all-dancing extravaganza combining sophisticated exhibits, spectacular design and a thick, creamy head of marketing hype.

To get here, head westwards beyond Christ Church, and you'll end up in the area known as the Liberties, home of the historic 26-hectare St James's Gate Brewery, which stretches along St James's St and down to the Liffey. On your way you'll pass No 1 Thomas St, where Arthur Guinness used to live, across the road from the 40m-tall St Patrick's Tower (Map pp90–1), built around 1757 and the tallest surviving windmill tower outside the Netherlands.

When Arthur started brewing in Dublin in 1759, he couldn't have had any idea that his name would become synonymous with Dublin around the world. Or could he? Showing extraordinary foresight, he had just signed a lease for a small disused brew-

G-FORCE GUINNESS

Ireland's new 9000-strong Nigerian community were dismayed to taste the 4.5% Guinness they discovered on arrival in Ireland, a limp and 'watery' version compared to the potent (and sweeter) 7.5% version at home. Nigeria is Guinness' third-largest market (after Ireland and Britain) and the increased volume harks back to the 18th century when fortified beer was produced to survive the ship's long journey to Africa. Guinness duly responded to the complaint and now the famous Dublin Guinness Foreign Extra satisfies the discerning Nigerian palate.

ery under the terms that he would pay just £45 annually for the next 9000 years, with the additional condition that he'd never have to pay for the water used.

In the 1770s, while other Dublin brewers fretted about the popularity of a new English beer known as porter – which was first created when a London brewer accidentally burnt his hops – Arthur started making his own version. By 1799 he decided to concentrate all his efforts on this single brew. He died four years later, aged 83, but the foundations for world domination were already in place.

At one time a Grand Canal tributary was cut into the brewery to enable special Guinness barges to carry consignments out onto the Irish canal system or to the Dublin port. When the brewery extensions reached the Liffey in 1872, the fleet of Guinness barges became a familiar sight. Pretty soon Guinness was being exported as far afield as Africa and the West Indies. As the barges chugged their way along the Liffey towards the port, boys used to lean over the wall and shout 'bring us back a parrot'. Dubliners still say the same thing

to each other when they're going off on holiday.

The company was once the city's biggest employer – in the 1930s up to 5000 people made their living at the brewery. Today, however, the brewery is no longer the prominent employer it once was; a gradual shift to greater automatisation has reduced the workforce to around 600.

One link with the past that hasn't been broken is the yeast used to make Guinness, essentially the same living organism that has been used since 1770. Another vital ingredient is a hop by the name of fuggles, which used to be grown exclusively around Dublin but is now imported from Britain, the US and Australia (everyone take a bow).

The brewery is far more than just a place where beer is manufactured. It is an intrinsic part of Dublin's history and a key element of the city's identity. Accordingly, the quasi-mythical stature of Guinness is the central theme of the brewery's museum, the Guinness Storehouse, which opened in 2000 and is the only part of the brewery open to visitors.

While inevitably overpriced and overhyped, this paean to the black gold is done exceptionally well. It occupies the old Fermentation House, built in 1904. As it's a listed building the designers could only adapt and add to the structure without taking anything away. The result is a stunning central atrium that rises seven storeys and takes the shape of a pint of Guinness. The head is represented by the glassed Gravity Bar, which provides panoramic views of Dublin to savour with your complimentary pint.

Before you race up to the top, however, you might want to check out the museum

THINKING THE UNTHINKABLE

Guinness and Dublin, Dublin and Guinness. The two sides of the same coin, united by history, tradition, symbolism and smell – the odour of roasting hops is one of the great olfactory sensations in the dirty aul' town. So when Diageo, the brewery's parent company, announced in June 2007 that they were 'considering a number of important investment decisions on upgrading and renewing its brewing facilities in Ireland in the coming years', the first ripples of panic spread throughout the city.

According to the company's own statistics, sales of the black stuff have fallen steadily in Ireland, with a 7% drop in the second half of 2006. In addition, the brewery sits on real estate currently worth in excess of €3 billion, and what successful business doesn't know how to put two and two together and come up with a staggering chunk of change? Diageo has assured us that it'll be 2008 before they make any decisions regarding the brewery, but rumours persist that the company will take the money and move to a Greenfield site on the outskirts of the city. Guinness, Grangegorman? Good God, no.

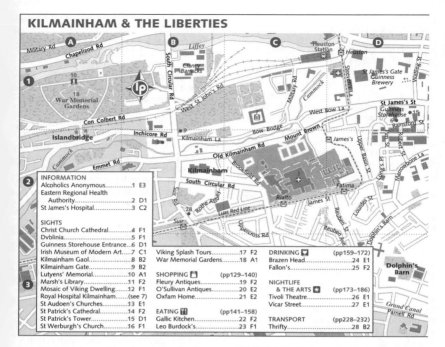

for which you've paid so handsomely. Actually, it's designed as more of an 'experience' than a museum. It has nearly four acres of floor space, featuring a dazzling array of audiovisual, interactive exhibits that cover most aspects of the brewery's story and explain the brewing process in overwhelming detail.

On the ground floor, a copy of Arthur Guinness' original lease lies embedded beneath a pane of glass in the floor. Wandering up through the various exhibits, including 70-odd years of advertising, you can't help feeling that the now wholly foreign-owned company has hijacked the mythology Dubliners attached to the drink, and it has all become more about marketing and manipulation than mingling and magic.

The climax, of course, comes when you emerge onto the circular Gravity Bar for your complimentary Guinness. It may well be the most technically perfect pint of Guinness you'll ever have – and the views are breathtaking – but if you're like us, you'll probably be more excited about getting back down to earth and having a pint with some real Dubliners.

ST PATRICK'S CATHEDRAL Map pp90–1
☎ 475 4817; www.stpatrickscathedral.ie; St Patrick's Close; adult/child/senior & student €5/free/4; ☉ 9am-6pm Mon-Sat, 9-11am, 12.45-3pm & 4.15-6pm Sun Mar-Oct, 9am-6pm Mon-Fri, to 5pm Sat, 10-11am & 12.45-3pm Sun Nov-Feb; ☐ 50, 50A or 56A from Aston Quay or 54 or 54A from Burgh Quay

Situated on the very spot that St Paddy himself rolled up his sleeves and dunked the heathen Irish into a well and thereby gave them a fair to middling shot at salvation, this is one of Dublin's earliest Christian sites and a most hallowed chunk of real estate. Although a church has stood here since the 5th century, this building dates from the turn of the 12th century and has been altered several times, most notably in 1864 when it was saved from ruin and, some might say, overenthusiastically restored. The interior is as calm and soothing as the exterior is sombre, and it's crammed with interesting curios, monuments and memorials. The picturesque St Patrick's Park, adjoining, was a crowded slum until it was cleared in the early 20th century.

It's likely that St Patrick's was intended to replace Christ Church as the city's cathedral

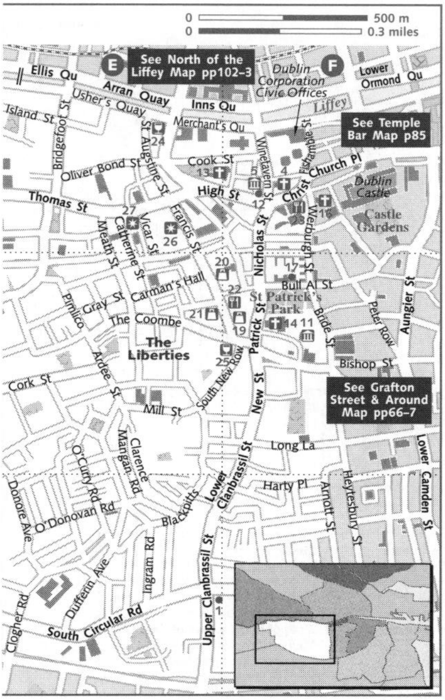
0 500 m
0 0.3 miles
E
See North of the Liffey Map pp102–3
F
Dublin Corporation Civic Offices
Lower Ormond Qu
Ellis Qu
Arran Quay
Usher's Quay
Inns Qu
Island St
Liffey
See Temple Bar Map p85
Merchant's Qu
Bridgefoot St
St Augustine St
24
Oliver Bond St
Cook St
13
5
4
Winetavern St
Fishamble St
Christ Church Pl
Dublin Castle
Thomas St
High St
12
Werburgh St
16
Castle Gardens
27
Catherine St
Vicar St
Meath St
26
Francis St
Nicholas St
20
17
Bull Al St
Carman's Hall
22
St Patrick's Park
Aungier St
Peter Row
Bride St
Pimlico
Gray St
The Coombe
21
19
14
11
The Liberties
25
Patrick St
South New Row
Bishop St
Cork St
Ardee St
See Grafton Street & Around Map pp66–7
Mill St
New St
Long La
Clarence Mangan Rd
O'Curry Rd
Lower Clanbrassil St
Lower Camden St
Harty Pl
Donore Ave
O'Donovan Rd
Blackpitts
Arnott St
Heytesbury St
Ingram Rd
Dufferin Ave
Upper Clanbrassil St
1
Clogher Rd
South Circular Rd

but the older church's stubborn refusal to be usurped resulted in the two cathedrals being virtually a stone's throw from one another. Separated only by the city walls (with St Patrick's outside), each possessed the rights of cathedral of the diocese. While St Pat's isn't as photogenic as its neighbour (it doesn't get the clicks, if you like), it probably one-ups its sexier-looking rival in historical terms.

It was built on unstable ground, with the subterranean River Poddle flowing beneath its foundations, and, because of the high water table, it does not have a crypt. The cathedral had been built twice by 1254 but succumbed to a series of natural disasters over the following century. Its spire was taken out in a 1316 storm, while the original tower and part of the nave were destroyed by fire in 1362 and rebuilt immediately after.

Its troubles were to be more than structural, however. Following Henry VIII's 16th-century hissy fit and the dissolution of the monasteries, St Patrick's was ordered to hand over all of its estates, revenues and possessions. The chapter (bureaucratic head of the church) was imprisoned until they 'agreed' to the handover, the cathedral's privileges were revoked and it was demoted to the rank of parish church. It was not restored to its previous position until 1560.

Further indignity arrived with Cromwell in 1649, when the nave was used as a stable for his horses. In 1666 the Lady Chapel was given to the newly arrived Huguenots and became known as the French Church of St Patrick. It remained in Huguenot hands until 1816. The northern transept was known as the parish church of St Nicholas Without (meaning outside the city), essentially dividing the cathedral into two distinct churches.

Such confusion led to the building falling into disrepair as the influence of the deanery and chapter – previously charged with the church's maintenance – waned. Although the church's most famous dean, Jonathan Swift (author of *Gulliver's Travels,* who served here from 1713 to 1745), did his utmost to preserve the integrity of the building, by the end of the 18th century it was close to collapse. It was just standing when the benevolent Guinness family stepped in to begin massive restoration in 1864.

Fittingly, the first Guinness to show an interest in preserving the church, Benjamin, is commemorated with a statue at the main entrance to the cathedral. Immediately inside to your left is the oldest part of the building, the baptistry, which was probably the entrance to the original building. It contains the original 12th-century floor tiles and medieval stone font, which is still in use. Inside the cathedral proper, you come almost immediately to the graves of Jonathan Swift and his long-term companion Esther Johnson, better known as Stella. The Latin epitaphs are both written by Swift, and assorted Swift memorabilia lies all over the cathedral, including a pulpit and a death mask.

Beginning clockwise around the cathedral, you can't miss the huge Boyle Monument, erected in 1632 by Richard Boyle, earl of Cork. It stood briefly beside the altar until, in 1633, Dublin's viceroy, Thomas Wentworth, earl of Strafford, had it shifted from its prominent position because he felt he shouldn't have to kneel to a Corkman. Boyle took his revenge in later years by orchestrating Wentworth's impeachment and execution. A figure in a niche at the

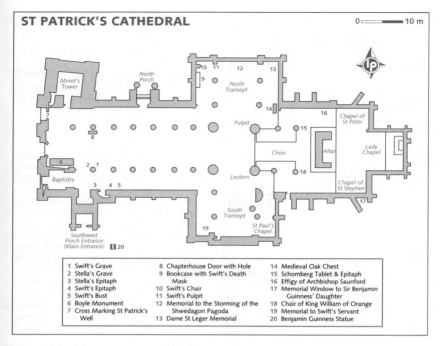

ST PATRICK'S CATHEDRAL

0 ▭▬▬ 10 m

Minot's Tower

North Porch

North Transept

Pulpit

Choir

Altar

Lectern

Baptistry

South Transept

Southwest Porch Entrance (Main Entrance)

St Paul's Chapel

Chapel of St Peter

Lady Chapel

Chapel of St Stephen

1 Swift's Grave	8 Chapterhouse Door with Hole	14 Medieval Oak Chest
2 Stella's Grave	9 Bookcase with Swift's Death	15 Schomberg Tablet & Epitaph
3 Stella's Epitaph	Mask	16 Effigy of Archbishop Saunford
4 Swift's Epitaph	10 Swift's Chair	17 Memorial Window to Sir Benjamin
5 Swift's Bust	11 Swift's Pulpit	Guinness' Daughter
6 Boyle Monument	12 Memorial to the Storming of the	18 Chair of King William of Orange
7 Cross Marking St Patrick's	Shwedagon Pagoda	19 Memorial to Swift's Servant
Well	13 Dame St Leger Memorial	20 Benjamin Guinness Statue

bottom left of the monument is the earl's son Robert who went on to become a noted scientist and discovered Boyle's Law, which sets out the relationship between the pressure and the volume of a gas.

In the opposite corner, there is a cross on a stone slab that once marked the position of St Patrick's original well, where the patron saint of Ireland rolled up his sleeves and got to baptising the natives.

Towards the north transept is displayed a door that has become a symbol of peace and reconciliation since it helped resolve a scrap between the earls of Kildare and Ormond in 1492. After a feud, supporters of the squabbling nobles ended up in a pitched battle inside the cathedral, during which Ormond's nephew – one Black James – barricaded himself into the chapterhouse. Kildare, having taken a deep breath and calmed down, cut a hole in the door between them and stuck his arm through it to either shake his opponent's hand, or lose a limb in his attempt to smooth things over. Luckily for him, James chose mediation over amputation and took his hand. The term 'to chance your arm' entered the English lexicon, the

door, complete with hole, was preserved for posterity and everyone lived happily ever after – except Black James, who was murdered by Kildare's son-in-law four years later.

The north transept contains various military memorials to Royal Irish Regiments, while the northern choir aisle has a tablet marking the grave of the duke of Schomberg, a prominent casualty of the Battle of the Boyne in 1690. Swift provided the duke's epitaph, caustically noting on it that the duke's own relatives couldn't be bothered to provide a suitable memorial. On the opposite side of the choir is a chair that was used by William of Orange when he came to the cathedral to give thanks to God for his victory over the Catholic James II during the same battle.

Passing through the south transept, which was once the chapterhouse where the earl of Kildare chanced his arm, you'll see magnificent stained-glass windows above the funerary monuments. The south aisle is lined with memorials to prominent 20th-century Irish Protestants, including Erskine Childers, president of Ireland from 1973 to 1974, whose father was executed by the Free State during the Civil War. The son never spoke of the struggle for Irish independence because, on the eve of his death, his father made him promise never to do anything that might promote bitterness among Irish people.

On your way around the church, you will also take in the four sections of the relatively new permanent exhibition, Living Stones, which explores the cathedral's history and the contribution it has made to the culture of Dublin. The cathedral managers are also hoping to provide tours of Minot's tower (approximately €7, limited to groups of eight) some time in the future, so it will be worth phoning ahead if you're interested.

MARSH'S LIBRARY Map pp90–1

☎ 454 3511; www.marshlibrary.ie; St Patrick's Close; adult/child/student €2.50/free/1.50; ⊗ 10am-1pm & 2-5pm Mon & Wed-Fri, 10.30am-1pm Sat; ☐ 50, 50A or 56A from Aston Quay, or 54 or 54A from Burgh Quay

It mightn't have the immediate appeal of a brewery or a big old church, but this magnificently preserved scholars' library, virtually unchanged in three centuries, is one of Dublin's most beautiful open secrets, and an absolute highlight of any visit. Few think to scale its ancient stairs to see its beautiful, dark oak bookcases, each topped with elaborately carved and gilded gables, and crammed with books. Here you can savour the atmosphere of three centuries of learning, slow into synch with the tick-tocking of the 19th-century grandfather clock, listen to the squeaky boards and record the scent of leather and learning. It's amazing how many people visit St Patrick's Cathedral next door and overlook this gem – they're mad, they don't deserve a holiday.

Founded in 1701 by Archbishop Narcissus Marsh (1638–1713) and opened in 1707, the library was designed by Sir Wil-

liam Robinson, the man also responsible for the Royal Hospital Kilmainham (p96). It's the oldest public library in the country, and contains 25,000 books dating from the 16th to the early 18th century, as well as maps, manuscripts (including one in Latin dating back to 1400) and a collection of incunabula (books printed before 1500). In its one nod to the 21st century, the library's current 'keeper', Dr Muriel McCarthy, is the first woman to hold the post.

Apart from theological books and bibles in dozens of languages, there are tomes on medicine, law, travel, literature, science, navigation, music and mathematics. One of the oldest and finest books is a volume of *Cicero's Letters to His Friends*, printed in Milan in 1472. The most important of the four main collections is the 10,000-strong library of Edward Stillingfleet, bishop of Worcester.

Most of Marsh's own extensive collection is also here, and there are various items that used to belong to Jonathan Swift (Dean of St Patrick's Cathedral), including his copy of *History of the Great Rebellion*. His margin notes include a number of comments vilifying Scots, of whom he seemed to have a low opinion. He also held a low opinion of Archbishop Marsh, whom he blamed for holding him back in the church. When Swift died in 1745, he was buried in St Patrick's Cathedral, near his former enemy.

Like the rest of the library, the three alcoves, in which scholars were once locked to peruse rare volumes, have remained virtually unchanged for three centuries. Don't worry though: the skull in the furthest one doesn't belong to some poor forgotten scholar, it's a cast of the head of Stella, Swift's other half. The library's also home to Delmas Conservation Bindery, which repairs and restores rare old books, and makes an appearance in Joyce's *Ulysses*.

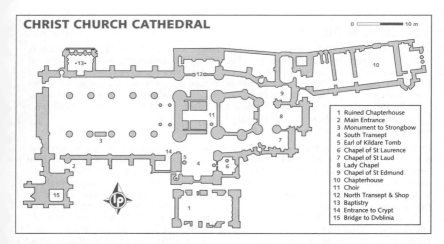

CHRIST CHURCH CATHEDRAL

0 ————————— 10 m

1 Ruined Chapterhouse
2 Main Entrance
3 Monument to Strongbow
4 South Transept
5 Earl of Kildare Tomb
6 Chapel of St Laurence
7 Chapel of St Laud
8 Lady Chapel
9 Chapel of St Edmund
10 Chapterhouse
11 Choir
12 North Transept & Shop
13 Baptistry
14 Entrance to Crypt
15 Bridge to Dvblinia

CHRIST CHURCH CATHEDRAL Map pp90–1
Church of the Holy Trinity; ☎ 677 8099; www
.cccdub.ie; Christ Church Pl; adult/concession
€5/2.50; ✆ 9.45am-5pm Mon-Fri, 10am-5pm Sat
& Sun; ⊟ 50, 50A or 56A from Aston Quay or 54 or
54A from Burgh Quay

Its hilltop location and eye-catching flying
buttresses make this the most photogenic
by far of Dublin's three cathedrals as well
as one of the capital's most recognisable
symbols.

A wooden church was first erected here
by Dunán, the first bishop of Dublin, and
Sitric, the Viking king, around 1030, at the
southern edge of Dublin's Viking settlement. In 1163, however, the secular clergy
were replaced by a group of Augustinian
monks installed by the patron saint of Dublin, Archbishop Laurence O'Toole. Six years
later, Strongbow's Normans blew into town
and got themselves into the church-building
business, arranging with O'Toole (and his
successor John Cumin) for the construction of a new stone cathedral that would
symbolise Anglo-Norman glory. The new
cathedral opened its doors late in the 12th
century, by which time Strongbow, O'Toole
and Cumin were long dead.

Above ground, the north wall, the tran-
septs and the western part of the choir are
almost all that remain from the original. It
has been restored several times over the
centuries and, despite its apparent uniformity, is a hotchpotch of different styles, ranging from Romanesque to English Gothic.

Until the disestablishment of the Church
of Ireland in 1869, senior representatives of

the Crown all swore their allegiance here.
The church's fortunes, however, were not
guaranteed. By the turn of the 18th century its popularity waned along with the
district as the upper echelons of Dublin
society fled north, where they attended a
new favourite, St Mary's Abbey. Through
much of its history, Christ Church vied
for supremacy with nearby St Patrick's
Cathedral, but both fell on hard times in
the 18th and 19th centuries. Christ Church
was virtually derelict – the nave had been
used as a market and the crypt had earlier
housed taverns – by the time restoration
took place. Whiskey distiller Henry Roe (see
p30) donated the equivalent of €30 million
to save the church, which was substantially
rebuilt from 1871 to 1878. Ironically, both
of the great Church of Ireland cathedrals
are essentially outsiders in a Catholic nation
today, dependent on tourist donations for
their very survival.

From its inception, Christ Church was the
State Church of Ireland, and when Henry
VIII dissolved the monasteries in the 16th
century, the Augustinian priory that managed the church was replaced with a new
Anglican clergy, which still runs the church
today.

From the southeastern entrance to the
churchyard you walk past ruins of the chapterhouse, which dates from 1230. The main
entrance to the cathedral is at the southwestern corner and as you enter you face
the ancient northern wall. This survived the
collapse of its southern counterpart but has
also suffered from subsiding foundations

(much of the church was built on a peat bog) and, from its eastern end, it leans visibly.

The southern aisle has a monument to the legendary Strongbow. The armoured figure on the tomb is unlikely to be of Strongbow (it's more probably the earl of Drogheda), but his internal organs may have been buried here. A popular legend relates an especially visceral version of the daddy-didn't-love-me tale: the half-figure beside the tomb is supposed to be Strongbow's son, who was cut in two by his loving father when his bravery in battle was suspect – an act that surely would have saved the kid a fortune in therapist's bills.

The southern transept contains the superb baroque tomb of the 19th earl of Kildare, who died in 1734. His grandson, Lord Edward Fitzgerald, was a member of the United Irishmen and died in the abortive 1798 Rising. The entrance to the Chapel of St Laurence is off the south transept and contains two effigies, one of them reputed to be of either Strongbow's wife or sister.

An entrance by the south transept descends to the unusually large arched crypt, which dates back to the original Viking church. Curiosities in the crypt include a glass display-case housing a mummified cat in the act of chasing a mummified mouse, frozen midpursuit inside an organ pipe in the 1860s. Also on display are the stocks from the old 'liberty' of Christ Church, used when church authorities meted out civil punishments to wrongdoers. The Treasury exhibit includes rare coins, the Stuart coat of arms and gold given to the church by William of Orange after the Battle of the Boyne. From the main entrance, a bridge, part of the 1871–78 restoration, leads to Dvblinia.

DVBLINIA Map pp90–1

☎ 679 4611; www.dublinia.ie; main entrance St Michael's Hill; adult/child/student €6.25/3.75/5.25; ☯ 10am-5pm Apr-Sep, 11am-4pm Mon-Sat, 10am-4pm Sun Oct-Mar; 🚌 50, 50A or 56A from Aston Quay or 54 or 54A from Burgh Quay

Inside what was once the Synod Hall, added to Christ Church Cathedral during its late-19th-century restoration, this is a lively and kitschy attempt to bring medieval Dublin to life using models, music, streetscapes and interactive displays. The ground floor has wax models depicting 10 episodes in Dublin's history, explained in a choice of five languages through headsets. Up one floor

is Viking World, which has a large selection of objects recovered from Wood Quay, the world's largest Viking archaeological site. There's also a huge model of 11th-century Dublin and a bunch of interactive exhibits such as a longboat that you can sit in and pretend to be a slave. There are also models of the medieval quayside and of a cobbler's shop. On the top floor is the Medieval Fayre, featuring merchants' wares, a medicine stall, an armourer's pavilion, a confessional booth and a bank. Finally, you can climb neighbouring St Michael's Tower and peek through its grubby windows for views over the city to the Dublin hills. There is also a pleasant café and the inevitable souvenir shop. Your ticket gets you into Christ Church Cathedral free, via the link bridge.

KILMAINHAM GAOL Map pp90–1

☎ 453 5984; www.heritageireland.ie; Inchicore Rd; adult/child €5/2; ☯ 9.30am-5pm Apr-Oct, 9.30am-4pm Mon-Sat, 10am-5pm Sun Nov-Mar; 🚌 23, 51, 51A, 78 or 79 from Aston Quay

If you have *any* interest in Irish history, especially the juicy bits about resistance to English rule, you will be shaken and stirred by a visit to this infamous prison. It was the stage for many of the most tragic and heroic episodes in Ireland's recent past, and the list of its inmates reads like a who's who of Irish nationalism. Solid and sombre, its walls absorbed the barbarism of British occupation and recount them in whispers to visitors.

It took four years to build, and the prison opened – or rather closed – its doors in 1796, when the first reluctant guests were led in. The Irish were locked up for all sorts of misdemeanours, some more serious than others. A six-year-old boy spent a month here in 1839 because his father couldn't pay his train fare, and during the Famine it was crammed with the destitute who had been imprisoned for stealing food and begging. But it is most famous for incarcerating 120 years of Irish nationalists, from Robert Emmet in 1803 to Eamon de Valera in 1923. All of Ireland's botched uprisings ended with the leaders' confinement here, usually before their execution.

It was the treatment of the leaders of the 1916 Easter Rising that most deeply etched the gaol into the Irish consciousness (also see p22). Fourteen of the rebel commanders were executed in the exercise yard, including James Connolly who was so badly injured at the time of his execution that he was strapped to a chair at the opposite end of the yard, just inside the gate. The places where they were shot are marked by two simple black crosses. The executions turned an apathetic nation on a course towards violent rebellion.

The gaol's final function was as a prison for the newly formed Irish Free State, an irony best summed up with the story of Ernie O'Malley, who managed to escape from the gaol when incarcerated by the British but was locked up again by his erstwhile comrades during the Civil War. This chapter is somewhat played down on the tour, and even the passing comment that Kilmainham's final prisoner was the future president, Eamon de Valera, doesn't reveal that he had been imprisoned by his fellow Irish citizens. The gaol was finally decommissioned in 1924.

Visits are by guided tour and start with a stirring audiovisual introduction, screened in the former chapel where 1916 leader Joseph Plunkett was wed to his beloved just 10 minutes before his execution. The lively, thought-provoking (but too crowded) tour takes you through the old and new wings of the prison, where you can see former cells of famous inmates, read graffiti on the walls and immerse yourself in the atmosphere of the execution yards.

Incongruously sitting outside in the yard is the *Asgard*, the ship that successfully ran the British blockade to deliver arms to nationalist forces in 1914. It belonged to, and was skippered by, Erskine Childers, father of the future president of Ireland. He was executed by Michael Collins' Free State army in 1922 for carrying a revolver, which had been a gift from Collins himself. There is also an outstanding museum dedicated to Irish nationalism and prison life. On a lighter, more musical note, *real* U2 fans will be chuffed to recognise the prison as the setting for the video to their 1982 single *A Celebration*; now that's a slice of history. Buffs of the other kind of history should allow at least half a day for a visit.

ROYAL HOSPITAL KILMAINHAM & IRISH MUSEUM OF MODERN ART
Map pp90–1

IMMA; ☎ 612 9900; www.imma.ie; Military Rd; admission free; ☼ 10am-5.30pm Tue-Sat, noon-5.30pm Sun; ☐ 24, 79 or 90 from Aston Quay
IMMA is the country's foremost gallery for contemporary Irish art, although it takes second billing to the majestic building in which it is housed. The Royal Hospital Kilmainham was built between 1680 and 1684 as a retirement home for veteran soldiers, a function it fulfilled until 1928, after which it was left to languish for half a century before being saved in a 1980s restoration.

The inspiration for the design came from James Butler, duke of Ormonde and Charles II's viceroy, who had been so impressed by Les Invalides on a trip to Paris that he commissioned William Robinson to knock up a Dublin version. What the architect designed was Dublin's finest 17th-century building and the highpoint of the Anglo-Dutch style of the day. It consists of an unbroken range enclosing a vast, peaceful courtyard with arcaded walks. A chapel in the centre of the northern flank has an elegant clock tower and spire. This was the first truly classical building in Dublin and marked the beginning of the Georgian boom. Christopher Wren began building London's Chelsea Royal Hospital two years after work commenced here.

The spectacularly restored hospital was unveiled in 1984, on the 300th anniversary of its construction. The next year it received the prestigious Europa Nostra award for 'distinguished contribution to the conservation of Europe's architectural heritage'. There are free guided tours of the museum's exhibits at 2.30pm on Wednesday, Friday and Sunday throughout the year, but we strongly recommend the free, seasonal heritage itinerary tour (50 minutes; 10am to 5.30pm Tuesday to Saturday, noon to 5.30pm Sunday July to September). It shows off some of the building's treasures, including the Banqueting Hall, with 22 specially commissioned portraits, and the stunning baroque chapel, with papier-mâché ceilings and a set of exquisite Queen Anne gates. Also worth seeing are the fully restored formal gardens.

In 1991 it became home to IMMA and the best of modern and contemporary Irish art. The blend of old and new works wonderfully, and you'll find contemporary Irish artists such as Louis Le Brocquy, Sean Scully, Richard Deacon, Richard Gorman and Dorothy Cross featured here. The permanent exhibition also features paintings from heavy hitters Pablo Picasso and Joan Miró, and is topped up by regular temporary exhibitions. There's a good café and bookshop on the grounds.

KILMAINHAM GATE Map pp90–1

📵 23, 51, 51A, 78 or 79 from Aston Quay

The Kilmainham Gate was designed by Francis Johnston (1760–1829) in 1812 and originally stood at the Watling St junction with Victoria Quay, near the Guinness Brewery, where it was known as the Richmond Tower. It was moved to its current position opposite the prison in 1846 as it obstructed the increasingly heavy traffic to the new Kingsbridge Station (now Heuston Station), which opened in 1844.

ST AUDOEN'S CHURCHES Map pp90–1

☎ 677 0088; Cornmarket, High St; adult/concession €2/1; 🕙 9.30am-5pm Jun-Sep; 📵 50, 50A or 56A from Aston Quay or 54 or 54A from Burgh Quay

It was only right that the newly arrived Normans would name a church after their patron saint Audoen (the 7th-century bishop of Rouen, aka Ouen), but they didn't quite figure on two virtually adjacent churches bearing his name, just west of Christ Church Cathedral. The more interesting of the two is the Church of Ireland, the only medieval parish church in the city that's still in use. It was built between 1181 and 1212, although a 9th-century burial slab in the porch suggests that it was built on top of an even older church. Its tower and door date from the 12th century and the aisle from the 15th century, but the church today is mainly a product of a 19th-century restoration.

As part of the tour you can explore the ruins as well as the present church, which has funerary monuments that were beheaded by Cromwell's purists. Through the heavily moulded Romanesque Norman door you can also touch the 9th-century 'lucky stone' that was believed to bring good luck to business.

St Anne's Chapel, the visitors centre, houses a number of tombstones of leading members of Dublin society from the 16th to the 18th centuries. At the top of the chapel is the tower, which holds the three oldest bells in Ireland, dating from 1423. Although the church's exhibits are hardly spectacular, the building itself is beautiful and a genuine slice of medieval Dublin.

The church is entered from the south off High St through St Audoen's Arch, which was built in 1240 and is the only surviving reminder of the city gates. The adjoining park is pretty but attracts many unsavoury characters, particularly at night.

Joined onto the Protestant church is the newer, bigger, 19th-century Catholic St Audoen's, an expansive church in which Father 'Flash' Kavanagh used to read Mass at high speed so that his large congregation could head off to more absorbing Sunday pursuits, such as football matches.

ST WERBURGH'S CHURCH Map pp90–1

☎ 478 3710; Werburgh St; 🕙 10am-4pm Mon-Fri; 📵 50, 50A or 56A from Aston Quay or 54 or 54A from Burgh Quay

Lying west of Dublin Castle, St Werburgh's Church stands upon ancient foundations (probably from the 12th century), but was rebuilt several times during the 17th and 18th centuries. The church's tall spire was dismantled after Robert Emmet's rising in 1803, for fear that future rebels might use it as a vantage point for snipers. Interred in the vault is Lord Edward Fitzgerald, who turned against Britain, joined the United Irishmen and was a leader of the 1798 Rising. In what was a frequent theme of Irish uprisings, compatriots gave him away and his death resulted from the wounds he received when captured. Coincidentally, Major Henry Sirr, the man who captured him, is buried out in the graveyard. On the porch you will notice two fire pumps that date from the time when Dublin's fire department was composed of church volunteers. The interior is rather more cheerful than the exterior, although the church is rarely used today. Phone, or see the caretaker at 8 Castle St, to see inside. Donations are welcome.

WAR MEMORIAL GARDENS Map pp90–1

☎ 677 0236; www.heritageireland.ie; South Circular Rd, Islandbridge; admission free; 🕙 8am-twilight Mon-Fri, from 10am Sat & Sun; 📵 25, 25A, 26, 68 or 69 from city centre, 🚉 Luas Red Line to Heuston

Hardly anyone ever ventures this far west, but they're missing a lovely bit of landscaping in the shape of the War Memorial Gardens, by our reckoning as pleasant a patch of greenery as any you'll find in the heart of the Georgian centre. Designed by Sir Edwin Lutyens, the memorial commemorates the 49,400 Irish soldiers who died during WWI – their names are inscribed in the two huge granite bookrooms that stand at one end. A beautiful spot and a bit of history to boot.

Eating p155; Drinking p169; Shopping p138; Sleeping p204

It has long been said that a 'real' Dubliner is born within the confines of the two canals that encircle the city centre – the older Grand Canal to the south and the newer Royal Canal to the north – but the rapid expansion of the city, coupled with the shockingly high price of central real estate makes it more a case of *older* Dubliners being born within the canal boundaries.

Built to connect Dublin with the River Shannon in the centre of Ireland, the Grand Canal makes a graceful 6km loop around south Dublin and enters the Liffey at Ringsend, through locks that were built in 1796. The large Grand Canal Dock, flanked by Hanover and Charlotte Quays, is now used by windsurfers and canoeists and is the site of major new development. Here you'll find the Waterways Visitor Centre, which illustrates the gleaming new development of the area that, for now, sits side by side with the workaday, historical and even quaint auld Dublin of Ringsend and Irishtown. At the northwestern corner of the dock is Misery Hill, once a very macabre place where it was the practice to bring the corpses of those already hanged at Gallows Hill, near Upper Baggot St, to be strung up for public display for anything from six to 12 months.

The canal hasn't been used commercially since 1960, but some stretches are attractive and enjoyable to stroll or cycle along. The poet Patrick Kavanagh was particularly enamoured with the 2km stretch from Mount St Bridge west to Richmond St, which has grassy, tree-lined banks and – as you might have guessed – a cluster of pubs. Among Kavanagh's compositions is the hauntingly beautiful *On Raglan Road*, which was put to music and sung most memorably by Luke Kelly of The Dubliners. In another, he requested that he be commemorated by 'a canal bank seat for passers-by'. His friends obliged with a seat beside the lock on the northern side of the canal. A little further along on the northern side you can sit down by Kavanagh himself, cast in bronze, comfortably lounging on a bench and staring at his beloved canal.

Beyond the Grand Canal and into the southern outer reaches of Dublin are inner suburbs that have developed along the main roads into the city. Lively Rathmines – for generations the favoured stomping ground of students and migrants from the rest of the country – has seen its stock rise higher and higher as gentrification marches ever onwards, converting student digs into chic studio apartments and cheap cafés into tapas bars. Barely half a mile away is Ranelagh, which makes Rathmines seem distinctly dowdy – its cosy village atmosphere barely disguises the elegance and sophistication of its bars, restaurants and wonderful Victorian and Edwardian architecture. For cashed-up Dubliners, this is definitely the place to live…unless they already reside in 'Dublin 4' further east, a postal address that is synonymous with money and affectation. Elegant and embassy-laden Ballsbridge is a great place to base yourself, especially if you don't mind being a 30-minute stroll or 10-minute bus ride from the city centre: it has some wonderful restaurants, a host of great bars and some of the most beautiful town-house hotels in the city.

NATIONAL PRINT MUSEUM Map p99

☎ 660 3770; www.iol.ie/~npmuseum; Garrison Chapel, Haddington Rd, Beggar's Bush; adult/concession €3.50/2; ☷ 9am-5pm Mon-Fri, 2-5pm Sat & Sun; ☷ DART to Grand Canal Dock, ☷ 7, 8 or 45 from city centre

You don't have to be into printing to enjoy this quirky little museum, where personalised guided tours are offered in a delightfully casual and compelling way. First watch a video relating to printing and its place in Irish history, then take a wander amid the smell of ink and metal, and through the various antique presses that are still worked for small jobs by a couple of retired printers doing it for the love of the craft. The guides are excellent and can tailor the tours to suit your special interests – for example, anyone interested in history can get a detailed account of the difficulties encountered by the rebels of 1916 when they tried to get the proclamation printed. Upstairs, there are lots of old newspaper pages recording important episodes in Irish history over the last century.

RATHFARNHAM CASTLE Off Map p99

☎ 493 9462; www.heritageireland.ie; Rathfarnham Rd, Rathfarnham; adult/concession €2/1; ☷ 9.30am-5.30pm May-Oct; ☷ 16, 17 from O'Connell St

Less castle and more fortified house, this was originally built by Adam Loftus, the

BEYOND THE GRAND CANAL

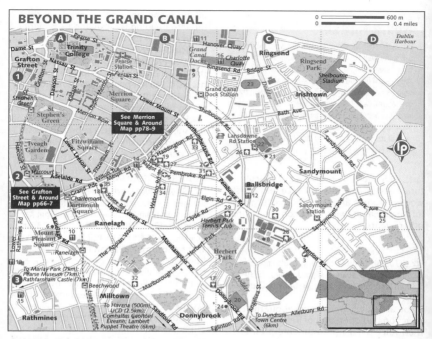

BEYOND THE GRAND CANAL

archbishop of Dublin, around 1583 and is most interesting as a restoration in progress. Several of the rooms – including 18th-century interiors by William Chambers – have been returned to their original splendour, while others are clearly struggling under the ravages of time. The guides have an infectious enthusiasm for the project. It's 6km south of the city centre.

ROYAL DUBLIN SOCIETY SHOWGROUND Map p99

☎ 668 9878; Merrion Rd, Ballsbridge; 🚌 7 from Trinity College

Founded in 1731, the Royal Dublin Society (RDS) was involved in the establishment of the National Museum, Library, Gallery and Botanic Gardens. The showground is used for various exhibitions throughout the year, but the main event is the Dublin Horse Show (p18), which reflects the society's agricultural background. It takes place in the first week of August and includes a prestigious international showjumping contest among other events.

WATERWAYS VISITOR CENTRE Map p99

☎ 677 7510; Grand Canal Quay; adult/concession €2.50/1.20; ⊗ 9.30am-5.30pm Jun-Sep, 12.30-5.30pm Wed-Sun Oct & May; ⓡ DART to Grand Canal Dock

If you absolutely must know about the construction and operation of Ireland's canals, then you'll dig a visit to this interpretive centre upstream from the Grand Canal Docks, which explores the history and personality of Ireland's canals and waterways through models (if they're working), audiovisual displays and panels. Otherwise,

admiring the 'box on the docks' – as this modern building is nicknamed – is plenty good enough for the average enthusiast of artificial waterways.

If you are here in summer and are wondering why it needs to employ a security guard, it's to keep local kids from storming up to the centre's roof and using it as a diving platform into the basin. Sometimes the kids content themselves with diving off the shed on the bridge, terrorising those on board the Viking Splash Tour boats that pass beneath.

PEARSE MUSEUM

☎ 493 4208; www.heritageireland.ie; St Enda's, Grange Rd, Rathfarnham; admission free; ⊗ St Enda's Park 10am-8pm May-Aug, 10am-7pm Apr & Sep-Oct, 10am-5.30pm Feb-Mar, 10am-4.30pm Nov-Dec; 🚌 16 from O'Connell St

This handsome Palladian mansion was home to St Enda's, an experimental Gaelic school established by nationalist poet and 1916 martyr Pádraig Pearse (for more on Pádraig Pearse, see the boxed text, p23). The fascinating exhibition focusing on Pearse's life and works was under the refurbisher's tarpaulin at the time of writing but due to reopen in mid-2008. The beautiful grounds, gardens and grottos surrounding the house are still open, but you'd want to be a big greenery fan to make the trek out here while the house is still closed.

Eating p156; Drinking p170; Shopping p139; Sleeping p206

What does a northsider use for protection? A bus shelter. Boom boom. Northsider/southsider jokes are a permanent fixture of the city's canon of humour, mostly because they highlight the perceived gap between the city's two halves, with the north side generally coming off second-best in all things save social ills and – as northsiders will happily tell you – true Dublin character. What does a southsider use for protection? Personality.

As gritty as the south side is glitzy, the north side is not just where Dubliners are at their most authentic, but where the great multicultural experiment is having its greatest success. A stroll through the street market on Moore St, once the epitome of auld Dublin, will reveal a weather-beaten street trader intoning 'five bananas for a euro' while young Koreans hawk phonecards from their shop hatches. On Parnell St, Nigerian teenagers rustle through beaded curtains into African salons for hair extensions while upstairs, their parents belt out gospel hymns in makeshift churches. Next door, Russians leave the supermarket laden with tinned caviar and *prianik* cookies.

This is the new Dublin, and it is slotting in comfortably alongside the older version of the north city centre, which radiates away from the grand dame of Dublin thoroughfares, the imperially wide O'Connell St. This famous street has played host to key episodes of Dublin's – and the nation's – history, none more so than the 1916 Easter Rising, when the proclamation announcing Ireland's independence was read out to a slightly bemused crowd from the steps of the General Post Office before the British Army pounded the building and its occupants into submission.

O'Connell St became Dublin's main street in 1794, when O'Connell Bridge was built and the city's axis shifted east. The north side was the residential area of choice at the start of the Georgian period, but when the hoi polloi got too close, the aristocracy doubled back over the Liffey and settled the new areas surrounding Leinster House. The Georgian squares named after Parnell and Mountjoy fell into rapid decline and were partly converted into slum dwellings. Although neglected, they still display a certain dishevelled charm and are gradually being restored. O'Connell St leads north to the large Parnell Sq, which is flanked by museums, public buildings and some fine, if rather run-down, Georgian residences.

West of O'Connell St along the refurbished river quays is the small but sterling Quartier Bloom, a little slice of genuine Italy in the heart of the city. Further along is the cobbled neighbourhood of Smithfield, an up-and-coming *quartier* of office blocks and residential apartments built around a main square that has been synonymous with markets since the 17th century and, in recent decades, was the scene of a bustling horse fair where deals were sealed with a spit in your hand. All gone now, we're afraid, hurriedly moved on because fruit 'n' veg and hoof inspections didn't quite fit the planned aesthetic. The 400,000-odd antique cobblestones that saw their fair share of horse manure over the decades were carefully removed, hand-cleaned and relaid alongside new granite slabs, giving the whole square a look that got an enthusiastic thumbs-up from pretty much everyone – except, we're guessing, the traditional traders themselves. Smithfield has yet to deliver the 21st-century neighbourhood of cool bars, restaurants and shops it was intended to be: instead, there are some great old-style pubs to hear great traditional music in, a couple of fabulous museums and a paeon to Irish whiskey. Don't forget to make your way further west again to the superb Collins Barracks (now a national museum).

If you're looking to base yourself on the north side, chances are you'll find yourself bedding down on or around B&B Row – Gardiner St, east of O'Connell St. This street has long been the preferred spot for those happy to trade luxury for an affordable bed, but even here the standards (and prices) have been raised, especially towards the southern end of the street; the options up toward Mountjoy Sq aren't recommended, if only because they're in a part of the 'hood that gets a little iffy after dark.

DUBLIN CITY GALLERY – THE HUGH LANE Map pp102–3

Municipal Gallery of Ireland; ☎ 874 1903; www. hughlane.ie; 22 North Parnell Sq; admission free; ☒ 9.30am-6pm Tue-Thu, 9.30am-5pm Fri & Sat, 11am-5pm Sun; ☐ 3, 10, 11, 13, 16, 19 or 22 from city centre

Whatever reputation Dublin may have as a repository of top-class art is in large part due to the collection at this magnificent

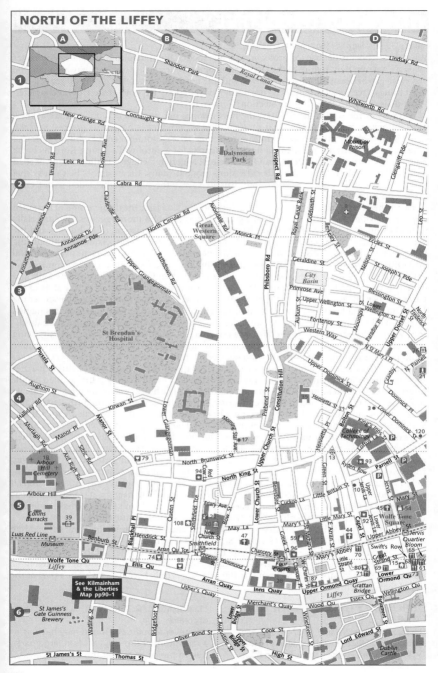

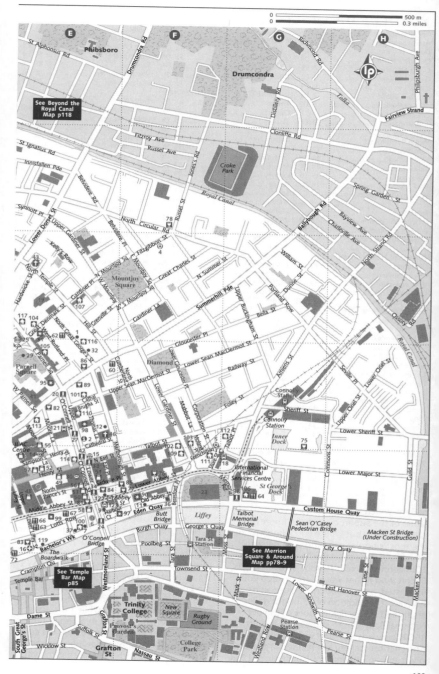

0   500 m
0   0.3 miles

E   F   G   H

St Alphonsus Rd   Phibsboro   Drumcondra Rd   Richmond Rd

Drumcondra

Tolka

Phibsburgh Ave

See Beyond the
Royal Canal
Map p118

Fitzroy Ave   Clonliffe Rd   Fairview Strand

Russel Ave   Distillery Rd

St Ignatius Rd

Innisfallen Pde   Croke
Park   Spring Garden St

Belvedere Rd   Royal Canal   Bayview Ave

Synnott Pl   North Circular Rd   Ballybough Rd   Chateville Ave

Lower Dorset   Upper Gardiner St

Kelly's Row   North Strand Rd

Hardwicke St   North Temple St   78   4   William St

43   Mountjoy Sq   W Mountjoy   Great Charles St   Ossory Rd

117 104   Gardiner Pl   N Mountjoy   N Summer St   Portland Row   Royal Canal

Mountjoy   Summerhill Pde   Duane St

Square   Upper Buckingham St

Denmark St   Grenville St   107   Gardiner La   Bella St

North Great George's   1   Amiens St

62   116   32   Gloucester Pl   Seville Pl   Lower Oriel St

105   86   Diamond   Lower Sean MacDermot St   Railway St   Sheriff St

Parnell   60   North   Connolly   Lower Oriel St

Square   Upper Sean MacDermot St   Station

95   89   Mabbot La   Foley St   Connolly

20 101   Canal   Corporation   Station   Sheriff St

82   Bridget   Inner   Lower Sheriff St

113   110   Dock   75

21   98   Talbot St   112   Commons St

ILAC   55   12   103   International   Lower Major St

Centre   42   15   102   Financial   Guild St

Sampson's   114   East St   109   Services Centre   St George's

La   57   49   Lower Abbey St   111   18   Dock   64

Henry St   24   86   9   Liffey   Custom House Quay

North   84   Old Abbey St   28   106

Prince's St   Middle Abbey St   Talbot   Lline St

66   99   67   Eden Quay   Memorial   Macken St

63   100   Butt   Bridge   Sean O'Casey   St

119   Row   Bridge   Pedestrian Bridge   Macken St Bridge

83   16   Bachelor's Wk   George's Quay   (Under Construction)

72   O'Connell   Burgh Quay   Tara St   City Quay

The   Bridge   Poolbeg St   Station

Boardwalk   See Merrion   East Hanover St

Crampton Qu   Square & Around   Lower Sandwith St

Temple Bar   Map pp78–9

See Temple   Westmoreland St   Townsend St   Mark St   Pearse

Bar Map   Station

p85   Trinity   New   Pearse St

Dame St   College   Square   Rugby

South Great   Ground   East Hanover St

George's St   Provost's   Westland Row

Garden   College   Pearse

Wicklow St   Grafton   Park   Station

Suffolk St   St   Nassau St

Grafton St

103

NORTH OF THE LIFFEY

gallery, which is not only home to works by some of the supernovas in the impressionist firmament, but where you'll find one of the most singular exhibitions to be seen anywhere: the *actual* studio of one of the 20th century's most famous artists, Francis Bacon. And if that wasn't art to keep you interested, a new modernist extension has seen the addition of 13 bright galleries spread across three floors of the old National Ballroom to show work from the 1950s onwards. Oh, and we should mention that the gallery has resided in the simply stunning Charlemont House since 1933,

which was designed by Georgian superstar architect William Chambers in 1763.

The gallery owes its 1908 origins to one Hugh Lane, whose failure to get any funding from an uninterested government and other commercial interests prompted WB Yeats to really have a go at the authorities and mercenary materialism in one of his most vitriolic poems, *September 1913*. Yeats was very annoyed, and while his disgust with those who 'fumble in a greasy till/and add the halfpence to the pence' was certainly justified, we wonder if his ire had anything to do with the fact that the very,

HUGH LANE

It's hardly surprising that wealthy Sir Hugh Lane (1875–1915) was miffed by the Irish and decided to bequeath his paintings to some other nation, as he was treated with less respect than he felt he deserved in his own land. Born in County Cork, he began to work in London art galleries from 1893, and five years later set up his own gallery in Dublin. He had a connoisseur's eye and a good nose for the directions of the market, which enabled him to build up a superb and valuable collection, particularly strong in impressionists.

Unfortunately for Ireland, neither his talents nor his collection were much appreciated, and in exasperation he turned his attention to opportunities in London and South Africa. Irish rejection led him to rewrite his will and bequeath some of the finest works in his collection to the National Gallery in London. Later he relented and added a rider to his will leaving the collection to Dublin but failed to have it witnessed, thus causing a long legal squabble over which gallery had rightful ownership. He was just 40 years old when he went down with the ill-fated *Lusitania* in 1915, after it was torpedoed by a German U-boat off the southern coast of Ireland.

very rich Lane was the nephew of Lady Gregory, Yeats' own patron?

Poor old Hugh Lane didn't get to enjoy his wealth or his art collection for too much longer, however, as he was a passenger on the ill-fated *Lusitania* and died in 1915 (see the boxed text, above). There followed a bitter wrangle over Lane's bequest, between the gallery he founded and the National Gallery in London. The collection was eventually split in a complicated 1959 settlement that sees some of the paintings moving back and forth. The conditions of the exchanges are in the midst of a convoluted negotiation, but for the time being the gallery has Manet's *Eva Gonzales*, Pissarro's *Printemps*, Berthe Morisot's *Jour d'Eté* and the most important painting of the entire collection (and one of our favourites of all time), Renoir's *Les Parapluies*.

Impressionist masterpieces notwithstanding, the gallery's most popular exhibit is the Francis Bacon Studio, which was painstakingly moved, in all its shambolic mess, from 7 Reece Mews, South Kensington, London, where the Dublin-born artist (1909–92) lived for 31 years. The display features some 80,000 items madly strewn about the place, including slashed canvasses, the last painting he was working on, tables piled with materials, walls daubed with colour samples, portraits with heads cut out, favourite bits of furniture and many assorted piles of crap. It's a teasing and tantalising, riveting and ridiculous masterpiece that provides the viewer – peering in at the chaos through thick Perspex – no real sense of the artist himself. Far more revealing is the 10-minute profile of him with Melvyn Bragg and the immensely sad photographs of Bacon's immaculately tidy bachelor pad, which suggest a deep, personal loneliness.

You can round off a (hopefully) satisfying visit with lunch in the superb café (p157) in the basement of the new extension, before making a stop in the well-stocked gift shop.

NATIONAL MUSEUM OF IRELAND – DECORATIVE ARTS & HISTORY
Map pp102–3

☎ 677 7444; www.museum.ie; Benburb St; admission free; ☼ 10am-5pm Tue-Sat, 2-5pm Sun; ☒ Luas Red Line to Museum, ☒ 25, 25A, 66, 67 or 90 from city centre

No wonder the British army were so reluctant to pull out of Ireland, when they were occupying this magnificent space, the oldest army barracks in Europe. The building – the museum bit can wait – was completed in 1704 according to the design of Thomas Burgh, whose CV also includes the Old Library (p69) in Trinity College and St Michan's Church (p110). Its central square held six entire regiments and is a truly awesome space, surrounded by arcaded colonnades and blocks linked by walking bridges. Following the handover to the new Irish government in 1922, the barracks was renamed to honour Michael Collins, a hero of the struggle for independence, who was killed that year in the Civil War; to this day most Dubliners refer to the museum as the Collins Barracks.

Any city would be hard-pressed to come up with a museum to match these surroundings, and the decorative arts don't exactly get the heart pumping. That said, the museum has done an exceptional job of presenting an impressive, if hardly remarkable, collection, featuring fashion, furniture, weaponry, folk life, silver, ceramics and glassware. Some of the best pieces are gathered in the *Curator's Choice* exhibition, a collection of 25 objects hand-picked by different curators, displayed with an account of why they were chosen.

The exhibitions are designed to offer a bird's-eye view of Ireland's social, economic and military history over the last millennium. It's a big ask – too big, say its critics – but well-designed displays, interactive multimedia and a dizzying array of disparate artefacts make for an interesting and valiant effort. On the 1st floor is the museum's Irish silver collection, one of the largest collections of silver in the world; on the 2nd floor you'll find Irish period furniture and scientific instruments, while the 3rd floor has simple and sturdy Irish country furniture. Modern-furniture-and-design lovers will enjoy the exhibition on iconic Irish designer Eileen Gray (1878–1976), one of the museum's highlights. One of the most influential designers of the 20th century, Gray's life and work are documented in the exhibit, which shows examples of her most famous pieces. The fascinating *Way We Wore* exhibit displays Irish clothing and jewellery from the past 250 years. An intriguing socio-cultural study, it highlights the symbolism jewellery and clothing had in bestowing messages of mourning, love and identity.

A new exhibition chronicling Ireland's Easter 1916 Rising is on the ground floor. Visceral memorabilia, such as first-hand accounts of the violence of the Black & Tans and post-Rising hunger strikes, the handwritten death certificates of the republican prisoners and their postcards from Holloway prison, bring to life this poignant period of Irish history.

OLD JAMESON DISTILLERY Map pp102–3

☎ 807 2355; www.jameson.ie; Bow St; adult/child/student €9.75/6/8; ⏱ tours every 35min 10am-5.30pm; 🚇 Luas Red Line to Smithfield, 🚌 67, 67A, 68, 69, 79 or 134 from city centre

Smithfield's biggest draw is devoted to *uisce beatha* (ish-kuh ba-ha, 'the water of life'). The whowhatnow? It's whiskey, the essential Irish spirit, which doesn't quite bestow life, but, if drunk enough, will undoubtedly take it away. Here, in the original home of one of its most famous and renowned distillers, you can get an excellent introduction to the history and culture of this most potent of drinks. Serious fans might be put off by the slickness of the tour and museum, which shepherds visitors through a compulsory tour of the re-created factory and into the ubiquitous gift shop.

The museum occupies a section of the old distillery, which kept the capital in whiskey from 1780 to 1971 (after which the remaining distillers moved to a new ultramodern distillery in Middleton, County Cork). The museum can only be visited on guided tours, which run every 35 minutes. They start with a short film and then, with the aid of models and exhibitions, explain everything you ever wanted to know about Irish whiskey, from its fascinating history to how it's made and why it differs from Scotch – ex-footballer (and Scot) Ally McCoist once joked that the Irish thought of everything, including putting an 'e' in whiskey. At the end of the tour you'll be invited into the Jameson Bar for a dram of complimentary whiskey. Stay alert and make sure to volunteer for the tasting tour, where you get to sample whiskeys from all around the world and train your palate to identify and appreciate the differences between each.

At the end of the tour, you're deposited in the shop, which was kinda the whole point of the tour in the first place you might reckon. If you do want to bring a bottle or two home, make sure you buy one that you can't get in your local. There are some 100 brands of Irish whiskey (not all sold here) but only three – Jameson, Bushmills and Tullamore Dew – are widely available. Our tip is Red Breast, pure pot still, the way all Irish whiskey used to be made, although the swashbuckling Power's is numero uno in Ireland and difficult to get elsewhere. You can also get a rare distillery reserve with your name printed on the label – kind of tacky, but neat, the way we like our whiskey.

There's also a good café and restaurant on the premises.

FOUR COURTS Map pp102–3

☎ 872 5555; Inns Quay; admission free; 🚇 Luas Red Line to Four Courts, 🚌 25, 25A, 66, 67, 90 or 134 from city centre

Impossible to miss if you're up this end of town, James Gandon's (1743–1823) masterpiece is a mammoth complex stretching 130m along Inns Quay. Construction on the Four Courts began in 1786, soon engulfing the Public Offices (built a short time previously at the western end of the same site), and continued until 1802. By then it included a Corinthian-columned central

DA NORT'SOYID & THE SOUTHSYDE

It is commonly assumed that the southside is totally posh and the northside a derelict slum – it makes the jokes easier to make and the prejudices easier to maintain. But the truth is a little more complex. The 'southside' generally refers to Dublin 4 and the fancy suburbs immediately west and south – conveniently ignoring the traditionally working class neighbourhoods in southwestern Dublin like Bluebell and Tallaght. North Dublin is huge, but the northside tag is usually applied to the inner suburbs, where incomes are lower, accents are more pronouncedly Dublin and – most recently – the influx of foreign nationals is more in evidence. All Dubliners are familiar with the posh twit stereotype born and raised on the southside, but there's another kind of Dubliner, usually from the middle-class districts of northern Dublin, who affects a salt-of-the-earth accent while talking about the 'gee-gees' and says things like 'tis far from sushi we was rared' while tucking into a *maki* roll.

block connected to flanking wings with enclosed quadrangles. The ensemble is topped by a diverse collection of statuary. The original four courts – Exchequer, Common Pleas, King's Bench and Chancery – branch off the central rotunda.

The Four Courts played a brief role in the 1916 Easter Rising without suffering damage, but it wasn't so lucky during the Civil War. When anti-Treaty forces seized the building and refused to leave, Free State forces led by Michael Collins shelled it from across the river. As the occupiers retreated, the building was set on fire and many irreplaceable early records were burned. These were the opening salvos in the Irish Civil War. The building wasn't restored until 1932.

Visitors are allowed to wander through, but not to enter the courts or other restricted areas. In the lobby of the central rotunda you'll see bewigged barristers conferring and police officers handcuffed to their charges waiting to enter court.

GENERAL POST OFFICE (GPO)
Map pp102–3

☎ 705 7000; www.anpost.ie; O'Connell St; ☼ 8am-8pm Mon-Sat; ᖷ Luas Red Line to Abbey St, 🚌 all cross-city buses

Imagine trying to post a letter at the country's main post office, only for a bunch of armed and most serious men interrupting your chore by declaring an Irish republic from the doorways before barricading themselves inside in anticipation of a week-long bombardment by the British Army. On Easter Monday 1916, the leaders of the Rising made the GPO their operational HQ, thus ensuring that this huge neoclassical building (designed by Francis Johnston in 1818) would become the focal point for all kinds of protests, parades and remembrances of the struggle for Irish independence.

It's not as if the GPO didn't earn it either: along with much of Lower O'Connell St, the building was left a smouldering wreck. You can still see pockmarks and bullet holes in the huge pillars supporting the Ionic portico, which spans the five central bays and is topped by three statues representing Fidelity, Hibernia and Mercury. The damage was so bad that it didn't reopen until 1929. For more on the Easter Rising, see p22.

In the spacious and light-filled interior there's a beautiful bronze statue, the *Death of Cuchulainn* (1935), depicting the legendary hero of Ulster, whose spirit was evoked in the poetry of Pádraig Pearse. He was an awesome warrior slain at the age of 27 after being tricked into an unfair fight. Even as he lay dead, nobody dared approach the body for fear of attack and it wasn't until ravens landed on him that they were convinced he was dead. The statue is dedicated to those who died in the Rising. Also inside is a series of communist noble-worker-style paintings depicting scenes from the Easter Rising. There are also lots of people going about the everyday business of buying stamps and posting letters. Finally, among all the flags hanging in here, notice that the Union Jack is hung behind the counter and out of reach; it had to be moved there because people kept setting it alight.

CUSTOM HOUSE Map pp102–3

☎ 888 2538; Visitor Centre, Custom House Quay; admission €1.30; ☼ 10am-12.30pm & 2-5pm Mon-Fri, 2-5pm Sat & Sun, closed Mon, Tue & Sat Nov–mid-Mar; 🚌 all cross-city buses

Georgian genius James Gandon (1743–1823) announced his arrival on the Dublin scene with this magnificent building (1781–91), constructed just past Eden Quay at a wide stretch in the River Liffey. When it was being built, angry city merchants and dockers from the original Custom House further upriver in Temple Bar were so menacing that Gandon often came to work wielding a broadsword. He was supported by the era's foremost property developer, Luke Gardiner, who saw the new Custom House as a major part of his scheme to shift the axis of the city eastwards from medieval Capel St to what was then Gardiner's Mall (now O'Connell St).

It's a colossal, neoclassical pile that stretches for 114m along the River Liffey. It can only be taken in and admired from the south side of the river, although its fine detail deserves closer inspection. Arcades, each with seven arches, join the centre to the end pavilions and the columns along the front have harps carved in their capitals. Motifs alluding to transport and trade include the four rooftop statues of Neptune, Mercury, Plenty and Industry, destroyed when the building was gutted in a five-day fire during the independence struggle in 1921, but replaced in 1991. The interior was extensively redesigned after 1921 and again in the 1980s. Below the frieze are heads representing the gods of Ireland's 13 principal rivers, and the sole female head, above the main door, represents the River Liffey. The cattle heads honour Dublin's beef trade, and the statues behind the building represent Africa, America, Asia and Europe. The building is topped by a copper dome with four clocks and, above that, a 5m-high statue of Hope.

Beneath the dome, the Visitor Centre features a small museum on Gandon and the history of the building.

Just outside the Custom House, on Custom House Quay, is a remarkable set of life-size bronze figures by Rowan Gillespie (1997), a memorial to the victims of the Famine (1845–49). The sullen, haunted figures are a powerful reminder of the worst tragedy in Irish history.

JAMES JOYCE CENTRE Map pp102–3

☎ 878 8547; www.jamesjoyce.ie; 35 North Great George's St; adult/child/student €5/free/4; ✆ 9.30am-5pm Mon-Sat, 12.30-5pm Sun; 🚌 3, 10, 11, 13, 16, 16A, 19, 19A or 22 from city centre Denis Maginni, the exuberant, flamboyant dance instructor and 'confirmed bachelor' immortalised by James Joyce in Ulysses, taught the finer points of dance out of this beautifully restored Georgian house, now a centre devoted to promoting and preserving the Joycean heritage. Although Jimmy probably never set foot in the house, he lived in the 'hood for a time, went to a local school and lost his virginity a stone's throw away in what was once Europe's largest red-light district. We couldn't imagine a more fitting location for the centre.

The centre owes its existence to the sterling efforts of Senator David Norris, a charismatic Joycean scholar and gay-rights activist who bought the house in 1982 and oversaw its restoration and conversion into the centre that it is today.

What it is today is more of a study centre than a museum, although there are a handful of exhibits that will pique the interest of a Joyce enthusiast. These include some of the furniture from Joyce's Paris apartment, which was rescued from falling into German hands in 1940 by Joyce's friend Paul Léon; a life-size re-creation of a typical Edwardian bedroom (not Joyce's, but one similar to what James and Nora would have used); and the original door of 7 Eccles St, the home of Leopold and Molly Bloom in Ulysses, which was demolished in real life to make way for a private hospital.

It's not much, but the absence of period stuff is more than made up for by the superb interactive displays, which include three short documentary films on various aspects of Joyce's life and work, and – the highlight of the whole place – computers that allow you to explore the content of Ulysses episode by episode and trace Joyce's life year by year. It's enough to demolish the myth that Joyce's works are an impenetrable mystery and render him as he should be to the contemporary reader: a writer of enormous talent who sought to challenge and entertain his audience with his breathtaking wit and use of language.

While here, you can also admire the fine plastered ceilings, some of which are restored originals while others are meticulous reproductions of Michael Stapleton's designs. Senator Norris fought a long, unrewarding battle for the preservation of Georgian Dublin, and it's wonderful to see others have followed his example – the street has been given a much needed face-lift and now boasts some of the finest Georgian doorways and fanlights in the city.

For information on James Joyce–related walking tours departing from the centre, see p241.

DUBLIN WRITERS MUSEUM Map pp102–3

☎ 872 2077; www.writersmuseum.com; 18 North Parnell Sq; adult/child/student €7/4.40/5.95; ☺ 10am-5pm Mon-Sat, 11am-5pm Sun, to 6pm Mon-Fri Jun-Aug; ☒ 3, 10, 11, 13, 16, 19 or 22 from city centre

Memorabilia aplenty and lots of literary ephemera line the walls and display cabinets of this elegant museum devoted to preserving the city's rich literary tradition. Although the busts and portraits of the greats in the gallery upstairs are worth more than a cursory peek, the real draw are the ground-floor displays, which include Samuel Beckett's phone (with a button for excluding incoming calls, of course), a letter from the 'tenement aristocrat' Brendan Behan to his brother, and a first edition of Bram Stoker's *Dracula*. The exhibits stop some three decades ago and the flat cabinet displays can literally become a pain in the neck, while we can't help thinking that a city with such a rich heritage of great writers deserves a more thorough and fitting tribute. Admission includes taped guides in English and other languages, which have the annoying habit of repeating quotes with actor's voices.

The building, comprising two 18th-century houses, is worth exploring on its own. Dublin stuccodore Michael Stapleton decorated the upstairs gallery. The Gorham Library next door is worth a peek and there's also a calming Zen garden. The museum café is a pleasant place to linger, while the base-ment restaurant, Chapter One (p156), is one of the city's best.

While the museum focuses on the dearly departed, the Irish Writers Centre (☎ 872 1302; 19 North Parnell Sq) next door provides a meeting and working place for their living successors.

SPIRE Map pp102–3

Soaring 120m over O'Connell St – and the rest of the city – this gigantic needle is impossible to miss, a risqué homage to the fight against one of Dublin's greatest social ills, heroin addiction. Yeah, right. Dubs excel at gallows humour, but the Spire is neither a joke nor a commemoration of anything in particular, except maybe the notion that for a spell in the 1990s the sky was the limit. But it's not just an ornament; it *is* apparently the highest sculpture in the world and, sarcasm aside, it's a hugely impressive feat of architectural engineering.

From a base of only 3m in diameter, it soars more than 120m into the sky and tapers into a 15cm-wide beam of light. It was the brainchild of London-based architect Ian Ritchie and is meant to be the centrepiece in a programme aimed at regenerating O'Connell St. And, for no reason other than it's tall and shiny, it actually does the trick rather nicely. Which doesn't stop Dubs making fun of it, calling it – among other names – the 'erection in the intersection', the 'stiletto in the ghetto' and the altogether brilliant 'eyeful tower'. When

O'CONNELL STREET STATUARY

Although overshadowed by the Spire, O'Connell St is lined with statues of Irish history's good and great (see Map p85). The big daddy of them all is the 'Liberator' himself, Daniel O'Connell (1775–1847), completed in 1880, whose massive bronze bulk soars high above the street at the bridge end. The four winged figures at his feet represent O'Connell's supposed virtues: patriotism, courage, fidelity and eloquence. Dubs began to refer to the street as O'Connell St soon after the monument was erected, but its name was only officially changed after independence.

Heading away from the river, past a monument to William Smith O'Brien (1803–64), leader of the Young Irelanders, is a statue that easily rivals O'Connell's for drama: just outside the GPO is the spread-armed figure of trade union leader Jim Larkin (1876–1947). His big moment came when he helped organise the general strike in 1913 – the pose catches him in full flow, urging workers to rise up for their rights. We're with you, comrade.

Next up and difficult to miss is the Spire (above), but just below it, on pedestrianised North Earl St, is the detached figure of James Joyce, looking on the fast and shiny version of 21st-century O'Connell St with a bemused air. Dubs have lovingly dubbed him the 'prick with the stick' and we're sure Joyce would have loved the vulgar rhyme.

Further on is the statue of Father Theobald Mathew (1790–1856), the 'apostle of temperance'. There can't have been a tougher gig in Ireland, but he led a spirited campaign against 'the demon drink' in the 1840s and converted hundreds of thousands to teetotalism.

The top of the street is completed by the imposing statue of Charles Stewart Parnell (1846–91), the 'uncrowned king of Ireland', who was an advocate of Home Rule and became a political victim of Irish intolerance. Despite his fall from grace, it's Parnell who gets the most imposing monument.

indicating that something isn't likely, some locals have taken to suggesting there was a better chance of 'Bertie Ahern shimmying bollock-naked up the Spire'.

CHIMNEY Map pp102–3

☎ 817 3820; Smithfield Village; adult/student & child/family €5/3.50/10; ☼ 10am-5pm Mon-Sat, 11am-5.30pm Sun; ⓡ Luas Red Line to Smithfield, 🚌 67, 67A, 68, 69, 79 or 134 from city centre

As part of the ongoing development of the Smithfield area, an old distillery chimney (nicknamed 'the flue with the view'), built by Jameson's in 1895, has been converted into Dublin's first and only 360-degree observation tower. A glass lift shuttles you to the top, where you get unique views of historic north Dublin. The commentary from the knowledgeable and humorous guide is excellent, which is a good job because Dublin's no oil painting.

ST MICHAN'S CHURCH Map pp102–3

☎ 872 4154; Lower Church St; adult/child/student €3.50/2.50/3; ☼ 10am-12.45pm & 2-4.45pm Mon-Fri, 10am-12.45pm Sat May-Oct, 12.30-3.30pm Mon-Fri Nov-Apr; ⓡ Luas Red Line to Four Courts, 🚌 134 from city centre

Macabre remains are the main attraction at this church, which was founded by the Danes in 1096 and named after one of their saints. The oldest architectural feature is the 15th-century battlement tower; otherwise the church was rebuilt in the late 17th century, considerably restored in the early 19th century and again after the Civil War.

The interior of the church, which feels more like a courtroom, is worth a quick look as you wait for your guide. It contains an organ from 1724, which Handel may have played for the first-ever performance of his *Messiah*. The organ case is distinguished by the fine oak carving of 17 entwined musical instruments on its front. A skull on the floor on one side of the altar is said to represent Oliver Cromwell. On the opposite side is the Stool of Repentance, where 'open and notoriously naughty livers' did public penance.

The tours of the underground vaults are the real draw, however. The bodies within are aged between 400 and 800 years, and have been preserved by a combination of methane gas coming from rotting vegetation beneath the church, the magnesium limestone of the masonry (which absorbs moisture from the air), and the perfectly constant temperature. The corpses have been exposed because the coffins in the vaults were stacked on top of one another and some toppled over and opened when the wood rotted. Among the 'attractions' is an 800-year-old Norman crusader who was so tall that his feet were lopped off so he could fit in a coffin. The guide sounds like he's been delivering the same, albeit fascinating, spiel for too long, but you'll definitely be glad you're not alone down there.

ARBOUR HILL CEMETERY Map pp102–3

Arbour Hill; admission free; ☼ 9am-4.30pm Mon-Sat, 9.30am-noon Sun; ⓡ Luas Red Line to Museum, 🚌 25, 25A, 66, 67 or 90 from city centre

Just north of Collins Barracks, this small cemetery is the final resting place of all 14 of the executed leaders of the 1916 Easter Rising (see p22). The burial ground is plain, with the 14 names inscribed in stone. Beside the graves is a cenotaph bearing the Easter Proclamation, a focal point for official and national commemorations. The front of the cemetery incongruously, but poignantly, contains the graves of British personnel killed in the War of Independence. Here, in the oldest part of the cemetery, as the gravestones toppled, they were lined up against the boundary walls where they still stand solemnly today.

HENRIETTA STREET Map pp102–3

🚌 25, 25A, 66, 67, 90 or 134 from city centre

Henrietta St dates from the 1720s and was the first project of Dublin's pre-eminent Georgian developer, Luke Gardiner. It was designed as an enclave of prestigious addresses (Gardiner himself lived at No 10), and remained one of Dublin's most fashionable streets until the Act of Union (1801). It's looking a little forlorn these days after spending much of the 20th century as tenement housing, where up to 70 tenants were crammed into each four-storey house. Some of the residences are in disrepair, yet it's still a wonderful insight into the evolution of Georgian residential architecture, and features mansions of varying size and style.

KING'S INNS Map pp102–3

☎ 874 4840; www.kingsinns.ie; Henrietta St; 🚌 25, 25A, 66, 67, 90 or 134 from city centre

Home to Dublin's legal profession, King's Inns occupies a classical building on Constitution Hill, which was built by James Gandon between 1795 and 1817, with Francis Johnston chipping in with the cupola. In 1541, when Henry VIII staked his claim to be King of Ireland as well as England, the country's lawyers took the title the Honourable Society of King's Inns and moved into a Dominican Monastery on the site of the modern-day Four Courts. When that building was erected they relocated here, where Irish barristers are still trained. It's only open to members and their guests.

GARDEN OF REMEMBRANCE Map pp102-3
☎ 874 3074; Parnell Sq; ☺ 8.30am-6pm Apr-Sep, 9.30am-4pm Oct-Mar; ◻ 3, 10, 11, 13, 16, 19 or 22 from city centre
This rather austere little park was opened by President Eamon de Valera in 1966 for the 50th anniversary of the Easter Rising. It is still known to some Dubs as the 'Garden of Mature Recollection', mocking the linguistic gymnastics employed by former favourite for president Brian Lenihan, who was caught out lying in a minor political scandal and used the phrase to try and wiggle his way out of it.

The most interesting feature in the garden is a bronze statue of the Children of Lir by Oisin Kelly, who according to Irish legend were turned into swans by their wicked stepmother. It was probably intended to evoke the famous lines penned by WB Yeats in his poem *Easter 1916*: 'All changed, changed utterly:/A terrible beauty is born.'

BELVEDERE HOUSE Map pp102-3
6 Great Denmark St; ◻ 3, 10, 11, 13, 16, 19 or 22 from city centre
Great Denmark St runs northeast towards Mountjoy Sq and passes the 18th-century Belvedere House at No 6. This has been used as the Jesuit Belvedere College since 1841, and one James Joyce studied here between 1893 and 1898, describing it later in *A Portrait of the Artist as a Young Man*. The building is renowned for its magnificent plasterwork by the master stuccodore Michael Stapleton and for its fireplaces by the Venetian artisan Bossi, but the only chance you'll get to admire these features is if you enrol for a class at this secondary school as the building is closed to the public. The plasterwork isn't *that* special.

ROTUNDA HOSPITAL Map pp102-3
☎ 873 0700; Parnell Sq; ☺ visiting hours 6-8pm; ◻ 3, 10, 11, 13, 16, 19 or 22 from city centre
Irish public hospitals aren't usually attractions, by any stretch of the imagination, but this one makes for an interesting walk-by or an unofficial wander inside if you're interested in Victorian plasterwork. It was the first maternity hospital in the British Isles – and once the world's largest – and was established by Dr Bartholomew Mosse in 1748, at a time when the burgeoning urban population was enduring shocking infant mortality rates.

It shares its basic design with Leinster House (p82) because the architect of both, Richard Cassels, used the same floor plan to economise. He added a three-storey tower, which Mosse intended to use for fundraising purposes (charging visitors an entry fee). He also laid out pleasure gardens, which were fashionable among Dublin's high society for a time, and built the Rotunda Assembly Hall to raise money. The hall is now occupied by the Ambassador Theatre, and the Supper Rooms house the Gate Theatre (p186).

Inside, the public rooms and staircases give some idea of how beautiful the hospital once was, and they lead to one of Dublin's largely hidden gems, the sumptuous Rotunda Chapel, built in 1758, and featuring superb coloured plasterwork by German stuccodore Bartholomew Cramillion. The Italian artist Giovanni Battista Capriani was supposed to supplement the work but his paintings were never installed, which is probably just as well because you can't imagine how this little space would have looked with even more decoration. If you intend visiting, you have to bear in mind that this is still a functioning hospital and you must be very quiet when coming to see the chapel. It's not terribly well sign-posted inside and is often locked outside visiting hours (although if you ask kindly or look like you're in desperate need of a prayer, somebody will let you in).

ST MARY'S ABBEY Map pp102-3
☎ 872 1490; Meeting House Lane; ◻ 11, 16 or 41 from city centre
Where now the glories of Babylon? All that remains of what was once Ireland's wealthiest and most powerful monastery is the chapterhouse, so forgotten that most Dubliners are unaware of its existence. In its

medieval day, this Cistercian abbey ran the show when it came to Irish church politics, although its reputation with the authorities was somewhat sullied when it became a favourite meeting place for rebels against the crown. On 11 June 1534, 'Silken' Thomas Fitzgerald, the most important of Leinster's Anglo-Norman lords, entered the chapterhouse and flung his Sword of State on the ground in front of the awaiting King's Council – a ceremonial two-fingered salute to King Henry VIII and his authority. Visitors today are slightly less dramatic, but they can enjoy a small exhibition and view a model of what the abbey looked like in the good old days. The easiest way to visit is by going to the City Hall (Map pp66–7) on Dame St and joining a free walking tour (10.30am, 1pm and 3.30pm Wednesday and Saturday). Otherwise, call to arrange a visit.

ST MARY'S CHURCH Map pp102–3
Mary St; 🚌 11, 16 or 41 from city centre
Designed by William Robinson in 1697, this is the most important church to survive from that period (although it's no longer in use and is closed to the public). John Wesley, founder of Methodism, delivered his first Irish sermon here in 1747 and it was the preferred church of Dublin's 18th-century social elite. Many famous Dubliners were baptised in its font, and Arthur Guinness was married here in 1793.

ST MARY'S PRO-CATHEDRAL Map pp102–3
☎ 874 5441; Marlborough St; admission free; ⊙ 8am-6.30pm; 🚌 3, 10, 11, 13, 16, 19 or 22 from city centre
Dublin's most important Catholic church is not quite the showcase you'd expect. It's in the wrong place for starters. This large neoclassical building, constructed from 1816 to 1825, was supposed to be on O'Connell St where the GPO now stands, but the local Protestant community – who pretty much ran the show back then – went nuts about the idea of it having such a prominent position. So it was built in a much less conspicuous side street, away from the main thoroughfare and smack in the middle of Monto, where purveyors of the world's oldest profession plied their trade (see the boxed text, below). In fact, it's so cramped for space around here that you'd hardly notice the church's six Doric columns, which were modelled on the Temple of Theseus in Athens, much less be able to admire them. The interior is fairly functional, and its few highlights include a carved altar by Peter Turnerelli and the alto relief representation of the Ascension by John Smyth. The best time to visit is 11am

MEETIN' IN MONTO

If you're listening to folk legends The Dubliners, you might come across a sing-along ditty called 'Monto (Take Her Up to Monto)', which is a playful reference to what was once Dublin's most notorious red-light district and the favoured destination of off-duty soldiers looking for a little night-time action. The name comes from Mountgomery St, which was just east of O'Connell St and where the light shone reddest. James Joyce lost his virginity here (as did many others) within spitting distance of the city's Catholic cathedral. A couple of years after independence the new, ultra-Catholic authorities decided to take action and closed all of the brothels. Catholic girls from the Legion of Mary marched through the streets attaching holy pictures to the doors of former dens of disrepute, and Mountgomery St, whose name was synonymous with pleasures of the flesh, was renamed the suitably chaste Cathedral St.

We'll leave you with the most scabrous verse of the whole song, which was never sung by The Dubliners – by the way, Póg mo thoin (pronounced 'pogue ma hone') means 'kiss my arse…'

The Queen she came to call on us,
She wanted to see all of us
I'm glad she didn't fall on us, she's eighteen stone.
"Mister Me Lord Mayor," says she,
"Is this all you've got to show me?"
"Why, no ma'am there's some more to see, Póg mo thoin!"

And he took her up Monto, Monto, Monto
Take her up to Monto, lan-ge-roo,
To you!

on Sunday when the Latin Mass is sung by the Palestrina Choir, with whom Ireland's most celebrated tenor, John McCormack, began his career in 1904.

The design of the church is shrouded in some mystery. In 1814 John Sweetman won a competition held to find the best design for the church, a competition that had actually been organised by his brother William. It's not certain whether John actually designed the building, since he was living in Paris at the time and may have bought the plans from the French architect Auguste Gauthier, who designed the similar Notre Dame de Lorette in northern France. The only clue as to the church's architect is in the ledger, which lists the builder as 'Mr P'.

Finally, a word about the term 'pro' in the title. It implies, roughly, that it is an 'unofficial cathedral'. More accurately it was built as a sort of interim cathedral to be replaced when sufficient funds were available. Church leaders never actually got around to it, leaving the capital of this most Catholic of countries with two incredible-but-under-used Protestant cathedrals and one fairly ordinary Catholic one. Irony one, piety nil.

ST GEORGE'S CHURCH Map pp102–3

Hardwicke Pl; 🚌 11, 16 or 41 from city centre
If you're on the north side, the steeple of this deconsecrated church may catch your eye. The church was built by Francis Johnston from 1802 in Greek Ionic style, and the 60m-high steeple was modelled on that of St Martin-in-the-Fields in London. Although this was one of Johnston's finest works, and the Duke of Wellington was married here, the church has been sorely neglected – probably because it's Church of Ireland and not Roman Catholic, it has to be said. The bells that Leopold Bloom heard in *that* book were removed, the ornate pulpit was carved up and used to decorate the pub Thomas Read's (p168), and the spire is in danger of crumbling, which has resulted in it being sheathed in scaffolding pending a patch-up job. The church is not open to the public.

PHOENIX PARK

Dubliners are rightly proud of this humungous patch of greenery at the northwestern edge of the city centre, a short skip from Heuston Station and the Liffey quays. The hugely impressive 709 hectares that comprise the park make up one of the largest set of inner-city green lungs in the world. To put it into perspective, it dwarfs the measly 337 hectares of New York's Central Park and is larger than all of the major London parks put together. The park is a magnificent playground for all kinds of activities, from running to polo, and it's a fitting home to the president of Ireland, the American ambassador and a shy herd of fallow deer who are best observed – from a distance – during the summer months. It is also where you'll find Europe's oldest zoo, not to mention dozens of playing fields for all kinds of sport. How's that for a place to stretch your legs?

From the Anglo-Norman invasion up to 1537, the park – whose name is a corruption of *fionn uisce* (clear water), rather than anything to do with the legendary bird – was part of the lands owned by the Knights of Jerusalem, keepers of an important priory on what is now the site of the Royal Hospital Kilmainham (p96). After King Henry VIII dissolved the monasteries, the lands passed into the hands of the king's viceroys. In 1671 the duke of Ormonde, James Butler, introduced a herd of fallow deer, 1000 pheasants and some partridge, and turned it into a royal deer park, soon enclosed by a wall. It remained the preserve of the British Crown and its Irish court until 1745, when the viceroy, Lord Chesterfield, threw it open to the public.

In an episode that set back the cause of Irish Home Rule, the British chief secretary for Ireland, Lord Cavendish, and his assistant were murdered in 1882 outside what is now the Irish president's residence, by an obscure Irish nationalist group called the Invincibles. Lord Cavendish's home is now called Deerfield, and is used as the US ambassador's residence.

Needless to say, this is very much a visit-only kind of neighbourhood – besides a tea-house in the park there are virtually no places to eat and absolutely no places to stay.

DUBLIN ZOO Map p115

☎ 677 1425; www.dublinzoo.ie; adult/concession/family €13/8.50/36; ☯ 9.30am-6pm Mon-Sat, 10.30am-6pm Sun Mar-Sep, 9.30am-dusk Mon-Fri, 9.30am-dusk Sat, 10.30am-dusk Sun Oct-Feb; ◙ 10 from O'Connell St, or 25 or 26 from Middle Abbey St

Established in 1830, the 12-hectare Dublin Zoo just north of the Hollow is one of the oldest in the world, and as thrilling or depressing as any other old zoo trying to drag itself into the 21st century. The zoo is well known for its lion-breeding programme, which dates back to 1857, and includes among its offspring the lion that roars at the start of MGM films. You'll see these tough cats, from a distance, on the 'African Plains', which were added a few years ago, doubling the size of the zoo and making it a much nicer place to stroll around in.

The zoo has several hundred different species, ranging from owls to hippos, most of which are housed in the old-fashioned part of the complex, which includes a 'World of Primates' section and 'Fringes of the Arctic', where similar animals have been grouped together as part of the zoo's modern restructuring. The one thing they haven't managed to fix, however, is the depression that seemingly afflicts the polar bears, who seem rightly incapable of coming to terms with the narrow confines of their world, a far cry from the northern tundra.

Still, the zoo has gone to great lengths to make itself visitor-friendly, and the presence of new babies or animals on breeding loans from other zoos will surely generate a couple of 'oohs' and 'aahs' from the kids. There are also plenty of children's activities, including a Meet the Keeper programme, which has events approximately every half-hour from 11am to 3.30pm, where children get to feed the animals and participate in other activities. Our favourite section is the City Farm, which brings you within touching distance of chickens, cows, goats and pigs, the luckiest animals here. There's also a zoo train and a nursery for infants.

Although there are places to eat, they're not very good and you'd be much better off bringing a picnic but, for God's sake, don't feed the animals.

ÁRAS AN UACHTARÁIN Map p115

☎ 617 1000; www.president.ie; admission by tour only; ◙ 10 from O'Connell St, or 25 or 26 from Middle Abbey St

The residence of the Irish president is a Palladian lodge that was built in 1751 and enlarged a couple of times since, most

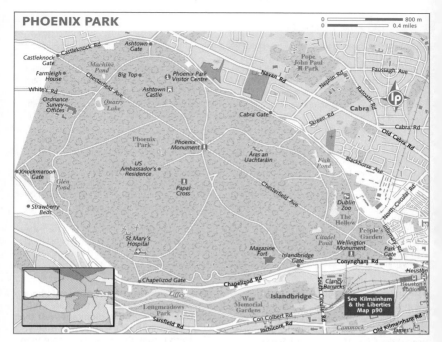

recently in 1816. It was home to the British viceroys from 1782 to 1922, and then to the governors general until Ireland cut ties with the British Crown and created the office of president in 1937. Queen Victoria stayed here during her visit in 1849, when she appeared not to even notice the Famine. The candle burning in the window is an old Irish tradition, to guide 'the Irish diaspora' home.

Tickets for the free one-hour tours (9.40am until 4.20pm on Saturdays only) can be collected from the Phoenix Park Visitor Centre (p116), where you'll see a 10-minute introductory video before being shuttled to the Áras itself to inspect five state rooms and the president's study. If you can't make it on a Saturday, just become elected president of your own country or become a Nobel laureate or something, and then wrangle a personal invite.

WORTH THE TRIP: STRAWBERRY BEDS

Running alongside the northern banks of the Liffey between the villages of Chapelizod and Lucan, roughly along the western edge of the Phoenix Park, are the Strawberry Beds, so-called on account of the fruits once grown here and sold along the side of the road. Before the days of flight, it was a popular honeymoon destination for Dubliners; the Chapelizod end was Joyce's favourite spot for contemplating the Liffey.

Only 6km west of the city centre, the Strawberry Beds are a totally unspoilt bit of countryside and one of the city's most beautiful getaway spots – in a time of unfettered development, it's a minor miracle that the entire area was declared a protected amenity.

To get here without your own wheels, take bus 25, 26 or 57 to Chapelizod village and then walk – or take a taxi – over the steep Knockmaroon Hill and down towards the beds. You can refuel at the Angler's Rest (☎ 820 4351; www.theanglersrest.ie; Knockmaroon; mains €9-12; ⏱ 11am-midnight Mon-Fri, from noon Sat & Sun), which specialises in seafood, or, further on, just have drinks at the utterly wonderful Strawberry Hall (☎ 821 0634; Strawberry Beds), reputedly Dublin's second-oldest pub and one of the best-kept secrets in town. This place alone makes it worth the trek.

PHOENIX PARK MISCELLANY

Chesterfield Ave runs northwest through the entire length of the park from the Parkgate St entrance to the Castleknock Gate. Near the Parkgate St entrance is the 63m-high Wellington Monument obelisk, which took almost 50 years to build because the duke fell from favour during its construction. It was finally completed in 1861. Nearby is the People's Garden, dating from 1864, and the bandstand in the Hollow. Across Chesterfield Ave from the Áras an Uachtaráin – and easily visible from the road – is the massive Papal Cross, which marks the site where Pope John Paul II preached to 1¼ million people in 1979 and drove around waving to the crowds in what was best described as a Tic-Tac box with wheels. In the centre of the park the Phoenix Monument, erected by Lord Chesterfield in 1747, looks so unlike a phoenix that it's often referred to as the Eagle Monument.

The southern part of the park has many football and hurling pitches; although they actually occupy about 80 hectares (200 acres), the area is known as the Fifteen Acres. To the west, the rural-looking Glen Pond corner of the park is extremely attractive.

At the northwestern end of the park near the White's Gate entrance are the offices of Ordnance Survey Ireland (OSI; ☎ 802 5300; www.osi.ie), the government mapping department. This building was originally built in 1728 by Luke Gardiner, who was responsible for the architecture in O'Connell St and Mountjoy Sq in north Dublin. In the building's map shop (☎ 802 5349; ⊙ 9am-4.45pm Mon-Fri) you can buy all of the OSI maps for any of the 26 counties of Ireland.

Back towards the Parkgate St entrance is the Magazine Fort (closed to the public) on Thomas's Hill. Like the nearby Wellington Monument, the fort was no quick construction, the process taking from 1734 to 1801. It provided useful target practice during the 1916 Easter Rising, and was raided by the Irish Republican Army (IRA) in 1940 when the entire ammunition reserve of the Irish army was nabbed, but recovered a few weeks later.

PHOENIX PARK VISITOR CENTRE
Map p115

☎ 677 0095; adult/concession/family €2.75/1.25/7;
⊙ 10am-6pm Apr-Sep, 10am-5pm Oct, 10am-5pm
Mon-Sat Nov & Dec, 10am-5pm Sat & Sun Jan-Mar;
🚌 37 or 29 from Middle Abbey St
In the north of the park, near the Ashtown Gate, this visitor centre occupies what were the stables of the papal nunciature, and explores the wildlife and history of the park through film and two floors of exhibits. Visitors are also taken on a tour of the adjacent four-storey Ashtown Castle, a 17th-century tower-house that was concealed inside the later building of the papal nunciature and was only 'discovered' when the latter was demolished in 1986. Box hedges surrounding the tower trace the ground plan of the lost building. Children keen on all things furry will love the Great Slumber Party exhibition upstairs, a walk-through tunnel that looks at the sleeping habits of animals such as foxes and badgers.

FARMLEIGH HOUSE Map p115

☎ 815 5900; www.farmleigh.ie; admission free;
⊙ 10.45am-5pm Sat, Sun & bank holidays Easter-Oct; 🚌 10 from O'Connell St, or 25 or 26 from Middle Abbey St

Situated in the northwest corner of Phoenix Park, this opulent house is the state's official B&B, where visiting dignitaries rest their very important heads – at least in theory. The truth is that after spending more than €52 million on purchasing and restoring the house, it was used to provide accommodation for just three weeks in the first two years after it opened in mid-2001. It has drawn savage criticism from some commentators who consider it money wasted on an already ugly house. It can only be visited by joining one of the 30-minute house tours.

The open days have been hugely popular with locals who, as tax payers, reckon it's as much their pad as anyone else's. The estate takes up 79 acres and there are many beautiful features. The main house is a bit blowsy and overblown but it's a pleasant enough example of Georgian–Victorian architecture. The real highlight is the garden, where regular shows are held. There is also an extensive programme of cultural events in summer, ranging from food fairs to classical concerts. Because the property is used for state business, schedules may change and you should telephone in advance.

BEYOND THE ROYAL CANAL

Eating p158; Drinking p172; Sleeping p208

Constructed from 1790, when the usefulness of such waterways was already on the wane, the Royal Canal was a total commercial flop. It was founded by Long John Binns, a director of the Grand Canal who quit the board in a huff after condescending remarks were made over his profession as a shoemaker. He established the Royal Canal principally for revenge, but it never made money and he became a bit of a laughing stock. Adding insult to injury, his waterway came to be known as the 'Shoemaker's Canal'. In 1840 the canal was sold to a railway company, and rail tracks still run alongside much of the canal's route.

Beyond the Royal Canal, which provides the northern boundary of the city centre, lie the down-to-earth Dublin suburbs of Glasnevin, Marino and Drumcondra, which is still the stomping ground of the Taoiseach Bertie Ahern. Although traditionally working- and lower-middle class suburbs, in recent years property prices have soared, transforming most of these 'burbs into some pretty choice postal districts.

Unless you have a particular interest in how Dubliners decorate their semidetached suburban houses, there are only a handful of sights to drag you beyond the Royal Canal's boundaries, but they're well worth the effort – and they're quite easy to get to by bus, unless of course you fancy a walk along the towpath that runs along the canal. You can join it beside Newcomen Bridge at North Strand Rd, just north of Connolly Station, and follow it to the suburb of Clonsilla and beyond, more than 10km away. The walk is particularly pleasant beyond Binns Bridge in Drumcondra. At the top of Blessington St, a large pond, used when the canal also supplied drinking water to the city, attracts water birds.

The mighty Croke Park, HQ of Gaelic games and home to a terrific museum of the association, offers a unique and compelling insight into the history and passion of these most Irish pastimes, while the architecturally magnificent Casino at Marino, the historic Glasnevin Cemetery and the soothing National Botanic Gardens are among the best attractions the city has to offer.

You can also crash in these neighbourhoods, most notably Drumcondra – which is on the road to the airport and has dozens of B&Bs in well-maintained Victorian and Edwardian houses – and Clontarf, which stretches out along the northern edge of Dublin Bay, offering the compelling prospect of waking with the scent of brine in your nostrils.

CROKE PARK & GAA MUSEUM Map p118

☎ 855 8176; www.gaa.ie; New Stand, Croke Park, Clonliffe Rd; museum only adult/child/student €5.50/3.50/4, museum & tour adult/child/student €9.50/6/7; ⏱ 9.30am-5pm Mon-Sat & noon-5pm Sun Apr-Oct, 10am-5pm Tue-Sat & noon-4pm Sun Nov-Mar; 🚍 3, 11, 11A, 16, 16A or 123 from O'Connell St

Uniquely important in Irish culture, the magnificent stadium at 'Croker' is the fabulous fortress that protects the sanctity and spirit of Gaelic games in Ireland, as well as being the administrative HQ of the Gaelic Athletic Association (GAA), the body that governs them. Sound a little hyperbolic? Well, the GAA considers itself not just the governing body of a bunch of Irish games, but the stout defender of a cultural identity that is ingrained in Ireland's sense of self (see the boxed text, p192). It goes without saying that this is the country's largest stadium; after being virtually rebuilt in recent years, it's actually the fourth-largest stadium in Europe,

with a capacity of some 82,000 people, and all for sports that are only played in this tiny little country! There are stadium tours available twice a day, although these are largely for hard-core GAA and sports stadia fans and are not available on match days. It's much better to get a ticket for a match, when you can watch these brilliant games, soak up the unique atmosphere and have a squiz at the arena. Hogan Stand ticket holders can visit the museum on match days.

In the 1870s, the site was developed as the 'City & Suburban Racecourse', but was bought by the GAA in 1913 and immediately renamed Croke Park in honour of the association's first patron, Archbishop Croke of Cashel. Since its foundation it has been entwined with Irish nationalism. The famous Hill 16, which is traditionally where the hardcore Dublin fans stand during matches, was so-called because its foundations were built with rubble taken from O'Connell St after the Easter Rising

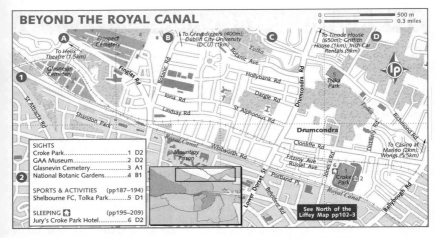

SIGHTS
Croke Park.................................1 D2
GAA Museum............................2 D2
Glasnevin Cemetery.................3 A1
National Botanic Gardens...........4 B1

SPORTS & ACTIVITIES (pp187–194)
Shelbourne FC, Tolka Park..........5 D1

SLEEPING (pp195–209)
Jury's Croke Park Hotel.............6 D2

of 1916. This was also the site of the first Bloody Sunday in Irish history, the greatest single atrocity of the War of Independence.

Bloody Sunday is one of the episodes recounted in the outstanding GAA Museum, where the history and culture of these most Irish of games is explored in fascinating, interactive style. As well as going into exhaustive detail about Gaelic games, the exhibitions feature audiovisual displays that are sure to get the hairs on the back of any GAA fan's neck to stand up, and many relics from other sports and episodes that have captured the mood of the nation. There are terminals set up where you can watch highlights from any All-Ireland football or hurling final that has been recorded, but the highlight, for us at least, is the opportunity to test one's skills with a football or a hurley and *sliothar* (small leather ball), and imagine the glories that might have been.

GLASNEVIN CEMETERY Map p118
☎ 830 1133; Finglas Rd; admission free; ⊙ 24hr; ⊟ 40, 40A or 40B from Parnell St
Make sure your visit coincides with one of the free tours (2.30pm Wednesday and Friday), which are provided by Dublin's most entertaining, informative and irreverent tour guide, the inimitable Lorcan Collins (also of the 1916 Rebellion tours, see p240), who'll bring you around all the most interesting sights in Ireland's largest cemetery – sometimes referred to as 'Croak Park'.

It was established in 1832 as a cemetery for Roman Catholics, who faced opposition when they conducted burials in the city's Protestant cemeteries. Many monuments and memorials have staunchly patriotic overtones, with numerous high crosses, shamrocks, harps and other Irish symbols. The single most imposing memorial is the colossal monument to Cardinal McCabe (1837–1921), archbishop of Dublin and primate of Ireland.

A modern replica of a round tower holds the tomb of Daniel O'Connell, who died in 1847 and was reinterred here in 1869, when the tower was completed. Charles Stewart Parnell's tomb is topped with a huge granite rock. Other notable people buried here include Sir Roger Casement, who was executed for treason by the British in 1916 and whose remains weren't returned to Ireland until 1964; the republican leader Michael Collins, who was assassinated during the Civil War; the docker and trade unionist Jim Larkin, a prime force in the 1913 general strike; and the poet Gerard Manley Hopkins.

There's a poignant 'class' memorial to the men who starved themselves to death for the cause of Irish freedom over the last century, including 10 men in the 1981 H Block hunger strikes. The most interesting parts of the cemetery are at the southeastern Prospect Sq end. The towers were once used to keep watch for body snatchers. The cemetery is mentioned in *Ulysses* and there are several clues for Joyce enthusiasts to follow.

NATIONAL BOTANIC GARDENS Map p118

☎ 837 7596; Botanic Rd, Glasnevin; admission free; ⏰ 9am-6pm Mon-Sat & 11am-6pm Sun Apr-Oct, 10am-4.30pm Mon-Sat & 11am-4.30pm Sun Nov-Mar; 🚍 13, 13A or 19 from O'Connell St, or bus 34 or 34A from Middle Abbey St

This 19.5-hectare treasure is a delightful blend of exoticism and tousled gentility. Although only established in 1795, the area was used as a garden long before it was christened so, and the area of Yew Walk (Addison's Walk) features trees dating back to the first half of the 18th century.

The architectural highlight in the gardens is a series of curvilinear glasshouses that date from 1843 to 1869. They were created by Dubliner Richard Turner, who was also responsible for creating the Palm House at London's Kew Gardens. Within these Victorian masterpieces you will find the latest in botanical technology, including a series of computer-controlled climates that reproduce environments from different parts of the world.

The gardens also have a palm house, which was built in 1884. Among the pioneering botanical work conducted here was the first attempt to raise orchids from seed, back in 1844. Pampas grass and the giant lily were first grown in Europe in these gardens.

CASINO AT MARINO Off Map p118

☎ 833 1618; Marino; adult/concession/family €2.90/1.30/7.40; ⏰ by guided tour only 10am-5pm May & Oct, 10am-6pm Jun-Sep, noon-4pm Sat & Sun Feb-Apr, Nov & Dec, noon-5pm Apr, closed Jan, last tour 45min before closing; 🚍 20A, 20B, 27, 27B, 42, 42C or 123 from city centre, 🚊 DART to Clontarf Rd

No, not that kind of casino; perhaps it's the images of blackjack and slot machines that make so many visitors overlook this bewitching 18th-century architectural folly, which is a *casino* in the Italian sense of the word, as in a 'house of pleasure' or summer home. Off Malahide Rd, it was built for the Earl of Charlemont (1728–99), who returned from his grand European tour with a huge art collection and a burning passion for the Italian Palladian style of architecture. He appointed the architect Sir William Chambers to build the casino, a process that spanned three decades and was never really concluded because the earl frittered away his fortune.

Externally, the building's 12 Tuscan columns, forming a templelike façade, and huge entrance doorway suggest that it encloses a simple single open space. Only when you go inside do you realise what a wonderful extravagance it is. The interior is a convoluted maze, planned as a bachelor's retreat, but eventually put to quite a different use. Flights of fancy include carved draperies, ornate fireplaces, chimneys for central heating disguised as roof urns, downpipes hidden in columns, beautiful parquet floors built of rare woods and a spacious wine cellar. All sorts of statuary adorn the outside, the amusing fakes being the most enjoyable. The towering front door is a sham, and a much smaller panel opens to reveal the interior. The windows have blacked-out panels to disguise the fact that the interior is a complex of rooms rather than a single chamber. Entry is by guided tour only, and the last tour departs 45 minutes before closing.

When the earl married, the casino became a garden retreat rather than a bachelor's quarters. The casino was designed to accompany another building where he intended to house the art and antiquities he had acquired during his European tour, so it's perhaps fitting that his town house on Parnell Sq, also designed by Sir William Chambers, is now the Dublin City Gallery (p101).

Despite his wealth, Charlemont was a comparatively liberal and free-thinking aristocrat. He never enclosed his demesne and allowed the public to use it as an open park. Nor was he the only eccentric in the area at that time. In 1792 a painter named Folliot took a dislike to the earl and built Marino Crescent at the bottom of Malahide Rd purely to block his view of the sea.

After Charlemont's death his estate, crippled by his debts, quickly collapsed. The art collection was dispersed and in 1870 the town house was sold to the government. The Marino estate followed in 1881 and the casino in 1930, though it was in a decrepit condition when the government acquired it. Not until the mid-1970s did serious restoration begin, and it still continues. Although the current casino grounds are a tiny fragment of the original Marino estate, trees around the building help to hide the fact that it's now surrounded by a housing estate.

BRAM STOKER DRACULA EXPERIENCE

☎ 805 7824; www.thebramstokerdraculaexper
ience.com; Bar Code, Westwood Club, Clontarf Rd;
adult/child/student €7/4/5; ☯ 4-10pm Fri, noon-
10pm Sat & Sun; ⓧ DART to Clontarf Rd, 🚌 20,
20B, 27, 27B, 29A, 31, 31A, 32, 32A, 32B, 42, 42A,
42B, 43, 127, 129 or 130 from Lower Abbey St

Abraham (Bram) Stoker (1847–1912) was
born and raised at 15 Marino Cres, in the
pretty seaside suburb of Clontarf, so it
makes perfect sense that the local fitness
club should be home to a museum dedicated to the author's life and, particularly,
to his most memorable creation. The sight
of Dublin's suburbanites struggling to
fend off the effects of age and gravity on a
Stairmaster may be scary enough, but Bram
Stoker's imagination was just that little
bit more extreme. The tour through his
fictional world mightn't keep you awake at
night, but it's pretty effective nonetheless,
as each of the various rooms have been
created to stimulate maximum discomfort
and fear. The journey begins in a 'Time
Tunnel to Transylvania', and transports unsuspecting visitors to such delightful destinations as Renfield's lunatic asylum and the
bowels of Castle Dracula, where a meeting
with the sharp-toothed one awaits. We
won't ruin the fun by telling you how it
was all put together; suffice to say that
technology and the warped imagination of
the designers have combined to startling
effect. There is also an exhibit dedicated to
the life of Bram Stoker.

If you present a same-day DART ticket,
you'll get a 25% discount on the entry
charge.

The walks included here take on three of the city's major themes, beginning with Dublin's well-earned reputation as a hive of literary genius, followed by a traipse through the city's faded Viking and medieval past. There's also the staggered walk that most people come to Dublin for – the pub crawl. Finally, we want you to explore the northern half of the city before straddling the southern boundary of the city centre and the suburbs.

LITERARY DUBLIN

1 Shaw Birthplace Start your walk just north of the Grand Canal at the Shaw Birthplace (p76). Barely visited, this elegant Victorian home was where Nobel Prize–winner George Bernard Shaw (1856–1950), author of *Pygmalion* (later hammered up and turned into the stage musical and film *My Fair Lady*), spent his early years.

2 Cornelius Ryan Birthplace Walk north along Synge St, take a left along Grantham St and at the very end, you can see Ryan's birthplace. There's not much to see, save the frontage of the house at 32 Heytesbury St where the author (1920–74) of *The Longest Day*, *The Last Battle* and *A Bridge Too Far* was born.

3 Bleeding Horse Retrace your steps along Grantham St and keep going along until you get to the intersection with Lower Camden St. Across Camden St is this popular watering hole, where a certain Captain Bligh, of *Mutiny on the Bounty* fame, lived upstairs for a time.

4 Sir Edward Carson Birthplace Walk along Charlotte St, take a left onto Harcourt St and head up to No 4. This is the birthplace of the founder of Northern Irish Unionism, who was a barrister in Dublin before going all political. Carson (1854–1935) made his legal bones by prosecuting Oscar Wilde in 1898, which ultimately resulted in the writer going to prison for homosexuality (which was illegal).

5 George (AE) Russell Residence Continue walking straight along West St Stephen's Green and onto North St Stephen's Green. Take a left onto Merrion Row and continue to Merrion Sq. The former residence of self-proclaimed poet, mystic, painter and co-operator George Russell (1867–1935) is at 84 Merrion Sq South.

6 WB Yeats Residence (Part One) The great poet, dramatist and nationalist agitator

WB Yeats (1865–1939) answered the door at 82 Merrion Sq South...

7 WB Yeats Residence (Part Two) ... Before moving around the square to 52 Merrion Sq East, although he later claimed not to like living on the square.

WALK FACTS

Start **Shaw Birthplace, 33 Synge St**
End **Dublin Writers Museum, North Parnell Sq**
Distance **3.5km**
Duration **2½ to three hours**
Fuel Stop **Palace Bar**
Transport 🚊 Luas to Harcourt St, 🚌 11, 11A, 13B or 48A from Trinity College.

LITERARY DUBLIN

8 Oscar Wilde House The self-professed genius (1854–1900) was born and raised at 1 Merrion Sq North (p82); fortunately, he grew up to prove himself right.

9 Bram Stoker House From the square's northern corner, walk straight down Nassau St. Kildare St runs off to your left, and No 36 was once the home of Bram Stoker (1847–1912), the creator of the greatest vampire of them all (er, *Dracula*).

10 Palace Bar Head back up Nassau St, past the main entrance to Trinity College and then down Westmoreland St. Off the street to your left, on Fleet St, is the Palace Bar (p169), traditionally a favourite haunt of journos and scribblers, including one Brendan Behan, who was regularly barred from here.

11 James Joyce Centre Cross the Liffey onto O'Connell St, take a right onto Lower Abbey St, then left into Marlborough St and head north until you reach North Great George's St. On your right, at No 35, in this lovingly restored period home, is the James Joyce Centre (p108), which is the home of all things Joycean.

12 Dublin Writers Museum Walk to the end of North Great George's St, head left into Great Denmark St and finish your literary walk at this interesting literary centre (p109) on the northern flank of Parnell Sq.

VIKING & MEDIEVAL DUBLIN

1 Essex Gate Begin your walk at the corner of Parliament St and Essex Gate, once a main entrance gate to the city. A bronze plaque on a pillar marks the spot where the gate once stood. Further along, you can see the original foundations of Isolde's Tower through a grill in the pavement, in front of the pub of the same name.

2 Church of St Francis Head west down Essex Gate and West Essex St until you reach Fishamble St; turn right towards the quays and left into Wood Quay. Cross Winetavern St and proceed along Merchant's Quay. To your left is the Church of St Francis, aka Adam & Eve's, after a tavern through which worshippers gained access to a secret chapel during Penal Law times in the 17th and 18th centuries.

3 Father Mathew Bridge Further down Merchant's Quay you'll spot this bridge, built in 1818 on the spot of the fordable crossing that gave Dublin its Irish name, Baile Átha Cliath (Town of the Hurdle Ford).

4 Brazen Head Take a left onto Bridge St and stop for a drink at Dublin's oldest pub (p169), dating from 1198 (although the present building dates from 1668).

5 St Audoen's Arch Take the next left onto Cook St, where you'll find one of the only remaining gates of 32 that were built into the medieval city walls, dating from 1240.

6 St Audoen's Church Climb through the arch up to the ramparts to see one of the city's oldest existing churches (p97). It was built around 1190, and is not to be confused with the newer Catholic church next door.

7 Dvblinia Leave the little park, join High St and head east until you reach the first corner. Here on your left is the former Synod Hall, now a museum (p95), where medieval Dublin has been interactively re-created.

8 Christ Church Cathedral Turn left and walk under the Synod Hall Bridge, which links it to one of the city's most important landmarks and, in medieval times, the most important church (p94) inside the city walls.

9 Tailors' Hall Exit the cathedral onto Christ Church Pl, cross over onto Nicholas St and turn right onto Back Lane. Proceed to Dublin's oldest surviving guild hall, built between 1703 and 1707 (though it says 1770 on the plaque) for the Tailors Guild. It's now the headquarters of An Taisce, the National Trust for Ireland.

10 St Patrick's Cathedral Do an about turn, head back along the lane and turn right into Nicholas St, which becomes Patrick St. To your left you'll see Dublin's most important cathedral (p90), which stood outside the city walls.

11 Marsh's Library Along St Patrick's Close, beyond the bend on the left, is this stunningly beautiful library (p93), named after Archbishop Narcissus Marsh, dean of St Patrick's. Further along again on your left is the Dublin Metropolitan Police building, once the Episcopal Palace of St Sepulchre.

VIKING & MEDIEVAL DUBLIN

12 Dublin Castle Finally, follow our route up Bride St, Golden Lane and Great Ship St, and finish up with a long wander around **Dublin Castle** (p74). Be sure not to miss the striking powder-blue **Bermingham Tower** and the nearby **Chester Beatty Library** (p70), south of the castle, which houses one of Dublin's most fascinating collections of rare books and manuscripts.

PINTLY PERAMBULATION

1 Merrion Hotel Before your walk, start with an elegant afternoon tea, complete with scones and cucumber sandwiches at this hotel (p201); it's the perfect lining for the road ahead.

2 Fitzwilliam Leave the Merrion Hotel, turn left and then right along Merrion Row. Walk around St Stephen's Green until you get to the Fitzwilliam (p198), which is the perfect place to kick off the boozing with a killer cocktail in hoity-toity style.

3 Dawson Lounge Retrace your steps back around the Green, take a left down Dawson St, then stop for a diminutive tipple in Dublin's smallest pub (p165).

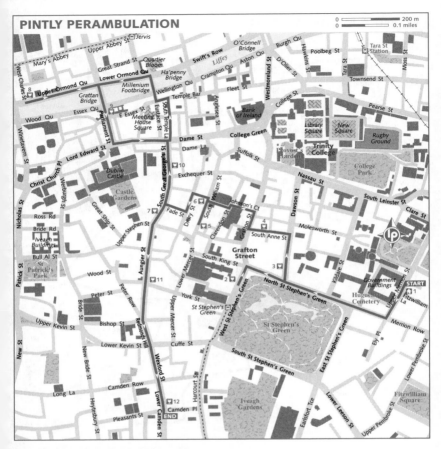

PINTLY PERAMBULATION

0 ——————— 200 m
0 ——————— 0.1 miles

WALK FACTS

Start **Merrion Hotel, Upper Merrion St**
End **Anseo, Camden St**
Distance **4km**
Duration **There's booze involved, so how long is a piece of string?**

4 Kehoe's Head north up Dawson St, take a left onto South Anne St and sink a pint of plain in one of the city centre's most atmospheric bars, Kehoe's (p165).

5 South William Turn right onto Grafton St, take a left onto Johnson's Ct and then another left into South William St. Head down to No

52 and order a drink in one of Dublin's coolest bars, South William (p164), the place to be seen.

6 Grogan's Castle Lounge Backtrack up South William St to No 15 to enjoy this pub (p165), favoured haunt of artists, frustrated writers and other bohemian types.

7 Long Hall Take a left onto Castle Market, left down Drury St and right onto Fade St. Cross South Great George's St and nip into the Long Hall (p165) to discuss the vicissitudes of life in a sombre Victorian setting.

8 Sin É Head up South Great George's St, and into South Temple Lane, cross the Millennium footbridge and turn left along the pleasant waterside boardwalk. Nearby is this narrow, deep bar (p171) with a big reputation for top-class music and a terrific night out.

9 Porterhouse Cross the Liffey at Grattan Bridge and stop for a tipple at our favourite of the quarter's drinking establishments (p168), which serves a range of great microbrews.

10 Globe Head south down Parliament St, turn left onto Dame St and then right onto South Great George's St. Stop off at the grand-daddy of Dublin's cool bars, the Globe (p164), still going strong.

11 Swan Stroll down South Great George's St, into Aungier St and pull up at the Swan (p166). Usually quiet and always beautiful, this terrific bar is very popular with locals and students from the nearby College of Surgeons.

12 Anseo Make the final push southwards, walking the length of the street until you get to Camden St and this seriously hip and totally unpretentious bar (p163) with fabulous DJs. If you've followed the tour correctly, you should no longer be referring to this guide. How many fingers?

TAKE A WALK ON THE NORTH SIDE

1 Mountjoy Square Start your walk in slightly dilapidated, yet elegant Mountjoy Sq, formerly one of Dublin's most beautiful and prestigious addresses.

2 St George's Church Take a left at the northwestern corner of the square and walk down Gardiner Pl, turning right onto North Temple St. Up ahead is this fine, but now deconsecrated Georgian church, designed by architect Francis Johnston (who lived close by in a now-demolished house at 64 Eccles St).

3 Abbey Presbyterian Church Take a left onto Hardwicke St and left again onto North Frederick St. On your right you'll spot this

WALK FACTS

Start Mountjoy Sq
End St Michan's Church, Church St
Distance 2.5km
Duration Two hours

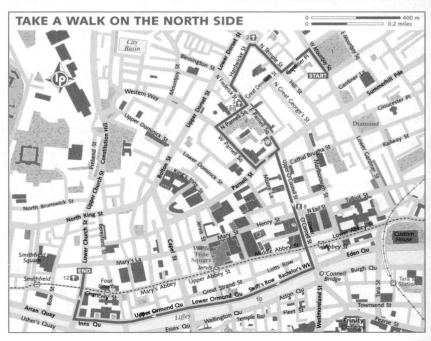

TAKE A WALK ON THE NORTH SIDE

125

distinctive building. Built in 1864, it's often referred to as Findlater's Church after the grocery magnate who financed the building's construction.

4 Garden of Remembrance The northern slice of Parnell Sq houses this garden (p111), opened in 1966 to commemorate the 50th anniversary of the 1916 Easter Rising.

5 Dublin City Gallery – The Hugh Lane North of the square, facing the park, is this excellent gallery (p101). Next door to the Dublin Writers Museum (p109), this is home to some of the best modern art in Europe as well as Francis Bacon's recreated studio.

6 Rotunda Hospital The southern part of Parnell Sq is occupied by this hospital (p111), a wonderful example of public architecture in the Georgian style, which was built in 1757.

7 Gate Theatre In the southeastern corner of the square is the Gate Theatre (p186). Part of the old Rotunda complex, it's now a major theatre for top-end drama.

8 Spire Head south down O'Connell St, passing by this 120m-high monument (p109). Erected in 2001, it has already become an iconic symbol of the city.

9 General Post Office On the other side of O'Connell St, this stunning neoclassical building (p107) towers over the street. Its role as HQ for the Easter Rising (p22) makes it an important historical site.

10 Ha'penny Bridge Head south until you hit the river, turn right and walk along the handsome boardwalk until you reach the city's most distinctive bridge (it got its name

from the charge that was levied on those who used it).

11 Four Courts Continue west along Ormond Quay to one of James Gandon's Georgian masterpieces (p106), home to the most important law courts in Ireland.

12 St Michan's Church Finally take a right onto Church St to admire this beautiful Georgian church (p110), with grisly vaults populated by the remains of the long departed.

ALONG THE GRAND CANAL

1 Portobello (☎ 475 2715; 33 South Richmond St) Begin at this popular watering hole, which was built to service the solid (and liquid) hungers of workers building the canal.

2 Portobello College Across the street is this technical college. Painter Jack B Yeats (1871–1957) – brother to William Butler – lived here in the years leading up to his death (see p45).

3 Patrick Kavanagh Statue Turn left at the Grand Canal and begin your stroll along the towpath. About 300m past Leeson St Bridge is the Kavanagh statue, relaxing on a bench. The Monaghan-born poet is immortalised in the spot he loved most in Dublin – where he couldn't get barred (see boxed text, left).

4 Searson's (☎ 660 0330; 42 Upper Baggot St) When you get to Baggot St Bridge take a right onto Baggot St and refuel at this popular bar.

5 St Stephen's Church Return to the canal and continue eastwards, diverting left at Mount St for St Stephen's Church (p83), a Greek Revival structure known as the 'Pepper Canister' on account of its curious shape.

6 National Print Museum Back on the towpath, turn right at Northumberland Rd and left onto Haddington Rd for this museum (p98). Housed in an old barracks, this is a surprisingly interesting museum, especially if you're a fan of old books.

7 Waterways Visitor Centre Turn left onto Upper Grand Canal St, then right into Grand Canal Quay for this centre (p100), where you can find out everything you could possibly want to know on the construction of the country's canals and waterways.

I'LL MEET YOU IN...

There's a famous story that tells of a meeting along the canal between Patrick Kavanagh and the hell-raising writer Brendan Behan. They chatted for a while, then Kavanagh suggested they go for a drink. He suggested a pub, to which Behan said 'no'. He was barred from that particular establishment, he explained, 'how about somewhere else?' Kavanagh asked Behan to recommend a spot, but when Behan did, Kavanagh demurely explained that *he* was barred from *that* pub. They shook hands and each went on their merry way.

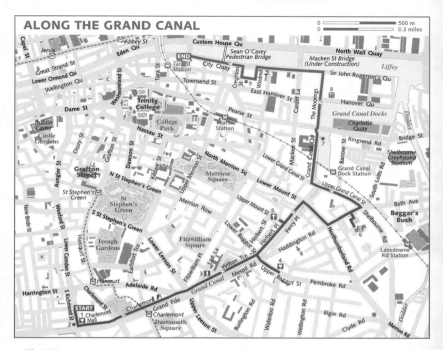

8 Ely HQ Before heading back to the city, stop for brunch or a drink at this supertrendy wine bar and restaurant (p155), which overlooks the Grand Canal Docks.

9 Windmill Lane Studios Walk north to Sir John Rogerson's Quay, turn left and left again at Windmill Lane. Here you'll find Dublin's very own Abbey Road Studios, where U2 have their offices and recorded all of their early records up to *The Unforgettable Fire*. Back on Roger-son's Quay, walk west along the quays and back into the city.

WALK FACTS

Start Portobello Pub, South Richmond St
End City Quay
Distance 5km
Duration Two to 2½ hours
Fuel Stop Searson's
Transport 🚊 Luas to Harcourt St, 🚌 16, 16A, 19, 19A, 65 or 83 from Trinity College & South Great George's St.

BLUELIST[1] (blu‚list) *v.*
to recommend a travel experience.
What's your recommendation? www.lonelyplanet.com/bluelist

SHOPPING

top picks

SHOPPING

It's official: Europe's busiest shopping street is...Dublin's very own Henry St, which gets an average of 16,000 people an hour, leaving Oxford St (London) and the Champs Elysées (Paris) in the ha'penny place. Retailers rejoice, but a stroll along the city's two main shopping strips on a Saturday afternoon will reveal a kind of manic madness as gaggles of teenagers, pram-pushing families, hurried couples and the odd elderly lady walk, push and shove their way up the street, their arms, prams and walking frames ladened down with bags full of stuff. Dubliners may have only recently acquired the kind of disposable income that makes retailers see them as ripe chickens ready for plucking, but the frantic nature of the city's shopping addiction suggests that they're far too busy making up for lost time to worry about next month's credit card bill.

Finding stuff to buy is not a struggle. If it's made in Ireland – or pretty much anywhere else – chances are you can find it here. Fashionistas can ogle at the Prada frocks in Brown Thomas, Dublin's most stylish department store, or head to the warren of streets west of Grafton St, Dublin's new epicentre of cool. It's lined with bars, espresso joints and more boutiques than you could shake a gold card at, and is a great spot to find designer gear by the Irish names mentioned previously. At its heart is Castle Market, where you can really let loose your retail chi.

Men's bespoke tailoring is rather thin on the ground. Designers have tried to instil a sense of classical style in the Dublin male, but the species doesn't seem too interested – any pressed shirt and leather shoe seems to suffice.

Not surprisingly, streetwear is very trendy and the most obvious buyers are the city's younger consumers, who pour into every midrange fashion outlet spread throughout the city centre and pore over the trendy, mass-produced clobber within. They spend their Saturdays, off-days and lunch hours ambling about Grafton St and its side streets on the south side, or Henry St and its surrounds on the far side of the Liffey; and then there's the consumer cathedral in the southern suburb of Dundrum, easily reached by Luas and open aggressively long hours, seven days a week. Stacked with every hot name in the retail black book it has raised the bar on shopping and turned it into a serious occupation.

At the other end of the fashion spectrum, you'll find all the knit and tweed you want at Avoca Handweavers (p132) or Blarney Woollen Mills (p134). But steer clear of that mass-produced junk whose joke value isn't worth the hassle of carting it home on the plane: trust us, there's no such thing as a genuine *shillelagh* (Irish fighting stick) for sale anywhere in town.

OPENING HOURS

The majority of the city's shops open 9.30am to 6pm Monday to Saturday. Thursday has late-night shopping, and most places stay open until 7pm or 8pm. With only a handful of exceptions, most shops also open from noon to 6pm on Sunday. Shopping centres keep the same hours with the rather pronounced exception of the Dundrum Town Centre, which opens until 9pm Monday to Friday and until 7pm on Saturday and Sunday.

DUTY FREE

Non-EU residents can claim VAT (Value Added Tax – a sales tax, around 20% of the purchase price) back on their purchases so long as the store operates either the Cashback or Taxback refund programme (they should display a sticker). You'll get a voucher with your purchase that must be stamped at the *last point of exit* from the EU. If you're travelling on to Britain or mainland Europe from Dublin, hold on to your voucher until you pass through your final customs stop in the EU; it can then be stamped and you can post it back for a refund of duty paid.

GRAFTON STREET & AROUND

Pedestrianised Grafton St has traditionally been *the* shopping street – but despite the sprinkling of older Dublin shops, the preponderance of British-owned chain stores means that you'll find the same kind of stuff you'll find almost anywhere else. To really get the most of the area's retail allure, it's best to get off Grafton St and head into the grid of streets surrounding it, especially to the west, where you'll find some of Dublin's most interesting outlets, from book stores to boutiques, as well as two extraordinary shopping centres. The Victorian structure of George's St Arcade houses a wonderful collection of pokey little shops and stalls while the exquisite Powerscourt Townhouse Shopping Centre is Dublin's most prestigious shopping mall.

BLUE ERIU   Map pp66–7   Beauty
☎ 672 5776; www.nueblueeriu.com; 7 South William St; ☯ 10am-6pm Mon & Fri-Sat, 10am-8pm Tue-Thu; 🚌 all city-centre
Less of a cosmetics shop and more a beauty experience with a Celtic twist, this supertrendy retreat serves up one of the best facials in town (or so we're told); the products used are strictly from the top shelf, including Kiehls, Chantecaille and Shu Uemura.

CATHACH BOOKS   Map pp66–7   Books
☎ 671 8676; www.rarebooks.ie; 10 Duke St; ☯ 9.30am-5.45pm Mon-Sat; 🚌 all cross-city
Our favourite bookshop in the city stocks a rich and remarkable collection of Irish-interest books, with a particular emphasis on 20th-century literature, including some rare first editions by the big guns: Joyce, Yeats, Beckett and Wilde.

DUBRAY BOOKS   Map pp66–7   Books
☎ 677 5568; 36 Grafton St; ☯ 10am-6pm Mon-Sat, to 8pm Thu, noon-6pm Sun; 🚌 all cross-city
Three roomy floors devoted to bestsellers, recent releases, coffee-table books and a huge travel section make this one of the better bookshops in town. It can't compete with its larger, British-owned rivals, but it holds its own with a helpful staff and a lovely atmosphere that encourages you to linger.

EASON'S – HANNA'S BOOKSHOP
Map pp66–7   Books
☎ 677 1255; 27-29 Nassau St; ☯ 9.30am-6pm Mon-Sat, to 8pm Thu, noon-6pm Sun; 🚌 all cross-city
It's across the street from the side entrance to Trinity College, so conveniently this large bookshop specialises in academic tomes, but you'll also find a good selection of other books. In the basement is a massive stationery shop.

HODGES FIGGIS   Map pp66–7   Books
☎ 677 4754; www.hodgesfiggis.ie; 57 Dawson St; ☯ 9.30am-7pm Mon-Sat, to 8pm Thu, noon-6pm Sun; 🚌 all cross-city
The mother of all Dublin bookstores has books on every conceivable subject for every kind of reader spread across its three huge floors, including a substantial Irish section (fiction, history, contemporary issues) on the ground floor.

MURDER INK   Map pp66–7   Books
☎ 677 7570; 15 Dawson St; ☯ 10am-5.30pm Mon-Sat, noon-5pm Sun; 🚌 all cross-city
All manner of murder mystery and crime novels are in this small specialist bookstore, which has categorisation down to a fine art – choose from historical mystery, romantic crime, sci-fi mystery, true crime and more.

STOKES BOOKS   Map pp66–7   Books
☎ 671 3584; 19 George's St Arcade; ☯ 11am-6pm Mon-Sat; 🚌 all cross-city
A small bookshop specialising in Irish history books, both old and new. Other titles, covering a range of subjects, include a number of beautiful, old, leather-bound editions.

WATERSTONE'S   Map pp66–7   Books
☎ 679 1415; 7 Dawson St; ☯ 9am-7pm Mon-Sat, to 8pm Thu, noon-6pm Sun; 🚌 all cross-city
Although it is large and multistoreyed, Waterstone's somehow manages to maintain that snugly, hide-in-a-corner ambience that book lovers adore. The broad selection of books is supplemented by five bookcases of Irish fiction, as well as poetry, drama, politics and history. There are book-signings every Thursday evening; check the board outside for details. There's also a lovely café on the 2nd floor.

GREAT OUTDOORS
Map pp66–7   Camping & Outdoors
☎ 679 4293; 20 Chatham St; ☯ 9.30am-5.30pm Mon-Sat, to 8pm Thu; 🚌 all cross-city
This is Dublin's best outdoors store, with gear for hiking, camping, surfing, mountaineering, swimming and more. Fleeces, tents, inflatable dinghies, boots and gas cookers – they're all here as well as an info-laden noticeboard and a superbly patient staff.

DECENT CIGAR EMPORIUM

Map pp66–7   Cigars

☎ 671 6451; 46 Grafton St; ⏰ 10am-6pm Mon-Sat, to 8pm Thu, 1.30-5.30pm Sun; 🚌 all city-centre

When the clamour of Grafton St gets too much, slip up this discreet staircase, recline in a plush leather armchair and run your nose along a sweet hand-rolled, long-filler cigar over a glass of decent red wine or a cup of Illy coffee. In a country that has a smoking ban, this is indeed a rare pleasure.

AVOCA HANDWEAVERS

Map pp66–7   Department Store & Irish Crafts

☎ 677 4215; www.avoca.ie; 11-13 Suffolk St; ⏰ 10am-6pm Mon-Sat, to 8pm Thu, 11am-6pm Sun; 🚌 all cross-city

Combining clothing, homewares, a basement food hall and an excellent top-floor café (p149), Avoca promotes a stylish but homey brand of modern Irish life – and is one of the best places to find an original present. Many of the garments are woven, knitted and naturally dyed at its Wicklow factory. The children's section, with unusual knits, fairy outfits, bee-covered gumboots and dinky toys, is fantastic.

BROWN THOMAS Map pp66–7 Department Store

☎ 605 6666; www.brownthomas.ie; 88-95 Grafton St; ⏰ 9am-8pm Mon-Fri, to 9pm Thu, to 7pm Sat, 10am-6pm Sun; 🚌 all cross-city

Soak up the Jo Malone–laden rarefied atmosphere of Dublin's most exclusive store, where presentation is virtually artistic. Here you'll find fantastic cosmetics, shoes to die for, exotic homewares and a host of Irish and international fashion labels such as Balenciaga, Stella McCartney, Lainey Keogh and Philip Treacy. The 3rd-floor Bottom Drawer outlet stocks the finest Irish linen you'll find anywhere.

DUNNES STORES Map pp66–7 Department Store

☎ 671 4629; 62 Grafton St; ⏰ 9am-6.30pm Mon-Sat, to 9pm Thu, noon-6pm Sun; 🚌 all cross-city, 🚇 St Stephen's Green

A favourite choice with Irish mothers for its affordable everyday family clothing. The Savida fashion range is remarkably on the pulse though and their excellent homewares department is giving Habitat a run for its money. Look for branches across the city including the new Home (Map pp66–7; ☎ 415 5044; South Great Georges St).

MARKS & SPENCER

Map pp66–7   Department Store

☎ 679 7855; 15-20 Grafton St; ⏰ 9am-6.30pm Mon-Sat, to 9pm Thu, noon-6pm Sun; 🚌 all cross-city

Good-quality clothing and virtually everything else that the body and house might need – at affordable prices – make this British chain store one of Dublin's most popular. There's a supermarket in the basement and a popular café on the ground floor.

ALIAS TOM Map pp66–7   Fashion & Designer

☎ 671 5443; Duke Lane; ⏰ 9.30am-6pm Mon-Sat, to 8pm Thu; 🚌 all cross-city

Dublin's best designer menswear store, where friendly staff guide you through casuals by bling labels Burberry and YSL Rive Gauche. Downstairs it's classic tailored suits and Patrick Cox shoes.

AVE MARIA Map pp66–7   Fashion & Designer

☎ 671 8229; 38 Clarendon St; ⏰ 9.30am-6pm Mon-Sat, to 8pm Thu; 🚌 all cross-city

If Tina Turner were in Dublin, she'd shop here. Glam up with neon net, sequinned and satin cocktail dresses from Queenie, Manoush and Consumer Guide, and some seriously bling costume jewels.

BT2 Map pp66–7   Fashion & Designer

☎ 605 6666; www.brownthomas.ie; 28-29 Grafton St; ⏰ 9am-6.30pm Mon-Sat, to 9pm Thu, to 7pm Sat, 10am-6.30pm Sun; 🚌 all cross-city

The kiddies' table in Brown Thomas' exquisitely laid-out dining room, BT2 is the annexe shop for the city's trendy young things, targeting an audience who want to look the contemporary part and set the tone for tomorrow. Brands include DKNY, Custom, Diesel, Ted Baker and Tommy Hilfiger.

CIRCUS STORE & GALLERY

Map pp66–7   Fashion & Designer

☎ 672 4736; www.circusstoreandgallery.com; 2nd fl, Powerscourt Townhouse Shopping Centre; ⏰ 10am-6pm Mon-Sat, to 8pm Thu; 🚌 all cross-city

If you are looking for the most elegant, one-off creations by Irish designers – from dresses for that fancy occasion to pins to tie up your hair – and fancy looking at some contemporary local art in the meantime, this wonderful new shop is perfect for you. You mightn't know any of the designers

HELEN JAMES, DESIGNER

Dublin-born designer Helen James, who cut her teeth cutting cloth for the likes of Donna Karan, Katayone Adeli and Club Monaco in New York, loves her boutiques and Dublin has enough to satisfy.

'My favourite shops are Costume (below), Smock (p137) and 5 Scarlett Row (p137). They're all great shops because they're imbued with the personality of their owners, who in turn make sure that the items they stock suit the shop and the customers who frequent them. As a shopper, you know that the boutique owner has you in mind when they go on buying trips.'

Her favourite Irish designers? Helen is quick to list them off: Leighlee, Eilis Boyle, Lucy Downes of Sphere One, Tim Ryan and Joanne Hynes. They're all talents who, with the exception of Joanne Hynes, have yet to really make an international splash – but their time will come.

Outside the city centre, Helen rates Havana (p138) in Donnybrook as one of the best boutiques in Ireland, and the place where you will find some of her favourite names in fashion. And with that, she was off to her favourite non-clothing shop, Fallon & Byrne, for some Aunt Jemima pancake mix.

represented here, but that's only because they're still busy making their time come.

COSTUME
Map pp66–7   Fashion & Designer
☎ 679 4188; 10-11 Castle Market; ☽ 10am-6pm Mon-Sat, to 7pm Thu, 2-6pm Sun; 🚌 all cross-city
Costume is considered a genuine pacesetter by Dublin's fashionistas; it has exclusive contracts with some of Europe's most innovative designers, such as Isabel Marant and Anna Sui. It also has the city's best range of Tempereley and American Retro. Local designers represented here are Helen James, whose Japanese-influenced obis are enormously popular, and Leighlee.

KILKENNY SHOP
Map pp66–7   Fashion & Designer, Irish Crafts
☎ 677 7066; www.kilkennyshop.com; 6 Nassau St; ☽ 8.30am-6pm Mon-Fri, to 8pm Thu, 9am-6pm Sat, 11am-6pm Sun; 🚌 all cross-city
A large long-running repository for contemporary, innovative Irish crafts, including multicoloured, modern Irish knits, designer clothing, Orla Kiely bags and some lovely silver jewellery. The glassware and pottery is beautiful and sourced from workshops around the country. A great source for presents.

LOUIS COPELAND
Map pp66–7   Fashion & Designer
☎ 872 1600; www.louiscopeland.com; 18-19 Wicklow St; ☽ 9am-5.30pm Mon-Sat, to 7.30pm Thu; 🚌 all cross-city
Dublin's answer to the famed tailors of London's Saville Row, this shop makes fabulous suits to measure, but also stocks plenty of ready-to-wear suits by a host of international designers.

TULLE
Map pp66–7   Fashion & Designer
☎ 679 9115; 29 George's St Arcade; ☽ 10am-6pm Mon-Sat, to 8pm Thu; 🚌 all cross-city
International designers with attitude – Sass and Bide, Wheels & Doll Baby, plus Fornarina and Sonia Rykiel – are stocked in this small outlet for fashion-savvy young gals, tucked away in the arcade. Don't be fooled by the plain frontage; this place is seriously cool.

ASIA MARKET
Map pp66–7   Food & Drink
☎ 677 9764; 18 Drury St; ☽ 10am-7pm Mon-Sat; 🚌 all cross-city
This large, friendly food emporium should be your first port of call if you want to whip up an Oriental feast. For a start it's really good value and you'll find everything here from kitchen implements to hard-to-come-by ingredients like grass jelly, habanero chillies, brown basmati rice or – should you wish – chicken's feet.

BRETZEL BAKERY
Map pp66–7   Food & Drink
☎ 475 2724; 1a Lennox St ☽ 8.30am-3pm Mon, 8.30am-6pm Tue, Wed & Fri, 8.30am-7pm Thu, 9am-5pm Sat, 9am-1pm Sun; 🚌 14, 15, 65, 83
The bagels might be a bit on the chewy side, but they've got their charms – as do the scrumptious selections of breads, savoury snacks, cakes and biscuits that have locals queuing out the door on weekends. Recertified as kosher since 2003, the bakery has been on this Portobello site since 1870.

FALLON & BYRNE
Map pp66–7   Food & Drink
☎ 472 1000; Exchequer St; ☽ 9.30am-7pm Mon-Sat, noon-6pm Sun; 🚌 18, 83
This upmarket food hall in the style of New York's Dean & Deluca falls short of

that Manhattan holy grail but still offers an abundance of delectable edibles such as white truffles from Alba, 30-year old balsamic vinegar and Wicklow organic veg. Downstairs, a marvellous wine cellar dispenses bottles for every occasion.

MAGILLS Map pp66–7 Food
☎ 671 3830; 14 Clarendon St ⏱ 9.30am-5.45pm Mon-Sat; 🚌 all cross-city, 🚊 St Stephen's Green
With its characterful old façade and tiny dark interior, Magills' old-world charm reminds you how Clarendon St must have once looked. At this family-run place, you get the distinct feeling that every Irish and French cheese, olive oil, packet of Italian pasta and salami was hand-picked.

SHERIDAN'S CHEESEMONGERS
Map pp66–7 Food
☎ 679 3143; 11 South Anne St; ⏱ 10am-6pm Mon-Fri, from 9.30am Sat; 🚌 all cross-city
If heaven were a cheese shop, this would be it. Wooden shelves are laden with rounds of farmhouse cheeses, sourced from around the country by Kevin and Seamus Sheridan, who have almost single-handedly revived cheese-making in Ireland. You can taste any one of the 60 cheeses on display and pick up some wild Irish salmon, Italian pastas and olives while you're at it.

BLARNEY WOOLLEN MILLS
Map pp66–7 Irish Crafts
☎ 671 0068; www.blarney.com; 21-23 Nassau St; ⏱ 9am-6pm Mon-Sat, 11am-6pm Sun; 🚌 all cross-city
This is the Dublin branch of the best-known Irish shop in the country – the actual mills are located in County Cork, within sight of the famous castle and its gab-bestowing rock. This branch shouldn't disappoint, with a particularly wide range of cut crystal, porcelain presents and its trademark woolly things.

CRAFTS COUNCIL GALLERY
Map pp66–7 Irish Crafts
☎ 679 7368; Powerscourt Townhouse Shopping Centre; ⏱ 10am-6pm Mon-Sat, to 8pm Thu, 11am-6pm Sun; 🚌 all cross-city
One of several craft shops in the Powerscourt building, this gallery has a fine selection of glassware, pottery and jewellery, although you'll need a flexible credit card.

HOUSE OF NAMES Map pp66–7 Irish Crafts
☎ 679 7287; www.houseofnames.ie; 26 Nassau St; ⏱ 10am-6pm Mon-Sat, to 8pm Thu, 11am-6pm Sun; 🚌 all cross-city
Impress your friends by serving them drinks on coasters emblazoned with your family's coat of arms, matching the sweatshirt you're wearing and, of course, the glasses or mugs your drinks are served in. All this and more can be yours from the House of Names, so long as you have a surname with Irish roots.

KNOBS & KNOCKERS Map pp66–7 Irish Crafts
☎ 671 0288; www.knobsandknockers.ie; 19 Nassau St; ⏱ 10am-6pm Mon-Sat, to 8pm Thu, 11am-6pm Sun; 🚌 all cross-city
Replica Georgian door-knockers are highly recommended as a great souvenir of your Dublin visit, but there are plenty of other souvenir door adornments to look at here.

ANGLES Map pp66–7 Jewellery
☎ 679 1964; Westbury Mall; ⏱ 10am-6pm Mon-Sat, to 7pm Thu; 🚌 all cross-city
You won't find Claddagh rings or charm bracelets here, just cabinets full of hand-made, contemporary Irish jewellery, most of it by up-and-coming Dublin craftspeople. Commissions are taken and can be sent on to you abroad.

APPLEBY Map pp66–7 Jewellery
☎ 679 9572; 5-6 Johnson's Ct; ⏱ 9.30am-5.30pm Mon-Sat, to 7pm Thu, to 6pm Sat; 🚌 all cross-city
The best known of the jewellery shops that line narrow Johnson's Court, Appleby's is renowned for the high quality of its gold and silver jewellery, which tends towards more conventional designs. This is the place to shop for serious stuff – diamond rings, sapphire-encrusted cufflinks and Raymond Weil watches.

BARRY DOYLE DESIGN JEWELLERS
Map pp66–7 Jewellery
☎ 671 2838; 30 George's St Arcade; ⏱ 10am-6pm Mon-Sat, to 7pm Thu; 🚌 all cross-city
Goldsmith Barry Doyle's upstairs shop is one of the best of its kind in Dublin. The handmade jewellery – using white gold, silver, and some truly gorgeous precious and semiprecious stones – is exceptional in its beauty and simplicity. Most of the pieces have Afro-Celtic influences.

VIVIEN WALSH Map pp66–7 — Jewellery
☎ 475 5031; Lower 24 Stephen St; ⏰ 11am-6pm Mon-Fri, to 7pm Thu, 10am-6pm Sat; 🚌 15, 16, 19, 83

One of Ireland's best-known jewellery designers, Vivien Walsh uses Swarovski crystal, glass, feathers, pearls and beads to create delicate, fantastical pieces that hark back to the 1920s and beyond. The elaborate necklaces, in vivid turquoise, pink, purple and green, are quite an investment, but simple bracelets can be had for under €40. French and Italian leather bags and shoes complement the displays.

WEIR & SON'S Map pp66–7 — Jewellery
☎ 677 9678; www.weirandsons.ie; 96-99 Grafton St; ⏰ 9am-5.30pm Mon-Sat, to 8pm Thu; 🚌 all cross-city

The largest jeweller in Ireland, this huge store on Grafton St first opened in 1869 and still has its original wooden cabinets and a workshop on the premises. There's new and antique Irish jewellery (including Celtic designs) and a huge selection of watches, Irish crystal, porcelain, leather and travel goods.

HMV Map pp66–7 — Music
☎ 679 5334; www.hmv.co.uk; 65 Grafton St; ⏰ 9am-7pm Mon-Wed & Sat, to 9pm Thu, to 8pm Fri, 11am-7pm Sun; 🚌 all cross-city

This giant entertainment retailer's main Dublin branch stocks CDs, vinyl, DVDs, games and even books across its three floors. It's exactly what you'd expect from a huge music store.

ROAD RECORDS Map pp66–7 — Music
☎ 671 7340; www.roadrecs.com; 16 Fade St; ⏰ 10am-6pm Mon-Sat, to 7pm Thu; 🚌 all cross-city

This small record shop, just south of the George's St Arcade, has all the latest indie sounds, both local and international. It's also a good place to get tickets for local gigs.

WALTON'S Map pp66–7 — Music
☎ 475 0661; 69-70 South Great George's St; ⏰ 9am-6pm Mon-Sat, to 7pm Thu; 🚌 all cross-city

This is the place to go if you're looking for your very own *bodhrán* (goat-skin drum) or indeed any other musical instrument

top picks

GUARANTEED IRISH

You want to buy something Irish-made to take home? This is our quick pick.
- Avoca Handweavers (p132) Our favourite department store in the city has myriad homemade gift ideas.
- Barry Doyle Design Jewellers (opposite) Exquisite handcrafted jewellery with unique contemporary designs.
- Cathach Books (p131) For that priceless 1st edition or a beautiful, leather-bound copy of Joyce's *Dubliners*.
- Louis Copeland (p133) Dublin's very own top tailor with his made-to-measure suits.
- Costume (p133) Elegance, originality and sophistication – and that's just the Irish designers represented at this fabulous shop.

associated with Irish traditional music. It also has an excellent selection of sheet music and recorded music.

DUBLIN CAMERA EXCHANGE
Map pp66–7 — Photography
☎ 478 4125; www.cameraexchange.ie; 63 South Great George's St; ⏰ 9am-6pm Mon-Sat, to 7pm Thu; 🚌 all city-centre

This is one of the best photographic equipment shops in town and a reputable developer of prints. Staff are friendly and knowledgeable, and will usually assist in answering any camera-related query, even if the equipment is not bought here. They have a smaller branch (Map pp66–7; ☎ 679 3410; 9B Trinity St) that also opens on Sunday from 1 to 5pm.

GEORGE'S ST ARCADE
Map pp66–7 — Shopping Arcade
www.georgesstreetarcade.ie; btwn South Great George's St & Drury St; ⏰ 9am-6.30pm Mon-Sat, to 8pm Thu, noon-6pm Sun; 🚌 all cross-city

Dublin's best nonfood market (there's sadly not much competition) is sheltered within an elegant Victorian Gothic arcade. Apart from shops and stalls selling new and old clothes, second-hand books, hats, posters, jewellery and records, there's a fortune teller, some gourmet nibbles and a fish and chipper who does a roaring trade.

WESTBURY MALL Map pp66–7 Shopping Arcade
Clarendon St; ⏰ **10am-6pm Mon-Sat, noon-5pm Sun;** 🚃 **all cross-city**
Wedged between the five-star Westbury Hotel and the expensive jewellery stores of Johnson's Ct, this small mall has a handful of pricey, specialist shops selling everything from Persian rugs to buttons and lace or tasteful children's wooden toys.

POWERSCOURT TOWNHOUSE SHOPPING CENTRE Map pp66–7 Shopping Centre
☎ **679 4144; 59 South William St;** ⏰ **10am-6.30pm Mon-Sat, to 9pm Thu, noon-6pm Sun;** 🚃 **all cross-city**
This absolutely gorgeous and stylish centre is in a carefully refurbished Georgian townhouse, originally built between 1741 and 1744 (see p76). These days it's best known for its cafés and restaurants but it still does a top-end, selective trade in high fashion, art, exquisite handicrafts and other chichi sundries.

ST STEPHEN'S GREEN SHOPPING CENTRE Map pp66–7 Shopping Centre
☎ **478 0888; King St S & St Stephen's Green;** ⏰ **9am-6pm Mon-Sat, to 9pm Thu, noon-6pm Sun;** 🚃 **all cross-city,** 🚈 **St Stephen's Green**
A 1980s version of a 19th-century shopping arcade, the dramatic, balconied interior and central courtyard are a bit too grand for the nondescript chain stores within. There's a Boots, Benetton and large Dunnes Store with supermarket though, as well as last-season designer warehouse TK Maxx.

HARLEQUIN Map pp66–7 Vintage Clothing & Accessories
☎ **671 0202; 13 Castle Market;** ⏰ **10.30am-6pm Mon-Sat, to 7pm Thu;** 🚃 **all cross-city**
A fantastically cluttered shop, jam-packed with authentic vintage clothing gems from the 1920s onwards as well as satin gloves, top hats, snakeskin bags and jet-beaded chokers.

JENNY VANDER Map pp66–7 Vintage Clothing & Accessories
☎ **677 0406; 50 Drury St;** ⏰ **10am-5.45pm Mon-Sat;** 🚃 **all cross-city**
More *Breakfast at Tiffany's* chic than the cast-offs from *Hair,* this second-hand store oozes elegance and sophistication. Discerning fashionistas and film stylists snap

up the exquisite beaded handbags, fur-trimmed coats, richly patterned dresses and costume jewellery priced as if it were the real thing.

MERRION SQUARE & AROUND

Isn't there enough shopping for you around Grafton St? Intrepid retail junkies who find themselves lost in officeland around Merrion Sq will be rewarded with one stand-out spot.

TOWER CRAFT DESIGN CENTRE Map pp78–9 Irish Crafts
☎ **677 5655; Pearse St;** ⏰ **9.30am-6pm Mon-Sat, to 8pm Thu;** 🚃 **all cross-city**
Housed in a 19th-century warehouse that was Dublin's first iron-structured building, this design centre has studios for local craftspeople. They produce jewellery in both contemporary and Celtic-inspired designs, and work with Irish pewter, ceramics, silk and other fabrics. Besides jewellery they knock out pottery, rugs, wall hangings, cards, leather bags and various other hand-crafted items. It's immediately opposite the Waterways Visitors Centre, off Lower Grand Canal St.

TEMPLE BAR

Dublin's most touristy neighbourhood has a pretty diverse mix of shops. Apart from the usual crap you might expect to find in any tourist trap, Temple Bar's stores traditionally specialise in pedalling secondhand clothing and flogging the weird and the (sometimes) wonderful; it's a place where you can get everything from a Celtic-design wall-hanging to a handcrafted bong. In recent years, however, the western end of the quarter has been developed and a number of new shops have opened up, mostly of the high-end luxury design kind, with prices to boot. A couple of Dublin's best markets take place in this area on Saturday (for more information see the boxed text, p139).

5 SCARLETT ROW
Map p85   Fashion & Designer, Shoes
☎ 672 9534; 5 Scarlett Row; ☻ 10am-6pm Mon-Sat, to 7pm Thu; 🚌 all cross-city
Beautiful, modern, exclusive, minimalist. If that's what you're after, try the creations of Eley Kishimoto, Zero, Irish designer Sharon Wauchob or menswear label Unis. Co-owner Eileen Shields worked with Donna Karan in New York before returning to found her own gorgeous shoe label, which retails here.

SMOCK Map p85   Fashion & Designer
☎ 613 9000; Smock Alley Ct, West Essex St; ☻ 10.30am-6pm Mon-Fri, 10am-6pm Sat; 🚌 all cross-city
This tiny designer shop sells quirky (and very exclusive) international women's-wear from investment labels Easton Pearson, Veronique Branquinho and AF Vandevorft, as well as a small range of interesting jewellery. Rumour has it that it might be moving to Drury St, closer to the action.

URBAN OUTFITTERS Map p85   Fashion & Music
☎ 670 6202; 4 Cecilia St; 🚌 all cross-city
With a blaring techno soundtrack, the only Irish branch of this American chain sells ridiculously cool clothes to discerning young buyers. Besides clothing, the shop stocks all kinds of interesting gadgets, accessories and furniture. On the 2nd floor you'll find a hypertrendy record shop (hence the techno).

DESIGNYARD Map p85   Irish Crafts, Jewellery
☎ 474 1011; Cow's Lane; ☻ 9.30am-6.30pm Mon-Fri, to 8pm Thu, 9am-6.30pm Sat, 10am-6pm Sun; 🚌 all cross-city
A high-end, craft-as-art shop where everything you see – glass, batik, sculpture, painting – is a one-off and handmade in Ireland. It also showcases contemporary jewellery stock from young international designers.

BIG BROTHER RECORDS Map p85   Music
☎ 672 9355; www.bigbrotherrecords.com; 4 Crow St; ☻ 11am-7pm Mon-Fri, to 8pm Thu, to 6pm Sat; 🚌 all cross-city
DJs, vinyl junkies and other creatures of the night can seek solace and the latest house, hip hop or dance groove in this basement store (beneath All-City Records) that never, ever sees daylight. And it's just the way they like it.

CLADDAGH RECORDS Map p85   Music
☎ 677 0262; www.claddaghrecords.com; 2 Cecilia St; 🚌 all cross-city
An excellent collection of good-quality traditional and folk music is the mainstay at this centrally located record shop. The profoundly knowledgeable staff should be able to locate even that elusive recording for you.

MUSEUM SHOPS

Most museums have a basic gift shop, but you'll find a few in Dublin that offer more than the usual baubles and trinkets, including the following.

Chester Beatty Library (p70; Dublin Castle) A wonderful little gift shop, with postcards, books, posters and other memorabilia of this extraordinary museum.

Dublin City Gallery – The Hugh Lane Shop (p101; Charlemont House, Parnell Sq N) A cultural playground for adults, where you can dig out cubist fridge magnets, huge po-mo hanging mobiles, masterpiece colour-by-number prints, cloth puppets, unusual wooden toys and beautiful art and pop culture hardbacks.

Irish Museum of Modern Art (p96; Military Rd) Offers a comprehensive selection of coffee-table books on Irish contemporary art.

National Gallery (p79; Merrion Sq) Sells books covering the whole history of Irish and European art.

Trinity Library Shop (Map p65; East Pavilion, Library Colonnades, Trinity College) The big sellers are the titles on the Book of Kells, but you can also get all kinds of other mementos and curios.

CLOTHING SIZES

Women's clothing

Aus/UK	8	10	12	14	16	18
Europe	36	38	40	42	44	46
Japan	5	7	9	11	13	15
USA	6	8	10	12	14	16

Women's shoes

Aus/USA	5	6	7	8	9	10
Europe	35	36	37	38	39	40
France only	35	36	38	39	40	42
Japan	22	23	24	25	26	27
UK	3½	4½	5½	6½	7½	8½

Men's clothing

Aus	92	96	100	104	108	112
Europe	46	48	50	52	54	56
Japan	S		M	M		L
UK/USA	35	36	37	38	39	40

Men's shirts (collar sizes)

Aus/Japan	38	39	40	41	42	43
Europe	38	39	40	41	42	43
UK/USA	15	15½	16	16½	17	17½

Men's shoes

Aus/UK	7	8	9	10	11	12
Europe	41	42	43	44½	46	47
Japan	26	27	27½	28	29	30
USA	7½	8½	9½	10½	11½	12½

Measurements approximate only, try before you buy

FLIP Map p85   Vintage Clothing

☎ 671 4299; 4 Upper Fownes St; ☼ 10am-6pm Mon-Wed & Fri, 10am-7pm Thu & Sat, 1.30-6pm Sun; 🚌 all cross-city

This hip Irish label takes the best male fashion moods of the 1950s and serves them back to us, minus the mothball smell. US college shirts, logo T-shirts, Oriental and Hawaiian shirts, Fonz-style leather jackets and well-cut jeans mix it with the genuine second-hand gear upstairs.

KILMAINHAM & THE LIBERTIES

Some of the most interesting – and wackiest – shopping is done along Francis St in the Liberties, the home of antiquarians and art dealers of every hue. Although you mightn't fancy transporting the hand luggage, you can have that original Edwardian fireplace you've always wanted, shipped to you by the shop.

FLEURY ANTIQUES Map pp90–1   Antiques

☎ 473 0878; www.fleuryantiques.com; 57 Francis St; ☼ 9.30am-6pm Mon-Sat; 🚌 123, 206, 51B

This blue-fronted antiques shop does a steady connoisseur's trade in all manner of oil paintings (there's something for virtually every taste), vases, candelabras, silverware, porcelain and decorative pieces from the 18th century right up to the 1930s.

O'SULLIVAN ANTIQUES Map pp90–1 Antiques

☎ 454 1143; 43-44 Francis St; ☼ 10am-5pm Mon-Sat; 🚌 123, 206, 51B

Fine furniture and furnishings from the Georgian, Victorian and Edwardian eras are the specialty of this respected antiques shop, where a rummage might also reveal some distinctive bits of ceramic and crystal, not to mention medals and uniforms from a bygone era that will win you first prize at the costume ball.

OXFAM HOME Map pp90–1   Antiques

☎ 402 0555; 86 Francis St; ☼ 10am-5.30pm Mon-Fri, 10am-1pm Sat; 🚌 123, 206, 51B

They say charity begins at home so get rummaging among the veneer cast-offs in this furniture branch of the charity chain where you might stumble across the odd 1960s Subbuteo table or Art Deco dresser. Esoteric vinyl from the '80s is another speciality of the house.

BEYOND THE GRAND CANAL

Every suburban village has its own little shopping centre, but only one can rule them all... Apart from Dundrum, there's also one of the city's best fashion boutiques.

HAVANA Off Map p99   Fashion & Designer

☎ 260 2707; 2 Anglesea House, 68 Donnybrook Rd; ☼ 10am-5.30pm Mon-Fri, 10am-1pm Sat; 🚌 7, 7B, 8

This is as exclusive as Dublin fashion boutiques get, but the rewards for a trek out here are the best of Irish design – Lucy Downe's Sphere One cashmeres, Joanne Hynes' elegant evening wear – as well as a host of other top international names. Shoes, jewellery and accessories fill out the rest of the stock.

DUNDRUM TOWN CENTRE

Off Map p99   Shopping Centre

☎ 299 1700; www.dundrum.ie; Sandyford Rd, Dundrum; ⏰ 9am-9pm Mon-Fri, to 7pm Sat, 10am-7pm Sun; ⛟ Dundrum or Ballaly, 🚌 bus 17, 44C, 48A or 75 from city centre

Europe's largest shopping and entertainment centre is either globalisation's hideous hydra or the greatest thing to happen to retail since the invention of money. There are more than 100 retail outlets, including virtually every imaginable high street shop, cinemas, restaurants and bars, baby-changing rooms and even a crèche so that you can keep the tiny 'uns amused while you load up on gear. A whole generation of Dubliners will grow up in its enormous shadow, the first true Dublin mall rats.

NORTH OF THE LIFFEY

With only a handful of exceptions, northside shopping is all about the high street chain store and the easy-access shopping centre, which is mighty convenient for Dubliners looking for everyday wear at decent prices, but will hardly make for a satisfying long-distance retail pilgrimage. But if you want to do as Dubliners do…

EASON'S Map pp102–3   Books

☎ 873 3811; 40 Lower O'Connell St; 🚌 all cross-city

The biggest selection of magazines and foreign newspapers in the whole country can be found on the ground floor of this huge bookshop near the GPO, along with literally dozens of browsers leafing through mags with ne'er a thought of purchasing one.

WINDING STAIR Map pp102–3   Books

☎ 873 3292; 40 Lower Ormond Quay; ⏰ 9.30am-6pm Mon-Sat; 🚌 all cross-city

There was a public outcry when this creaky old place closed a few years ago. It's just reopened its doors and Dublin's bohemians, students and literati can once more thumb the fine selection of new and

---

DUBLIN MARKETS

In recent years Dublin has gone gaga for markets. Which is kind of ironic, considering that the city's traditional markets, like Moore St, were ignored by those same folks who now can't get enough of the homemade hummus on sale at the new gourmet spots. It's all so…continental.

Blackrock Market (off Map pp62-3; Main St, Blackrock; ⏰ 11am-5.30pm Sat, 10am-5.30pm Sun; ⛟ Blackrock) The long-running Blackrock Market takes place in an old merchant house and yard in the seaside village, and has all manner of stalls selling everything from New Age crystals to futons.

Book Fair (Map p85; Temple Bar Sq; ⏰ 10am-5pm Sat) Bad, secondhand potboilers, sci-fi books, picture books and other assorted titles invite you to rummage about on Saturday afternoons. If you look hard enough, you're bound to find something worthwhile.

Cow's Lane Market (Map p85; ⏰ 10am-5.30pm Sat) A real market for hipsters, on the steps of Cow's Lane, this market brings together over 60 of the best clothing, accessory and craft stalls in town. Buy cutting-edge designer duds from the likes of Drunk Monk, punky T-shirts, retro handbags, costume jewellery by Kink Bijoux and even clubby baby-wear. It's open from June to September; the rest of the year it moves indoors to St Michael's and St John's Banquet Hall, just around the corner.

Meeting House Square Market (Map p85; Meeting House Sq; ⏰ 10am-5pm Sat) From sushi to salsa, this is the city's best open-air food market, a compact stroll through gourmet lane where you can pick, prod and poke your way through the organic foods of the world. There are tastes of everywhere, from cured Spanish chorizos and paellas to Irish farmhouses cheeses, via handmade chocolates and freshly made crepes, homemade jams and freshly squeezed juices.

Moore Street Market (Map pp102-3; Moore St; ⏰ 8am-4pm Mon-Sat) An open-air, steadfastly 'Old Dublin' market, with fruit, fish and flowers. Traditional vendors hawk cheap cigarettes, tobacco and chocolate among the new wave of Chinese and Nigerians selling phone cards and hair extensions. Don't try to buy just one banana though – if it says 10 for €1, that's what it is.

Smithfield Fish Market (Map pp102-3; Michan St; ⏰ 7am-3pm Mon-Sat) One of Dublin's most traditional markets, this is the place to come for the freshest fish in town. Hang about long enough and you'll undoubtedly run into some of the city's best chefs picking up the makings of the evening's menu.

second-hand books crammed into heaving bookcases. When you've had enough of browsing, head up the winding stairs to the excellent restaurant (p157).

ARNOTT'S Map p85 — Department Store

☎ 805 0400; 12 Henry St; ☼ 9am-6.30pm Mon-Sat, to 9pm Thu, noon-6pm Sun; ▣ all cross-city

Occupying a huge block with entrances on Henry, Liffey and Abbey Sts, this is our favourite of Dublin's department stores. It stocks virtually everything you could possibly want to buy, from garden furniture to high fashion, and it's all relatively affordable.

CLERY'S & CO Map pp102–3 — Department Store

☎ 878 6000; O'Connell St; ☼ 9am-6.30pm Mon-Sat, to 9pm Thu, noon-6pm Sun; ▣ all cross-city

This elegant department store is Ireland's most famous retailer, a real Dublin classic. Recently restored to its graceful best, it has sought to shed its conservative reputation by filling its shelves with funkier labels to attract younger buyers.

DEBENHAM'S Map pp102–3 — Department Store

☎ 873 0044; www.debenhams.com; 54-62 Henry St; ☼ 9am-6.30pm Mon-Sat, to 9pm Thu, noon-6pm Sun; ▣ all cross-city

This UK giant hit these shores in 2006; bold and glass-fronted on the outside with street-smart fashion labels like Zara, Warehouse and G-Star inside, as well as the obligatory homewares and electrical sections.

PENNEY'S Map pp102–3 — Department Store

☎ 888 0500; www.primark.co.uk; 47 Mary St; ▣ all cross-city

Ireland's cheapest department store is a northside favourite, a place to find all kinds of everything without paying a fortune for it – it's the best place in town for men's socks and jocks. True, the stuff here isn't guaranteed to last, but at prices like these, why quibble over quality? There's also another branch (☎ 656 6666; 26 O'Connell St).

WALTON'S Map pp102–3 — Music

☎ 874 7805; 2 North Frederick St; ▣ 36 or 36A

This is the main branch of the well-known Walton's music stores (p135).

CLARK'S Map pp102–3 — Shoes

☎ 872 1841; www.clarks.com; 25 Henry St; ▣ all cross-city

This well-known shoe store stocks not only its own brand but others too; it also has an excellent selection of Birkenstocks. The branch (☎ 872 7665; 43 O'Connell St) on O'Connell St stocks women's shoes only.

SCHUH Map pp102–3 — Shoes

☎ 873 0621; www.schuh.ie; 10 O'Connell St; ▣ all cross-city

Two floors of footwear, from trainers to formal shoes, and pretty much everything in-between. The labels represented here are of the high-street variety, so don't expect Manolo or Gucci.

JERVIS CENTRE Map pp102–3 — Shopping Centre

☎ 878 1323; Jervis St; ☼ 9am-6pm Mon-Sat, to 9pm Thu, noon-6pm Sun; ▣ Jervis

An ultramodern, domed mall that's a veritable shrine to the British chain store. Boots, Top Shop, Debenhams, Argos, Dixons, M&S and Miss Selfridge all get a look-in.

BLUELIST[1] (blu,list) *v.*
to recommend a travel experience.
What's your recommendation? www.lonelyplanet.com/bluelist

EATING

top picks

- **Bang Café** (p152)
- **Chapter One** (p156)
- **Good World** (p148)
- **Gruel** (p154)
- **Larder** (p154)
- **L'Gueuleton** (p147)
- **Lock's** (p147)
- **Silk Road Café** (p150)
- **Tea Rooms** (p153)
- **Town Bar & Grill** (p145)

EATING

Of all of the transformations brought on by prosperity, none has been so dramatic, so downright *revolutionary*, as how Dubliners deal with grub. Gone are the days when food was nothing more than a biological necessity to be endured – or enjoyed after a bellyful of pints. Now, it's all 'did you hear about that new Vietnamese place? You absolutely *have* to go, the spring rolls are divine, just like the ones in that little place in Hanoi we ate in a couple of years ago.' Food – how it's eaten, where it's eaten, even how it's talked about – is the new drug of choice for so many Dubliners that in some social circles you aren't so much *what* you eat but *where* you eat.

Eating out – once the preserve of the idle rich, business-lunch crew and extraordinary celebration – has become a remarkably popular pastime, enjoyed by Dubliners in their thousands nightly in the hundreds of restaurants, bistros and brasseries that have opened their doors in recent years to an increasingly picky audience who fancy themselves natural-born food critics.

And in Dublin, critics have a field day – and not simply because giving out is a favourite sport. Not so long ago, your average Dubliner would have accepted steak as hard as shoe leather surrounded by veggies boiled beyond recognition because to complain would have appeared ungrateful. No more. The opening of so many eateries has turned a dormant dining town into a culinary bear-pit, where restaurateurs paying exorbitant rents are in a perpetual dogfight for the patronage of a clientele that no longer feels awkwardly grateful crossing the hearth of the latest themed epicurean fantasy.

Of which there are an awful lot. The city is now awash with super-cool restaurants sporting fab décor, funky menus and staff who really should be strutting the length of a catwalk. But décor, beauty and plenty of press do not necessarily a good restaurant make. Substance is usually more important than style to your average Dublin diner, and you can rely on at least half the population to point out that the Emperor is, in fact, stark bollock naked. Thankfully, a growing number of chefs and restaurateurs have cottoned on to this fact and are working to increasingly higher standards.

HISTORY

Irish food is great until it's cooked, laughed generations of travellers who used to visit these shores *in spite* of the grub. They were right and it was a thing to be mocked. The cuisine was thrown together by an indifferent, almost penitent race and was best characterised by charred chops, mushy vegetables and an overreliance on an overrated tuber. But although the reputation lingers, the cap no longer fits, for nowhere is Dublin's renaissance more obvious than at the table.

Ironically, although never renowned for its culinary dash, Ireland has always been blessed with a wealth of staples and specialities, and its meat, seafood and dairy produce have long been feted around the world. It was what to do with these riches that baffled generations of Irish mothers. Then, in the twilight of the 20th century, as Ireland rode the wave of its economic boom, a brigade of talented cooks and dedicated foodies went back to consult the original model for Irish cuisine. They added a pinch of this, took back a bit of that

and came up with what the media quickly described as New Irish Cuisine. In truth, there was very little new about this cuisine at all; it was more a confident return to a tradition that combined the finest local ingredients with simple cooking techniques.

It aroused the taste buds of the nation, and Dublin diners in particular suddenly became more discerning and adventurous. They started banging on their tables, sending the old rubbish back to the kitchen and demanding something to savour rather than to just soak up the drink. Restaurants had to lift their game if they were going to cash in on the new culture of dining out, and cooks sought influences from all over to satisfy the adventurous appetites of their cashed-up clientele. In the space of a decade, Ireland's gastronomy was transformed. Of course, you can still find leathery meat, shrivelled fish and vegetables so overcooked that they can barely cling to the prongs of a fork, but you're more likely to experience simple and sophisticated fare that will make your head spin and your palate sing.

ETIQUETTE

Conviviality is the most important condiment at the Dublin table. Meal times are about taking the load off your feet, relaxing and enjoying the company of your fellow diners. There is very little prescribed or restrictive etiquette. In fact, the only behaviour likely to cause offence could be your own haughtiness. Dubliners will happily dismiss any faux pas but if they think you have ideas above your station, they're quick to bring you back down to earth.

SPECIALITIES

Although many old Dublin staples have been consigned to the scrapheap of culinary history, some have earned their longevity while others are kept around for the sake of the tourists.

Perhaps the most feared Irish speciality is the fry – the heart attack on a plate that is the second part of so many B&B deals. It's really three meals in one – who can say no to a plate of fried bacon, sausages, black pudding, white pudding, eggs and tomatoes, washed down with lots of tea or coffee and usually accompanied by a basket of toast? But hysterical health fears have seen the fry disappear from the menus of most Dubliners and, with only a handful of exceptions, your best chance of a fry is in the hotel breakfast room.

The most Dublin of dishes is coddle, a working-class concoction of rashers, sausages, onions, potato and plenty of black pepper. Another specific to the capital is gurr cake, which 19th-century bakers made out of stale bread and cakes mixed with candied peel and dried mixed fruit. Because it was very cheap, it became popular with street urchins 'on the gurr' from school. The term 'gurrier' entered the Dublin dialect to describe rough tearaways. Bacon and cabbage – once the epitome of bad, flavourless Irish cooking – is making a comeback, but its rich and delicious reincarnation proves that there was never anything wrong with the produce, just the person boiling it to death.

The most famous Irish bread, and one of the signature tastes of Ireland, is soda bread. Irish flour is soft and doesn't take well to yeast as a raising agent, so Irish bakers of the 19th century leavened their bread with bicarbonate of soda. Combined with buttermilk, it makes a superbly light-textured and tasty bread, and is often on the breakfast menus at B&Bs.

Scones, tarts and biscuits are specialities too. Barm brack (from the Irish for 'speckled bread') is a spicy, fruity cake long associated with Halloween. Various charms are traditionally baked in the brack, and the one you get decides your destiny for the following year. Discover the ring and you'll get married, bite into the penny and you'll be wealthy (which is some consolation for the cracked tooth); the pea denotes impending poverty while a little stick cheerfully prophesises domestic violence.

Soda bread is a wonderful platform for smoked salmon, and you should take every opportunity to sample the fruits of the Irish seas, be it on a platter or wrapped in batter from a traditional chipper. Of course, you should also sample the cockles and mussels that Molly Malone made famous, oysters from the west coast, and Dublin Bay prawns – which are actually local lobsters and taste superlative at their best. If you get a chance, be sure to down a Dublin lawyer. Before you go getting yourself into trouble, this is a lobster dish cooked with whiskey and cream.

Better known is the national edible icon, Irish stew, the slow-simmered one-pot wonder of lamb, potatoes, onions, parsley and thyme (note, no carrots). In summer look out for mountain lamb from Connemara or Kerry.

Savour the dairy produce, which is some of the best you'll taste anywhere (all that rain's got to be good for something); the butter is deliciously rich and the thick and luscious cream is a joy to behold. The resurgence of cheese-making has been one of the most exciting culinary developments of recent years and Irish farmhouse cheeses win many international awards and plaudits.

WHERE TO EAT

The epicentre of decent dining is on the south side of the city centre, where the vast majority of Dublin's best and most popular eateries sit cheek by jowl with each other. The most concentrated restaurant area is Temple Bar, but except for a handful of places the bulk of eateries offer bland, unimaginative fodder and cheap set menus for tourists. Merrion Row, St Stephen's Green and the swathe of streets west of Grafton St have plenty of options, but prohibitively high rents round these parts have forced restaurateurs to serve their specialities a little further afield, including south along the Grand Canal and east towards Grand Canal Dock.

The same pecuniary logic has forced a re-evaluation of the north side as a gourmet hotspot. Besides the plethora of greasy diners, crappy fast-food outlets and a few grand dames that have been part of the scene for decades, the north side has seen the arrival of some pretty fancy restaurants and – most excitingly – a whole new world of genuinely ethnic cuisines, from Chinese to Polish, especially along Parnell St, which runs a perpendicular line off the northern end of O'Connell St.

If you're really lucky – or just smile and make nice with the right people – you'll get the chance to share a homecooked meal, which remains the best way to cut right to the heart of this unique culture. Irish cuisine isn't just about sampling sensational seafood, fine farmhouse cheeses and mountain-bred lamb, it's defined by the warmth and conviviality around the dinner table, the chat over a cup of tea and the sizzle of the traditional Sunday roast.

PRACTICALITIES
Opening Hours

Dubliners follow a fairly rigid fuelling schedule; they like to eat their evening meal early, generally between 7pm and 9.30pm, while lunch goes down between 1pm and 2pm. Cafés are open 8.30am to 6.30pm Monday to Saturday, and 10am to 6pm Sunday. Most restaurants are open Monday to Saturday for lunch between noon and 3pm, and dinner from 5.30pm until 10.30pm, although many midrange restaurants stay open throughout the day. Top-end joints are more likely to close for Saturday lunch. Throughout these listings you can presume every place is open daily, unless otherwise specified. While we've noted where places stray from the standard, if you're going out of your way it's always safest to telephone ahead.

How Much?

It's a frustrating cliché at this stage, but food is bloody expensive in Dublin and you'll rarely get what you'd consider value for money (unless you're earning sterling or yen). Go to a smart restaurant, order three courses á la carte and wash them down with a decent European red, and two of you will be lucky to get change out of €150. On the other hand, choose well and you get a memorable meal for half that. For around €15 you can eat surprisingly well, although you won't get much more than a bowl of soup and what goes between two slices

PRICE GUIDE

€€€	Over €25 for a main course
€€	€15-25 for a main course
€	€15 or less for a main course

of bread for less than €10. The city's better restaurants only get interesting if you're willing to part with €15 to €25 for a main course, while for that special meal you will need to fork out even more. As a rule, wine is very expensive and will add the guts of €20 to your bill for even a basic red – go for a known vintage and you'll be charged twice that.

In these pages, we've given you an even spread of the city's eateries, from the choicest cheap to choosiest chic – scan them well before you go out.

Booking Tables

Reserving a table has become just about compulsory for most of the city's restaurants from Thursday to Saturday, and for the hippest ones all week. Many of the latter have also gone for the multiple-sittings system, which means 'yes, we have a table for you at 7pm but could you please vacate by 9pm?' In response, some places have snubbed the reservations system entirely in favour of the (equally annoying) get-on-the-list, get-in-line policy that usually encourages a pre-dinner drink in a nearby pub.

Tipping

It's industry standard these days to tip between 10% and 12% of the bill, unless the waiter has dumped the dinner in your lap and given you the finger, while the gratuity for exceptional service is only limited by your generosity and/or level of inebriation. If you're really unhappy don't be afraid to leave absolutely nothing, though it will very rarely come to that.

The rule of thumb is simple: the classier the restaurant, the classier the service, but even at midrange and basic places you will be treated with courtesy and attention. Dubliners are not especially obsequious and generally eschew the kind of I'm-your-slave-for-the-evening take on serving tables, but that doesn't mean that you won't get quality service with politeness and a smile. The real treat among Dublin waitstaff is a bit of personality – they might be serving your table but they're not afraid to have a laugh and share a joke.

Self-Catering

Dubliners' new taste for food extends to cooking and market shopping, and a number of artisan street markets have opened up in recent years. If you're keen to self-cater – or just to take advantage of a sunny afternoon and an empty park – the most famous and authentic market is on Moore St, where the colour of the produce is matched by the language of the dentally challenged spruikers. The more discerning shopper should head south of the river where there are a few terrific delis, cheesemongers and bakeries.

GRAFTON STREET & AROUND

There's no doubt about it: south of the Liffey is where all the eating action is at…well mostly anyway. It is impossible to walk 10 paces south of the river without coming across a menu in a window. The diversity of eating options will satisfy most palates and the wide variety in taste is matched by a range in prices, from good and groovy cheap eats to world-class cuisine.

THORNTON'S Map pp66–7   French, Irish €€€
☎ 478 7015; www.thorntonsrestaurant.com; Fitzwilliam Hotel, St Stephen's Green; 3-course set lunch €45, 5-course tasting menu €85; ⓥ closed Sun & Mon

Kevin Thornton shrugged his shoulders when Michelin saw fit to strip him of one of his two stars, and replied by ordering a refurb of his *über*-trendy room on the 1st floor of the Fitzwilliam Hotel overlooking St Stephen's Green. The food – a mouthwatering Irish interpretation of new French cuisine – remains as good as ever, offering a mix of succulent seafood and gamey dishes like roast woodcock. Want to watch a grown-up squirm? Ask for ketchup.

SHANAHAN'S ON THE GREEN
Map pp66–7   American €€€
☎ 407 0939; www.shanahans.ie; 119 West St Stephen's Green; steaks €36-45; ⓥ from 6pm Mon-Thu & Sat-Sun, from noon Fri

'American-style steakhouse' hardly does justice to this elegant restaurant where JR Ewing and his cronies would happily have done business. Spread across three floors of a stunning Georgian building are four elegant dining areas, where impeccable service and a courteous bonhomie attract the great, the good and the not-so-good to its well-laid-out tables. Although the menu features seafood, this place is all about meat, notably the best cuts of impossibly juicy and tender Irish Angus beef you'll find anywhere on the island. The mountainous onion rings are the perfect accompaniment, while the sommeliers are among the best in the business.

JACOB'S LADDER Map pp66–7 Modern Irish €€€
☎ 670 3865; www.jacobsladder.ie; 4-5 Nassau St; mains about €30; ⓥ closed Sun & Mon

Looking over the playing fields of Trinity College – which counts as a view in Dublin – this fashionably formal restaurant is spread over two floors and is renowned for its exquisite and innovative Irish cuisine, which flirts with modern European influences. The food is a winner, with entrées like grilled goat's cheese and mains such as mackerel and potato terrine guaranteed to impress.

TOWN BAR & GRILL
Map pp66–7   Modern European €€-€€€
☎ 662 4724; www.townbarandgrill.com; 21 Kildare St; mains €23-39; ⓥ closed lunch Sun

On any given night, you're likely to share the low-ceilinged basement dining room with a selection of Ireland's most affluent and influential people, who conduct their oh-so-important affairs barely above a murmur. But the slight stuffiness of the place is swept aside by the simply mouth-watering food, which ranges from basics like lambs' liver to slow-roasted rabbit or sweet pepper–stuffed lamb. The only stars it has are homegrown ones, but this is our favourite meal in town.

PEPLOE'S Map pp66–7   Wine Bar €€-€€€
☎ 676 3144; 16 St Stephen's Green; mains €23-29; ⓥ closed Sun

Lots of air-kissing and comparing of shopping-bag contents takes place at this sophisticated and sumptuous wine-bar, which is basically Dublin's answer to London's Ivy Rooms. It's all about elegance and attention to detail – check out the sumptuous tableware – and not really about the perfectly adequate continental cuisine, which is merely a complement to the superb wine list.

TROCADERO Map pp66–7 International €€-€€€

☎ 677 5545; www.trocadero.ie; 3 St Andrew's St; mains €19-30; ☻ dinner only, closed Sun

There used to be a time when the Troc was the only place in town for a splash-out celebratory meal, hopefully alongside the glitterati of Dublin's screens and stages. No more, but the thespians, hacks, musos and TV execs are still partial to this warm and friendly Art Deco restaurant that won't challenge your taste buds but rarely fails to deliver old favourites, just as your mother dreamt of making them.

BALZAC Map pp66–7 French €€-€€€

☎ 677 8611; 35 Dawson St; mains €18-30; ☻ 6-11pm

It's official: one of the best chefs in Ireland is Paul Flynn, who made his name with the simply stunning Tannery in Dungarvan, County Waterford. His first Dublin venture will only serve to cement his growing reputation. The elegant old-world dining room is a fitting setting for the superb cuisine on offer; how about oysters mignonette followed by champagne and truffle risotto?

TIGER BECS Map pp66–7 Thai €€-€€€

☎ 677 8677; www.lastampa.ie; 36 Dawson St; mains €18-27; ☻ dinner Mon-Sat, plus lunch Mon-Sat Dec only

Below SamSara (p163), this long and cavernous restaurant serves high-end Thai nosh to Dublin's beautiful young things. The lamb massaman, a mild curry from southern Thailand, is a popular choice on a menu that sparkles but doesn't often shine. You'll probably feel you're paying a little too much for the sense of style, but nevertheless this loud, buzzing venue has oodles of atmosphere and is a great place to launch yourself into a night on the razzle.

FALLON & BYRNE

Map pp66–7 Contemporary European €-€€€

☎ 472 1000; www.fallonandbyrne.com; 11-17 Exchequer St; deli mains €6-9, brasserie mains €17-28; ☻ deli 9am-8pm Mon-Sat, 11am-6pm Sun; brasserie noon-4.30pm & 6.30-10.30pm Mon-Wed, to 11.30pm Thu-Sat, 11am-4pm Sun

Dublin's very own Dean and Deluca–style upmarket food hall (see p133), wine cellar and restaurant has been an absolute smash hit since it opened in 2006. The queues for the delicious deli counter are constant (which is partly due to the often inefficient staff), while the chic buzzy brasserie upstairs – with long red banquettes, a diverse menu of creamy fish pie, beef carpaccio or roast turbot and excellent service – hasn't failed to impress either.

AYA Map pp66–7 Japanese €-€€€

☎ 677 1544; www.aya.ie; Clarendon St; mains €12-28; ☻ to 10.30pm

Aya looks like it belongs in downtown Tokyo, with its chic, designer ambience and revolving sushi bar favoured by shoppers laden down with bags from the attached Brown Thomas store, and anyone else looking to gossip over raw fish and sake. Problem is, the sushi belt consists mainly of fruit plates, desserts and mostly non-sushi bites; the few bits you do get are generally of the salmon and fake-crab type. If you want the real deal, you have to order à la carte, and even then it's not that brilliant. Still, it is a great place to meet and greet and it looks just fabulous.

SABA Map pp66–7 Japanese €-€€€

☎ 679 2000; www.sabadublin.ie; 26-28 Clarendon St; mains €12-28; ☻ to 11.30pm

The name means 'happy meeting place' and so far this Thai–Vietnamese fusion restaurant has proven to be just that, packed virtually every night with all sorts tucking into the extensive Southeast Asian menu amid the kind of contemporary décor that screams designer cool. We thought both the menu and the look were good without being exceptional, but it's really popular, so what the hell do we know?

YAMAMORI Map pp66–7 Japanese €€

☎ 475 5001; www.yamamorinoodles.ie; 71-72 South Great George's St; sushi €3-3.50, mains €16-25; ☻ closed lunch Sun

Hip, inexpensive and generally pretty good, Yamamori rarely disappoints with its bubbly service and vivacious cooking that swoops from sushi and sashimi to whopping great plates of noodles, with plenty in between. It's a great spot for a sociable group – including vegetarians – although you'll have to book at the weekend to be one of the happy campers. They've recently opened a mostly-sushi branch north of the river (p157) that we think is just that little bit nicer.

LOCK'S Map pp66–7 · French €€
☎ 454 3391; www.locksrestaurant.ie; 1 Windsor Tce; mains €16-23; ☽ dinner only, closed Sun

When chef Troy Maguire left the immensely popular L'Gueuleton (right) in early 2007 to team up with ex-Bang manager Kelvin Rynhardt to take over one of the steady stalwarts of the Dublin dining scene, the bar was suddenly set very, very high. Would Lock's shake off its old-town dust? Could Maguire recreate the informal-but-superb French *campagnard* cooking that made his former kitchen such a huge hit? Would Lock's be as cool as Bang used to be? And would the prices stay this side of decent? Thankfully, yes on all counts, and while it's still early days, Lock's promises to be one of the most sought-after tables in town for years to come.

CEDAR TREE Map pp66–7 · Lebanese €€
☎ 677 2121; 11a St Andrew's St; mains €17-22; ☽ to midnight

An old stalwart of Dublin's restaurant scene, this marvellously low-key Lebanese eatery is still a top spot to while away an evening in the company of friends, delicious meze (falafel, spicy sausage, dips), meatballs, kofta and several bottles of red wine. The service here is warm and personable.

JAIPUR Map pp66–7 · Indian €€
☎ 677 0999; www.jaipur.ie; 41 South Great George's St; mains €19-21

A stylish and contemporary room sets the scene for some of the best Indian cuisine in town. Critics rave about the subtle and varied flavours produced by Jaipur's kitchen, which is down to its refusal to skimp on even the smallest dash of spice; what you get here is as close to the real deal as you'll get anywhere outside India.

EL BAHIA Map pp66–7 · Moroccan €€
☎ 677 0213; 1st fl, 37 Wicklow St; mains €16-18; ☽ closed lunch Sun

Dark and sultry, Ireland's only Moroccan restaurant looks a little like how we imagine a desert harem might be. Or maybe we just got carried away with the Moroccan sounds and smells. There are some rather fetching geometric designs on the ceilings and walls, and the gimme-gimme food includes the likes of tasty *tajines* (stews), couscous and *bastile* (pastry stuffed with chicken), while the sweet-and-spicy Moroccan coffee is an unusual treat.

L'GUEULETON Map pp66–7 · French €-€€
☎ 675 3708; 1 Fade St; mains €11-23; ☽ closed Sun

Dubliners have a devil of a time pronouncing the name (which means 'a gluttonous feast' in French) and have had their patience tested with the no-reservations-get-in-line-and-wait policy, but they just can't get enough of this restaurant's robust take on French rustic cuisine that makes twisted tongues and sore feet a small price to pay. The steak is sensational, but the Toulouse sausages with *choucroute* and Lyonnaise potatoes is a timely reminder that when it comes to the pleasures of the palate, the French really know what they're doing.

IMPERIAL CHINESE RESTAURANT
Map pp66–7 · Chinese €-€€
☎ 677 2580; 12a Wicklow St; lunch from €4, mains €13-22; ☽ noon-midnight

This long-established restaurant is a favourite with the Chinese community and is noted for its lunchtime dim sum and its we-don't-smile-but-we're-efficient service. If you're looking for some genuine Chinese dishes in an authentic atmosphere, there's no better time to go than Sunday, when the Imperial serves brunch Chinese-style in what is known as yum cha, or 'drink tea', the traditional accompaniment to dim sum.

ODESSA Map pp66–7 · Mediterranean €-€€
☎ 670 7634; www.odessa.ie; 13 Dame Ct; mains €13-20; ☽ 11.30am-4.30pm Sat & Sun, 6pm-late daily

Odessa and the hungover brunch go hand in hand like Laurel and Hardy. But this stylish eatery's dining credentials have long been maintained by its excellent dinner menu, which combines solid favourites like the homemade burger with more adventurous dishes like roast fillet of hake served with chorizo, clams, white bean stew and Serrano ham. Although it's been around for more than a decade, the loungy atmosphere with comfy sofas and retro standard lamps have kept it a perennial fave with the cool crowd.

SIXTY6 Map pp66–7 · International €-€€
☎ 400 5878; 66 South Great George's St; mains €12-20; ☽ 8am-11.30pm Mon-Sat, from 11am Sun

This swanky New York–style brasserie is one of the most popular party-dinner spots in town – the kind of place at which you'd want to celebrate your birthday with friends. It does a mean rotisserie chicken, four different ways at any given time. Besides its signature dish, the meat-heavy menu features things like lamb shank and a particularly good bit of liver. For that special occasion, there's a whole roast pig, but you need to order seven days in advance and be in a group of eight.

DUNNE & CRESCENZI Map pp66–7   Italian €-€€
☎ 677 3815; www.dunneandcrescenzi.com; 4 South Frederick St; mains €9-20; ☺ closed Sun
This exceptional Italian eatery delights its regulars with a basic menu of rustic pleasures, such as *panini*, a single pasta dish and a superb plate of mixed antipasto drizzled in olive oil. It's always full, and the tables are just that little bit too close to one another but the coffee is perfect and the desserts are sinfully good.

CHEZ MAX Map pp66–7   French €-€€
☎ 633 7215; 1 Palace St; mains €13-19; ☺ from 7.30am
Guarding the main gate to Dublin Castle is a French café that is Gallic through and through, from the fixtures imported from gay Paree to the beautiful, sultry staff who ignore you until they're ready and then turn the sexy pout into a killer smile. The lunchtime *tartines* – basically open sandwiches – are good enough to get us misty-eyed for Montmartre, but its coffees are a timely reminder that while the French do an awful lot really, really well, they still don't know how to make a decent brew.

CAFÉ MAO Map pp66–7   Asian €-€€
☎ 670 4899; www.cafemao.com; 2-3 Chatham Row; mains €12-19; ☺ to 10.30pm
Mao's often spicy mix of Vietnamese and Thai specialities, cooked to order and served with a musical soundtrack that declared its super-cool credentials, really did the business until a fire gutted the place in early 2006. A whole year and a half went by before the reopening, but once again Dubliners could feast on the likes of nasi goreng and *bulkoko* – best enjoyed alfresco in fine weather. A long-time favourite of the trendy lunchtime crowd.

BISTRO Map pp66–7   Modern European €-€€
☎ 671 5430; 4-5 Castle Market; mains €10-19
The real draw at this place is its outdoor seating in summer, on a lively pedestrian-

ised strip behind the George's St Arcade. An excellent menu of fish, pasta and meat specials, a well-stocked wine cellar and efficient service make this the warm weather choice for alfresco dining.

CHILLI CLUB Map pp66–7   Thai €-€€
☎ 677 3721; 1 Anne's Lane; mains €13-18; ☺ lunch & dinner
Cosy, comfy and a million miles from the hubbub of modern Dublin – well, a block – this is one of the longest-serving Thai restaurants in town. It has built its reputation on unfailingly good – and unremittingly hot – curries, satays and soupy broths served in a slightly cramped but stylish room. A great choice for a quiet first date!

CLARENDON CAFÉ BAR
Map pp66–7   Contemporary European €-€€
☎ 679 2909; www.clarendon.ie; Clarendon St; mains €12-18; ☺ noon-8pm Mon-Sat, to 6pm Sun
Spread across three stylishly designed floors, the Stokes brothers (of Bang fame; see p152) have given pub food a go at the Clarendon, and come up trumps: the chicken burger with guacamole is about the plainest thing on a menu that changes regularly. The only difference between here and a proper restaurant is that the waitstaff won't flinch when you order lager to go with your meal.

GOOD WORLD Map pp66–7   Chinese €-€€
☎ 677 5373; 18 South Great George's St; mains €11-18; ☺ to 3am
A hands-down winner of our best-Chinese-restaurant competition, the Good World has two menus, but to really get the most of this terrific spot, steer well clear of the Western menu and its unimaginative dishes. With listings in two languages, the Chinese menu is literally packed with dishes and delicacies that keep us coming back for more.

WAGAMAMA Map pp66–7   Japanese €-€€
☎ 478 2152; www.wagamama.ie; South King St; mains €11-18; ☺ lunch & dinner
There's ne'er a trace of raw fish to be seen, but this popular chain dishes up some terrific Japanese food nonetheless. Production-line rice and noodle dishes served pronto at canteen-style tables mightn't seem like the most inviting way to dine, but boy this food is good, and the basement it's served up in is surprisingly

light and airy – for a place with absolutely no natural light.

LÉON Map pp66–7 French €-€€
☎ 670 7238; 33 Exchequer St; mains €11-17; ☺ breakfast & lunch

Unashamedly baroque in style and unmistakably French in substance, this wonderful new brasserie has us humming Edith Piaf as we tuck into the sublime fresh salmon blini or the lovely *salade paysanne*. Round it off with a genuinely sinful pastry. The fruit tarts are excellent but for something truly divine you'll have to tuck in the belly and tackle a *réligeuse*, a chocolate or coffee pastry so named because it looks like a nun in her habit. They are so damned good that you *will* be singing '*non, je ne regrette rien…*'.

JUICE Map pp66–7 Vegetarian €-€€
☎ 475 7856; www.juicerestaurant.ie; Castle House, 73 South Great George's St; smoothies €5, mains €12-16; ☺ to late Fri & Sat, closed Sun

Lighten up, folks, it's just food! If the staff at this trendy, self-conscious vegetarian restaurant lost some of their attitude and smiled occasionally, we might actually forget the cool-out and focus on the terrific Pacific Rim–style cuisine, as well as tasty stir-fries, soups, wraps, soya desserts, organic wines and, of course, delicious fresh juices and smoothies. Isn't yoga supposed to be *relaxing*?

VILLAGE Map pp66–7 Pub Grub, International €
☎ 475 8555; www.thevillagevenue.com; 26 Wexford St; mains €10-15; ☺ noon-8pm Mon-Sat

Forget plain old pub grub; even an accomplished chef would be proud of the menu at one of Dublin's most popular pub venues. How about pan-fried piri piri perch with vegetable ratatouille for €14.95? A great choice for lunch or early dinner.

AVOCA Map pp66–7 Café €
☎ 677 4215; www.avoca.ie; 11-13 Suffolk St; mains €11-14; ☺ breakfast & lunch

This airy 1st-floor café was one of Dublin's best-kept secrets (because of an absence of any obvious signs) until discovered by the Ladies Who Lunch. If you can battle your way past the designer shopping bags to a table, you'll relish the simply delicious, rustic delights of organic shepherd's pie, roast lamb with couscous, or sumptuous salads from the Avoca kitchen. There's also

a takeaway salad bar and hot counter in the basement. For more information on the handicrafts, see p132.

CAFÉ BARDELI Map pp66–7 Italian €
☎ 672 7720; www.cafebardeli.ie; Bewley's Bldg, Grafton St; mains €10-14; ☺ breakfast, lunch & dinner

With two branches in the south city centre, the folks behind Café Bardeli have created a winning formula: great crispy pizzas with imaginative toppings such as spicy lamb and tzatziki, fresh homemade pastas or salads like broccoli, feta and chickpea, all served within the stylish environs of what were once branches of Dublin's most beloved café, Bewley's. No reservations allowed, so prepare to wait on a busy night. There's a second city branch (Map pp66–7; ☎ 677 1646; 12-13 Sth Great George's St; ☺ lunch & dinner) and another in Ranelagh (see p156).

PIZZA MILANO Map pp66–7 Italian €
☎ 670 7744; www.pizzaexpress.ie; 38 Dawson St; pizzas €10-13; ☺ lunch & dinner

There are four branches of this large and pretty stylish pizza emporium spread throughout the city centre, all sharing a similar menu, but this one is our favourite because of the alfresco dining area on Dawson St and the on-site free child-minders, who entertain your little ones while you eat, on Sunday between noon and 4.30pm.

LA MAISON DES GOURMETS
Map pp66–7 French €
☎ 672 7258; 15 Castle Market; mains €5-12; ☺ 9am-6pm, to 8pm Thu

This thoroughly Francophile café changed hands in 2006 and suffered a dip in form, but it remains a wonderful spot to enjoy a *tartine*, salad specials or a plate of charcuterie. It also has a fine range of pastries, baked goodies and herbal teas. We prefer sitting on the street outside, where you can watch the world go by on Castle Market; the upstairs room is just that little bit too lacking in atmosphere.

LISTONS Map pp66–7 Deli €
☎ 405 4779; 25 Camden St; lunch €5-12; ☺ closed Sun

The lunchtime queues streaming out the door of this place are testament to its reputation as Dublin's best deli. Its sandwiches (with fresh and delicious fillings), roasted-vegetable quiches, rosemary potato cakes and sublime salads will have you coming back again and again – the only problem is there's too much choice! On fine days, take your gourmet picnic to the nearby Iveagh Gardens (p75).

SILK ROAD CAFÉ Map pp66–7 Middle Eastern €
☎ 407 0770; www.cbl.ie; Chester Beatty Library, Dublin Castle; mains around €11; ⏰ 11am-4pm Mon-Fri

Museum cafés don't often make you salivate, but this vaguely Middle Eastern–North African–Mediterranean gem is the exception. On the ground floor of the Chester Beatty Library, it is the culinary extension of the superb collection upstairs, gathering together exotic flavours into one outstanding menu that is about two-thirds veggie. Complementing the house specialities like Greek moussaka and spinach lasagne are daily specials like *djaj mehshi* (chicken stuffed with spices, rice, dried fruit, almonds and pine nuts and served with okra and Greek yoghurt). For dessert, there's Lebanese baklava and coconut kataif, or you could opt for the juiciest dates this side of Tyre. All dishes are halal and kosher.

BOTTEGA TOFFOLI Map pp66–7 Italian €
☎ 633 4022; 34 Castle St; sandwiches & salads €8-11; ⏰ 10am-6pm Tue-Sat

Tucked away on a side street running alongside Dublin Castle, which you'd miss unless you were specifically looking for it, is this superb new Italian café. It's the home of one of the best sandwiches you'll eat in town – beautifully cut prosciutto, baby tomatoes and rocket salad drizzled with imported olive oil on a homemade *piadina* bread that is just too good to be true.

MARKET BAR Map pp66–7 Spanish €
☎ 677 4835; Fade St; mains €7-11

This one-time sausage factory, now fashionable watering hole (see p163), also has a super kitchen knocking out Spanish tapas and other Iberian-influenced bites in a light-filled, cavernous room, which is just perfect for a slow lunch. The dishes also come in convenient half-size portions, so you can mix and match without feeling like you've gorged.

BOBO'S Map pp66–7 Burger Bar €
☎ 400 5750; 22 Wexford St; burgers around €10; ⏰ 9.30am-11pm Mon-Sat, from 1pm Sun

Cow-hide leather banquettes suggest a

CAFÉ CULTURE & BEST COFFEES

Dublin's coffee junkies are everywhere, looking for that perfect barista fix that will kill the hunger until the next one. Sure, you can top up in the likes of O'Briens, Café Sol, Insomnia, West Coast Coffee Company and the recently arrived Starbuck's, but why drink a crappuccino when you can get a proper caffeine high at the following places:

Brown's Bar (Map pp66–7; ☎ 679 5666; Brown Thomas, Grafton St) Not as cool as it used to be, thank God, this is in Dublin's finest department store and is the best place to stop for a mid-shop reviver.

Butler's Chocolate Café (Map pp66–7; ☎ 671 0591; 24 Wicklow St) Heavenly hedonistic; the coffee might not be the *very* best in town, but the combination of a delicious handmade chocolate and damn good coffee is hard to beat. Actually, sod the coffee and double up with its famous hot chocolate for an unforgettable treat. There are branches around the south side.

Coffee Society (Map pp102–3; ☎ 878 7984; 2 Lower Liffey St) It looks most uninviting from the outside and only has paper cups, so it's a good job that this place has some of the best coffee-to-go in the city. There are various branches around town.

Milk Bar (Map pp66–7; ☎ 487 8450; 18 Montague St; ⏰ closed Sat & Sun) Don't go to Iveagh Gardens (p75) without visiting this groovy little sandwich bar, which serves some of the best coffee in Dublin. The blend is a little mild, but if its standard offerings don't hit the mark, these are the most benevolent baristas in Dublin and are happy to tweak their coffee – a little cooler, warmer, stronger, milkier, sweeter – until you get your fix exactly how you like it.

Queen of Tarts (Map pp66–7; ☎ 670 7499; Cork Hill; breakfast €6-9; ⏰ lunch to 1-2pm Sat & Sun) Diet dodgers rejoice, for this doughty little café is to cakes what Willie Wonka was to chocolate, and you'll think you're in a dream when you just see the displays of tarts, meringues, crumbles, cookies and brownies, never mind taste them. There are also great brekkies – such as potato-and-chive cake with mushroom and egg – the coffee's splendid and the service sweet. A treasure.

burger joint with a difference, and Bobo's is just that: a dozen different kinds of organic burgers with Irish names flesh out the menu at this cute spot that promotes the notion that fast food can be healthy. The burgers are exceptional but the home-cut chips, which promise so much in their old-fashioned metal bucket, are very disappointing.

CAKE SHOP Map pp66–7 — Pastries €
☎ 633 4477; Pleasant Pl; mains €4-8;
🕙 10am-6pm
Dublin's best-kept pastry secret is this great little café on a tiny lane parallel to Camden St. The easiest way in is through Daintree (61 Camden St) stationery shop; through the back is the self-contained yard, which in good weather is the best spot to enjoy a coffee and a homemade cake.

HONEST TO GOODNESS
Map pp66–7 — Café €
☎ 677 5373, George's St Arcade; mains €6;
🕙 9am-6pm Mon-Sat, noon-4pm Sun
A devastating fire kept this wonderful café under wraps for much of 2007, but it finally reopened and went back to the business of dispensing wholesome sandwiches, imaginative breakfasts and homemade soups and smoothies. Add to that delicious home-baked goodies and fair-trade coffee, all at rock bottom prices. Niiice.

NUDE Map pp66–7 — Sandwich Bar €
☎ 675 5577; 21 Suffolk St; wraps €5-6;
🕙 closed Sun
This fabulous and environmentally friendly take on Dublin fast food looks like the juice bar at the end of the universe. The massive kitchen is fronted by a space-age counter and the communal benches are very human and sociable. Just checking out the huge pre-packaged display, with all its juices, salads and cold dishes, makes your vitamin count surge, while the hot menu mainly features hunky and healthy Asian-style filled wraps.

LARALU Map pp66–7 — Food Stall €
George's St Arcade, Drury St; sandwiches €5;
🕙 10am-6pm Mon-Sat
Offering a carefully selected range of deli delights very much in keeping with its 'slow food' philosophy, this popular counter at the Drury St entrance of the George's St Arcade offers healthy soups (including wheat- and dairy-free options), sandwiches and specials like slow-cooked Moroccan lamb and Thai chicken curry with cardamom and coconut. The coffees are superb and the Valhrona hot chocolate is the best in town.

LEMON Map pp66–7 — Creperie €
☎ 672 9044; 66 South William St; crepes from €4.50; 🕙 to 7pm, 8pm Thu
Dublin's best pancake joint has branches on both sides of Grafton St, one on South William and the other on Dawson St (☎ 672 8898; 60 Dawson St). Each serves up a wide range of sweet and savoury crepes – those paper-thin ones stuffed with a variety of goodies and smothered in toppings – along with super coffee in a buzzy atmosphere that is popular with literally everyone.

SIMON'S PLACE Map pp66–7 — Café €
☎ 679 7821; George's St Arcade; 🕙 to 5pm, closed Sun
Hogging a prime corner spot off the very groovy George's St Arcade (p135), Simon's Place is a bustling café that serves up big, chunky sandwiches, nutritious, rich soups and decent pastries. The coffee is only satisfactory, but the cute European staff are more than all right. Avoid the downstairs part, which is dark and dingy.

MERRION SQUARE & AROUND

The best of Dublin's restaurants are gathered in the area surrounding Merrion Square, which is also full of sandwich bars catering to the busy lunchtime business trade. You'll never land a table at any of the top end spots without making a reservation first.

RESTAURANT PATRICK GUILBAUD
Map pp78–9 — French €€€
☎ 676 4192; www.restaurantpatrickguilbaud.com; Merrion Hotel, 21 Upper Merrion St; 2-/3-course set lunch €35/47, mains €48-90; 🕙 closed Mon & Sun
Handing out the title of 'Best in the Country' involves some amount of personal choice, but few disagree that this exceptional restaurant is a leading candidate, not least those good people at Michelin, who have put two stars in its crown. As a result,

this is the most prestigious restaurant in the country, where the service is formal, the setting elegant, the wine list awesome and the fare proudly French. While the food is innovative it's rarely too fiddly, just beautifully cooked and superbly presented. The lunch menu is an absolute steal, at least in this stratosphere.

L'ECRIVAIN Map pp78–9 French €€€
☎ 661 1919; www.lecrivain.com; 109a Lower Baggot St; mains €47-53; ⌚ closed Sun, lunch Sat
A firm favourite with the bulk of the city's foodies, L'Ecrivain trundles along with just one Michelin star to its name, but the plaudits just keep coming. Head chef Derry Clarke is considered a gourmet god for the exquisite simplicity of his creations, which put the emphasis on flavour and the use of the best local ingredients – all given the French once over and turned into something that approaches divine dining.

UNICORN Map pp78–9 Italian €€€
☎ 676 2182; www.unicornrestaurant.com; 12b Merrion Ct, Merrion Row; mains €28-45; ⌚ closed Sun
Saturday lunch at this Italian restaurant in a laneway off Merrion Row is a tradition for Dublin's media types, socialites, politicos and their cronies who guffaw and clink glasses in conspiratorial rapture. At lunch many opt for the extensive antipasto bar, but we still prefer the meaty á la carte menu – a particular favourite are the kidneys on a bed of risotto, but there are pastas and fish dishes to cater to all palates.

DOBBINS Map pp78–9 French €€€
☎ 676 4679; www.dobbins.ie; 15 Stephen's Lane; mains €26-35; ⌚ closed Sun, lunch Sat
This old stalwart, opposite a row of council houses, was where the privileged came for lunch before the Celtic Tiger brought privilege to half the city. Its traditional French fare, homely setting and old-fashioned hospitality have served it well over the last quarter of a century, and it's still a favourite with politicians, journalists and spin doctors (often at the same table).

DAX Map pp78–9 Fench €€€
☎ 676 1494; 23 Upper Pembroke St; mains €22-35; ⌚ lunch & dinner Tue-Fri, dinner only Sat

Olivier Meisonnave, convivial ex-maître d of Thornton's stepped out on his own with Irish chef Pól ÓhÉannraich to open this posh-rustic restaurant named after his home town, north of Biarritz. In this bright basement venue, serious foodies will be able to sate their palate on sea bass with celeriac purée, pork wrapped in serrano ham or truffle risotto.

BANG CAFÉ Map pp78–9 Modern European €€-€€€
☎ 676 0898; www.bangrestaurant.com; 11 Merrion Row; mains €18-33; ⌚ closed Sun
The biggest problem with hype is that disappointment is invariably nipping at its heels, and so it is with this stylish spot owned by the handsome Stoke twins – but only just. The innovative and meaty modern European menu was once credited with trailblazing a touch of London to an eager Dublin palate, but that was 10 years ago and the city's trendy diners have grown a little blasé with the always excellent fare on offer here. It's still very popular, so reservations are a must, even for lunch.

DIEP LE SHAKER Map pp78–9 Asian €€-€€€
☎ 661 1829; www.diep.net; 55 Pembroke Lane; mains €19-29; ⌚ closed Sun, lunch Sat
Diep le Shaker is a modern, light-filled space that is tucked down an alley off prestigious Pembroke St. It is popular with the local business crowd, establishment movers and shakers, and people generally consumed by their own self-importance. It's the ugly side of the Celtic Tiger. The predominantly Thai grub is inventive and excellent, but you get the impression you're paying for the company and it ain't worth it.

ELY Map pp78–9 Wine Bar €€-€€€
☎ 676 8986; www.elywinebar.ie; 22 Ely Pl; mains €15-29; ⌚ lunch & dinner Mon-Sat
Scrummy homemade burgers, bangers and mash, or wild smoked salmon salad are some of the dishes you'll find in this basement restaurant. Meals are prepared with organic and free-range produce from the owner's family farm in County Clare, so you can rest assured of the quality. There's a large wine list to choose from, with more than 70 sold by the glass. There are two more branches on either side of the Liffey – see p157 and p155.

top picks

IRISH CUISINE

- Chapter One (p156)
- Winding Stair (p157)
- Tea Rooms (below)
- Jacob's Ladder (p145)
- Avoca (p149)

TEMPLE BAR

Scattered among the panoply of crap, overpriced and underwhelming eateries in Temple Bar are some excellent spots to get a bite that will suit a variety of tastes and depth of pocket.

TEA ROOMS Map p85 · Modern Irish €€€

☎ 670 7766; www.clarence.ie; Clarence, 6-8 Wellington Quay; mains €31-37; ⏲ closed lunch Sat
Designed to resemble a church, the Clarence's Tea Rooms are spacious with a soaring ceiling and double-height windows, flooding the room with natural light. Appropriately, Mathieu Melin's innovative menu commands respect, with an ambitious marriage of classic French cuisine and typically Irish produce. How about traditional Cork city crubeens (pig's trotters), soft quail eggs and potato salad topped with mustard dressing followed by chartreuse of red leg partridge, smoked sausage, savoy cabbage and carrot, and juniper flavoured jus? The three-course Market Menu, available before 8pm Monday to Thursday, is excellent value at €39.

MERMAID CAFÉ Map p85 · Seafood €€-€€€

☎ 670 8236; www.mermaid.ie; 22 Dame St; mains €19-28
The largely seafood-serving Mermaid is one of the city's favourite restaurants, as much for the superb cuisine as for the friendly and informal atmosphere. The menu is loaded with inventive ingredient-led organic food, such as roast monkfish tail with sweet potato and chorizo mash and roast poussin with cassava chips, lentils and shallots. But what makes this place that little bit extra special is the atmosphere, fostered as much by the excellent staff as by little touches like free coffee refills at brunch. Call now and make a booking.

EDEN Map p85 · Modern European €€-€€€

☎ 670 5372; Meeting House Sq; mains €23-27; ⏲ lunch & dinner
The epitome of Temple Bar chic, Eden's minimalist look – designed to look something like the interior of an (empty) swimming pool – and contemporary European menu has earned plenty of kudos over the last decade. The menu, which offers dishes as diverse as braised lamb shank with Moroccan spices and organic beef and Guinness stew, is generally excellent, but we enjoy it best at brunch on the much-sought-after ground-floor terrace. Try to avoid the upstairs dining room, which can get very hot.

TANTE ZOÉ'S Map p85 · Cajun, Creole €€-€€€

☎ 679 4407; www.tantezoes.com; 1 Crow St; mains €16-26; ⏲ closed Sun
This well-established favourite serves up a Mardi Gras for the senses almost every night, with its menu of gumbos, jambalayas, bayou steaks, Cajun-blackened this and Creole-infused that. It ain't subtle and it won't win a lot of gourmet foodie awards, but the crowd couldn't care less: they come to laisser rouler les bons temps and that's exactly what they get.

CHAMELEON Map p85 · Indonesian €€

☎ 671 0362; www.chameleonrestaurant.com; 1 Lower Fownes St; mains €15-25, 6-dish set menu €30; ⏲ dinner, closed Mon
Friendly, cute and full of character, Chameleon is draped in exotic fabrics and serves up perky renditions of Indonesian classics, such as satay, gado gado and nasi goreng. If you can't decide what dish to have, you can always plump for the rijsttaffel, a selection of several dishes with rice. The top floor has low seating on cushions, which is perfect for intimate group get-togethers.

IL BACCARO Map p85 · Italian €€

☎ 671 4597; Meeting House Sq; mains €15-22; ⏲ dinner daily, also lunch Sat
Want a free Italian lesson? Drop into this fabulous trattoria and eavesdrop in this rustic piece of the Old Boot, where the food is exuberantly authentic, and includes bruschetta, homemade pasta, Italian sausage, cannelini beans and the like. The Italian wines are buonissimi.

VEGGIE BITES

Veggies are having it increasingly easier in Dublin as the capital has veered away from the belief that food isn't food until your incisors have had to rip flesh from bone and towards an understanding that healthy eating leads to, well, longer lives. There's a selection of general restaurants that cater to vegetarians beyond the token dish of mixed greens and pulses – places like Nude (p151), Yamamori (p146), Chameleon (p153) and Jacob's Ladder (p145). Solidly vegetarian places include the following:

Blazing Salads (Map pp66–7; ☎ 671 9552; 42 Drury St; mains €3–7) Organic breads (including many special diet varieties), Californian-style salads, smoothies and pizza slices can all be taken away from this delicious deli.

Cornucopia (Map pp66–7; ☎ 677 7583; 19 Wicklow St; mains from €7) For those escaping the Irish cholesterol habit, Cornucopia is a popular wholefood café turning out healthy goodies. There's even a hot vegetarian breakfast as an alternative to muesli.

Fresh (Map pp66–7; ☎ 671 9552; top fl, Powerscourt Townhouse Shopping Centre; lunch €6-12) This long-standing restaurant serves a variety of salads and filling, hot daily specials. Many dishes are dairy- and gluten-free, without compromising on taste. The baked potato, topped with organic cheese (€5.50), comes with two salads, is very reasonable and is a hearty meal in itself.

Govinda's (www.govindas.ie; mains €7-10) Aungier St (Map pp66–7; ☎ 475 0309; 4 Aungier St); Merrion Row (Map pp78–9; ☎ 661 5095; 18 Merrion Row); Middle Abbey St (Map pp102–3; ☎ 872 7463; 83 Middle Abbey St) An authentic beans-and-pulses place run by the Hare Krishna, with three branches in the city centre. Its cheap, wholesome mix of salads and Indian-influenced hot daily specials are filling and tasty.

AR VICOLETTO Map p85   Italian €-€€
☎ 670 8662; 5 Crow St; mains €13-25; ☺ lunch & dinner Mon-Sat, from 3pm Sun
When it's good, this cosy little *osteria* is very, very good, with excellent Italian dishes washed down with splendid Italian reds and enjoyed in a convivial atmosphere. But it's a little inconsistent and sometimes the standard menu of pasta, meaty mains and seafood misses the mark. At these times it doesn't seem like good value at all, although the warm Gorgonzola salad never disappoints. Absolutely worth the risk.

MONTY'S OF KATHMANDU
Map p85   Nepalese €-€€
☎ 670 4911; www.montys.ie; 28 Eustace St; mains €14-18; ☺ closed lunch Sun
It has won a ton of ethnic dining awards, but Monty's still leaves us a little flat. The food is good if not exceptional, focusing primarily on Nepalese dishes like *gorkhali* (chicken cooked in chilli, yoghurt and ginger) or *kachela* (raw marinated meat). The atmosphere is muted, but on weeknights it can tend towards the moribund.

GRUEL Map p85   International €-€€
☎ 670 7119; 68a Dame St; breakfast €4, lunch €3.50-8, brunch €5-12, dinner mains €11-18; ☺ breakfast, lunch & dinner Mon-Fri, brunch & dinner Sat & Sun
Noisy, cosy and beloved by its ever-lengthening list of devotees, Gruel is one of the best dishes in town, a deli–cum–rustic trattoria that has them queuing out the door. They come for the super-filling, taste-defying, lunchtime roast-in-a-roll – a rotating list of slow roast organic meats stuffed into a bap and flavoured with homemade relishes – and the exceptional evening menu, where pasta, fish and chicken are given the exotic once-over. It doesn't accept bookings, so just go, queue and share elbow space with the table behind you; it's worth every effort.

LARDER Map p85   International €-€€
☎ 633 3581; 8 Parliament St; mains €10-18; ☺ lunch & dinner
This new caff-by-day, restaurant-by-night eatery has a positively organic vibe to it, with its wholesome porridge breakfasts, gourmet sandwiches like serrano ham, gruyere and rocket, and Japanese speciality suki teas (try the China gunpowder). They're confident about their food – even listing their suppliers – and so are we.

BAR ITALIA Map p85   Italian €
☎ 679 5128; www.baritalia.ie; Bookend, 4 Essex Quay; lunch €6-12; ☺ to 6pm
One of a new generation of eateries to show the more established Italian restaurants how the Old Country *really* eats, Bar Italia is a favourite with the lunchtime

crowd, who come for the ever-changing pasta dishes, homemade risottos and excellent Palombini coffee. Its larger sister restaurant is across the river in the Italian Quarter (see p157).

ZAYTOON Map p85   Middle Eastern €
☎ 677 3595; 14-15 Parliament St; chicken shish-kebab meal €10; ⏲ to 4am
It's the end of the night and you've got a desperate case of the munchies. Head straight for this terrific kebab joint and gobble the house speciality, the chicken shish-kebab meal, complete with chips and a soft drink.

KILMAINHAM & THE LIBERTIES

Gourmet experiences are a little thin on the ground west of the south city centre, but if you are traipsing towards the Guinness Storehouse, IMMA or Kilmainham Gaol and are looking for something to sustain you, there are two spots worth considering.

GALLIC KITCHEN Map pp90–1   French, Café €
☎ 454 4912; www.gallickitchen.com; 49 Francis St; meals around €8; ⏲ to 5pm, closed Sun
'Our food is so fucking good you won't believe it' advises the sign on the front wall of this little bakery shop. Standing at a bench, devouring a goat's-cheese brioche, salmon roulade, smoked haddock quiche and chocolate pecan tart, we – wait for it – tend to agree.

LEO BURDOCK'S Map pp90–1   Fish & Chips €
☎ 454 0306; 2 Werburgh St; fish & chips €7-9; ⏲ to 11pm
You will often hear that you haven't eaten in Dublin until you've queued in the cold for

---

DINING ON THE CANAL

One of the most atmospheric ways to experience the Grand Canal – and enjoy a fine dinner – is on an evening barge trip. Board La Peniche (Map p99; ☎ 087 790 0077; www.lapeniche.ie; Grand Canal, Mespil Rd; mains €15-19; ⏲ lunch & dinner Tue-Fri, dinner only Sat), sit on deck with its twinkly lights and enjoy fine Belgian wine and food while your skipper navigates the locks.

---

a cod 'n' chips wrapped in paper from the city's most famous chipper. Total codswallop, of course, but there's something about sitting on the street, balancing the bag on your lap and trying to eat the chips quickly before they go cold that smacks of Dublin in a bygone age. It's nice to revisit the past, especially if you don't have to get stuck there.

BEYOND THE GRAND CANAL

If you fancy a change of pace, head to the inner southern suburbs ringing the Grand Canal, including Ranelagh, Ballsbridge and around the Grand Canal Basin itself, where you can find some excellent nosh.

ELY HQ Map p99   Contemporary European €€-€€€
☎ 633 9986; www.elywinebar.ie; Hanover Quay, Forbes St, Grand Canal Basin; mains €18-29; ⏲ lunch & dinner Mon-Sun
As part of the ongoing development of Dublin's docklands, Ely opened a branch of its successful city-centre restaurant in what they assume will be one of the hippest spots in town. The new restaurant is suitably impressive – lots of exposed concrete coupled with modern designer touches more often seen in a high-end Bangkok restaurant – and the food is made to match, even if the menu isn't all that adventurous and you won't eat anything that will absolutely blow your socks off. Still, it's a good spot to eat off a hangover.

FRENCH PARADOX Map p99   French €€
☎ 660 4068; 53 Shelbourne Rd; mains €16-18; ⏲ closed Sun
This bright and airy wine bar, over an excellent wine shop of the same name, serves fine authentic French dishes such as cassoulet, a variety of pâté de foie gras, cheese and charcuterie plates, and large green salads. All are there to complement the main attraction: a dazzling array of fine wines, mostly French unsurprisingly, sold by the bottle, glass or even 6.25cL taste! A little slice of Paris in Dublin 4.

OCEAN Map p99   Seafood €-€€
☎ 668 8862; Charlotte Quay Dock, Ringsend; mains €12-18
Once the docks are redeveloped, Ocean will have one of the best views in town (hence

THE PUB CARVERY

Dublin's greatest contribution to its own gourmet heritage has been the pub lunch, invariably made up of three kinds of meat, three kinds of potato, overboiled cabbage and carrots and lashings of droopy gravy, all kept warm under the toxic glow of the heat lamp. And if you needed something a little lighter, how about a ham-and-cheese toastie wrapped in plastic? Ah yes, the good old days – but they're still with us. The cuts of meat have improved, the cooking time for veg has been reduced by half and a whole bunch of new delights have been added to the menu, including curries and – shock, horror – fresh salad. Besides those pubs whose cuisine is so good that they stand alone as proper restaurants (and are included in our main reviews), we recommend the following pubs for their better class of pub grub.

You'll get solid steak and chips at the Stag's Head (p166) and good pasta at the ever-fashionable Bailey (p162). Davy Byrne's (p163) has been associated with food since Leopold Bloom dropped in for a Gorgonzola sandwich and a burgundy in *Ulysses*; a century later, oysters, salmon and other seafood make up the fare. Dublin's oldest pub, the Brazen Head (p169), does a mean carvery and a summer alfresco menu.

the floor to ceiling windows). The problem is, it's already charging for the view while it – and the food – aren't quite there yet. Standards include oysters, crab salad and a langoustine (lobster) cocktail, but portions are small and the convoluted cooking unreliable. That said, there's a nice terrace, should the sun stick its head out.

CAFÉ BARDELI Map p99 Italian €

☎ 496 1886; www.cafebardeli.ie; 62 Ranelagh Rd; mains €10-14; 🕑 12.30-11pm Mon-Sat, to 10pm Sun

If it ain't broke, do it again: CBD hit Ranelagh a few years back with the same no-fuss menu that made its city-centre sisters such roaring successes on Grafton and South Great George's Sts (see p149) and it just hasn't looked back.

MASH Map p99 International €

☎ 497 9463; Castlewood Ave, Rathmines; mains around €12; 🕑 closed Sun

This tiny, eclectic place is run by Bobby and Jerome, possibly the friendliest hosts in the capital. It is well regarded for its tasty, homemade dishes and cosy atmosphere, and the small menu features daily specials such as Thai chicken curry, roast red snapper, organic steaks or the popular range of Mash potato cakes, all made with TLC and served with a smile.

JO'BURGER Map p99 Burger Bar €

☎ 491 3731; www.joburger.ie; 137 Rathmines Rd, Rathmines; burgers €7.95-11.50; 🕑 noon-midnight

A playful, kids-in-the-70s theme (the menus are pasted into children's almanacs), DJs playing great music loud enough to hear but not too loud to be annoying, and a sensational burger menu make this the coolest, hippest, best burger joint in the city. The organic burgers – beef, lamb, fish, veggie – come in a variety of options, all with funky names. The mapetla has beetroot salad, rocket and relish; the zondi comes with green thai curry mayo, coriander and chilli.

NORTH OF THE LIFFEY

Like just about every facet of Dublin life, cafés and restaurants north of the Liffey tend to be more down-to-earth than their southern counterparts. O'Connell St itself is lined with fast-food factories, although there are a couple of cracking restaurants close by. The area around Parnell St has exploded in the last couple of years and is now chock-a-block with ethnic eateries, mostly Chinese.

CHAPTER ONE Map pp102–3 Modern Irish €€€

☎ 873 2266; www.chapteronerestaurant.com; Dublin Writers Museum, 18-19 Parnell Sq; mains €33-70; 🕑 closed Sun, lunch Sat

One of the best restaurants in Dublin, this venerable old trooper sets its ambitions no further than modern Irish cuisine, which it has realised so brilliantly that those Michelin lads saw fit to throw one of their sought-after stars its way. Menus change regularly but the dishes are always top-notch, the service first class and the atmosphere reassuringly reserved. Get there before 7pm for the three-course pre-theatre special (€35), a favourite with those heading to the Gate (p186) around the corner.

RHODES D7 Map pp102–3 British €€-€€€

☎ 804 4441; www.rhodesd7.com; Mary's Abbey; mains €23-30; 🕑 lunch & dinner Tue-Sat, closed dinner Sun & Mon

The northside got its first real taste of trendy dining when celebrity TV chef Gary Rhodes decided that this was the spot to open his first Irish venture. While you won't spot the Tintin-haired one sweating it out in this big, brash restaurant's kitchen, he did devise the menu and his British staples – cheddar rarebit, roast cod with lobster champ – have been given an Irish twist, which really just means that the ingredients are local.

ELY CHQ Map pp102–3 Contemporary European €€-€€€
☎ 672 0010; www.elywinebar.ie; IFSC, Docklands; mains €18-29; ☺ lunch & dinner Mon-Sun
The International Financial Services Centre (IFSC) finally has a decent restaurant to cater to the throngs of blackberry-addicted power-diners who need sustenance to fuel their busy lives – and this gorgeous tobacco warehouse conversion is the perfect spot to take a break. Ironically, the only criticism of the place is that the service is a little bit slow, although that doesn't matter too much in the evening, when there are fewer suits in a hurry.

HALO Map pp102–3 Modern Irish €€-€€€
☎ 878 2999; www.morrison.ie; Morrison Hotel, Lower Ormond Quay; mains €23-27; ☺ dinner only
Housed in this superslick hotel, the visually stunning Halo has soaring ceilings, a wall of mirrors and striking artwork, but don't let this distract you from the Ireland–meets–continental Europe fusion fare that includes the likes of fillet of sea bream and Carlow lamb rump. Its critics complain that the menu competes with the staff to see who can be more stuffy, but in truth it's the moneyed clientele that win hands down.

WINDING STAIR Map pp102–3 Modern Irish €€-€€€
☎ 873 3292; www.winding-stair.com; 40 Lower Ormond Quay; mains €15-26; ☺ noon-4pm & 6-10pm Tue-Sat, from 1pm Sun
There was much tearing of hair and gnashing of teeth when this Dublin institution closed a few years ago. Thankfully it re-opened in 2006 with the same simple décor and warm atmosphere but with the addition of an excellent wine list and wonderful Irish menu – creamy fish pie, bacon and organic cabbage, steamed mussels or Irish farmyard cheeses – all prepared with much TLC.

YAMAMORI SUSHI Map pp102–3 Japanese €€
☎ 475 5001; 38-39 Lower Ormond Quay; sushi €3-3.50, mains €16-25; ☺ lunch & dinner Sun-Wed, dinner Thu-Sat

Sushi arrives on the northside and immediately proves successful, but that's hardly surprising considering that its southside sister has been doing the Japanese thang with great aplomb for a very long time. The menus in both are largely the same, but we prefer this newer location – right on the river – because it's just that little bit more airy and spacious. The bento boxes are a popular choice, but we really just can't get enough of the sushi moriawase (€20).

BAR ITALIA Map pp102–3 Italian €
☎ 874 1000; 28 Lower Ormond Quay, Quartier Bloom; mains €9-15
The food here is exactly the same as that served by its sister spot across the river (see p154) but what's with the attitude? When we visited, the waitstaff were brusque to the point of rudeness, a complaint that was echoed by others during our research. More's the pity, because this could be a terrific place.

ALILANG Map pp102–3 Korean €
☎ 874 6766; 102 Parnell St; mains €8-13; ☺ to late
With elements of Chinese, Japanese and Thai cuisine, this Korean restaurant on multicultural Parnell St has plenty to whet Western appetites. Tasty dishes like padun (a seafood pancake), cod-and-tofu hotpot and barbecued meats are brought to your table with gas burner, skillet and spicy marinade, for you to tuck in DIY-style, making the food a talking piece. Although the bright and shiny décor may not be conducive to romantic first dates, the atmosphere at Alilang is strangely inviting. Steer clear of the dull wine list in favour of the Korean Hite beer.

DUBLIN CITY GALLERY – THE HUGH LANE Map pp102–3 International €
☎ 874 1903; www.hughlane.ie; 22 North Parnell Sq; mains €8-12; ☺ to 6pm Mon-Thu, to 5pm Fri-Sun
There's hardly a better way to ruminate the art in the gallery than over lunch in the new gallery café, an airy room in the basement next to a small garden. The menu tends largely towards the healthy eating side of things, offering a range of scrumptious savoury tarts and exotic seasonal salads.

PANEM Map pp102–3 Café €

☎ 872 8510; 21 Lower Ormond Quay; mains €7-10; to 5pm, closed Sun

Pasta, focaccia and salads are the standard fare at this diminutive quay-side café, but the specialities are wickedly sweet and savoury pastries, which are all made on-site. The croissants and brioche – filled with Belgian chocolate, almond cream or hazelnut *amaretti* – are the perfect snack for a holiday stroll along the Liffey Boardwalk. Lunchtimes are chaotic.

COBALT CAFÉ & GALLERY

Map pp102–3 Café €

☎ 873 0313; 16 North Great George's St; mains €6-10; closed Sun

A splendid little café just opposite the James Joyce Centre (p108), the Cobalt occupies the ground floor of an elegant Georgian building and serves honest-to-goodness sandwiches stuffed with lots of lovely fillings. The big fireplace is the spot to warm those winter toes.

LA TAVERNA DI BACCO Map pp102–3 Italian €

☎ 873 0040; Quartier Bloom; salads & sandwiches €5-8, mains €8-9; closed lunch Sun

Football-mad developer Mick Wallace has managed to single-handedly create a thriving new Italian quarter with cafés and eateries popping up all over Quartier Bloom, the new lane from Ormond Quay to Great Strand St. La Taverna and Enoteca Delle Langhe (Map pp102–3; ☎ 888 0834), just a few doors up, serve simple pastas, antipasti and Italian cheeses along with the delicious produce of Wallace's own vineyard and others in Piemonte.

SOUP DRAGON Map pp102–3 Soup Bar €

☎ 872 3277; 168 Capel St; soups €5-10; closed Sun

Eat in or takeaway one of 12 tasty varieties of homemade soups, including shepherd's pie or spicy vegetable gumbo. Bowls come in three different sizes and prices include fresh bread and a piece of fruit. Kick-start your day (or afternoon) with a healthy all-day breakfast selection: fresh smoothies (€4.25), generous bowls of yogurt, fruit and muesli (€4.50) or poached egg in a bagel (€3.70).

EPICUREAN FOOD HALL

Map pp102–3 International €

Lower Liffey St; closed Sun

This place is essentially just a food court, but some of Dublin's best eateries have outlets here, and it's a worthy daytime stop-off for a snack, a coffee, lunch or specialist supplies. The food court is perfect if you're not sure what you feel like or if there's discord among your number, because once you get here you can choose between bagels, Italian, French, Mexican, Japanese, Indian and Lebanese, to name just a few.

BEYOND THE ROYAL CANAL

Every Dublin suburb has its foreign eatery – Chinese and Italian are the big faves – but, in terms of restaurants, there isn't much to recommend in the northern wildlands outside of the trendy burghs of Malahide (p216) and Howth (p214). With one very notable exception…

WONGS Off Map p118 Chinese €€

☎ 833 4400; 436 Clontarf Rd; mains €17-18; closed lunch Mon-Sat

This top-rated Chinese restaurant, 5km from the city centre, is a family-run classic with subdued décor and friendly service that raises the bar on warmth and courtesy. The menu is not especially adventurous – it sticks to tried and tested dishes that won't offend the conservative Irish palate – but what it does serve is generally excellent. Our absolute favourite is the duck in a carved-out pineapple shell surrounded by pieces of the fruit and dripping with sauce. Upstairs is a *teppanyaki* room – a private dining room where the food is cooked in the middle of the seated group – for that special occasion or business dinner.

BLUELIST[1] (blu.list) *v.*
to recommend a travel experience.
What's your recommendation? www.lonelyplanet.com/bluelist

DRINKING

top picks

- **Anseo** (p163)
- **Dice Bar** (p171)
- **Gravediggers (aka Kavanagh's)** (p172)
- **Grogan's Castle Lounge** (p165)
- **James Toner's** (p167)
- **Kehoe's** (p165)
- **Long Hall** (p165)
- **Shakespeare** (p171)
- **South William** (p164)
- **Sin É** (p171)

DRINKING

Simply put, the pub is the heart of Dublin's social existence and we're guessing the experience of it ranks pretty high on your list of why you're here. The pub is the broadest window through which you can examine and experience the very essence of the city's culture, in all its myriad forms. It's the great leveller where status and rank hold no sway, where generation gaps are bridged, inhibitions lowered, tongues loosened, schemes hatched, songs sung, stories told and gossip embroidered. It's a unique institution: a theatre and a cosy room, a centre stage and a hideaway, a debating chamber and a place for silent contemplation. It's whatever you want it to be, and that's the secret of the great Irish pub.

Talk – whether it is frivolous, earnest or incoherent – is the essential ingredient. Once tongues are loosened and the cogs of thought oiled, your conversation can go anywhere and you should follow it to its natural conclusion. An old Irish adage suggests you should never talk about sport, religion or politics in unfamiliar company. But just be mindful and you needn't restrict yourself too much. While it's a myth to say you can walk into any Dublin pub and be befriended, you probably won't be drinking on your own for long – unless that's what you want of course. There are few more spiritual experiences than a solitary pint in a Dublin pub in the midafternoon.

There are pubs for every taste and sensibility, although the traditional haunt populated by flat-capped pensioners bursting with insightful anecdotes is disappearing under a modern wave of designer bars and themed locales that wouldn't seem out of place in any other city in the world. All the while, of course, the Irish pub theme is being exported throughout the world like a McPub; if the trend continues Dublin might be the last place to come if you're looking for a spit-and-sawdust boozer.

It's not all doom and gloom, however; some truly great modern bars have opened in recent years to reassure the nostalgic among us that Dublin's reputation as pub capital of the world is in safe hands.

PUB ETIQUETTE

The rounds system – the simple custom where someone buys you a drink and you buy one back – is the bedrock of Irish pub culture. It's summed up in the Irish saying: 'It's impossible for two men to go to a pub for one drink.' Nothing will hasten your fall from social grace here like the failure to uphold this pub law. The Irish are extremely generous and one thing they can't abide is tightfistedness.

Another golden rule about the system is that the next round starts when the first person has finished (preferably just about to finish) their drink. It doesn't matter if you're only halfway through your pint, if it's your round get them in.

Your greatest challenge will probably be trying to keep up with your fellow drinkers, who may keep buying you drinks in every round even when you've still got a clatter of unfinished pints in front of you and you're sliding face first down the bar.

Banter is the fibre of sociability. 'Slagging', or teasing, is the city's favourite pastime and a far more reliable indicator of the strength of friendship than virtually any kind of compliment: a fast, self-deprecating wit and an ability to take a joke in good spirits will win you plenty of friends.

IRISH DRINKS

You can get every conceivable international brew and distillation of booze that is made for export – and the vast majority of Dubliners are happy to declare a foreign tipple as their favourite, with one exception. You would be criminally negligent if you didn't wet your teeth with at least one local liquid, the black stuff that virtually symbolises the city.

A Pint of Plain

They've been brewing beer in Ireland possibly since the Bronze Age and definitely since the arrival of Christianity. The most famous beer of all though, stout, was in fact brewed in Britain, and became known as porter because of its popularity among London market porters. A mere accident of geography, say Dubliners, all the while pointing to the very large Guinness brewery (p88) that has occupied the same premises at St James' Gate since 1759 and whose product is as much a part of the furniture of the Dublin pub as the counter-top itself.

If you're looking for another taste and want to avoid the same beers you can get in any other city, seek out the blossoming micro-brews. In the following listings we have included pubs serving speciality beers on draught – proof that the pub is serious about their beers.

Whiskey, not Whisky

Irish whiskey shares equal billing as the national drink, but in the home it is paramount and if your host produces their best bottle it means you're either very welcome, very wealthy or very lucky. Besides the spelling and the fact that it is distilled three times, Irish whiskey differs from its Scotch cousins in that Scottish malt barley is dried over peat fires, which gives the drink its smoky flavour, whereas Irish malt is dried in smokeless kilns. Finally, while most punters (including most Dubs) would be hard pressed to name more than a handful of Irish whiskeys, at last call there were almost 100 different types, albeit brewed by only three distilleries – Jameson's, Bushmills and Cooley's. If the history, creation (and the drinking) of whiskey is your bag, check out the Old Jameson Distillery (p106).

WHERE TO DRINK

There are about 1000 pubs across the city, so there's bound to be one to suit every mood. Many visitors begin – and sadly end – their exploration of the city's pub scene within the cobbled confines of Temple Bar, the city's most frequented nightlife quarter. It's busy, sure, but the pubs here cater to out-of-towners rather than locals, frantically selling a plastic paddy version of the Dublin experience that most locals avoid like the plague. Still, if the 'Ibiza in the Rain' cheesefest is what you're looking for, you won't be disappointed.

The pubs around Grafton St and St Stephen's Green are a mix of authentic Dublin boozers and stylish contemporary bars that cater to a broad range of punters, from penniless students cadging pints of cider off one another to moneyed execs buying rounds of Mojitos for the table. If the former is more your bag, stay west and southwest of Grafton St, especially along the newish corridor of cool that extends from Aungier St south to Wexford and Camden Sts. If a more designer drink is to your liking, Dawson St, east of Grafton St, and Ballsbridge and Donnybrook, beyond the Grand Canal, have plenty of bars to suit those tastes.

The area around Merrion Square has pubs and bars that are popular with office workers winding down – but that's not nearly as unattractive a proposition as it might sound elsewhere. Most Dubliners like to leave work behind once they cross the pub's hearth and many a wild Friday night is regretted on a Saturday morning!

The quays north and south of the river, for so long in a state of perilous abandonment, have come to life in recent years and now play host to a number of excellent pubs well worth checking out. There are many unreconstructed boozers north of the Liffey, although O'Connell St and its environs are not particularly pleasant or safe places to hang around at night, and you should keep your wits about you when out and about.

But we won't leave this section on that note. From centuries-old taverns to slick DJ bars, there's plenty to please in Dublin these days whether you're supping Guinness, quaffing wine or sipping cocktails. While some still bemoan the loss of the traditional and the proliferation of slick designer bars, we've accepted the development now and like to think that it leaves more room for us in our favourite snugs.

Finally, if you're looking for traditional music pubs, you'll find them listed in the Nightlife chapter, under Live Music Bars (p183).

IRISH DRINK IS MADE TO MEASURE

When drinking stout, beer or ale, the usual measure is a 'pint' (568mL). Half a pint is called a 'glass' and these are generally drunk by women – or visitors from Italy and Spain, unless of course they buy one pint to share among the whole group. Sound sexist and chauvinistic? Truth is that even if they only want a half, and are in a rush, most Dublin males will buy a half-measure and pour into a pint glass rather than be seen drinking from the half-pint glass. That's not to say that the pint glass is the sole preserve of the Dublin male; many a member of the Fair City's fairer sex are equally comfortable with the bigger measure, without any eyebrows being raised.

If you come to Ireland via Britain and drink spirits (or 'shorts' as they're called here), watch out: the English measure is a measly 25mL, while in Dublin you get a whopping 35mL, nearly 50% more.

PRACTICALITIES
Opening Hours & Licensing Laws

Last orders are at 11.30pm Monday to Thursday, 12.30am Friday and Saturday and 11pm Sunday, with 30 minutes drinking-up time each night. However, many central pubs have secured late licences to serve until 1.30am, 2.30am and – in the case of those with a super-special 'theatre licence' – until 3am. As part of the 2003 licensing laws, happy hours have been banned and pubs instructed to get tougher on underage drinkers (so if you look young, bring ID).

Tipping

The American-style gratuity has never been a part of Irish drinking culture, mostly because hard-pressed drinkers in less prosperous times would have needed every penny to continue keeping reality at bay. At best, a regular may opt to leave coppers on the bar for the bartender to pick up, but this practice would only happen in quieter bars among locals.

Which of course doesn't mean that you *can't* tip. If you want to reward your hard-working barkeep for good service (watch them sweat on a busy night and you'll know how hard it is) feel absolutely free to do so. They'll probably look at you with bemused gratitude.

Non-Smoking

Ireland went smoke-free in March 2004 (with smoking banned in all workplaces, including pubs). For more info, see the boxed text (p19).

GRAFTON STREET & AROUND

Amid the designer shops and trendy eateries of the Grafton St area, a few top-notch Victorian pubs combine elegance and traditional style to pull in punters from far and near. Dawson St is popular with straight professional types, the area immediately west of Grafton St has something for everyone, and trendy Wexford and Camden Sts tick the arty, alternative box.

BA MIZU Map pp66–7   Contemporary Bar
☎ 674 6712; www.bamizu.com; Powerscourt Townhouse Shopping Centre, South William St
Tucked away beside the grand entrance to Powerscourt Townhouse is one of the showiest feathers in South William St's well-plumed cap o' cool. Head downstairs to an intimate lobby dominated by a central square bar and surrounded by cosy nooks, perfect for ice breaking on first dates.

BAILEY Map pp66–7   Contemporary Bar
☎ 670 4939; www.baileybar.ie; 2 Duke St
Perpetually popular with self-appointed shakers and movers – and a few frustrated office workers looking to shake and move – the Bailey has wall-mounted light boxes and comfortable seating, perfect for an evening schmooze. Outside gas braziers allow you to sit on the pavement and observe the street life by day. It also does a mean trade in continental lunches.

BANK Map pp66–7   Contemporary Bar
☎ 677 0677; www.bankoncollegegreen.com; 20-22 College Green
This architecturally dazzling bar occupies the site of a former Victorian bank and has opulent decoration, including a stained-glass ceiling, hand-carved plasterwork and mosaic-tiled floors to occupy your eyes while you wait for your pint of Guinness to settle. The atmosphere is conversational, and the bar staff are excellent.

CAFÉ EN SEINE Map pp66–7   Contemporary Bar
☎ 677 4369; www.capitalbars.com; 40 Dawson St
Dublin's 'in' bar when it opened in 1995, Café en Seine lost its place but was then overhauled into one of the most spectacular bars in the drinking world. It is decorated in an opulent, wildly extravagant 19th-century style, which includes glass panelling and real 12m-high trees! The highlight, though, is propping up the beautiful wood-and-marble bar and checking out the beautiful people.

CARNIVAL Map pp66–7   Contemporary Bar
☎ 405 3604; 11 Wexford St; ☽ 2pm-midnight Sun-Thu, to 1am Fri & Sat; ☐ 83, 123
A party atmosphere and a candle-lit, down-at-heel room with lots of cosy corners makes Dermot Doran's latest bar venture, Carnival, a great place to meet people. Don't expect to chat though – the music from those DJs playing everything from Magic Numbers to Kraftwerk (Thursday to Sunday) will drown out those witticisms.

DAKOTA Map pp66–7   Contemporary Bar

☎ 672 7696; 8 South William St

Surprisingly chilled out for a superpub, Dakota is distinguished by dimmed lights, funky tunes, crafty cocktails and a slick modern layout. Unfortunately, we found the weekend bouncers to be goons, the beer patchy and the bar staff so frosty that if you stuck your tongue out at them it might stick.

DAVY BYRNE'S Map pp66–7   Contemporary Bar

☎ 677 5217; www.davybyrnes.com; 21 Duke St

The place where Leopold Bloom popped in for a Gorgonzola sandwich and a glass of burgundy. Davy Byrne's makes the most of its Joycean connection, but the contemporary version bears about as much resemblance to the boozer mentioned in *Ulysses* as it does a hole in the wall. It is popular with out-of-towners and gets especially packed on rugby weekends.

HORSESHOE BAR Map pp66–7   Contemporary Bar

☎ 676 6471; Shelbourne Hotel, St Stephen's Green

The refurb of the Shelbourne has brought us a brand new Horseshoe Bar, a thoroughly modern version of the old one beloved of politicians, hacks and journalists, where many an important decision was made, celebrated and even regretted around the horseshoe-shaped bar.

MARKET BAR Map pp66–7   Contemporary Bar

☎ 613 9094; www.marketbar.ie; 14a Fade St

An architectural beauty, this giant redbrick and iron girder room that was once a Victorian sausage factory is now a large, breezy bar that stands as a far more preferable alternative to many of the city's superbars. Unlike virtually every other new pub in town, there's no music. It also does a roaring trade in Spanish-influenced pub grub (see p150).

ODEON Map pp66–7   Contemporary Bar

☎ 478 2088; www.odeon.ie; Old Harcourt St Station, 57 Harcourt St

This former train station is light, airy, and jam-packed with Art Deco elegance and Red Bull–loaded punters getting ready for a gig next door at Tripod. The comfy sofas are too scarce but its the kind of place to be parading or standing along its impossibly long bar rather than sitting down

anyway. Sunday afternoons are all about indulgence and taking it nice and easy with Bloody Marys, the newspapers and comfort foods.

RON BLACK'S Map pp66–7   Contemporary Bar

☎ 672 8231; www.ronblacks.ie; 37 Dawson St

The youngest of the three superbars along this strip, along with SamSara (below) and Café en Seine (opposite), Ron Black's is packed with affluent young players who think that leisure time is cutting a deal with a drink in their hand. It's the Celtic Tiger love story in all its designer drama: budding business impresario spots young commercial property agent across the dark wood bar, glides across the floor and takes a seat next to her on the comfy couch…and it's love and planning permission for all eternity. We should be so lucky.

SAMSARA Map pp66–7   Contemporary Bar

☎ 671 7723; www.lastampa.ie; 35-36 Dawson St

This huge Middle Eastern–themed drinking emporium is packed at weekends with gorgeous young things and thingies, air-kissing and comparing their designer ware. The seats are too uncomfortable and there's an overwhelming vibe of 'me, me, me!' but you can get through it by meditating on samsara – the endless cycle of suffering and reincarnation. Or just enjoy the eye candy.

ANSEO Map pp66–7   DJ Bar

☎ 475 1321; 28 Camden St

Unpretentious, unaffected and incredibly popular, this cosy alternative bar – which is pronounced 'an-*shuh*', the Irish for 'here' – is a favourite with those who live by the credo that to try too hard is far worse than not trying at all. Wearing cool like a loose garment, the punters thrive on the mix of chat and terrific DJs, who dig into virtually every crate to provide the soundtrack, whether it be Peggy Lee or Lee Perry.

BIA BAR Map pp66–7   DJ Bar

☎ 405 3563; 30 Lower Stephen St

In the last couple of years, this trendy watering hole has become massively popular. We thought at first it was to do with the excellent music policy that has brought some of the city's best DJs to exercise their craft at the decks. Sure, that helped, but then it dawned on us: it's the huge beer garden at

top picks

DJ BARS

- Anseo (p163) **Old and new favourites.**
- Dice Bar (p171) **Dive bar with eclectic music.**
- Village (right) **Good music every night.**
- Hogan's (p176) **Contemporary dance music.**
- Sin É (p171) **Down-to-earth ambience and great music.**

the back that really brings them in, for not only does it allow some al fresco drinking, but it's one of the few bars where you don't have to stand on the street to have a smoke.

GLOBE Map pp66–7   DJ Bar
☎ 671 1220; www.globe.ie; 11 South Great George's St
In 2007 the first of the city's wave of 'cool' bars changed hands after nearly 15 years of the same ownership; while the new crowd have promised not to mess with a winning formula, some change is inevitable, be it in the New York dive–style décor, the relaxed, friendly attitude or both. The bar doubles as a chill-out room for the excellent Rí Rá (p177).

HOGAN'S Map pp66–7   DJ Bar
☎ 677 5904; 35 South Great George's St
Once an old-style traditional bar, Hogan's is now a gigantic boozer spread across two floors. Mid-week it's a relaxing hang-out for young professionals and restaurant and bar workers on a night off. But come the weekend the sweat bin downstairs pulls them in for some serious music courtesy of the usually excellent DJs.

NO 4 DAME LANE Map pp66–7   DJ Bar
☎ 679 0291; 4 Dame Lane
This two-storey designer bar took forever to get going – one of the pitfalls of trying to manufacture cool – but once it did it really took off, especially at weekends, when clubby kids and young professionals dressed as clubby kids try to hold a conversation above the loud DJ-led music. Upstairs is even louder, but that's OK, because – judging by some of the conversations we eavesdropped on – the music is often better than the chat. It has a late licence, so you don't have to bother with a nightclub.

SOLAS Map pp66–7   DJ Bar
☎ 478 0583; 31 Wexford St
Good DJs every night of the week are the primary attraction at this trendy little bar along trendy Wexford St; at weekends the music is loud and you'll most likely struggle to hear what's being said. Mid-week the place is quieter but you might find yourself stopping the conversation with a 'hold on a minute, I love this song!'

SOUTH WILLIAM Map pp66–7   DJ Bar
☎ 679 3701; www.southwilliam.ie; South William St
The city's hippest new bar has it all behind its huge glass frontage: top class music, great DJs, a downstairs club with a rotating list of guest DJs from all over, and even pies created by Troy Maguire from Lock's (p147).

VILLAGE Map pp66–7   DJ Bar
☎ 475 8555; www.thevillagevenue.com; 26 Wexford St
Packed to overflowing every weekend, this large modern bar is where the lovely lads and gorgeous gals show off their plumage in a fun-time courting ritual that has the rest of them queuing up at the door to join in. There are live bands (see p183) and excellent DJs nightly, and Sunday night's Songs of Praise is the city's best karaoke night. The nightclub bit of the venue (see p177) opens Thursday to Saturday.

DRAGON Map pp66–7   Gay Bar
☎ 478 1590; www.capitalbars.com; 64 South Great George's St
High-concept, high-octane and simply loaded with attitude, the Dragon is the slightly trendier alternative to the long-established George down the street (George and the Dragon; get it?). But neon lighting, loud music and drunken couples slobbering all over each other do not a memorable bar make. Next.

GEORGE Map pp66–7   Gay Bar
☎ 478 2983; www.capitalbars.com; 89 South Great George's St
The purple mother of Dublin's gay bars is a long-standing institution, having lived through the years when it was the only place in town where the gay crowd could, well, be gay. There are other places to go, but the George remains the best, if only for

tradition's sake. Shirley's legendary Sunday night bingo is as popular as ever.

BRUXELLES Map pp66–7 — Traditional Pub
☎ 677 5362; 7-8 Harry St

Although it has largely shed its heavy metal and alternative skin, Bruxelles is still a raucous, fun place to hang out and there are different music areas. It's comparatively trendy on the ground floor, while downstairs is a great, loud and dingy rock bar with live music each weekend. Just outside, a bronze Phil Lynott is there to remind us of Bruxelles' impeccable rock credentials (see the boxed text, p182).

DAWSON LOUNGE Map pp66–7 — Traditional Pub
☎ 677 5909; 25 Dawson St

To see the smallest bar in Dublin, go through a small doorway, down a narrow flight of steps and into two tiny rooms that always seem to be filled with a couple of bedraggled drunks who look like they're hiding. Psst, here's a secret: a certain sunglassed lead singer of a certain ginormous Irish band is said to love unwinding in here from time to time.

GROGAN'S CASTLE LOUNGE
Map pp66–7 — Traditional Pub
☎ 677 9320; 15 South William St

This place is known simply as Grogan's (after the original owner), and it is a city-centre institution. It has long been a favourite haunt of Dublin's writers and painters, as well as others from the alternative bohemian set, most of whom seem to be waiting for the 'inevitable' moment when they are finally recognised as geniuses. A peculiar quirk of the pub is that drinks are marginally cheaper in the area with a stone floor than in the carpeted lounge, even though they are served by exactly the same bar!

INTERNATIONAL BAR
Map pp66–7 — Traditional Pub
☎ 677 9250; www.international-bar.com; 23 Wicklow St

This tiny pub with a huge personality is a top spot for an afternoon pint. It has a long bar, stained-glass windows, red velour seating and a convivial atmosphere. Some of Ireland's most celebrated comedians stuttered through their first set in the Comedy Cellar (p178), which is, of course, upstairs.

KEHOE'S Map pp66–7 — Traditional Pub
☎ 677 8312; 9 South Anne St

This is one of the most atmospheric pubs in the city centre and a favourite with all kinds of Dubliners. It has a beautiful Victorian bar, a wonderful snug, and plenty of other little nooks and crannies. Upstairs, drinks are served in what was once the publican's living room – and looks it!

LONG HALL Map pp66–7 — Traditional Pub
☎ 475 1590; 51 South Great George's St

Luxuriating in full Victorian splendour, this is one of the city's most beautiful and

MARC BEREEM, PUBLICAN

'The days of the traditional Dublin pub, where all they do is serve a good pint of Guinness are gone. The contemporary bar has to offer more, but it can't lose sight of the past either.' A bold statement, but Marc Bereem knows a thing or two about the city's bars. As one of the two brothers who own arguably Dublin's coolest bar, the South William (opposite), Bereem (early 30s) believes that the essence of a great Dublin pub is not the old-fashioned look but the personality behind the bar.

'If the staff feel a sense of ownership of the place and are to serve and entertain the clientele, then you have the makings of a great bar.' Marc is pretty adamant as to why so many other modern bars are so infinitely forgettable: 'Most of them are owned by companies who don't care about anything other than the bottom line.'

This is hardly the case with the South William, lovingly designed by Marc and his younger brother Conor in a style influenced as much by their extensive travels as their love of the simple lines of a traditional boozer. 'We wanted to create a simple space where young creative people would feel inspired…by the food, the music and the décor, which has lots of little things we collected over the years.'

The South William opened its doors in December 2006 and so far, so very good. Its mix of New York bar, trendy Parisian café and Dublin boozer hits the spot just right and manages to avoid the label of trying too hard. But where does Marc go when he wants a night off? 'My favourite pub is Peter's, which is conveniently just up the street!' Why aren't we surprised that he's chosen such a quiet and classy pub as his favourite?

best-loved pubs. Check out the ornate carvings in the woodwork behind the bar and the elegant chandeliers. The bartenders are experts at their craft, an increasingly rare attribute in Dublin these days.

MCDAID'S Map pp66–7 Traditional Pub
☎ 679 4395; 3 Harry St

One of Dublin's best-known literary pubs, this classic boozer was Brendan Behan's 'local' (until he was barred) and it still oozes character. The pints are perfect, and best appreciated during the day when it's not full of our type. Thankfully, there's no music – just conversation and raucous laughter.

NEARY'S Map pp66–7 Traditional Pub
☎ 677 8596; 1 Chatham St

One of a string of off-Grafton St, classic Victorian boozers once patronised by Dublin's legless literati, Neary's is a perfect stop-off day or night. It combines great service, a bohemian atmosphere and attractively worn furnishings, and is popular with actors from the nearby Gaiety Theatre (p186).

OLD STAND Map pp66–7 Traditional Pub
☎ 677 7220; 37 Exchequer St

Refreshingly unreconstructed, this is one of the oldest pubs in Dublin and seems to be just sauntering along at the same pace it was 10 years ago, as if the whole Celtic Tiger thing never happened. It's named after the old stand at Lansdowne Rd Stadium, and is a favourite with sports fans and reporters.

O'NEILL'S Map pp66–7 Traditional Pub
☎ 679 3671; 2 Suffolk St

This rambling old pub near Trinity College has plenty of nooks and crannies, as well as punters to fill them. The odd combination of students and stockbrokers lends the place a chaotic atmosphere. There are also hefty portions of decent pub grub.

PAVILION Map pp66–7 Traditional Pub
☎ 896 1000; Trinity College

One of the most enjoyable drinking experiences in town can be had on a pleasant summer's day on the balcony of the Pav, the cricket pavilion overlooking Trinity's playing fields. Grab a beer and a sandwich before settling down to enjoy the spectacle on display: a cricket match or just the other punters getting drunk and trying to play Frisbee.

PETER'S PUB Map pp66–7 Traditional Pub
☎ 677 8588; 1 Johnston Pl

A pub for a chat and a convivial catch up, this humble and friendly place is more like Peter's Living Room, and is one of the few remaining drinking dens in this area that hasn't changed personality in recent years, or gone chasing the new money.

STAG'S HEAD Map pp66–7 Traditional Pub
☎ 679 3701; 1 Dame Ct

The Stag's Head was built in 1770, remodelled in 1895 and sold in 2004. Fortunately, the new owners knew better than to change one bolt of this superb pub, so picturesque that it often appears in films and also featured in a postage-stamp series on Irish bars. While you're waiting for your steak and chips you may find yourself philosophising in the ecclesiastical atmosphere, as James Joyce did. It's probable that some of the fitters that worked on this pub would have also worked on churches in the area, so the stained-wood-and-polished-brass similarities are no accident. A bloody great bar, no doubt.

SWAN Map pp66–7 Traditional Pub
☎ 647 5272; 70 Aungier St

John Lynch's pub (known to all as the Swan) is home to two kinds of punter: the in-for-a-pint-and-a-chat tippler that doesn't venture far from the Victorian front bar; and the more animated younger person, who finds solace and music in the side bar. A beautiful marriage that works because neither troubles the other.

WHELAN'S Map pp66–7 Traditional Pub
☎ 475 8555; www.whelanslive.com; 28 Wexford St

The traditional pub attached to the popular live music venue (see p183) was one of the best places to wind down a week over a pint and a chat, until it closed its doors for a major refurb. What it'll become is anyone's guess – we just hope that it keeps its old-fashioned ambience.

OLESYA'S WINE BAR Map pp66–7 Wine Bar
☎ 672 4087; 18 Exchequer St; ☽ noon-midnight

With over 100 different wines available by the glass and about 400 by the bottle, this lovely wine bar is perfect if you fancy a liquid evening but want to avoid a crowded pub. Take a seat, order some wine and wash it down with something from the accompanying menu, even though we were disappointed with the size of the cheeseboard.

MERRION SQUARE & AROUND

Away from the city centre there are a number of fine pubs that are worthy of the trek. Many fill up with office workers straight after (or just before) clocking-off time and then get quieter as the night progresses.

WHITE HORSE INN
Map pp78–9   Contemporary Bar
☎ 672 7597; 1 George's Quay
This excellent quayside bar has been re-invented in recent times as a cool spot for the clubby crowd, thanks largely to the A: M Club, an early morning party that starts at 7am every Saturday for those who don't want to say goodnight just yet. At more sociable hours, the bar dances to a soulful, jazzy soundtrack Thursday to Saturday night.

DOHENY & NESBITT'S
Map pp78–9   Traditional Pub
☎ 676 2945; 5 Lower Baggot St
A standout, even in a city of wonderful pubs, Nesbitt's is equipped with antique snugs and is a favourite place for high-powered gossip among politicians and journalists; Leinster House (p82) is only a short stroll away.

HARTIGAN'S Map pp78–9   Traditional Pub
☎ 676 2280; 100 Lower Leeson St
This is about as spartan a bar as you'll find in the city, and is the daytime home to some serious drinkers, who appreciate the quiet, no-frills surroundings. In the evening it's popular with students from the medical faculty of University College Dublin (UCD).

JAMES TONER'S Map pp78–9   Traditional Pub
☎ 676 3090; 139 Lower Baggot St
Toner's, with its stone floors and antique snugs, has changed little over the years and is the closest thing you'll get to a country pub in the heart of the city. The shelves and drawers are reminders that it

top picks

TOP-SHELF HOTEL BARS

You don't have to be a high-paying guest to enjoy the luxury of a fancy hotel bar. The following are the best places in town to be seen with a drink in hand.

- **Central Hotel (p200)** The 2nd-floor Library Bar is a genuine Victorian/Edwardian drawing room.
- **Four Seasons Hotel (p204)** A must for anyone aspiring to be a part of the Dublin scene.
- **Dylan Hotel (p204)** The Dylan Bar is the latest place to schmooze over a Bellini.
- **Shelbourne (p198)** Politicians and journos trade tales and secrets in the Horseshoe Bar.
- **Westbury Hotel (p198)** Strangely ignored by most, which is probably why visiting celebs feel comfortable relaxing in this large and beautiful bar.

once doubled as a grocery shop. The writer Oliver St John Gogarty once brought WB Yeats here, after the upper-class poet – who only lived around the corner – decided he wanted to visit a pub. After a silent sherry in the noisy bar, Yeats turned to his friend and said, 'I have seen the pub, now please take me home.' We always suspected he was a little too precious for normal people, and he would probably be horrified by the good-natured business crowd making the racket these days too. His loss.

KENNEDY'S Map pp78–9   Traditional Pub
☎ 677 0626; 10 George's Quay
Not to be confused with the home of the terrific underground nightclub on Westland Row (see p176), this is a proper traditional pub where literally nothing has changed in 50 years, including some of the clientele. Tread softly and speak even quieter so as not to disturb the contemplative atmosphere of a bar that seems oblivious to what's happened to Dublin in the last 20 years.

MULLIGAN'S Map pp78–9   Traditional Pub
☎ 677 5582; 8 Poolbeg St
This brilliant old boozer was established in 1782 and has barely changed over the years. In fact, the last time it was renovated was when Christy Brown and his rowdy clan ran amok here in the film My Left Foot. It has one of the finest pints of Guinness in Dublin and a colourful crew of regulars. It's

just off Fleet St, outside the eastern boundary of Temple Bar.

O'DONOGHUE'S Map pp78–9   Traditional Pub
☎ 661 4303; 15 Merrion Row

Once the most renowned traditional music bar in all Dublin, this is where the world-famous folk group the Dubliners refined their raspish brand of trad in the 1960s. On summer evenings a young, international crowd spills out into the courtyard beside the pub. It's also a famous rugby pub and the Dublin HQ for many Irish and visiting fans.

TEMPLE BAR

Temple Bar's loud and busy pubs are a far cry from authentic, but they're undoubtedly fun – that is if your idea of fun is mixing it with a bunch of lads and lasses from the North of England, egging each other on to show off their family jewels and daring one another to drain 10 Fat Frogs in a row, all in front of a bemused audience of Spanish and Italian tourists, all sharing three glasses of Guinness. You've been warned!

AULD DUBLINER Map p85   Contemporary Bar
☎ 677 0527; 17 Anglesea St

Predominantly patronised by tourists, 'the Auld Foreigner', as locals have dubbed it, has a carefully manicured 'old-world' charm that has been preserved – or refined – after a couple of renovations. It's a reliable place for a singsong and a laugh, as long as you don't mind taking 15 minutes to get to and from the *jax* (toilet).

BOB'S Map p85   Contemporary Bar
☎ 677 5482; 35 East Essex St

This used to be known as Bad Bob's, but after a 2000 renovation the owners went on the straight and narrow, which in this case meant chasing the new money. It's a typical Dublin superpub, with three floors, bland modern décor, young groups and shirty security staff.

FRONT LOUNGE Map p85   Contemporary Bar
☎ 670 4112; 33-34 Parliament St

The unofficially gay 'Flounge' is a sophisticated and friendly bar that is bright and airy during the week and positively mobbed on weekends. It's by no means an exclusive place, but its clientele is predominantly gay and preposterously handsome.

MESSRS MAGUIRE Map p85   Contemporary Bar
☎ 670 5777; 1-2 Burgh Quay

This uber-bar and microbrewery is spread across three levels, connected by a truly imperious staircase, and is a disconcerting mix of young and old, intimate and brash. Its own beers are worth contemplating, but not on the weekend when the place is absolutely jammers.

OCTAGON BAR Map p85   Contemporary Bar
☎ 670 9000; Clarence Hotel, 6-8 Wellington Quay

Temple Bar's trendiest watering hole is where you'll find many of Dublin's celebrities (including mates of the owner's, U2) and hangers-on, swaggering and sipping expertly made cocktails in front of stylish wood panelling and amid perpetual daylight. Drinks are expensive, but if such things concern you, don't even try getting past the bouncers.

PORTERHOUSE BREWING COMPANY
Map p85   Contemporary Bar
☎ 679 8847; 16-18 Parliament St

The second-biggest brewery in Dublin, the Porterhouse looks like a cross between a Wild West bar and a Hieronymus Bosch painting – all wood and full of staircases – on the fringe of Temple Bar. We love it, and although it inevitably gets crowded, this pub is for the discerning drinker and has lots of its own delicious brews, including its Plain Porter (some say it's the best stout in town) as well as unfamiliar imported beers.

TEMPLE BAR Map p85   Contemporary Bar
☎ 677 3807; 48 Temple Bar

The most photographed pub façade in Dublin, perhaps the world, the Temple Bar (aka Flannery's) is smack bang in the middle of the tourist precinct and is usually choc-a-bloc with visitors. It's good craic though, and presses all the right buttons, with traditional musicians, a buzzy atmosphere and even a beer garden. It's also one of the most expensive pubs in Dublin.

THOMAS READ'S Map p85   Contemporary Bar
☎ 670 7220; 1 Parliament St

The clientele at this spacious and airy bar, spread across two levels, seems to favour a selection of wine and coffee over beer.

During the day, it's a great place to relax and read a newspaper. For a more traditional setting its annexe, the Oak, is still a great place for a pint.

TURK'S HEAD Map p85   Contemporary Bar
☎ 679 9701; 27-30 Parliament St
This superpub is decorated in two completely different styles – one really gaudy, the other a re-creation of LA circa 1930 – and is one of the oddest and most interesting in Temple Bar. It pulsates nightly with a young pumped-up crowd of mainly tourists, out to boogie to chart hits. Be mindful of hidden steps all over the place.

BROGAN'S Map p85   Traditional Pub
☎ 679 9570; 75 Dame St
Only a couple of doors down from the Olympia Theatre (p182), this is a wonderful old-style bar where conversation – not loud music – is king. The beer is also pretty good.

OLIVER ST JOHN GOGARTY
Map p85   Traditional Pub
☎ 671 1822; 58-59 Fleet St
You won't see too many Dubs ordering drinks in this bar, which is almost entirely given over to tourists, who come for the carefully manufactured slice of authentic traditionalism…and the knee-slappin', toe-tappin' sessions that run throughout the day (see p184). The kitchen serves up dishes that most Irish cooks have consigned to the culinary dustbin.

PALACE BAR Map p85   Traditional Pub
☎ 677 9290; 21 Fleet St
With its mirrors and wooden niches, this is one of Dublin's great Victorian pubs and used to be the unofficial head office of the

Irish Times. Throughout the 1990s it steadfastly refused to accommodate the cubs of the Celtic Tiger and has always had a reputation as a place where yuppie bullshit is barred. While the Temple Bar vibe is encroaching on it a little, the staff's razor-sharp sarcasm can still bring uppity patrons down the required peg or two. Upstairs is where you'll hear some of the city's best traditional music (see p184).

KILMAINHAM & THE LIBERTIES

Like what's happening in the rejuvenated Smithfield across the river, some of the pubs in Dublin's oldest area are now being rediscovered by new crowds jaded with the superpub phenomenon.

BRAZEN HEAD Map pp90–1   Traditional Pub
☎ 679 5186; 20 Lower Bridge St
Reputedly Dublin's oldest pub, the Brazen Head has been serving thirsty patrons since 1198 when it set up as a Norman tavern. Though its history is uncertain, the sunken level of the entrance courtyard clearly indicates how much street levels have altered since its construction. It's a bit away from the city centre, and the clientele is made up of foreign-language students, tourists and some grizzly auld locals. Robert Emmet was believed to have been a regular visitor, while in *Ulysses*, James Joyce reckoned 'you get a decent enough do in the Brazen Head'.

FALLON'S Map pp90–1   Traditional Pub
☎ 454 2801; 129 The Coombe
Just west of the city centre, in the heart of medieval Dublin, this is a fabulously old-fashioned bar that has been serving a great pint of Guinness to a most discerning clientele since the end of the 17th century. Prize fighter Dan Donnelly, the only boxer ever to be knighted, was head bartender here in 1818. It's a genuine Irish bar filled with Dubs.

BEYOND THE GRAND CANAL

Southern suburban bars are among the most popular in town, especially those in the chi chi Dublin 4 area, where the bold and the beautiful swap tales of new cars bought with old money over vodka gimlets and gin and tonics.

ICE BAR Map p99   Contemporary Bar

☎ 665 4000; Four Seasons Hotel, Simmonscourt Rd
Not to be confused with the Dice Bar (opposite) in a taxi – practise your elocution because the bars are worlds apart in every sense. Young, single 20-somethings with infinite disposable incomes come here to see and be seen, making this either the most sought-after destination in town or somewhere to avoid like a bad dose of plague. Flash your convertible-beemer car keys at the door for speedy access. The all-white chichi interior with central chrome and marble bar is softened by some lovely, specially commissioned wall hangings by Irish artists. Vodka-based cocktails are the house speciality.

KIELY'S Map p99   Contemporary Bar

☎ 283 0209; 22 Donnybrook Rd
Fans of satirist Paul Howard's lovable D4 monster Ross O'Carroll Kelly will instantly recognise the favourite hangout of the rugby-loving southsider, where the fortunes of Drico, Shaggy and the Darce are discussed in earnest by hardbodies wrapped in Leinster jerseys…and that's just the girls. If you're going to the next-door Donnybrook Rugby Ground, this is the perfect pre- and post-match place to be.

O'BRIEN'S Map p99   Traditional Pub

☎ 668 2851; 8-9 Sussex Tce, Upper Leeson St
The unofficial HQ of media types and advertising execs, old-fashioned O'Brien's is the embodiment of all the aspirations of the Celtic Tiger, a place where prosperity and forward-thinking can flourish amid the powerfully nostalgic reminders of a time gone by. Which pretty much means that

O'Brien's hasn't changed its décor all that much, but the bathrooms are absolutely spotless.

SEARSON'S Map p99   Traditional Pub

☎ 660 0330; www.searsons.ie; 42-44 Upper Baggot St
What could easily be dismissed as yet another characterless superpub, with the warmth and ambience of a train station, is actually a pretty decent bar with the option of Old Man pub at the front and trendy, modern bar at the back. Something for everyone then: lunchtimes it's packed with office workers, weekend nights it's packed with the same crowd in jeans and designer shirts and, when the rugby's on, the Irish green. Two Havana Clubs and Coke, please.

NORTH OF THE LIFFEY

The northside's pubs just don't get the same numbers of visitors as their southside brethren, which just means that if you're looking for a truly authentic pub experience, you're more likely to get it here. Around O'Connell St you'll also get the rough with the smooth, and we suggest you keep your wits about you late at night so as to avoid the potential for trouble that sadly besets the city's main thoroughfare after dark.

FLORIDITA Map pp102–3   Contemporary Bar

☎ 878 1032; www.floriditaireland.ie; Irish Life Mall, Lower Abbey St
Ernest Hemingway's favourite Havana bar is now a multinational chain, and the newest branch of the super-slick bar-club-restaurant opened in the distinctly uncool Irish Life Mall in 2007. Real live Cuban musicians provide the backbeat to a night of rum, cigars and Latin American cuisine.

MORRISON BAR Map pp102–3   Contemporary Bar

☎ 878 2999; Upper Ormond Quay
This is the north side's version of the Octagon Bar (p168), only far more difficult to get into if you don't look the part. If you haven't spent a fortune on your outfit (or managed to fake it), forget it. You wouldn't have enjoyed the luxurious John Rocha–designed dark-oak and cream interior, the views over the Liffey, the suave and sophisticated clientele. Nah, you didn't miss much.

PRAVDA Map pp102–3 — Contemporary Bar
☎ 874 0076; www.pravda.ie; 35 Lower Liffey St

As un-Irish as you could probably get, this huge, multilevel Russian-themed bar was all the rage when it opened a few years ago. It has got a party atmosphere and is a great pick-up joint for young tourists, but you can forget about conversation at night (because the music is so loud) and the bouncers seem especially dim-witted.

SHAKESPEARE Map pp102–3 — Contemporary Bar
☎ 878 8650; 160 Parnell St

This marvellous bar is a great example of the meeting of two very different worlds, in this case a traditional old Dublin bar and the Korean love of all things karaoke and contemporary. We can't think of a more successful and enjoyable example of Dublin's new multicultural identity.

VOODOO LOUNGE
Map pp102–3 — Contemporary Bar
☎ 873 6013; 37 Arran Quay

Run by the same crew as Dice Bar (below), the Voodoo Lounge is a long, dark bar with decadent, Gothic Louisiana–style décor, great service, a friendly atmosphere and looooo-uuud music, just the way the fun-lovin' crowd likes it.

DICE BAR Map pp90–1 — DJ Bar
☎ 674 6710; 79 Queen St

Co-owned by Huey from the Fun Lovin' Criminals, the Dice Bar looks like something you might find on New York's Lower East Side. Its dodgy locale, black-and-red painted interior, dripping candles and stressed seating, combined with rocking DJs most nights, make it a magnet for Dublin's beautiful beatnik crowds. It has Guinness and local microbrews.

SIN É Map pp102–3 — DJ Bar
☎ 878 7009; 14-15 Ormond Quay

Phew. This quayside bar opened just in time, just before the essential ingredient of all great Dublin bars was abandoned in favour of whatever designer gimmickry was all the rage that month. Well done for remembering that ambience is the key, not fancy mirrors where pretentious gobshites can keep an eye on their oh-so-important look. This place has no real décor, but who cares? It buzzes almost nightly with a terrific

mix of students, professionals, the hip and the uncool. The DJs are uniformly excellent.

FLOWING TIDE Map pp102–3 — Traditional Pub
☎ 874 0842; 9 Lower Abbey St

This beautiful, atmospheric old pub is directly opposite the Abbey (p184) and is popular with theatre-goers – it can get swamped around 11pm, after the curtain comes down. They blend in with some no-bullshit locals who give the place a vital edge, and make it a great place for a drink and a natter.

GILL'S Map pp102–3 — Traditional Pub
☎ 855 4128; 555 North Circular Rd; 🚍 10, 38 or 122

Just a stone's throw from Croke Park, this unashamedly old-fashioned boozer was one of Brendan Behan's favourites and the place where his friends chose to wake his passing when he died. If you're on your way to Croker for a match, or just want to try out a good old-style pub, there are few better.

GLIMMER MAN Map pp102–3 — Traditional Pub
☎ 677 9781; 14-15 Manor St, Stoneybatter; 🚍 38, 39 or 39A

It's slightly out of the way, to the west of Smithfield, but this is a terrific neighbourhood bar that has benefited from the influx of foreign nationals to the area in recent years. In warm weather, the beer garden out the back is a great place to enjoy a pint.

NEALON'S Map p85 — Traditional Pub
☎ 872 3247; Capel St

The warm and cosy décor of this traditional pub is matched by the exceptionally friendly staff. It's a bit of old Dublin on a street getting ready to take off, so catch it while you can. There's live jazz on Sunday.

OVAL Map p85 — Traditional Pub
☎ 872 1259; 78 Middle Abbey St

This is a great little pub, where young and old come together in conversation and rich, creamy pints go down a treat. The Tardis effect is evident once you walk through the door: it is much bigger than it looks from the outside, spreading over three floors.

PATRICK CONWAY'S
Map pp102–3 — Traditional Pub
☎ 873 2687; 70 Parnell St

This gem of a pub has been lining up drinks since 1745 and joyous fathers – including

Colm Meaney's character in *The Snapper* (see p43) – have been skulling celebratory pints at its bar since the day the Rotunda Maternity Hospital opened across the road in 1757. Upstairs is the fantastic Boom Boom Room (p182), one of the best places in the city for good live music.

SACKVILLE LOUNGE
Map pp102–3   Traditional Pub
☎ 874 5222; Sackville Pl
This tiny 19th-century one-room, wood-panelled bar lies just off O'Connell St and is popular with actors from the nearby Abbey and Peacock theatres (see p184), as well as a disproportionate number of elderly drinkers. It's a good pub for a solitary pint.

SEAN O'CASEY'S Map pp102–3   Traditional Pub
☎ 874 8675; 105 Marlborough St
The antithesis of the Dublin superpub, this is the kind of place where the male drinkers (and there seems to be *only* male drinkers) look up and grunt when you walk through the door. It's a Kerry pub, decked out in the county's Gaelic Athletic Association (GAA) colours, and is particularly lively when Kerry are playing in Croke Park.

WELCOME INN Map pp102–3   Traditional Pub
☎ 874 3227; 93 Parnell St
This musty, scruffy, wonderful bar has been a favourite with the city's college slackers for a couple of generations. They love the oversized lounge and its assorted cast of characters, which these days include groups of Spanish and Italian tourists looking to check out Dublin alcoholics up close.

ENO WINES Map pp102–3   Wine Bar
☎ 636 0616; Irish Financial Services Centre, Mayor Sq
A wine bar in a financial services centre sounds like a formula for insufferable pre-tentiousness, but this remarkable venture is unique to the city so we thought we'd give it a try – and we weren't disappointed. Basically, this is a wine-tasting centre where you buy a card for whatever amount you like and are then free to try any of the 60-plus wines that are available, deducting the cost of it from your card as you go along. The Shiraz is to die for, darling.

BEYOND THE ROYAL CANAL
It is just beyond the north side's canal that you can find some of the best traditional pubs in Dublin, and these places are highly recommended.

GRAVEDIGGERS (AKA KAVANAGH'S)
Off Map p118   Traditional Pub
☎ 830 7978; 1 Prospect Sq, Glasnevin; 🚌 13
The gravediggers from the adjacent Glasnevin Cemetery (p118) had a secret serving hatch so that they could drink on the job – hence the pub's nickname. Founded in 1833 by one John Kavanagh and still in the family, this pub is one of the best in Ireland, virtually unchanged in 150 years. In summer time the green of the square is full of drinkers basking in the sun, while inside the hardened locals ensure that ne'er a hint of sunshine disturbs some of the best Guinness in town. An absolute classic.

RYAN'S Map pp62–3   Traditional Pub
☎ 677 6097; 28 Parkgate St; 🚆 Heuston
Near Phoenix Park, this is one of only a handful of city pubs that has retained its Victorian décor virtually intact, complete with ornate bar and snugs. An institution among Dublin's public houses, this is truly worth the trip.

BLUELIST[1] (blu₁list) *v.*
to recommend a travel experience.
What's your recommendation? www.lonelyplanet.com/bluelist

NIGHTLIFE & THE ARTS

top picks

- Abbey Theatre (p184)
- Boom Boom Room (p182)
- Button Factory (p175 & p182)
- Devitt's (p184)
- Dublin Fringe Festival (p185)
- JJ Smyth's (p181)
- Screen (p179)
- Tripod (p177 & p183)
- Village (p183)
- Whelan's (p183)

Wait a minute…we've already included a chapter devoted to drinking, what else is there that falls under 'nightlife' in this town? Doesn't *everybody* come here to drink the beer and discover their inner poet? Even the most hard-nosed business deal is discussed and delivered at some point with a pint (or two) in one of the city's 1000-or-so boozers.

Believe it or not, there is life beyond the pub or, more accurately, *around* it. Dublin's status as an entertainment giant has been hyped out of all proportion by the tourist authorities and other vested interests, but it is – for its size at least – a pretty good town to amuse yourself in, with a range of options to satisfy most tastes. There are comedy clubs and opera nights, recitals and readings, cinemas and concert halls. There is the theatre, where you can enjoy a light-hearted musical alongside the more serious stuff by Beckett, Yeats and O'Casey – not to mention a host of new talents. There is music, and lots of it – you can trawl through the listings virtually every day and find a live gig, from classical to contemporary, featuring musicians both homegrown and internationally renowned. There are festivals, dozens of them running throughout the year, devoted to film, theatre, literature, dance and music. And when everything else has closed its doors for the night, you can go back to the pub, or negotiate your way past club bouncers, and strut your funky stuff on a packed dance floor. Whatever it is that floats your boat, you can be sure you will find a version of it in Dublin.

A word to the wise: if you really want to get a full slice of what's available, look beyond Temple Bar. We're not saying you should avoid it – a night of sloppy hedonism should always feature on the schedule – but we do believe that the district is a victim of its own success. The south side remains the part of Dublin with most to offer, but ignore the north side at your peril; not only does it have the city's most important theatres, but the nightlife is constantly evolving, thanks in large part to the influx of nationals from all over the world who have added new flavour to the business of having fun.

BOOKINGS

Theatre, comedy and classical concerts are usually booked directly through the venue. Tickets for touring international bands and big-name local talent are either sold at the venue or through a number of booking agencies, including Big Brother Records (Map p85; ☎ 672 9355; www .bigbrotherrecords.com; 4 Crow St), which sells tickets to smaller alternative gigs and DJ sets (see also p137), HMV (Map pp66–7; ☎ 24hr credit-card booking line 679 5334; 65 Grafton St), which sells tickets to pop and rock gigs (see also p135), and Ticketmaster (Map pp66–7; ☎ 0818 719 300, 456 9569; www.ticketmaster.ie; St Stephen's Green Shopping Centre), which sells tickets to every genre of big- and medium-sized show – but be aware that it charges between 9% and 12.5% service charge *per ticket*.

CLUBBING

Dublin's veteran clubbers will fondly reminisce about the good old days of the early 1990s, when exploring the underground fuelled by ecstasy (lovingly referred to as 'disco biscuits') and dancing to the pounding beats of white-label floor-killers virtually defined a whole generation's experience of what a good night out really was. Then dance music went mainstream, venue owners cottoned on to the fact that there was a lot of money to be made from kids in Day-Glo tops and crazy smiles, and the scene more or less fell into the safe mainstream and hasn't budged since.

In Dublin, the big problem has been the late-night bar licence (see the boxed text, opposite), which sees pay-in clubs run only about an hour later than free-entry late-night bars, prompting thousands of punters to keep their euros in their pockets and stay put, where the music is just as loud and the booze is (marginally) cheaper.

The other issue here is variety. Dublin is just too small and ground rents too expensive for a club owner to push out the boat and promote a night of Afro-beat or Nu Jazz that might only attract a few dozen devotees: cost margins dictate the bottom line, which invariably means quantity over quality and the overwhelming dominance of a tried-and-tested menu of unchallenging dance music, rock and chart stuff. Which doesn't mean to say that there aren't great DJs who play really great music (see the boxed text, p176), but most

WHAT'S ON

To make sense of Dublin's entertainment options, a number of resources will come in handy. Listings of virtually every event appear in the following websites and publications – available at all newsagents except for the *Dublin Event Guide*, which is found in hostels, cafés and bars.

Newspapers

Dublin Event Guide (www.eventguide.ie; free) A comprehensive fortnightly listings newspaper.

Evening Herald (www.unison.ie; €1) The Thursday edition features listings of pop and rock concerts, movies and other popular activities.

Hot Press (www.hotpress.com; €3.50) Dublin's premier weekly entertainment magazine lists all gigs and events.

In Dublin (www.indublin.ie; €1.50) A monthly look at the city's events, with solid listings.

Irish Times (www.ireland.com; €1.50) The Friday edition has an excellent pull-out section called the *Ticket*, with reviews and listings of upcoming events.

Websites

Dublinks (www.dublinks.com) Good for all kinds of entertainment in the capital.

Dublinpubscene.com (www.dublinpubscene.com) An exhaustive list of where to go for night-time fun, including club nights.

Entertainment.ie (www.entertainment.ie) A catch-all listings page detailing what's on.

Events of the Week (www.eventsoftheweek.com) An excellent website that does exactly what it says and is updated weekly.

MCD (www.mcd.ie) Ireland's biggest promoter provides a comprehensive list of upcoming gigs.

of them play irregular one-off club nights or stick to bar sets. Check out the Drinking chapter (p164) for details of the best DJ bars.

Yet the city's reputation as a clubber's capital endures, which is almost entirely down to the atmosphere generated by the clubbers themselves. Dubliners love to dance and will not let the total absence of rhythm or style get in the way of getting down – a lack of inhibition brought on by a long night's drinking. The other bonus is the city's fixed position on the gigging schedules of some of the world's best DJs, who complement the cream of local talent and help generate some truly memorable nights.

The busiest club nights are Thursday to Saturday, but there's something going on vir-

tually every other night of the week except Sunday. The listings publications and websites (see above) have comprehensive, night-by-night coverage of who and what's playing where and when. Admission to most places is between €5 and €8 Monday to Thursday, rising to up to €15 or €20 Friday and Saturday. For discounts, look out for the thousands of fliers that are distributed around most of the city centre's pubs.

BUTTON FACTORY Map p85
☎ 670 0533; Curved St; admission €8-12;
Thu-Sun
Temple Bar's newest venue is a top-class joint for late-night clubbing (to 3.30am) that deserves a merit badge on two counts:

OPENING HOURS

It's difficult to be one of Europe's coolest clubbing cities if everything has to shut down just as the night is getting going everywhere else. So difficult, in fact, that Dublin clubs are not too cool at all. Unless a club has a 'theatre licence' granted to venues that have 'live' performances – a handy loophole abused by some of the city's clubs by having something like a snake charmer walk around the crowded dancefloor for 10 minutes every couple of months – then the needles come off the decks at 2.30am sharp and everyone has to clear out within half an hour. The authorities listen to the complaints about a nanny state and then do nothing about it; there are much more powerful forces exerting influence than a bunch of clubbers looking to stretch the good times by a couple of hours, namely the publicans themselves, who hate the idea of late openings and will fight tooth and nail to resist them.

top picks

CLUB NIGHTS

- **Backlash** (Pod, opposite; www.backlash.ie; Thursday) The loose collective of Irish DJs and producers that make up Bodytonic are behind this great night, where you're as likely to hear anything from house, electro and techno to soul, hip-hop and drum and bass.

- **Pogo** (Pod, opposite; Saturday) Barry Redsetta is lord of the dancefloor with his superb mix of house, electro, breaks and funky techno. He is supported by Irish and international guests, including local boy DJ Arveene (see p40), one of our favourites.

- **Soundstream** (Rogue, opposite; Friday) Deep, deep techno brought to you by the always excellent D1 crew – they usually feature an invited international guest as well as their own brilliant DJs.

- **Strictly Handbag** (Rí Rá, opposite; Monday) Dublin's longest-running club night is the Irish version of London's super-popular School Disco, only better. This excellent tribute to the '80s is a weekly reminder that underneath the dodgy hair and synthesizer beats were some incredibly good dance songs.

- **Underground@Kennedy's** (Kennedy's, right; Friday) A rotating menu of top-class sounds from visiting DJs and local favourites including the likes of techno maestro Billy Scurry.

firstly for offering something to the left of the usual Temple Bar cheese; and secondly for being swanky and carpeted. Great sound, big room, terrific spot.

COPPER FACE JACKS Map pp66–7

☎ 475 8777; www.jackson-court.ie; Jackson Court Hotel, 29-30 Harcourt St; admission €6-12

Dublin's ultimate meat market packs them in and has a reputation for being the destination of choice for off-duty police officers, nurses and anyone looking to avoid music that didn't chart. Don't let the presence of the law put you off though. From what we've heard, they're the biggest miscreants of the lot, especially if there are nurses about!

GAIETY THEATRE Map pp66–7

☎ 677 1717; www.gaietytheatre.com; South King St; admission €12; 🕒 11pm-4am Fri & Sat

More than 800 punters cram into the theatre (see p186) after hours for dancing

and plenty of drinking. It's loose, fun and very popular. The music is a mix of Latin and soul.

HOGAN'S Map pp66–7

☎ 677 5904; 35 South Great George's St; admission free; 🕒 11pm-2.30am Thu-Sun

The basement of this popular bar is now home to Under The Stairs, a free club loosely run by local legend Billy Scurry and featuring a rotating mix of home-grown and visiting DJs. The emphasis is on soul, funk, hip hop and disco – all of which serves to keep the dancefloor going.

HUB Map p85

☎ 670 7655; www.thehubmezz.ie; 11 Eustace St; admission €6-15

The Arctic Monkeys, We Are Scientists and comedian Jimmy Carr have all graced the decks at the legendary rock-indie-electronic night Trashed on Tuesdays, hosted by Trev Radiator. Otherwise it's a mixed bag of indie hits and drinks promos for all and sundry.

KENNEDY'S Map pp78–9

☎ 661 1124; 31-32 Westland Row; admission €10; 🕒 Fri-Sat

Not to be confused with the adamantly old-fashioned pub of the same name on the quays, Kennedy's suitably sweaty and darkened basement is home to the Underground, which plays regular host to a rotating menu of top-class hip hop, techno and house, played by some of the best local and international DJs around. Very much for those in the know.

LILLIE'S BORDELLO Map pp66–7

☎ 679 9204; www.lilliesbordello.ie; Adam Ct; admission €10-20

Dublin's most prestigious nightclub is all about exclusivity – it claims greatness not so much by whom it caters to (Dublin's power brokers, their ligger mates and visiting celebs) but by whom it refuses entry to (ie everyone else). And, just to prove that even when you've arrived there's always somewhere else to go, those on the inside really wish they could get into the ultra-VIP Jersey Lil's, where some visiting mega-rapper might be swishing Cristal and dropping it like it's hot. Even if they let us in, we wouldn't want to stay – the music is rubbish.

POD Map pp66–7

☎ 478 0025; www.pod.ie; 35 Harcourt St; admission €5-20; ☺ Wed-Sat

The name is still the same, but the one-time legendary dance club (in Dublin terms, anyway) has been resized and incorporated within the confines of John Reynold's newest entertainment venue, made up of three attached but separate rooms. The much smaller Pod is still home to club nights, ranging from Wednesday's indie faves at Antics to the always excellent dancefest that is Pogo (Saturday).

RENARD'S Map pp66–7

☎ 677 5876; www.renards.ie; South Frederick St; admission €8-15

Snooty Renard's offers little in terms of interesting music (it mostly has pop hits and old classics), but it is a top spot for a little social credibility. The problem, however, is that most of the celebs – including some of U2 and their entourage when they're in town – are safely ensconced in the upstairs lounge, while the ordinary plebs have to make do with the main room. Frankly, the main floor is far better than the stuffy, slightly depressing celebrity lounge, unless, of course, Bono is buying the drinks.

RÍ RÁ Map pp66–7

☎ 677 4835; www.rira.ie; Dame Ct; admission €5-12

One of the true veterans of the nightclub scene, Rí Rá – one half of the Irish expression *rí rá agus ruaile buaile* (ree raw aw-gus roola boola), which translates roughly as 'devilment and good fun' – changed hands in 2007, with the new owners promising the same mix of laid-back grooves and funky beats that made it one of the most popular in town. Monday night's Strictly Handbag, with its great menu of '80s music, has been going for more than a dozen years.

ROGUE Map p85

☎ 675 3971; 64 Dame St; admission €8-12; ☺ Mon-Sat

Relative newcomer on the block, Rogue is an intimate two-floored venue and home to the Bodytonic crew, who specialise in expertly mixed disco, house and electro. Expect to hear melodic and deep house and techno at the excellent Discotonic on Saturday nights.

SPIRIT Map pp102–3

☎ 877 9999; www.spiritdublin.com; 57 Middle Abbey St; admission €5-20; ☺ Thu-Sat

A veritable temple to hardcore clubbing and the New Age mantra of mind-body-spirit, this three-floored club belies its touchy-feely promos with an edginess that can sometimes verge on nasty – or maybe that's just the coke-fuelled paranoia that so many of the clubbers seem to display. Strictly for the hardened clubber.

TRIPOD Map pp66–7

☎ 478 0025; www.tripod.ie; 35 Harcourt St; admission €5-20; ☺ Wed-Sat

It's all very confusing, but this newish venue – part of the overall centre that also includes the Pod and Crawdaddy (p182) – mostly hosts live music. Wednesday and Thursday nights are student nights, with the DJs playing a safe-but-fun mix of chart stuff, R'n'B and indie.

VILLAGE Map pp66–7

☎ 475 8555; 26 Wexford St; www.thevillagevenue.com; admission €8-10; ☺ Thu-Sat

When the live music ends (see p183), the club kicks off and takes 600-odd groovers through a consistent mix of new and old tunes, dancefloor classics and whatever else will shake that booty. A great venue, an eager crowd and a top night out overall.

COMEDY

The Irish can be hilarious. Off-the-cuff, in the pub, their real speciality is deflationary, iconoclastic humour as used within that other great art form, storytelling. It's all about pacing and not taking yourself too seriously. On a stage, though, they tend to take themselves far too seriously.

SODOM & BEGORRAH

Ah, those Dubs and their word plays. One of our favourites was coined by the country's first film censor, James Montgomery, appointed in 1932. He took his job very seriously and dedicated himself to protecting Irish audiences from the 'californication' of American films (Red Hot Chilli Peppers, eat your hearts out). He also cast a suspicious eye on the activities of the Gate and Abbey theatres, which he dubbed Sodom and Begorrah. Brilliant.

Still, a few names have risen out of the mire of mother-in-law jokes and earned that elusive tag of great comic. Besides stars like Dermot Morgan and Ardal O'Hanlon – who gave us the utterly brilliant *Father Ted* – these include the observational genius of Dara O'Briain, the laconic wit of Dylan Moran, the superb Deirdre O'Kane and the utterly brilliant Tommy Tiernan.

The highlight of the comedy year is the annual Bulmers International Comedy Festival (www.bulmerscomedy.ie), which takes place at 20-odd venues over three weeks, usually in September, and features a barrel-load of local and international talent. Big laughs.

BANKER'S Map pp66–7

☎ 679 3697; 16 Trinity St; admission €5; ✆ 9-11pm
A Friday-night improv club takes place in the basement of this bar near Trinity College. It has yet to establish itself as a success, but it's a good spot to watch wet-behind-the-ears wannabe comics go through their (often terrified) paces. And who said *Schadenfreude* wasn't fun?

COMEDY DUBLIN

☎ 872 9199; www.comedydublin.com; admission €8; ✆ from 8pm
Some of Dublin's best comic talents have grouped together to create a comedy troupe that takes to the stage on Sunday nights in the Belvedere (Map pp102–3; ☎ 872 9199; Great Denmark St) and Tuesday nights in Sheehan's (Map pp66–7; ☎ 677 1914; 17 Chatham St). Some of their stuff is hilarious.

HA'PENNY BRIDGE INN Map p85

☎ 677 0616; 42 Wellington Quay; adult/concession €6/5; ✆ 9-11pm
From Tuesday to Thursday you can hear some fairly funny comedians (as well as some truly awful ones) do their stuff in the upstairs room of this Temple Bar pub. Tuesday night's Battle of the Axe (☎ 086 815 6987; www.battleoftheaxe.com), an improvisation night that features a lot of 'crowd participation' (read 'trading insults'), is the best of them.

INTERNATIONAL BAR Map pp66–7

☎ 677 9250; 23 Wicklow St; admission €7.50; ✆ 9-11pm
The upstairs room above this pub (see p165) hosts three comedy nights a week. Monday night is Comedy Improv, the best of the lot,

where the audience throws up subjects for the established comedians to work with. Wednesday night is Comedy Cellar, Ardal O'Hanlon's original creation, where blossoming talent is given the chance to find out if their material is up to scratch, and Thursday night is the International Comedy Club, hosted by Aidan Bishop, which generally has a line-up of good comedians.

LAUGHTER LOUNGE Map p85

☎ 1800 266 339; www.laughterlounge.com; 4-6 Eden Quay; reserved/unreserved seat €30/25; ✆ doors open 7.30pm
This newly refurbished comedy theatre is the place to see those comics too famous for the smaller pub stages but not famous enough to sell out the city's bigger venues. Think comedians on the way up (or on the way down).

FILM

Ireland boasts the highest number of young cinemagoers in all of Europe. Forty years ago, O'Connell St and the surrounding streets were literally awash with cinemas, but now most of them have long since disappeared. This has left many film-hungry Dubliners queuing up in the foyer of a suburban multiplex, waiting to be fed a diet of first-run blockbusters and the odd independent movie. Of the four cinemas left in the city centre, however, two offer a more challenging list of foreign releases and art-house films.

Save yourself the hassle of queuing and book your tickets online, especially for Sunday-evening screenings of popular first-run films. Out on the piss Friday and Saturday nights, most Dubliners have neither the energy nor

DUBLIN INTERNATIONAL FILM FESTIVAL

If you're around in early spring (late February to early March), most of Dublin's cinemas participate in the Jameson Dublin International Film Festival (☎ 679 1616; www.dubliniff.com), a two-week showcase for new films by Irish and international directors, and a good opportunity to see classic movies that hardly get a run in cinemas. A major criticism of the festival, however, is that many of the films included in the schedule would have earned a cinema release regardless, making it more difficult for small-budget films to find a slot.

MOVIES IN THE SQUARE

Every Saturday night throughout the summer (from June to August), Temple Bar's Meeting House Sq hosts free screenings of films beginning at 8pm. The movies on offer are usually classics and are often preceded by an Irish short. For tickets, contact the Temple Bar Information Centre (Map p85; ☎ 677 2255; www .visit-templebar.ie; 12 East Essex St).

the cash for more of the same, so it's a trip to the cinema at the end of the weekend. Admission prices are generally €5 to €6 for afternoon shows, rising to €8.50 after 5pm. If you have a student card, you pay only €5 for all shows.

CINEWORLD MULTIPLEX Map pp102–3
☎ 0818 304 204; www.cineworld.ie; Parnell Centre, Parnell St
This 17-screen cinema replaced many smaller cinemas and shows only commercial releases. The seats are comfy, the concession stand is huge and the selection of pick 'n' mix could induce a sugar seizure. It lacks the style of the older-style cinema, but we like it anyway.

IRISH FILM INSTITUTE Map p85
☎ 679 3477; www.irishfilm.ie; 6 Eustace St
The Irish Film Institute (IFI) has a couple of screens and shows classics and new art-house films, although we question some of their selections: weird and controversial can be a little tedious if the film is crap. The complex also has a bar, a café and a bookshop. Weekly (€1.70) or annual (€20) membership is required for some uncertified films that can only be screened as part of a 'club' – the only way to get around the censor's red pen. It's a great cinema, but sometimes it can be a little pretentious.

SAVOY Map pp102–3
☎ 0818 776 776; www.savoy.ie; Upper O'Connell St
The Savoy is a five-screen, first-run cinema, and has late-night shows at weekends. Savoy Cinema 1 is the largest in the country and its enormous screen is the perfect way to view really spectacular blockbuster movies.

SCREEN Map pp78–9
☎ 671 4988; www.screencinema.ie; 2 Townsend St
If you like art-house movies or foreign films that wouldn't get a run in a multiplex,

this is your best bet. Devoid of the self-awareness that afflicts the IFI, this place puts the emphasis on well-made films rather than experimental ones.

KARAOKE

Even in Dublin you can rule the mike for a night of out-of-tune balladeering and all-round fun.

UKIYO Map pp66–7
☎ 633 4071; www.ukiyobar.com; 7-9 Exchequer St; per hr €25
The basement rooms of this trendy sake bar can fit up to 10 people each for a night of singalong fun from the 30,000-odd songs on the menu (in a variety of languages).

VILLAGE Map pp66–7
☎ 475 8555; 26 Wexford St; www.thevillage venue.com; admission free; ☉ Sun
Sunday nights are the ever-popular Songs of Praise, hosted by Rory, Murt and Sister Barbara: just put down your name and choice and wait for your turn to get up and belt out songs like Whitesnake's 'Here I Go Again'.

LIVE MUSIC
CLASSICAL

Classical music is constantly fighting an uphill battle in Dublin, with inadequate funding, poor management and questionable repertoires all contributing to its limited appeal. Resources are appalling, and there's neither the talent nor the funding to match their European counterparts. But before lambasting Ireland's commitment to classical forms, it's well worth bearing in mind that this country has never had a tradition of classical music or lyric opera – the musical talents round these parts naturally focused their attentions on Ireland's homegrown repertoire of traditional music. And still they managed to produce one of the great lyric tenors of the 20th century in Count John McCormack (1884–1945).

But it's not all doom and gloom. Classical music is small fry, but it's getting better all the time, thanks to the efforts of promoters who attract performers and orchestras from abroad; one local success has been the Anna Livia International Opera Festival (☎ 661 7544; www .dublinopera.com), which celebrates its fifth edition in September 2008 with two productions running on alternate nights for two weeks: Verdi's *Rigoletto* and *Samson and Delilah* by Saint-Saëns.

Bookings for all classical gigs can be made at the venues or through Ticketmaster and HMV (see Bookings, p174).

BANK OF IRELAND ARTS CENTRE Map pp66–7

☎ 671 1488; www.bankofireland.ie; Foster Pl; admission free

The arts centre hosts a regular Wednesday lunch-time recital at 1.15pm, usually featuring a soloist with accompaniment. The performers are excellent. It also hosts an irregular evening programme of concerts; call for details.

DUBLIN CITY GALLERY – THE HUGH LANE Map pp102–3

☎ 874 1903; www.hughlane.ie; 22 North Parnell Sq

From September to June, the art gallery (see p101) hosts up to 30 concerts of contemporary classical music. Concerts start at noon on Sunday.

GAIETY THEATRE Map pp66–7

☎ 677 1717; www.gaietytheatre.com; South King St

Amid its repertoire of popular plays (see p186) the Gaiety occasionally plays host to the more salubrious sounds of classical music, including some outstanding performances by Opera Ireland (www.operaireland.com).

HELIX Off Map p118

☎ 700 7000; www.thehelix.ie; Collins Ave, Glasnevin; 🚌 11, 13A or 19A

Based in Dublin City University, the impressive Helix theatre hosts, among other things, a fantastic array of international operatic and classical recitals and performances. Check the website for details.

NATIONAL CONCERT HALL Map pp66–7

☎ 475 1572; www.nch.ie; Earlsfort Tce

Leaden acoustics and a none-too-aesthetic conversion of University College Dublin's old lecture hall are the main criticisms levelled at Ireland's premier orchestral venue, but the cream of the classical crop perform here throughout the year as part of a rich and various programme of concerts and recitals. There's also a series of excellent

lunchtime concerts (€9) from 1.05pm to 2pm on Tuesday, June to September.

ROYAL DUBLIN SOCIETY SHOWGROUND CONCERT HALL Map p99

☎ 668 0866; Merrion Rd, Ballsbridge; 🚌 7 from Trinity College

The RDS (see p99) hosts a rich line-up of classical music and opera throughout the year.

JAZZ

Sadly, jazz is a marginal art form in Dublin and mostly the preserve of a small clique of loyal listeners; for most others it's nothing more than background music. The small scene is nonetheless pretty active, promoting gigs and sponsoring the visits of international artists, although for the most part the gigs are held in pubs. Keeping the jazz flame burning is the Improvised Music Company (☎ 877 9001; www.improvisedmusic.ie), whose website will keep you abreast of the jazzy goings on in the city, including a yearly series of summer lunchtime gigs at a number of changing venues.

AVOCA HANDWEAVERS Map pp66–7

☎ 677 4215; 11-13 Suffolk St; admission free; 🕑 noon-4pm Sun

Sunday brunch has some live jazz accompaniment at this gorgeous department store (see p132). The restaurant (p149) is upstairs.

BLEU NOTE Map pp102–3

☎ 878 3371; www.bleunote.ie; 61-62 Capel St; admission €8-14; 🕑 9-11.30pm Mon-Thu & Sun, to 2.30am Fri-Sat

The self-proclaimed Dublin home of jazz and blues, the Bleu Note has performed a minor bit of syntactical trickery to ensure that it 'borrows' from the world-famous New York club without actually stealing from it, a balancing act it's in no danger of doing with the musical policy, which remains firmly on the safe side. Blues-infused New Orleans jazz is about as far out as this venue will go. There are two live gigs nightly on Friday and Saturday.

CAFÉ EN SEINE Map pp66–7

☎ 677 4567; 40 Dawson St; admission free; 🕑 2-4pm Sun, 9-11pm Mon

A tidy jazz band for Sunday brunch and some Big Band Swing on Monday nights fill out the musical menu at one of Dublin's

DANCING IN THE STREETS

We're not kidding – some of the best performances in town are on the street. Grafton St is the buskers' Carnegie Hall, operating an unforgiving theory of natural selection by separating the gifted wheat from the crappy chaff. And believe us, some of these performers are absolutely sensational. During the day is the best time to hear the really good stuff – the plucky string quartets, rapid-fire lick merchants and other solo performers, including the juggling fire-eater and the group of break-dancers body-popping the change out of your pockets. Once the shutters come down, the talent slinks away – presumably to spend their well-earned coins – and are generally replaced by the B-team, mostly performers who should be applauded for their efforts and little else.

The other great busker's hangout is Temple Bar, where performers tend to be a little more informal, in keeping with the slightly more relaxed crowd that surrounds them. Fire dancers, African drummers and other suitably left-of-centre performances make up the bill, but you'll also find impromptu performances by tourists themselves – how nice it is to join in with a group of Italian kids singing Dylan tunes phonetically.

Finally, the pavement opposite the main entrance to Trinity College is popular with artists, who can be seen of a Saturday, adding lines and colour to their re-creations of Renaissance masterpieces.

biggest and most wildly extravagant bars (see p162). The Belle Epoque décor make it easy to imagine that you're actually at one of F Scott and Zelda Fitzgerald's decadent parties.

GLOBE Map pp66–7

☎ 671 1220; www.globe.ie; 11 South Great George's St; admission free; ⏰ 5.30-7.30pm Sun
This trendy café-bar (see p164) has a popular Sunday afternoon session. The atmosphere is usually terrific, and the players are generally pretty good, even though you're unlikely to hear John Coltrane's successor.

JJ SMYTH'S Map pp66–7

☎ 475 2565; 12 Aungier St; admission €8-12; ⏰ 8-11.30pm Thu & Sun
The best place in Dublin to hear good jazz is at this pub, located in an upstairs lounge where the stage is almost on top of the punters. Sunday's Pendulum Club, run by the Improvised Music Company, is a consistently good night. The intimacy of the place, coupled with the generally high standard of musicians performing here, make this a definite must for any fans of the genre.

POPULAR

Dublin rocks. The city is now a definite stop on the international touring schedule of virtually every rock and pop act in the world. In part it's because Dublin is no longer a pissant capital, but mostly it's because promoters promise big fees (the cost of which is duly handed down to you, the out-of-pocket fan) and big crowds (it seems the high fees offer

little deterrent!) to anyone willing to stand in front of thousands of screaming, cheering fans who do a damn fine job of making you feel like you're the biggest star in the world. From Dolly Parton to Arcade Fire, they've all come, sung and gone away very, very happy.

A far cry from the days of yore, before Dublin produced any rock star worthy of the name. Then, in the mid-1970s, along came Phil Lynott and Thin Lizzy (see the boxed text, p182), followed by Bob 'don't fuck with me' Geldof and the Boomtown Rats. As popular as they were, they were but the pre-show routine for four young lads from Ballymun, who took to the stage in 1978 with dodgy haircuts and even dodgier clobber. The clobber is still pretty suspect, but U2 are officially the world's biggest band, and have raised the bar to such an impossibly high level that no-one even bothers to wonder where the 'next U2' will come from any more, and most will happily settle for a few crumbs from the fabulous U2 cake. Still, their success has inspired plenty of bands and the local scene has developed a vitality and confidence never before seen – even if some of the contemporary acts would do well to leave the confidence alone and work a little on their songwriting.

Big and small, Dublin has venues to suit every taste and crowd requirement. Check the newspapers for upcoming events. The city is also awash with music festivals, especially in summer – check p16 for the list of the ones you don't want to miss.

You can sometimes buy tickets at the venue itself, but you're probably better off going through an agent. Prices for gigs range dramatically, from as low as €5 for a tiny local act to anywhere up to €140 for the really big international stars.

BOOM BOOM ROOM Map pp102–3

☎ 873 2687; www.theboomboomroom.tv; Patrick Conway's, 70 Parnell St

Most people run for the hills when they hear the words 'avant garde' and 'music' in the same sentence, but we urge you to keep still, for this venue has done more to reflect the cultural diversity of the new Dublin – with its absolutely fabulous blend of folk, jazz, blues, electronica and other diverse styles – than any other. Dubliners are always bemoaning the absence of somewhere they can listen to something genuinely new and different; that just means they haven't climbed the stairs above Patrick Conway's (p171) to one of the coolest music venues in town.

BUTTON FACTORY Map p85

☎ 670 0533; Curved St

This venue offers a wide selection of musical acts, from traditional Irish music to drum and bass (and all things in between), to a non-image-conscious crowd. One night you might be shaking your glow light to a thumping live set by a top DJ and the next you'll be shifting from foot to foot as an esoteric Finnish band drag their violin bows over their electric guitar strings.

CRAWDADDY Map pp66–7

☎ 478 0225; www.pod.ie; 35a Harcourt St

Named after the London club where the Stones launched their professional careers in 1963, Crawdaddy is an intimate bar-venue that specialises in putting on rootsy performers – from African drum acts to avant garde Jazz artists and Flamenco guitarists. It's part of the Pod/Tripod entertainment complex.

GAIETY THEATRE Map pp66–7

☎ 677 1717; www.gaietytheatre.com; South King St; ☯ 11pm-4am Fri & Sat

This old Victorian theatre is an atmospheric place to come and listen to late-night jazz, rock or blues on weekends; performing bands are generally put on as part of the nightclub entertainment (p176).

MARLAY PARK Off Map p99

☎ 1890 925 100; Rathfarnham, Dublin 24; 🚌 15C, 16, 16A, 16C or 17 from city centre

In recent years, this park in the south Dublin suburb of Rathfarnham has been transformed into a major outdoor venue for some fairly heavy-hitting international acts, with Daft Punk, Aerosmith and The Who just some of the acts who played here in 2007. But it also hosts slightly more muted affairs throughout the summer. The yearly Bud Rising festival takes place here too (see p16).

OLYMPIA THEATRE Map p85

☎ 679 3323; 72 Dame St

This beautiful Victorian theatre generally puts on light plays, musicals and pantomime (see p186), but also caters to a range of mid-level performers and fringe talents that are often far more interesting than the superstar acts – this is one of the best places for a more intimate gig.

POINT DEPOT Map pp62–3

☎ 836 3633; www.thepoint.ie; East Link Bridge, North Wall Quay

The premier indoor venue for all rock and pop acts playing in Dublin, this 8000-capacity warehouse closed its doors for a major facelift in 2007. It will reopen at the end of 2008, and we only hope that it

---

THE PEOPLE'S ROCKER

Just in case you didn't recognise the bronze figure outside Bruxelles (p165), it is none other than the greatest of all Dublin rockers, Thin Lizzy frontman Phil Lynott (1949–86). Lynott's immense popularity with Dubliners is not especially hard to fathom – not only did Thin Lizzy lead the Irish charge onto the international rock stage but they turned out to be one of the best bands of their time – though it is reflective of more than just Lynott's talent or success. Dubliners loved Lynott because he was always one of their own, a true Dub who remembered where he came from long after his star had risen. And, just to prove that Dubliners aren't so easily understood, they loved him because he was an outsider – a black kid raised in a working-class Dublin suburb during the 1950s and '60s – and a tortured genius who died young from drugs and alcohol, but who left a musical legacy that we should all be proud of and cherish. So, find a copy of Live and Dangerous and listen to 'Still in Love with You'; U2 fans may disagree, but it never did get better than this.

By the way, take a close look at Philo's face: isn't it uncannily like the face on the James Joyce statue (p109) on North Earl St? Joyce with an afro or wha'?

manages to fix the problems that made it one of the most unsatisfactory venues to see our favourite gigs, mostly because the stage was so bloody far away.

SUGAR CLUB Map pp78–9
☎ 678 7188; www.thesugarclub.com; 8 Lower Leeson St; admission €8-10; ☺ Tue-Sun
Table service and a cocktail bar draw in a slightly more sophisticated (read older) crowd who come for the cabaret-style acts performing here regularly.

TRIPOD Map pp66–7
☎ 478 0025; www.tripod.ie; 35 Harcourt St; admission €15-40; ☺ Wed-Sat
R'n'B stars, reggae masters, indie guitar heroes, dance music monsters… You can see a full range of live shows at this excellent venue, which has quickly developed a reputation as one of the best in the city, as much for the quality of its acts as the acoustics and surroundings.

VICAR STREET Map pp90–1
☎ 454 5533; www.vicarstreet.com; 58-59 Thomas St
Smaller performances take place at this intimate venue near Christ Church Cathedral. It has a capacity of 1000, between its table-serviced group seating downstairs and theatre-style balcony. Vicar Street offers a varied programme of performers, with a strong emphasis on soul, folk, jazz and foreign music.

VILLAGE Map pp66–7
☎ 475 8555; www.thevillagevenue.com; 26 Wexford St
An attractive midsize venue that is a popular stop for acts on the way up and down, the Village has gigs virtually every night of the week, featuring a diverse range of rock bands and solo performers. It's also a good showcase for local singer-songwriters.

WHELAN'S Map pp66–7
☎ 478 0766; www.whelanslive.com; 25 Wexford St
Whelan's is such an institution with Irish singer-songwriters and other lo-fi performers that the press often refer to them as the 'Whelan's clique'. This includes the likes of Glen Hansard and the Frames, Paddy Casey, Mark Geary, Damien Dempsey and Mundy.

A TEMPORARY SOLUTION…
During the Point Depot's refit, the big gigs in Dublin will be held in a huge, 5000-capacity Big Top (Map p115) in Phoenix Park. We hope it's such a success that they keep it up even after the Point has reopened. For details of gigs and tickets, contact the agents listed under Bookings (p174).

TRADITIONAL & FOLK
Dublin's ambivalent relationship with traditional music stems from its peculiar separation from the heart of traditional Irish culture; the capital has always seemed more concerned with the cultural goings on across the water in Britain and, latterly, continental Europe. Many middle-class Dubliners, eager to bask in a more 'cosmopolitan' light, have dismissed the genre as the preserve of rural types with nicotine-coloured fingers and beer-stained beards, all the while packing their own CD collections with the folk and traditional music of *other* cultures – inevitably found in the 'world music' section of their local CD store.

The irony has become all too apparent and in recent years there has been a slow (and often grudging) acknowledgement that one of the richest and most evocative veins of traditional expression is on their very doorstep – and it's *not* Riverdance, or any of the other versions of sex-and-reels that have led to Irish music becoming popular all over the world.

The best place to hear traditional music is in the pub, where the 'session' – improvised or scheduled – is still best attended by foreign visitors who appreciate the form far more than most Dubs and will relish any opportunity to drink and toe-tap to some extraordinary virtuoso performances.

Also worth checking out is the Temple Bar Trad Festival (☎ 677 2397; www.templebartrad.com), which takes place in the pubs of Temple Bar over the last weekend in January.

COBBLESTONE Map pp102–3
☎ 872 1799; www.cobblestonedublin.com; 77 North King St; admission free
This pub in the heart of Smithfield has a great atmosphere in its cosy upstairs bar, where there are superb nightly music sessions performed by traditional musicians (especially Thursday) and up-and-coming folk acts.

COMHALTAS CEOLTÓIRÍ ÉIREANN Off Map p99

☎ 280 0295; www.comhaltas.com; 32 Belgrave Sq, Monkstown; admission €5-10; ✆ Mon, Wed & Fri; ⊞ DART to Monkstown

The Friday evening traditional *céilidh* (communal dance) is the big draw at this informal venue, which is really a community club for the preservation of the traditional form, be it played or danced. Other nights feature regular sessions, but you'll find something just as good in the city centre.

DEVITT'S Map pp66-7

☎ 475 3414; 78 Lower Camden St; admission free; ✆ from 9.30pm Thu-Sat

Devitt's – aka the Cussak Stand – is one of the favourite places for the city's talented musicians to display their wares, with sessions as good as any you'll hear in the city centre. Highly recommended.

HA'PENNY BRIDGE INN Map p85

☎ 677 0616; 42 Wellington Quay; adult/concession €6/5; ✆ 9-11pm Fri

An excellent session takes place upstairs on Friday at this lovely pub, best known for its comedy nights (see p178).

HUGHES' BAR Map pp102-3

☎ 872 6540; 19 Chancery St; admission free; ✆ from 9pm

Traditional purists love the nightly sessions at this pub, which by day caters to barristers, solicitors and their clients from the nearby Four Courts (p106) – all of whom probably need a pint, but for different reasons! Although the playing is very good, the atmosphere is a little lacking and the sessions can be a bit dead.

OLIVER ST JOHN GOGARTY Map p85

☎ 671 1822; 58-59 Fleet St; admission free; ✆ from 2pm

The best thing about this popular Temple Bar watering hole (see p169) is not that it's ram-packed with tourists or that the 'craic' is slightly manufactured, but that the sessions run virtually all day from 2pm, making this the only place you'll hear trad before nightfall. And it's pretty good stuff too.

PALACE BAR Map p85

☎ 677 9290; 21 Fleet St; admission free; ✆ from 8.30pm Tue, Wed & Sun

Some of the best traditional music in Dublin can be heard at the excellent sessions laid on in the gorgeous upstairs lounge of this venerable boozer. If you want to hear the real deal in the city centre, this is the place.

THEATRE

Dublin has a reputation for being a theatrical heavyweight, and while it's true that Irish theatre is going through something of a revival after several decades in the doldrums, theatre remains under threat by the overwhelmingly oppressive force of commerce. The prohibitively high price of real estate has drastically impeded theatre's ability to stretch its legs by reducing the amount of available space for theatrical ventures to operate in.

Despite the recent revival, no new theatres have opened up and companies have been forced to improvise – usually by going outdoors or co-opting non-theatrical spaces like pubs or offices. It makes for some interesting experimentation, but the jury is out on whether it makes for lasting theatre.

Theatre bookings can usually be made by quoting a credit-card number over the phone, then you can collect your tickets just before the performance. Expect to pay anything between €12 and €25 for most shows, with some costing as much as €30. Most plays begin between 8pm and 8.30pm. Check www.irish theatreonline.com and other online listings (see p175) to see what's playing.

ABBEY THEATRE Map pp102-3

☎ 878 7222; www.abbeytheatre.ie; 26 Lower Abbey St; admission €25

Ireland's national theatre has had its fair share of trouble and strife in recent years, marking its 2004 centennial with virtual bankruptcy and the possibility of closure. Enter a new regime under director Fiach MacConghail, and the Abbey is alive and well once again, financially secure and equipped with a whole new seating rig that has transformed the old theatre from a venue that we endured to one we positively enjoy. Under MacConghail's strict tutelage, the Abbey is rigorously following a twin stream of rendering old classics by the great stalwarts of the Irish theatrical firmament (JM Synge, Sean O'Casey et al) and supporting the work of new playwrights like Mark O'Rowe, Marina Carr and contemporary international stars like Sam Shepard. The old box – built to replace the original building that burnt down in the 1950s – will eventually be abandoned in favour of a move down to the new Docklands development, but that won't happen for a few years yet. Monday performances are cheaper. Work by up-and-coming writers and more experimental theatre is staged in the adjoining Peacock Theatre (☎ 878 7222; admission €12-16).

CIVIC THEATRE

☎ 462 7477; www.civictheatre.ie; The Square, Tallaght; adult/child €20/16; 🚊 Tallaght
This purpose-built 350-seat theatre is inconveniently located in the southern suburb of Tallaght, but its state-of-the-art facilities are top-notch and include an art gallery. The plays it puts on, an interesting mix of Irish and European works, are uniformly good. The easiest way to get here is by Luas: the theatre is at the terminus of the red line.

DRAÍOCHT THEATRE

☎ 885 2622; www.draiocht.ie; Blanchardstown Shopping Centre; adult/child €15/12; 🚌 38, 38A, 39, 39X, 236 or 239
This multipurpose arts centre (named after the Irish word for 'magic') is one of the most interesting venues in the city. Two

THEATRE FESTIVALS

Dublin Fringe Festival (☎ 1850 374 643; www.fringefest.com; admission up to €20) Initially a festival for those shows too 'out-there' or insignificant to be considered for the main festival, this is now a three-week extravaganza with more than 100 events and over 700 performances. The established critics may keep their ink for the bigger do, but we strongly recommend the Fringe for its daring and diversity.

Dublin Theatre Festival (☎ 677 8439; www.dublintheatrefestival.com; admission €15-35) For two weeks in October most of the city's theatres participate in this festival, originally founded in 1957 and today a glittering parade of quality productions and elaborate shows.

separate theatres feature all kinds of work, from reinterpretations of classic plays to brand-new material by cutting-edge writers and performers.

FOCUS THEATRE Map pp78–9

☎ 676 3071; 6 Pembroke Pl; adult/child or student €20/15
The small Focus Theatre is committed to showcasing the work of new Irish playwrights, which is thoroughly laudable even

SMALLER THEATRES & WORKSHOPS

Ark (p86) This children's centre has a 150-seat venue that stages shows for kids aged between three and 14.

Bewley's Café Theatre (Map pp66–7; ☎ 086 878 4001; www.bewleyscafetheatre.com; Bewley's Bldg, 78/79 Grafton St; adult/concession €15/13; 🕑 1.10pm) Fancy a bowl of soup and a sandwich with your theatre ticket? This marvellous space puts on interesting, experimental work by Irish playwrights in a suitably bohemian atmosphere. Mind your slurping.

Crypt Arts Centre (☎ 671 3387; www.cryptartscentre.org; Dublin Castle) The beautiful church crypt in Dublin Castle (p74) has a space used by adventurous young Irish companies for experimental work.

International Bar (Map pp66-7; ☎ 677 9250; 23 Wicklow St; 🕑 6-8.30pm) Early evening plays in the upstairs space of this bar (p165) by non-established actors can offer up some worthwhile stuff; they're on early because they have to clear the room for the established comedy shows (see p178).

Lambert Puppet Theatre (off Map p99; ☎ 280 0974; www.lambertpuppettheatre.com; 5 Clifton Lane, Monkstown; adult/child €12.50/9; 🚉 DART to Monkstown/Salthill, 🚌 7, 7A or 8 from Trinity College) You think Gameboy and Xbox have spoilt the magic of puppetry for your kids? Let the Lambert prove you wrong with its excellent performances, staged every Saturday (and daily at Christmas and Easter).

New Theatre (Map p85; ☎ 670 3361; www.thenewtheatre.com; 43 East Essex St; admission from €15) Sitting above the left-wing Connolly Books, this refurbished little theatre puts on a pretty palatable fare of 'fun' plays and in-your-face work that might challenge social conventions but will hardly disturb the more serious critics.

Samuel Beckett Theatre (Map p65; ☎ 608 2266; www.tcd.ie; Trinity College; admission €5-20) Used mainly by drama students, the theatre also features the occasional show by established troupes. It's all pretty cerebral stuff.

WHO WANTS BECKETT'S COAT?

The last great shadow cast by an Irish dramatist was that of Samuel Beckett (1906–89), who moved from Dublin to Paris before he wrote a single word. Thereafter, only Brian Friel has really come close to inheriting the mantle of the 'greatest Irish playwright'. Today, Irish theatre is at an exciting but uneasy crossroads. A new generation of talented dramatists has certainly emerged since 1990 – Conor McPherson, Mark O'Rowe, Marie Jones and Marina Carr among them – but their path to theatrical greatness is littered with the high expectations of critics and a media that is uncomfortable with the fact that Irish theatre currently has no outstanding behemoth, and that is chomping at the bit to proclaim the next Beckett, Wilde or Shaw. There are plenty of dramatists about (see p41), but if we had to pick one who has the mark of greatness rather than merely the rubber stamp of commercial success, it would be Eugene O'Brien, whose first play, *Eden*, was one of the best to hit a Dublin stage since Vladimir and Estragon sat around waiting for a guy who never showed up.

if the quality of the work isn't always top notch. Still, the company offers challenging work and is well worth checking out.

GAIETY THEATRE Map pp66–7

☎ 677 1717; www.gaietytheatre.net; South King St; adult/child or student €35/20 plus booking fee
The Gaiety's programme of plays is strictly of the fun-for-all-the-family type: West End hits, musicals, Christmas pantos and classic Irish plays keep the more serious-minded away, but it leaves more room for those simply looking to be entertained.

GATE THEATRE Map pp102–3

☎ 874 4045; www.gate-theatre.ie; 1 Cavendish Row, East Parnell Sq; admission from €25
The city's most elegant theatre, housed in a late-18th-century building, features a generally unflappable repertory of classic American and European plays. Orson Welles' first professional performance was here, and James Mason played here early in his career. Even today it is the only theatre in town where you might see established international movie stars work on their credibility with a theatre run.

OLYMPIA THEATRE Map p85

☎ 677 7744; www.olympia.ie; 72 Dame St; admission from €21
You won't find serious critics near the place, but the much-loved Olympia, a Victorian beauty that began life as a music hall, attracts the crowds for its programme of variety shows and musicals. One of its

most popular runs was *I, Keano*, a (not very) comic rendition of the travails of Ireland's greatest-ever soccer player and the virtual civil war he provoked by falling out with the management of the national team on the eve of the 2002 World Cup.

PAVILION THEATRE

☎ 231 2929; www.paviliontheatre.ie; Pavilion Complex, Dun Laoghaire; adult/child €22/14; Ⓓ Dun Laoghaire
Like the Draíocht Theatre (p185) and Civic Theatre (p185), this modern space in the seaside suburb of Dun Laoghaire offers a dynamic programme of theatre and performance art.

PROJECT ARTS CENTRE Map p85

☎ 1850 260 027; www.project.ie; 39 East Essex St; adult/child €18/15
This is the city's most interesting venue for challenging new work – be it drama, dance, live art or film. Three separate spaces, none with a restricting proscenium arch, allow for maximum versatility. You never know what to expect, which makes it all that more fun: we've seen some awful rubbish here, but we've also seen some of the best shows in town.

TIVOLI THEATRE Map pp90–1

☎ 454 4472; 135-136 Francis St; adult/child or student €20/18
This commercial theatre offers a little bit of everything, from a good play with terrific actors to absolute nonsense with questionable comedic value.

SPORTS & ACTIVITIES

top picks

- A match at **Croke Park** (p192)
- A round of golf in **Druid's Glen** (p189)
- Heineken Cup rugby in **Donnybrook** (p194)
- A night at the dogs in **Shelbourne Park** (p193)
- A massage in **Melt** (p188)

SPORTS & ACTIVITIES

Just as soon as you thought that the alpha and omega of all social activity in this city occurred within an arm's length of licensed premises, you might be shocked to know that Dubliners treat their sport – both watched and played – like religion. For some, it's all about faith through good works like jogging, amateur football and yoga; for most everyone else, observance is enough, especially from the living room armchair or the pub stool.

Sporting facilities are pretty good, but for the most part they're in private hands – there are only a handful of public tennis courts in the whole city, for instance (and they're not that good) – which means that you'll have to pay some kind of fee or membership to participate in most sports. We assume you're only visiting, so there's little point in telling you how to join one of the city's myriad soccer, rugby or GAA teams; instead, you'll have to settle on watching them play.

HEALTH & FITNESS

Dublin's become far more body-conscious than ever. Gym memberships have soared – although most city-centre gyms are private affairs that require three- to six-month membership commitments. No hotel worth its handful of stars opens its doors these days without having somewhere for guests to stretch a muscle or two, while anywhere that wants to rock five stars has to provide the ultimate in self-care: the spa. We're suckers for the kinds of mysterious treatments administered to a body that just murmurs in delight, but we leave a dangling, cynical question mark over some of these mystical Indian- and Irish-named treatments that are little more than an oily massage to whale music. The gyms and spas listed here are all open to the public. Get healthy and beautiful at the following places:

BELLAZA CLINIC Map p99
☎ 496 3484; www.bellazabeauty.com; 27 Ranelagh Rd, Ranelagh; treatments €50-600; 9.30am-6pm Mon-Wed & Fri-Sat, to 8pm Thu; Ranelagh

Cult facialist Sue Machesney uses all her considerable skills to treat, repair, nurture and love all kinds of skins – using facials, vein zapping, laser hair removals and other non-surgical methods that leave you feeling beautiful without the post-op feeling.

FOUR SEASONS SPA Map p99
☎ 665 4000; www.fourseasons.com; Four Seasons Hotel; Simmonscourt Rd, Ballsbridge; 9am-9pm

Every conceivable treatment, from a basic 55-minute facial to the three-hour Swiss Bliss, working the body from head to toe with a range of La Prairie products, is available at this top spa in arguably the city's finest hotel. Day packages (€150 to €400) also allow you full use of the gym, swimming pool and fitness facilities.

MANDALA DAY SPA Map pp66–7
☎ 671 7099; www.mandala.ie; La Stampa, 35 Dawson St; 70min massage €120; 10am-6pm Mon-Tue & Sat-Sun, to 9pm Wed-Thu, to 8pm Fri

It sells itself as the 'essence of Eastern solace', but even the cringeworthy feng shui nonsense doesn't detract from the fact that this is a terrific little spa where you genuinely can iron out those stress creases and get back in touch with your inner softness (there is such a thing as too much spa treatment).

MARKIEVICZ LEISURE CENTRE
Map pp78–9
☎ 672 9121; www.dublincity.ie; Townsend St; adult/child €5.50/2.80; 7am-10pm Mon-Thu, 7am-9pm Fri, 9am-6pm Sat, 10am-4pm Sun

This excellent fitness centre has a swimming pool, a workout room (with plenty of gym machines) and a sauna. You can swim for as long as you please, but children are only allowed at off-peak times (10am to 5.30pm Monday to Saturday).

MELT Map p85
☎ 679 8786; www.meltonline.com; 2 Temple Lane; massage per 30min €45, 1hr €50-55; 9am-7pm Mon-Sat

A full range of massage techniques – from Swedish to shiatsu and many more in between – are doled out by expert practitioners at Melt, aka the Temple Bar Healing Centre. Also available are a host of other left-of-centre healing techniques, including acupuncture, Reiki and polarity therapy. It's all very alternative, but the touchy-feely vibe never obscures the fact that these folks really know what they're doing.

WELLS SPA

☎ 0402 36444; www.brooklodge.com; Brook Lodge, Macreddin, Co Wicklow; whole-day packages €230-270; 🚌 Bus Eireann 133 from city centre to Rathdrum

OK, so it's not technically in Dublin, but this extraordinary spa in a luxurious country house is the favourite chill-out spot for Dublin's high-flyers. Mud and flotation chambers, Finnish and aroma baths, Hammam massages and a full range of Decleor & Carita treatments make this one of the top spas in the country. Whole-day treatments include a light lunch and full use of all the pool and gym facilities. Your credit card will never have nestled in softer hands. It is 3km west of Rathrum in the village of Macreddin.

ACTIVITIES

It's tough to join in a sport if you're breezing through the city; there are virtually no opportunities to join in besides a round of golf, which is always popular.

GOLF

Pádraig Harrington's unlikely play-off win of the 2007 Open Championship at Carnoustie is the most momentous event in recent Irish golfing history, eclipsing even the successful hosting of the 2006 Ryder Cup at Kildare's famous K Club. Indeed, although Ireland has always been renowned for its outstanding courses – mostly seaside links – in recent years a slew of new developments has seen the arrival of the modern, American-style resort course, most of them an easy drive from Dublin. The following are the best courses:

CARTON HOUSE Map p213

☎ 505 2000; www.cartonhouse.com; Maynooth, Co Kildare; green fees Mon-Wed €115, Thu-Sun €135)

Two outstanding courses designed by Colm Montgomerie and Mark O'Meara respectively.

top picks

DUBLIN SPORTING MOMENTS

- Dubliner Pádraig Harrington winning the Open Championship in 2007 – the first Irish golfer to win a major since Fred Daly in 1947.
- Dublin beating Kerry in the 1976 All-Ireland Final, the only victory in four finals meetings that decade against the Kingdom.
- Ireland beating England 1-0 in 1988 during the European Championship finals in Stuttgart, the first – and only – time the Irish soccer team has ever beaten England competitively.
- The Irish rugby team beating England by a record-margin 43-13 on 24 February 2007 at Croke Park: history and victory wrapped up in one delicious moment.
- England losing at anything, preferably sports that they think they're good at (hey, Dubliners love a little *Schadenfreude*).

DRUID'S GLEN Map p213

☎ 287 3600; www.druidsglen.ie; Newtownmountkennedy, Co Wicklow; green fee €180

One of the older breed of championship courses, this is a spectacular place to play with some stunningly beautiful holes.

HERITAGE Map p213

☎ 0578-645 500; www.theheritage.com; Killenard, Co Laois; green fee Mon-Wed €115, Thu-Sun €135

This new Seve Ballesteros–designed resort has an outstanding course, a five-star hotel and a top spa in and around the American-style club house.

K CLUB Map p213

☎ 601 7297; www.kclub.com; Kildare Hotel & Golf Club, Straffan, Co Kildare; green fee Jan-Apr & Oct-Dec €160, May-Sep €370

Host of the Ryder Cup in 2006 and the annual European Open in late July/early August, the two courses here are among the best in the country.

SPECTATOR SPORT

Sport has a special place in the Irish psyche, probably because it's one of the few occasions when an overwhelming expression of emotion won't cause those around you to wince or shuffle in discomfort. Sit in a pub while a match is on and watch the punters foam at the mouth as they yell pleasantries at the players on the screen, such as 'they should pay me for watching you!'

What is absolutely true, however, is that sport – for the few who play and the majority who are happy to watch it on TV or from the sidelines – is a major bonding activity in Dublin, and it's by no means an exclusively male domain. Ask any adult in Dublin for their top five sporting moments and they could probably reel them off as quickly as they could remember their five closest friends.

FOOTBALL

Dublin is football mad, although local fans – and the national broadcaster – are much more enthusiastic about the likes of Manchester United, Liverpool and Glasgow Celtic than the struggling pros and part-timers that make up the Eircom League of Ireland (www.leagueofireland .com). It's just too difficult for domestic teams to compete with the multimillionaire glitz and glamour of the English Premiership, which has always drawn off the cream of Irish talent. The current crop of Dubliners playing in England include Damien Duff (Newcastle

United), Robbie Keane (Tottenham Hotspur, where he is captain) and Paul McShane (Sunderland).

Nevertheless, if you want to feel the excitement of actually attending a game rather than just watching it on TV, Dublin is currently home to five teams in the League of Ireland Premier division (see the boxed text, below). The season runs from April to November; tickets are easily available at all grounds.

The national side, made up of Irish players playing nowhere near the League of Ireland, has had some notable successes, especially in the late 1980s and 1990s, but things haven't gone so well since their last appearance in a major tournament, the World Cup of 2002. They are – in the words of Irish soccer's governing body, the Football Association of Ireland (FAI; ☎ 676 6864; www.fai.ie) – in a 'period of rebuilding', but most fans are pissed off with the whole organisation and their perceived mismanagement of the national team. In 2006 they fired manager Brian Kerr and promised a 'world class replacement'. In came ex-player Steve 'Stan' Staunton, whose management experience didn't extend much further than picking up the training cones in his role as assistant at lowly English side Walsall. Stan oversaw a hapless qualifying campaign for

---

LOCAL FOOTBALL TEAMS

Local die-hards will insist that 'real' football is played on bumpy pitches by 'honest' semi-pros who aren't wandering about the pitch thinking about their image rights. You can find out for yourself between April and November by going to see one of the Dublin clubs in action.

Bohemians FC (Map pp62–3; ☎ 868 0923; www.bohemians.ie; Dalymount Park, Phibsboro; adult/child €15/5; 🚌 10, 19 or 19A) Known as the Gypsies, this club is the north side's pride and joy, and one of only two totally professional teams playing in the league.

St Patrick's Athletic (Map pp62–3; ☎ 454 6332; www.stpatsfc.com; Richmond Park, Inchicore, Dublin 8; adult/child from €15/10; 🚇 Drimnagh or Goldenbridge, 🚌 19, 51, 51B, 68 or 69) Four league titles in the 1990s, and one since the turn of the century…the Saints are an accomplished club whose ground is known as the Stadium of Lights, in tribute to the infinitely more impressive ground once played on by Benfica.

Shamrock Rovers FC (☎ 709 3620; www.shamrockrovers.ie; 35 Boyne House, Greenmount Office Park, Harold's Cross, Dublin 6; adult/child €15/10; 🚌 3, 11, 11A, 13, 16 or 16A) The Hoops' tale is a cautionary one: once the dominant club in Irish soccer, the team hasn't won the league in years and it doesn't even have a permanent home ground. It's playing at Tolka Park pending the long-awaited construction of their own ground in Tallaght, which remains caught up in planning row limbo.

Shelbourne FC (Map p118; ☎ 837 5536; www.shelbournefc.ie; Tolka Park, Richmond Rd, Drumcondra; adult/child €15/5; 🚌 3, 11, 11A, 13, 16 or 16A) Premier League champions in 2006, Shels was ignominiously booted out of the top division straight afterwards for financial irregularities, lost all its good players and spent all of 2007 struggling in Division 1 – which is really the second division.

UCD (off Map p99; ☎ 716 2142; www.ucdsoccer.com; Belfield, Clonskeagh; adult/child from €10/5; 🚌 10, 10A) The Students have been yo-yoing up and down the league but in 2007 found themselves respectively mid-table in the Premier Division. They play in the lovely Belfield stadium, part of the University College Dublin campus.

THE FAST & THE FURIOUS

Gaelic games are fast, furious and not for the faint-hearted. Challenges are fierce, and contact between players is extremely aggressive. Both games are played by two teams of 15 players whose aim is to get the ball through what resembles a rugby goal: two long vertical posts joined by a horizontal bar, below which is a soccer-style goal, protected by a goalkeeper. Goals (below the crossbar) are worth three points, whereas a ball placed over the bar between the posts is worth one point. Scores are shown thus: 1-12, meaning one goal and 12 points, giving a total of 15 points.

Gaelic football is played with a round, soccer-size ball, and players are allowed to kick it or hand-pass it, like Australian Rules football. Hurling, which is considered by far the more beautiful game, is played with a flat ashen stick or bat known as a hurley or *camán*. The small leather ball, called a *sliothar*, is hit or carried on the hurley; hand-passing is also allowed. Both games are played over 70 action-filled minutes.

Both sports are county-based games. The dream of every club player is to represent his county, with the hope of perhaps playing in an All-Ireland final, the climax of a knockout championship that is played first at a provincial and then interprovincial level.

And if you thought that only men would be so bold as to get involved, you'll be surprised to know that there's also an equally tough women's version of hurling called camogie, which is now being promoted as 'chicks with sticks' in an attempt to rejuvenate the sport. Women's football is growing all the time, with the Dublin senior team one of the country's best, along with Waterford, Mayo and Monaghan.

Euro 2008, which cost Ireland qualification and, eventually, Stan's own job. The winter of 2007 looked bleak indeed for the Irish national team.

Still, Ireland's misfortunes don't stop the fans from filling the stadium to see them play. Until the redevelopment of their long-time home at Lansdowne Road (which should be ready by 2011), the Irish will play their home games in the magnificent Croke Park stadium (p117). Tickets range from €25 to €50, but fan interest and corporate buyouts make getting a ticket for a really competitive match pretty tough without having to deal with a tout.

GAELIC FOOTBALL & HURLING

Gaelic games are at the core of Irishness; they are enmeshed in the fabric of Irish life and hold a unique place in the heart of its culture. Their resurgence towards the end of the 19th century was entwined with the whole Gaelic revival and the march towards Irish independence. The beating heart of Gaelic sports is the Gaelic Athletic Association (GAA), set up in 1884 'for the preservation and cultivation of National pastimes'. The GAA is still responsible for fostering these amateur games and it warms our hearts to see that after all this time – and amid the onslaught of globalisation and the general commercialisation of sport – they are still far and away the most popular sports in Ireland.

They are simultaneously the most divisive and unifying activity in Irish culture. Although the GAA club is at the heart and soul of virtually every parish in the country, in Dublin the organisation holds its greatest

sway in the northern half of the city and the traditionally working- and lower-middle-class enclaves on the south side.

Here football – commonly referred to as 'gaah' (but only by Dubs) – is king, and hurling is a game for country folk and crazy people with a death wish. This is probably because, while Dubs are very good at football, they're light years behind the very best practitioners of what they disparagingly call 'stick-fighting'. We've outlined the basic rules in a boxed text (above).

Support for the Dubs verges on the fanatical, but it's a support that grows from the ground up, beginning with the local parish club that virtually everyone – man, woman and child – in the community can be a member of. And, because the GAA is a volunteer-based amateur organisation, local communities come together to raise money for the club, through cake sales, raffles, bingo nights and other fund-raising efforts that further strengthen the ties that bind.

Community bonding aside, club matches are intensely competitive and provoke fierce local rivalries, especially among the major teams in north Dublin: Na Fianna from the Finglas/Glasnevin area, St Brigid's from Castleknock and St Vincent's from Raheny. Throw in a little southside rivalry with Kilmacud Crokes and the support can get pretty vocal. But when the best players from the club teams are selected to put on the blessed blue jersey, local rivalries are cast aside and replaced by intercounty ones as supporters unite behind their county. As fervent as this rivalry is, and as polarised as the support may be, there's rarely a cross word between opposing fans who are ultimately united in their love of the game and shared heritage; there's nothing like it anywhere else in the world, and we love it.

They might be good at football, but the Blues haven't held Sam in their mitts since 1995 – 'Sam' being the Sam Maguire Cup, awarded to the winner of the All-Ireland Football Championship, contested at a county level from April onwards to the final in Croke Park on the third Sunday of September. They have won a few Leinster finals in the last few years, but they can't seem to cross that final hurdle and add to their tally of 22 All-Ireland wins, an impressive haul that is second only to their great nemesis Kerry, who added yet another win in 2007 to make it a face-rubbing 35.

The All-Ireland's poorer cousin is the National Football League (and National Hurling League), which runs from February until mid-April. All of the county teams fight it out for the title of their respective divisions in a tournament that is generally seen as the warm-up for the All-Ireland Championship, which begins a couple of weeks after the league has wrapped up its affairs.

Dublin plays all of its championship matches at the newly remodelled Croke Park (p117), Ireland's largest stadium and the venue for both semifinals and the final, irrespective of whether the Dubs are involved. League matches, however, are played at the far less impressive Parnell Park (off Map pp62–3; Clantarkey Rd, Donnycarney; adult/child €10/7; 🚌 20A, 20B, 27, 27A, 42, 42B, 43 or 103 from Lower Abbey St or Beresford Pl).

While tickets for the NFL and NHL are easy to come by (you can just buy one at the grounds), they're tougher to get for the championship games, particularly past the quarter-final stages. Dublin's hurling team usually gets pounded long before then, but the football team is generally expected to reach the quarterfinals at least. Ticket prices range from €28 in the stand and €16 in the terrace for the early rounds, €37 and €17 respectively for the quarterfinals, €42 and €28 for the semis, and €65 and €35 for the final – although good luck hunting down a ticket for the big game. Kids are entitled to a €6 juvenile ticket, but then must be seated in the stand; if you want to take your kid into the terrace, you'll have to pay full price. The stand is more comfortable and usually has better views, but if the Dubs are playing and you want to get right into the partisan thick of things, go for the Hill 16 terrace.

The website for all Dublin-related info is www.hill16.ie.

WHEN HISTORY REALLY MATTERS

At 5.31pm on 24 February 2007, history was made. It happened at Croke Park, when the band struck the first notes of 'God Save the Queen'. The English rugby team stood proudly to attention, and the 82,000 in the crowd applauded respectfully before settling down to a long-anticipated Six Nations match between Ireland and 'the old enemy'.

A quarter century ago, the above paragraph would have seemed the stuff of heretical fantasy, a perverse dream that would – could – never, ever come true. Before that day, the last official representatives of Britain to set foot inside Croke Park did so on 1 November 1920, when soldiers opened fire on the crowd in retaliation for the earlier killing of 14 British agents. Fourteen people, including a player and two young boys, died. In the intervening 76 years, the Republic of Ireland came into being and the Gaelic Athletic Association admirably went about the task of establishing itself as the premier sporting and cultural association in the country, with a wide-ranging influence that included a ban on all 'foreign' (read: English) games in its holiest cathedral, Croke Park.

The Irish did play football and rugby – quite successfully in recent decades – but they did so away from GAA-controlled pitches, with internationals played at Lansdowne Road, owned by the Irish Rugby Football Union (IRFU). But Lansdowne Road began a long-overdue reconstruction in 2007, leaving the rugby crowd and the Football Association of Ireland (FAI) with a major dilemma: with no alternative stadium in Ireland to stage internationals, they were confronting the possibility of staging home games in . . . gasp . . . Britain!

The GAA had refused to even talk about it for a couple of years, but in April 2005 they voted – by the slenderest of margins – to allow temporary use of Croke Park to their rival associations. And so 24 February 2007 came, and with it history of the most momentous kind. Eighty minutes later, another bit of history: Ireland had won, 43-13, by the biggest margin ever.

A neat and fitting end to a powerful bit of history. But in the interests of (often) boring accuracy, it must be mentioned that the English were not the first team to play an English game at Croke Park: two weeks earlier, the French earned that particular honour with a hard-fought win over a spirited Irish side who were over-awed by the sense of occasion. But it was the English that really mattered. As always.

HORSE & GREYHOUND RACING

Dubliners love the gee-gees, but most of all, they love betting on them. There are several picturesque racecourses within easy driving distance of the city centre and there are good quality meetings throughout the year.

The flat racing season runs from March to November, while the National Hunt season – when horses jump over things – is October to April. There are also some events in summer.

Traditionally the poor-man's punt, greyhound racing (the dogs), has been smartened up in recent years and partly turned into a corporate outing. It offers a cheaper, more accessible and more local alternative to horse racing. The action all happens at the following venues:

CURRAGH Map p213

☎ 045-441 205; www.curragh.ie; County Kildare; admission €16-55; 🚌 special from Busáras
The home of Irish racing, 35km west of Dublin, hosts five classic flat races between May and September: the 1000 Guineas, 2000 Guineas, Oaks, St Leger and Irish Derby.

FAIRYHOUSE Map p213

☎ 825 6167; www.fairyhouseracecourse.com; Ratoath, County Meath; admission €14-22; 🚌 special from Busáras
The National Hunt season has its yearly climax with the Grand National, held here on Easter Monday. The course is 25km north of Dublin.

HAROLD'S CROSS PARK Map pp62–3

☎ 497 1081; 151 Harold's Cross Rd; admission €8; 🕗 from 8pm Mon, Tue & Fri; 🚌 16
This greyhound track is close to the city centre and offers a great night out for a fraction of what it would cost to go to the horses.

LEOPARDSTOWN Map p213

☎ 289 3607; www.leopardstown.com; Foxrock; admission €12-55; 🚌 special from Eden Quay
Specialising in both flat and steeplechase races, Leopardstown's big event is the prestigious Hennessey Gold Cup in February.

PUNCHESTOWN Map p213

☎ 045-897 704; www.punchestown.com; Naas, Co Kildare; admission from €15
Although it specialises mostly in flat racing, Punchestown is home to the extremely popular Steeplechase Festival in April. The course is 40km southwest of the city.

SHELBOURNE PARK Map p99

☎ 668 3502; www.shelbournepark.com; South Lotts Rd; admission €8; 🕗 7-10.30pm Wed, Thu & Sat; 🚌 3, 7, 7A, 8, 45 or 84
All the comforts, including a restaurant in the covered stand overlooking the track, make going to the dogs one of the best nights out in town. Table service – including betting – means that you don't even have to get out of your seat. Shelbourne Football Club (see the boxed text, p190) doesn't play here; its home is Tolka Park. Don't worry, even some Dubs get confused.

RUGBY

Have a look at any of Ross O'Carroll-Kelly's hilarious tales of life in Dublin and you'll understand how important rugby is in certain social circles, especially the affluent ones of SoCoDu (that's South County Dublin to you and me). Attendance at one of the dozen or so rugby-playing schools in Dublin is advantage enough, but being a rugby star, especially at Blackrock College, the *primus inter pares* of rugger schools, is a virtual guarantee of status, recognition and a bloody good career.

Rugby is but a sporting extension of a privileged caste, but it helps to be passionate about the game, especially the fortunes of Leinster, the provincial side. It's currently captained by the Mr Dreamy of most young rugger bugger huggers (as the girls who like rugby and rugby players are so affectionately known), Brian O'Driscoll (who was born and raised on the north side). Drico also happens to be the main man on the Irish national team, which pretty much ensures that a bit of Dublin 4 will one day bear his name.

The association with privilege has pretty much always been there with rugby, until the game decided to go global, kick its branding into a whole new gear and Dublin began witnessing some pretty successful local teams at both inter-provincial and international level. Irish rugby's governing body, the Irish Rugby Football Union (IRFU; Map p99; ☎ 660 0779; www.irishrugby.ie; 62 Lansdowne Rd), has done a brilliant job of selling rugby outside its traditional domain, so much so that the game has finally generated a genuinely national interest.

The Six Nations championship sees Ireland pitted against Scotland, Wales, France, Italy and the old enemy, England, in an annual league that in recent years has seen Ireland beat everyone except the French. Ireland's three home matches – played between February and April – are currently being staged at Croke Park (p117) while their own Lansdowne Road stadium is being rebuilt – the work should be done by 2011. Tickets for internationals are like gold dust – they're generally divided between corporate buyers and the network of small clubs throughout the country, of which you need to be a member if you want a ticket. You can try getting them through the IRFU (which also has a limited online purchasing service), but chances are you'll draw a blank.

Leinster has had similar fortunes to the national side – good, but not quite good enough. They have performed steadily in the European Cup, the premier provincial tournament that sees sides from the Six Nations countries play each other from December to May. The 2006 season culminated in a final that their great rivals Munster won. Leinster has done better in the lesser Celtic League (played against teams from Scotland and Wales), which runs from September to January, but mostly because everyone is gearing up for the European Cup. If you want to see them play, you can do so at the Donnybrook Rugby Ground (Map p99; ☎ 269 3224; www.leinsterrugby.ie; Donnybrook Rd; adult/child from €20/10). Tickets for both competitions are available at Elvery's (Map pp66–7; ☎ 679 4142; Suffolk St), another outlet (Map pp66–7; ☎ 679 1141; Dawson St); and at the Spar (Map p99; ☎ 269 3261; 54-56 Donnybrook Rd) opposite the rugby ground; or online from the IRFU or Leinster rugby.

lonely planet Hotels & Hostels

Want more Sleeping recommendations than we could ever pack into this little ol' book? Craving more detail – including extended reviews and photographs? Want to read reviews by other travellers and be able to post your own? Just make your way over to **lonelyplanet.com/hotels** and check out our thorough list of independent reviews, then reserve your room simply and securely.

SLEEPING

top picks

- **Aberdeen Lodge** (p205)
- **Four Seasons** (p204)
- **Grafton House** (p200)
- **Herbert Park Hotel** (p205)
- **Irish Landmark Trust** (p203)
- **Isaacs Hostel** (p208)
- **Number 31** (p201)
- **Pembroke Townhouse** (p205)
- **Shelbourne** (p198)
- **Trinity College** (p200)

Dublin's a pricey city to bed down in, easily the equal of any of Europe's most popular destinations. The other bit of bad news is that until you reach the upper price brackets, you're not always getting great value for money. The tourist boom also means that in high season – from around May to September – getting the room you want, at a reasonable price, can be a challenge. Always book ahead unless you're happy to stay out in 'the sticks' and grapple with a two-hour traffic-choked journey into town.

That's the bad news. The good news is that the city's popularity, coupled with the country's overall prosperity, has seen the overall landscape of accommodation improve and diversify dramatically over the last few years. There are now hotels that can compete with the world's best, while a host of others have cottoned on to the fact that the contemporary traveller doesn't think worn sheets are part of the charm and that grapefruit isn't some kind of exotic fruit that has no place at the breakfast buffet. Those that haven't just don't get a mention, least of all in these pages. As ever, we've only selected what we consider the best options in each category for your delectation.

So where to stay? If you're only in Dublin for the weekend, you'll want to be in the city centre or a short stroll away. The prices are higher, but pay the money. Believe us, it's worth it. Besides the obvious advantage of being central, you will avoid the potential nightmare of transport to and from the suburbs. The construction of the Luas tram line has made some suburbs far more accessible, but public transport more or less disappears shortly after midnight, with the exception of hourly night buses packed full of drunken youngsters (an experience that can often be a cutting-edge anthropological experiment). Get a taxi, you'll think, and we say good luck: there's you and thousands of others all queuing up in the wee hours for the same thing. Still, some of our favourite properties – the ones with all the charm and character – are just outside the city centre in the outlying suburbs south of the Grand Canal, so you may have to rely on some kind of motorised transport if you can't handle the 20- to 30-minute walk.

So, what exactly is available in this fair city?

ACCOMMODATION STYLES

Top-end and deluxe hotels fall into two categories – period Georgian elegance and cool, minimalist chic. No matter what the décor, you can expect luxurious surrounds, king-size beds, satellite TV, in-room DVDs, full room service, broadband or wi-fi and discreet, professional pampering. While the luxury of the best places is undeniable, their inevitable affiliation to the world's most celebrated hotel chains has introduced the whiff of corporate homogeneity into the carefully ventilated air.

Dublin's midrange accommodation is more of a mixed bag, ranging from no-nonsense but soulless chains to small B&Bs in old Georgian town houses. These days, hotel connoisseurs the world over have discovered the more intimate, but equally luxurious, boutique hotel, where the personal touch is maintained through less rooms, each of which is given lavish attention. Dublin's town houses and guesthouses – usually beautiful Georgian homes converted into lodgings – are this city's version of the boutique hotel, and there are some truly outstanding ones to choose from.

These are beautifully decked out and extremely comfortable, while at the lower end, rooms are simple, a little worn and often rather overbearingly decorated. Here you can look forward to kitsch knick-knacks, chintzy curtains, lace doilies and clashing floral fabrics so loud they'll burn your retinas. Breakfast can range from home-baked breads, fruit and farmhouse cheeses to a traditional, fat-laden fry-up.

Budget options are few and far between in a city that has undergone a dramatic tourist revolution and if you want to stay anywhere close to the city centre you'll have to settle for a hostel. Thankfully, most of these maintain a pretty high standard of hygiene and comfort. Many offer various sleeping arrangements, from a bed in a large dorm to a four-bed room or a double. There are plenty to choose from, but they tend to fill up very quickly and stay full.

Groups, families or those on extended stays may prefer to do their own thing so you'll also find a list of central self-catering apartments (p199).

CHECK-IN & CHECK-OUT TIMES

Check-out at most establishments is noon, but some of the smaller guesthouses and B&Bs require that you check out a little earlier, usually around 11am. Check-in times are usually between noon and 2pm.

ROOM RATES

Hardly surprising, but the closer to the centre you stay, the more you'll pay – and in Dublin we're talking as much as the most expensive cities in Europe. With prices, it's not just quality that counts, but position. For instance, a large-roomed comfortable B&B in the north-side suburbs may cost you as little as €45 per person, while the owners of a small, mediocre guesthouse within walking distance of Stephen's Green won't blink when asking €70 for the box room. A quality guesthouse or midrange hotel can cost anything from €90 to €200, while the city's top accommodation places don't get interested for less than €200. At the other end of the scale there's the ubiquitous hostel, the bedrock of cheap accommodation: their standards have uniformly gone up, but so have their prices and a bed will cost anything from €13 to as much as €30.

Most budget to midrange places charge low and high season rates, and prices are bumped up during holidays, festivals or sporting events. And now for the good news. Many hotels have a weekend or B&B rate that can save you as much as 40% on the rack rate; others offer similar discounts for midweek stays. At top-end hotels, check what discounts are available on the published rack rates by phoning or checking their website; you'll be surprised how much even the poshest of places will stoop for custom in low season so it's always worth asking.

BOOKINGS

Finding a bed is pretty tough in any price range, especially between April and September. If you can make a reservation, it will make life easier. If you arrive without accommodation, staff at Dublin Tourism's walk-in booking offices (see p243) will find you a room for €4 plus a 10% deposit. Sometimes this may require a great deal of phoning around so it can be money well spent.

If you want to book a hotel from elsewhere in Ireland or abroad, the easiest way is to go through Gulliver Info Res, Dublin Tourism's computerised reservations service, via their website www.visitdublin.com or book directly yourself from the accommodation's own website. See p243 for a list of Dublin Tourism offices and Gulliver contact numbers.

There are also great savings if you book online (see the boxed text, below). These rates are generally available year-round, but are tougher to find during high season. Be sure to book ahead and ask for a pre-booking rate.

LONGER-TERM RENTALS

Finding long-term accommodation in Dublin is difficult for Dubliners, never mind visitors from abroad. Gulliver Ireland's Reservation Service (☎ 1800 668 668; www.gulliver.ie) specialises in reserving accommodation. However, while it can find places for up to six months, or even a year, it charges a non-refundable deposit of 10% of the total price.

There are several letting agencies in Dublin. Abbott & Matthews Letting & Management (Map pp66–7; ☎ 679 2434; www.abbottmatthews.com; 40 Dame St) specialises in long- and short-term leases of apartments and houses, furnished or unfurnished. One-bedroom apartments rent for between €800 and €1500 per month. Home Locators (Map pp66–7; ☎ 679 5233; www.homelocators.ie;

ROOM RATES

The categories used in this chapter indicate the cost per night of a standard double room in high season.

€€€	over €200
€€	€90-200
€	under €90

BOOKING SERVICES

Advance Internet bookings are your best bet for deals on accommodation. These are just a handful of services that will get you a room at a competitive rate.

All Dublin Hotels (www.all-dublin-hotels.com)

Dublin City Centre Hotels (http://dublin.city -centre-hotels.com)

Dublin Hotels (www.dublinhotels.com)

Dublin Tourism (www.visitdublin.com)

Go Ireland (www.goireland.com)

Hostel Dublin (www.hosteldublin.com)

Under 99 (www.under99.com)

35 Dawson St) has a wide selection of properties on its books; it charges a €10 registration fee and then helps you locate suitable accommodation.

A few British newspapers, notably the *Daily Telegraph*, carry advertisements for long-term rentals in Dublin. Websites such as www.daft.ie are well worth checking too.

GRAFTON STREET & AROUND

Grafton St itself has only one hotel – one of the city's best – but you'll find a host of choices in the area surrounding it. Not surprisingly, being so close to the choicest street in town comes at a premium, but the competition for business is fierce, which ensures that quality is top rate.

WESTBURY HOTEL Map pp66–7   Hotel €€€
☎ 679 1122; www.jurysdoyle.com; Grafton St; s/d/ste from €210/245/750; ▣ all cross-city; ℗ ✄ ▣ ♿

Visiting celebs looking for some quiet time have long favoured the Westbury's elegant suites, where they can watch TV from the Jacuzzi before retiring to a four-poster bed. Mere mortals tend to make do with the standard rooms, which are comfortable enough but lack the sophisticated grandeur promised by the luxurious public spaces – which are a great spot for an afternoon drink.

SHELBOURNE Map pp66–7   Hotel €€€
☎ 676 6471; www.marriott.co.uk; 27 St Stephen's Green; r from €255; ▣ all cross-city; ℗ ✄ ▣ ♿

Two years, one renovation and many millions later, an old friend sorely missed has returned and the city's most iconic hotel is once again the best address in town, as it has been since it was founded in 1824. If the sumptuous elegance of the grandly restored public spaces and carefully re-designed rooms weren't enough, then perhaps it will be the thought that you're bedding down where the Irish Constitution was drafted in 1921 and about which Elizabeth Bowen wrote her novel *The Hotel*. They've added a new restaurant and oyster bar, but afternoon tea in the refurbished Lord Mayor's Lounge remains one of the best experiences in town.

BROWNE'S TOWNHOUSE
Map pp66–7   Boutique Hotel €€€
☎ 638 3939; www.brownesdublin.com; 22 St Stephen's Green; s/d from €195/250; ▣ all cross-city; ✄ ▣

This exquisite Georgian home is a slice of country house living in the middle of the city. The elegant rustic theme is pursued throughout; each of the rooms has a four-poster bed and stylish antique furniture. The fabulous Thomas Leighton Suite is best of the lot, successfully recreating the kind of style and plush comfort enjoyed by the 18th-century's rich and powerful – updated to suit the needs of the 21st-century equivalent.

HILTON Map pp66–7   Hotel €€€
☎ 402 9988; www.hilton.com; Charlemont Pl; r €240; ▣ Charlemont; ℗ ▣ ♿

What is it about hotels that assume that just because you're here on business you couldn't care less about style, décor or the basics of good taste? The Hilton group's Dublin offering is comfortable, convenient – right on the Grand Canal by a Luas stop – and corporate…but about as pretty as a photocopier. You'll sleep just fine here, but that's about it. We expected more.

BROOKS HOTEL Map pp66–7   Hotel €€€
☎ 670 4000; www.sinnotthotels.com; 59-62 Drury St; s/d from €190/240; ▣ all cross-city; ℗ ✄

About 120m west of Grafton St, this small, plush place has an emphasis on familial, friendly service. The décor is nouveau classic with high-veneer-panelled walls, decorative bookcases and old-fashioned sofas, while bedrooms are extremely comfortable and come fitted out in subtly coloured furnishings. The clincher for us though is the king- and superking-size beds in all rooms, complete with…a pillow menu. Go figure. The intimate Jasmine bar and on-site cinema are popular with media industry schmoozers.

FITZWILLIAM HOTEL Map pp66–7   Hotel €€€
☎ 478 7000; www.fitzwilliam-hotel.com; St Stephen's Green; r from €200; ▣ all cross-city; ℗ ✄ ▣ ♿

You couldn't pick a more prestigious spot on the Dublin Monopoly board than this minimalist Terence Conrad–designed number overlooking the Green. Ask for a corner room on the 5th floor (502 or 508)

HOME AWAY FROM HOME

Self-catering apartments are a good option for visitors staying a few days, for groups of friends, or families with kids. Apartments range from one-room studios to two-bed flats with lounge areas, and include bathrooms and kitchenettes. There are some good, central places:

Clarion Stephen's Hall (Map pp78–9; ☎ 638 1111; www.premgroup.com; 14-17 Lower Leeson St; s/d €165/310; 🚇 all cross-city; Ⓟ 🍽 💻) Deluxe studios and suites, with in-room safe, fax, modem facilities and CD players.

Latchfords (Map pp78–9; ☎ 676 0784; www.latchfords.ie; 99-100 Lower Baggot St; per week €575-860; 🚇 all cross-city) Studios and two-bedroom flats in a Georgian town house.

Home From Home Apartments (Map pp78–9; ☎ 678 1100; www.yourhomefromhome.com; The Moorings, Fitzwilliam Quay; per night/week from €220/660) Deluxe one- to three-bedroom apartments in the southside city centre.

Oliver St John Gogarty's Penthouse Apartments (Map p85; ☎ 671 1822; www.gogartys.ie; 18-21 Anglesea St; weekend €600; 🚇 all cross-city) Perched high atop the pub of the same name, these one- to three-bedroom places have views of Temple Bar.

with balmy balcony: that is, if you're not living it large in the new €3200-a-night penthouse with personal trainer/shopper/chef thrown in. The hotel is also home to one of the city's best restaurants, Thornton's (p145).

RADISSON SAS ROYAL HOTEL

Map pp66–7   Hotel €€-€€€

☎ 898 2900; www.royal.dublin.radissonsas.com; Golden Lane; r Sun-Thu €159-239, Fri-Sat €194-274; 🚇 all cross-city; Ⓟ 🍽 💻 ♿

The stunning new Dublin flagship of this well-respected Scandinavian group is an excellent example of how sleek lines and muted colours can combine beautifully with luxury to ensure a memorable night's stay. From the hugely impressive public areas (the bar alone is worth the visit) to the sophisticated bedrooms – each with flat-screen digital TVs embedded in the wall to go along with all the other little touches – this is bound to be one of the most popular options for the business traveller. There's free wi-fi throughout the building.

STEPHEN'S GREEN HOTEL

Map pp66–7   Hotel €€

☎ 607 3600; www.ocallaghanhotels.com; St Stephen's Green; r €200; 🚇 all cross-city; Ⓟ 🍽 💻 ♿

Past the glass-fronted lobby are 75 thoroughly modern rooms that make full use of the visual impact of primary colours, most notably red and blue. This is a business hotel *par excellence*; everything here is what you'd expect from a top international hotel (including a gym and a business centre), but what you won't find elsewhere is the marvellous view of St Stephen's Green

below. There are extraordinary online deals available.

LA STAMPA HOTEL

Map pp66–7   Boutique Hotel €€

☎ 677 4444; www.lastampa.ie; 35 Dawson St; r weekday/weekend €160/200; 🚇 all cross-city; Ⓟ 🍽 💻

La Stampa is an atmospheric little hotel on trendy Dawson St with 29 Asian-influenced white rooms with Oriental rattan furniture and exotic velvet throws. They've just added an Ayurvedic spa, Mandala (p188), but to fully benefit from your restorative treatments, ask for a top-floor bedroom away from the revelling at SamSara bar below.

TRINITY LODGE Map pp66–7   Guesthouse €€

☎ 617 0900; www.trinitylodge.com; 12 South Frederick St; s/d from €140/180; 🚇 St Stephen's Green

Martin Sheen's grin greets you on entering this cosy, award-winning guesthouse. Not that he's ditched movies for hospitality – he enjoyed his stay (and full Irish breakfast presumably) at the classically refurbished Georgian pad so much that he let them take his mugshot. Room 2 has a lovely bay window.

HARRINGTON HALL Map pp66–7 Guesthouse €€

☎ 475 3497; www.harringtonhall.com; 69-70 Harcourt St; s/d €134/173; 🚇 Harcourt; Ⓟ 🍽 💻 ♿

Want to fluff up the pillows in the home of a former Lord Mayor of Dublin? The traditional Georgian style of Timothy Charles Harrington's home – he wore the gold chain from 1901 to 1903 – has thankfully been retained and this smart guesthouse stands out for its understated elegance. The 1st- and 2nd-floor rooms have their original fireplaces and ornamental ceilings.

MERCER HOTEL Map pp66–7 Hotel €€

☎ 478 2179; www.mercerhotel.ie; Lower Mercer St; s/d from €99/160; 🚌 all cross-city; Ⓟ ✖

Not a stone's throw from Grafton St, a fairly plain frontage hides a pretty decent hotel, with largish rooms dressed in antiques, giving the whole place an elegant, classical look. There are a dizzying array of room deals available; the off-peak rates are sensational.

CAMDEN COURT HOTEL
Map pp66–7 Hotel €€

☎ 475 9666; www.camdencourthotel.com; Camden St; s/d from €110/145; 🚌 all cross-city; Ⓟ ✖ 🖥 ⚑

Big and bland ain't such a bad thing this close to St Stephen's Green, especially if the mainstay of your clientele is the business crowd. They like the standardised rooms but *love* the amenities, which include a 16m pool, health club (with Jacuzzi, sauna and steam room) and a fully equipped gym.

STAUNTON'S ON THE GREEN
Map pp66–7 Guesthouse €€

☎ 478 2300; www.stauntonsonthegreen.ie; 83 St Stephen's Green; s/d from €88/140; 🚌 all cross-city

Bargains and a St Stephen's Green address are mutually exclusive, so surely there must be a catch to this handsome Georgian house two doors down from the Department of Foreign Affairs smack in the middle of the most expensive spot in town? There isn't really, not unless the worn décor reminiscent of another decade really bothers you. The place is clean, the staff are friendly and professional, and the front-facing rooms have floor-to-ceiling windows overlooking the Green. Any closer and you're sleeping with the Lord Mayor.

TRAVELLING WITH CHILDREN

Finding reasonable accommodation for a young family can be difficult in Dublin. Your best bet is a larger chain hotel (where a flat room rate usually applies), a serviced apartment, or a hostel where you can house the whole family in one room, usually with en suite. Almost all deluxe and top-end hotels offer 24-hour babysitting services and extra beds or cots.

CENTRAL HOTEL Map pp66–7 Hotel €€

☎ 679 7302; www.centralhotel.ie; 1-5 Exchequer St; s/d from €100/135; 🚌 all cross-city; Ⓟ

The rooms are a modern – if miniaturised – version of Edwardian luxury. Heavy velvet curtains and custom-made Irish furnishings (including beds with draped backboards) fit a little too snugly into the space afforded them, but they lend a touch of class. Note that street-facing rooms can get a little noisy. The wonderful Library Bar, all leather armchairs and roaring fireplaces, is also one of the finest spots for an afternoon drink in the whole city. Location-wise, the name says it all.

GRAFTON HOUSE Map pp66–7 Guesthouse €€

☎ 679 2041; www.graftonguesthouse.com; 26-27 South Great George's St; s/d from €60/120; 🚌 all cross-city; 🖥

This slightly off-beat guesthouse in a Gothic-style building gets the nod in all three key categories: location, price and style. Just next to George's St Arcade, the Grafton offers the traditional friendly features of a B&B (including a terrific breakfast), coupled with a funky design – check out the psychedelic wallpaper. Hard to beat at this price.

GRAFTON CAPITAL HOTEL
Map pp66–7 Hotel €€

☎ 475 0888; www.capital-hotels.com; Lower Stephen's St; r from €115; 🚌 all cross-city; Ⓟ ✖ ♿

It's hardly recognisable as such today, but this centrally located hotel just off Grafton St is actually a couple of converted Georgian town houses. Its 75 modern rooms are designed along the lines of function before form, which makes them perfect for the weekend visitor who wants to bed down somewhere central and still keep some credit-card space for a good night out. Breakfast is included.

TRINITY COLLEGE
Map pp66–7 Campus Residence €

☎ 608 1177; www.tcd.ie; Accommodations Office, Trinity College; s/d from €37/70; ☷ mid-Jun–Sep; 🚌 all cross-city; Ⓟ 🖥 ♿

The closest thing to living like a student at this stunningly beautiful university is crashing in their rooms when they're on holidays. The location is second-to-none, and the rooms are large and extremely comfortable. Rooms and two-bed apartments in the newer block have their own bathrooms; the others in the older (and more beautiful) blocks share facilities, though there are private sinks. Breakfast is included.

AVALON HOUSE Map pp66-7   Hostel €
☎ 475 0001; www.avalon-house.ie; 55 Aungier St; 🚇 all cross-city; dm/s/d €18/32/64
Before there was tourism, this large, listed Victorian building catered to the thin trickle of adventurers who landed in Dublin. They flood in now, and Avalon House is one of the city's most popular hostels, a welcoming house with pine floors, high ceilings and large, open fireplaces that create the ambience for a good spot of meet-the-backpacker lounging. Some of the cleverly designed rooms have mezzanine levels, which are great for families. Book well in advance.

MERCER COURT CAMPUS ACCOMMODATION
Map pp66-7   Campus Residence €
☎ 478 0328; www.mercercourt.ie; Lower Mercer St; r from €42; ☿ end Jun-end Sep only; 🚇 all cross-city; 🖳 ⚟
Owned and run by the Royal College of Surgeons, this is the most luxurious student-accommodation option in the city. Cheaper than Trinity, but just as central, it's close to Grafton St and St Stephen's Green. The rooms are modern and up to hotel standard.

MERRION SQUARE & AROUND

It's the most sought-after real estate in town, so it's hardly surprising that it's home to the lion's share of the city's top hotels. But what price to sleep amid Dublin's Georgian heritage, within a gentle stroll of the best restaurants, bars and attractions the city has to offer? You'll pay upwards of €130 for even a basic room round these parts, but there are some truly outstanding hotels to make your expense worthwhile.

MERRION Map pp78-9   Hotel €€€
☎ 603 0600; www.merrionhotel.com; Upper Merrion St; r from €470; 🚇 all cross-city; 🅿 ⚟ 🖳 ⚟ ⚟
This resplendent five-star hotel, in a terrace of beautifully restored Georgian town houses, opened in 1988 but looks like it's been around a lot longer. Try to get a room

top picks

COMFIEST PILLOWS

Our favourite pillows to rest our weary heads on are in...
- Brooks Hotel (p198)
- Merrion (left)
- Aberdeen Lodge (p205)
- Morrison Hotel (p206)
- Westin Dublin (p203)

in the old house (with the largest private art collection in the city), rather than the newer wing, to sample its truly elegant comforts. Located opposite government buildings, its marble corridors are patronised by politicos, visiting dignitaries and the odd celeb. Even if you don't stay, come for the superb afternoon tea (€32), with endless cups of tea served out of silver pots by a raging fire.

NUMBER 31 Map pp78-9   Boutique Hotel €€€
☎ 676 5011; www.number31.ie; 31 Leeson Cl; s/d/tr €200/320/480; 🚇 11, 11a, 13b, 46, 58, 58c; 🅿
Probably the city's most distinctive property, this is the former home of modernist architect Sam Stephenson (see p50), who created here a stunning homage to the style and cool of the 1960s: cue the theme music to *Austin Powers*. As you enter this magnificent home, only five minutes' walk from St Stephen's Green, with its sunken sitting room, leather sofas, mirrored bar, Perspex lamps and ceiling-to-floor windows, you are enveloped in an oasis of stylish calm. Its 21 bedrooms are split between the retro coach house, with its fancy rooms, and the more gracious Georgian house, through the garden, where rooms are individually furnished with tasteful French antiques and big comfortable beds. Gourmet breakfasts with kippers, homemade breads and granola are served in the conservatory. Yeah, baby!

QUALITY HOTEL Map pp78-9   Hotel €€
☎ 643 9500; www.qualityhoteldublin.com; Cardiff Lane; r €109-359; 🚇 1,2 or 3; 🖳 ⚟ ⚟
It's a little bit removed from the action in the middle of the yet-to-be-hip waterfront development area, but the name does not lie: this

top picks

HOTEL BARS

These are our favourite hotels to hole up in with a drink:

- Radisson SAS Royal Hotel (p199) **Bangkok-style bar.**
- Merrion (p201) **Best afternoon tea.**
- Shelbourne (p198) **Drink like a lord.**
- Four Seasons (p204) **Ice, baby, Ice.**
- Westbury Hotel (p198) **I recognise him/her/them!**

is one of the best midrange options in the city. The rooms are large and extremely comfortable, but the real appeal is the amenities: two restaurants, a top-class fitness centre complete with sauna and a 22m swimming pool, the largest hotel pool in town.

LONGFIELD'S Map pp78–9   Boutique Hotel €€
☎ 676 1367; www.longfields.ie; 9-10 Lower Fitzwilliam St; s/d €125/195; ☐ 11, 11a, 13b, 46, 58 or 58c; ☐ ☐
This 26-room hotel, between Merrion and Fitzwilliam Sqs, is a little slice of Georgian heaven. It feels more like a private home than a commercial property, as each room is carefully decorated with period antiques, beautiful fabrics and elegant fittings. The rooms on the lower floors are bigger than the ones above, and some have four-poster or half-tester beds.

CONRAD DUBLIN Map pp78–9   Hotel €€
☎ 602 8900; www.conradhotels.com; Earlsfort Tce; r from €185; ☐ all cross-city; ☐ ☒ ☐
Kudos to the Conrad: Dublin's first truly international business hotel has worked hard to keep up with the ever-growing needs of its primary clientele, folks in suits. The king-size rooms have every gizmo and gadget your computer, PDA or mobile phone might ever need, while the state-of-the-art fitness centre should take good care of the rest of you. The hotel offers a dizzying array of special discount rates – at the last minute, room prices are often slashed by half – for both business and leisure travellers.

DAVENPORT HOTEL Map pp78–9   Hotel €€
☎ 607 3500; www.ocallaghanhotels.com; Merrion Sq; r from €180; ☐ all cross-city; ☐ ☒ ☐ ☐

Certain travel writers may fantasise that this fine and elegant hotel somehow belongs in the family, but it just ain't so: it is located in Merrion Hall, which was built in 1863 for the religious Plymouth Brethren. It is still a popular spot for meetings, only of a more commercial kind, and its 114 rooms are tailored to suit the needs of the business visitor (voicemail, ISDN line, wi-fi and European and American sockets are all standard). Leisure travellers also like the large rooms, which come with orthopaedic beds. There's a well-equipped workout room downstairs.

BUSWELL'S HOTEL Map pp78–9   Hotel €€
☎ 614 6500; www.quinnhotels.com; 23-27 Molesworth St; r from €130; ☒ St Stephen's Green; ☐ ☒ ☐
In business since 1882, this elegant hotel, made up of five Georgian town houses, is a Dublin institution. Like the Shelbourne (p198), it has a long association with politicians, who wander across the road from Dáil Éireann to wet their beaks at the hotel bar. The 69 bedrooms have all been given the once-over, but the owners have thankfully resisted the temptation to contemporise the furnishings and have left its Georgian charm more or less intact.

O'NEILL'S TOWNHOUSE Map pp78–9   Pub €€
☎ 671 4074; www.oneillsdublin.com; 36-37 Pearse St; s/d €65/130; ☐ all cross-city
There's only one thing better than living above a pub: living in one. The pub in question – where you'll have to settle for the first option – is O'Neill's, a Victorian beauty that is a long-time favourite with the students of Trinity College next door. The eight rooms above the pub are snug and decorated without too much imagination, but they're warm and cosy. Most importantly, the owners are friendly and very helpful. It's central and convenient.

GEORGIAN HOTEL Map pp78–9   Boutique Hotel €€
☎ 661 8832; www.georgianhotel.ie; 18-22 Lower Baggot St; s/d from €80/99; ☒ St Stephen's Green; ☐ ☒
Ideally located just a few steps from St Stephen's Green, this boutique hotel, in a 200-year-old Georgian building, has successfully combined the intimacy of a traditional Dublin guesthouse with the meticulous luxury of a high-end hotel. Breakfast costs an extra €15.

TEMPLE BAR

If you're here for a weekend of wild abandon and can't fathom anything more than a quick stumble into bed, then Temple Bar's choice of hotels and hostels will suit you perfectly. Generally speaking the rooms are small, the prices large and you should be able to handle the late-night symphonies of die-hard revellers.

CLARENCE HOTEL Map p85   Hotel €€€
☎ 407 0800; www.theclarence.ie; 6-8 Wellington Quay; r €350, ste €640-2400; 🚍 all cross-city; Ⓟ 🖳 ♿
If you were hoping to find TV sets cascading from windows, groupie-clad tour buses or any other evidence of the Clarence's rock star associations, you'll be sorely disappointed as Bono and Edge's discreet little bolthole is anything but that – although we suspect that the penthouse's rooftop hot tub has seen its fair share of frolics. The genteel atmosphere is more 1930s gentleman's club with 50-odd lavish-albeit-smallish rooms, decorated with simple elegant furnishings and original artwork by their friend (and former member of Irish cult band the Virgin Prunes) Guggi.

IRISH LANDMARK TRUST
Map p85   Self-Catering €€€
☎ 670 4733; www.irishlandmark.com; 25 Eustace St; 1 night €403, weekend €807, weekly €1925; 🚍 all cross-city
If you're travelling in a group, instead of renting a bunch of doubles in a hotel that you'll barely remember a week after you've gone home, why not go for this fabulous 18th-century heritage house, gloriously restored to the highest standard by the Irish Landmark Trust charity? You'll have this unique house all to yourselves. It sleeps up to seven in its double, twin and triple bedrooms. Furnished with tasteful antiques, authentic furniture and fittings (including a grand piano in the drawing room), this kind of period rental accommodation is something really unique.

WESTIN DUBLIN Map p85   Hotel €€€
☎ 645 1000; www.westin.com; Westmoreland St; r from €360; 🚍 all cross-city; Ⓟ 🌠 🖳 ♿
Formerly a grand branch of the Allied Irish Bank, this fine old building was gutted and reborn as a stylish upmarket hotel. The rooms, many of which overlook a beautiful atrium, are decorated in elegant mahogany and soft colours that are reminiscent of the USA's finest. You will sleep on 10 layers of the Westin's own trademark Heavenly Bed, which is damn comfortable indeed. The hotel's most elegant room is the former banking hall, complete with gold leaf plasterwork on the ceiling, now used for banquets. Breakfast will set you back €28.

MORGAN HOTEL Map p85   Boutique Hotel €€€
☎ 679 3939; www.themorgan.com; 10 Fleet St; r €140-400; 🚍 all cross-city; 🖳
Designer cool can often be designer cold and the hypertrendy Morgan falls on the right side of the line, but only just. It's the kind of place Victoria Beckham would have liked – before she made the real cash. The facilities are top rate, and all rooms come equipped with satellite TV, video, stereo and minibar. Aromatherapy treatments and massages are extra, as is breakfast (€20).

PARAMOUNT HOTEL Map p85   Hotel €€€
☎ 417 9900; www.paramounthotel.ie; cnr Parliament & Essex Sts; s/d €150/250; 🚍 all cross-city; Ⓟ
Behind the Victorian façade, the lobby is a faithful re-creation of a 1930s hotel, complete with dark-wood floors, deep-red leather Chesterfield couches and heavy velvet drapes. The 70-odd rooms don't quite bring *The Maltese Falcon* to mind, but they're handsomely furnished and very comfortable. Downstairs is the Turk's Head (p169), one of the area's most popular bars. Highly recommended.

ELIZA LODGE Map p85   Guesthouse €€
☎ 671 8044; www.dublinlodge.com; 23-24 Wellington Quay; s/d/ste from €76/130/200; 🚍 all cross-city; 🌠
It's priced like a hotel, looks like a hotel, but it's still a guesthouse. The 18 rooms are comfortable, spacious and – due to its position right over the Millennium Bridge – come with great views of the Liffey. The penthouses even have Jacuzzis.

ASTON HOTEL Map p85   Hotel €€
☎ 677 9300; www.aston-hotel.com; 7-9 Aston Quay; s/d from €90/120; 🚍 all cross-city; Ⓟ 🖳 ♿
This small, friendly hotel makes big use of pine furniture and primary colours, which give the public spaces and rooms a fairly

light, modern air. Rooms come with private bathroom and are equipped with cable TV, and two are wheelchair accessible. A buffet breakfast is included. Parking is by arrangement with a local car park.

DUBLIN CITI HOTEL Map p85 Hotel €€
☎ 679 4455; www.dublincitihotel.com; 46-49 Dame St; s/d Sun-Thu from €79/89, Fri-Sat €120/159; 🖳 all cross-city
An unusual turreted 19th-century building right next to the Central Bank is home to this cheap and cheerful hotel. Rooms aren't huge but are simply furnished and have fresh white duvets. Prices are reasonable considering it's only a stagger (literally) from the heart of Temple Bar, hic.

ASHFIELD HOUSE Map p85 Hostel €
☎ 679 7734; www.ashfieldhouse.ie; 19-20 D'Olier St; dm/s/d from €14/45/78; 🖳 all cross-city; 🖳
A stone's throw from Temple Bar and O'Connell Bridge, this modern hostel in a converted church has a selection of tidy four- and six-bed rooms, one large dorm and 25 rooms with private bathroom. It's more like a small hotel, but without the price tag. A continental-style breakfast is included – a rare beast indeed for hostels. Maximum stay is six nights.

BARNACLES TEMPLE BAR HOUSE
Map p85 Hostel €
☎ 671 6277; www.barnacles.ie; 1 Cecilia St; dm/d from €18.50/40; 🖳 all cross-city; 🅿
Bright and spacious, in the heart of Temple Bar, this hostel is immaculately clean, has nicely laid-out dorms and doubles with private bathrooms and, that rare commodity, in-room storage. Because of its location, rooms are quieter at the back. Top facilities include a comfy lounge with an open fire. Linen and towels are provided. A contender for the south side's best hostel, it also has a discount deal with a nearby covered car park.

GOGARTY'S TEMPLE BAR HOSTEL
Map p85 Hostel €
☎ 671 1822; www.gogartys.com; 18-21 Anglesea St; dm from €18, d with/without bathroom €45/40; 🖳 all cross-city; 🅿
Sleeping isn't really the activity of choice for anyone staying in this compact, decent hostel in the middle of Temple Bar, next to the pub of the same name. It tends to

get booked up with stag and hen parties so, depending on your mood, bring your earplugs or bunny ears. Six self-catering apartments are also available.

KINLAY HOUSE Map p85 Hostel €
☎ 679 6644; www.kinlayhouse.ie; 2-12 Lord Edward St; dm/d from €19/34; 🖳 all cross-city
An institution among the city's hostels, this former boarding house for boys has massive, mixed 24-bed dorms, as well as smaller rooms. Its bustling location next to Christ Church Cathedral and Dublin Castle is a bonus, but some rooms suffer from traffic noise. There are cooking facilities and a café, and breakfast is included. Not for the faint-hearted.

BEYOND THE GRAND CANAL

Just beyond the prohibitive reaches of city-centre real estate are some of Dublin's most beautiful guesthouses and hotels. They're spread out through the residential suburbs that stretch elegantly south of the Grand Canal, most notably in Ballsbridge and Donnybrook. Here you'll find the best examples of Dublin's take on the boutique hotel.

DYLAN Map p99 Hotel €€€
☎ 660 3001; www.dylan.ie; Eastmoreland Pl; r from €395; 🖳 5, 7, 7A, 8, 18, 27X or 45; 🅇 🖳 🅖
Dublin's glamourpusses got all weak at the knees when this luxury boutique hotel threw open its doors in 2006, inviting us to sample the 'sensual' pleasures within. While we certainly want to get sexy between their crisp Frette linen sheets, there's something just a little too much about the place. The 38 rooms and six suites are all individually styled in what might best be termed designer OTT – baroque meets Scandinavian sleek by way of neo-Art Nouveau and glammed up 1940s Art Deco. There's no denying the sheer luxury of the place, but the all-styles-in-one is just a little too much.

FOUR SEASONS Map p99 Hotel €€€
☎ 665 4000; www.fourseasons.com; Simmonscourt Rd, Ballsbridge; r from €295; 🖳 5, 7, 7A, 8, 18 or 45; 🅿 🖳 🅐 🅖
The muscular, no-holds-barred style of American corporate inn-keeping is in full

force at this huge hotel, which has raised the hospitality bar to a whole new level of service. Its over-the-top look – lots of marble effect, fancy chandeliers and carefully pruned floral arrangements – has its critics, who think it garish, but there's no denying the sheer quality of the place. For many, this is the best hotel in town. We're suckers for a slightly more demure luxury, so we'll stick it in the top three. It's in the grounds of the Royal Dublin Showgrounds.

HERBERT PARK HOTEL
Map p99   Hotel €€€

☎ 667 2200; www.herbertparkhotel.ie; Merrion Rd, Ballsbridge; s/d from €230/270; 🚌 5, 7, 7A, 8, 18 or 45; P 🖥 ♿

We'll forgive them the stripey wallpaper in the bedrooms (and it's not the worst) because this place has so much else going for it. A bright, modernist foyer opens onto two buzzing bars; gorgeous Herbert Park is right on your doorstep; there are spacious comfortable rooms; and, in our opinion, the best (and most reasonably priced) suites in town, designed with chichi New York in mind and with huge balconies overlooking Dublin's most exclusive bit of greenery.

PEMBROKE TOWNHOUSE
Map p99   Boutique Hotel €€

☎ 660 0277; www.pembroketownhouse.ie; 90 Pembroke Rd; s/d €155/240; 🚌 5, 7, 7A, 8, 18 or 45; P 🖥 ♿

This super-luxurious town house is a wonderful example of what happens when traditional and modern combine to great effect. A classical Georgian house has been transformed into a modern boutique hotel, with each room carefully appointed to reflect the best of contemporary design and style, right down to the modern art on the walls and the lift to the upper floors. May we borrow your designer?

ABERDEEN LODGE
Map p99   Guesthouse €€

☎ 283 8155; www.halpinsprivatehotels.com; 53-55 Park Ave; s/d/ste from €90/140/200; 🔵 Sydney Parade; P

Not only is this one of Dublin's absolutely best guesthouses, but it's a carefully guarded secret, known only to those lucky enough to dare stay a short train ride from the city centre. Their reward is a luxurious house with stunning rooms, most of which

come with either a four-poster, a half-tester or a brass bed to complement the authentic Edwardian furniture and tasteful art on the walls. The suites even have fully working Adams fireplaces. To top it off, there's a level of personalised service as good as any you'll find in any of the city's top hotels.

SCHOOLHOUSE HOTEL
Map p99   Boutique Hotel €€

☎ 667 5014; www.schoolhousehotel.com; 2-8 Northumberland Rd; s/d €169/199; 🚌 5, 7, 7A, 8, 18 or 45; P 🍴 🖥

A Victorian schoolhouse dating from 1861, this beautiful building has been successfully converted into an exquisite boutique hotel that is (ahem) ahead of its class. Its 31 cosy bedrooms named after famous Irish people, all have king-sized beds, big white duvets and loudly patterned headboards. The Canteen bar and patio bustles with local business folk in summer.

MERRION HALL
Map p99   Boutique Hotel €€

☎ 668 1426; www.halpinsprivatehotels.com; 54 Merrion Rd, Ballsbridge; s/d from €89/158; 🚌 5, 7, 7A, 8, 18 or 45; P

This ivy-clad Edwardian house, directly across the street from the Royal Dublin Showground, has 12 superbly appointed rooms, each decorated with restored period furniture. The suites have four-poster beds and whirlpool baths. A nice touch in all the rooms are the aromatherapeutic toiletries, a far cry from the usual savonettes.

WATERLOO HOUSE
Map p99   Guesthouse €€

☎ 660 1888; www.waterloohouse.ie; 8-10 Waterloo Rd; s/d €65/118; 🚌 5, 7, 7A, 8, 18 or 45; P ♿

A short walk from St Stephen's Green, off Baggot St, this plush guesthouse spread over two ivy-clad Georgian houses has 17 rooms classically furnished in authentic Georgian style and immaculately kept right through to the manicured gardens and breakfast conservatory. There's a serene atmosphere here and the prices represent exceptional value for the swanky D4 address.

ARIEL HOUSE
Map p99   B&B €€

☎ 668 5512; www.ariel-house.net; 52 Lansdowne Rd; r from €99; 🚌 5, 7, 7A, 8, 18 or 45; P

With 28 rooms, all with their own bathroom, this is hardly your average B&B, but not many B&Bs are listed Victorian homes that have been given top rating by Fáilte Ireland either. Every room is individually decorated with period furniture, which lends the place an air of genuine luxury. Ariel House beats almost any hotel.

SANDFORD TOWNHOUSE
Map p99   Guesthouse €

☎ 412 6880; 52 Sandford Rd, Ranelagh; s/d from €50/70; 🚇 Ranelagh; 🅿

The pleasant suburb of Ranelagh is one of the most desirable addresses in town, a self-contained village with decent pubs and some terrific restaurants. This elegant Victorian home, with three large rooms, is a terrific choice, made all the better by the presence of the nearby Luas, which makes getting in and out of town a cinch.

NORTH OF THE LIFFEY

It's a truism that you'll get more for your buck on the north side, but as the north inner city continues to get a facelift so its desirability has grown. The fancy hotels of yesteryear don't seem as out of place anymore and a number of excellent new hotels have made the area an interesting spot to bed down in again. East of O'Connell St is Gardiner St, where virtually every second building is a B&B. Once proudly unfussy and basic, they've had to up the game and introduce a better standard of comfort – although the further north you go the dodgier they get. Watch yourself around Upper Gardiner St and the area immediately around Connolly Station and Busáras, the central bus station.

GRESHAM HOTEL Map pp102–3   Hotel €€€
☎ 874 6881; www.gresham-hotels.com; Upper O'Connell St; r €200, ste €450-2500; 🚌 all cross-city; 🅿 🛒 🖥 ♿

This landmark hotel shed its traditional granny's parlour look with a major overhaul some years ago. Despite its brighter, smarter, modern appearance and a fabulous open-plan foyer, its loyal clientele – elderly groups on shopping breaks to the capital and well-heeled Americans – has stuck firmly. Rooms are spacious and well serviced, though the décor is a little brash.

MORRISON HOTEL Map pp102–3   Hotel €€€
☎ 887 2400; www.morrisonhotel.ie; Lower Ormond Quay; r €285-580, ste €1400; 🚌 all cross-city, 🚇 Luas Red Line to Jervis; 🅿 🛒 🖥

The Morrison recently upped the ante in the Hip Hotel stakes with the addition of 48 new bedrooms in the adjoining former printworks. Fashion designer John Rocha's loosely Oriental style is still evident in the zen-like furnishings but extras like Apple Mac plasma screens, iPod docking stations and Aveda goodies clinch it for us. For a few quid extra, nab a far superior studio den in the new wing with balcony and enough space to throw a party.

CLARION HOTEL Map pp102–3   Hotel €€€
☎ 433 8800; www.clarionhotelifsc.com; Custom House Quay; r €265, ste €395-1000; 🚇 Connolly Station; 🅿 🛒 🖥 🛒

This swanky business hotel in the heart of the Irish Financial Services Centre has beautiful rooms decorated in contemporary light oak furnishings and a blue-and-taupe colour scheme that is supposed to relax the mind after a long day of meetings. We prefer to relax with a swim in the Sanovitae health club downstairs.

LYNHAM'S HOTEL Map pp102–3   Hotel €€
☎ 888 0886; www.lynams-hotel.com; 63-64 O'Connell St; s/d €100/170; 🚌 all cross-city

Bang in the middle of O'Connell St, beside the General Post Office, this smart, friendly little hotel is a gem. All 42 rooms are nicely furnished with country pine furniture and tasteful fabrics. Room No 41 is a lovely triple with an additional camp bed, handy for groups who want to share. Midweek rates are cheaper.

COMFORT INN SMITHFIELD
Map pp102–3   Hotel €€

☎ 485 0900; www.comfortinndublincity.com; Smithfield Village; r €130-150; 🚇 Luas Red Line to Smithfield

This functionally modern hotel with big bedrooms and plenty of earth tones to soften the contemporary edges is your best bet in this part of town. We love the floor-to-ceiling windows: great for checking out what's going on below in the square.

TOWNHOUSE Map pp102–3   Boutique Hotel €€
☎ 878 8808; www.townhouseofdublin.com; 47-48 Lower Gardiner St; s/d/tr €70/115/132; 🚇 Connolly Station

The ghostly writing of Irish-Japanese author Lafcadio Hearn may have influenced the Gothic-style interior of his

GAY STAY

Most of the city's hotels wouldn't bat an eyelid if same-sex couples checked in, but the same can't be said of many of the city's B&Bs. Tongues would wag, however, if a mixed-gender couple checked into Frankies Guesthouse (Map pp66–7; ☎ 478 3087; www.frankiesguesthouse.com; 8 Camden Pl; r from €80), an old mews house with 12 homey rooms complete with cable TV, a full Irish breakfast and a plant-filled roof terrace.

former home. A dark walled, gilt-framed foyer with jingling chandelier leads into 82 individually designed, comfy rooms. Some rooms in the new wing at the back are larger with balconies overlooking the small Japanese garden. It shares a dining room with the Globetrotters Tourist Hostel (p208) next door.

ACADEMY HOTEL Map pp102–3   Hotel €€
☎ 878 0666; www.academyhotel.ie; Findlater Pl; r from €130; 🚌 all cross-city; Ⓟ 💻 📶
Recently acquired by the Best Western group and thoroughly upgraded to solidly three-star level, the Academy has well-appointed rooms with light, modern furnishings that will afford you a comfortable if unmemorable night's sleep. The deluxe suites come with free wi-fi and flat-screen digital TVs. There's discounted parking at the covered car park next door.

WALTON'S HOTEL Map pp102–3   Hotel €€
☎ 878 3131; www.waltons-hotel.ie; 2-5 North Frederick St; s/d from €80/120; 🚌 36 or 36A; Ⓟ ♿
Better known for their legendary musical instrument shop next door, the Walton family opened this friendly hotel in an effort to preserve the traditional Georgian heritage of the building. With the help of the Castle Hotel (right) they have done just that. This is an excellent choice with a superb location overlooking Findlater's Church and the Rotunda Hospital, and 43 clean, spacious rooms. Children under 12 stay for free.

BROWN'S HOTEL Map pp102–3   Hotel €€
☎ 855 0034; www.dublin-hotel.net; 80-90 Lower Gardiner St; s/d €89/115; 🚈 Connolly Station
A popular hotel along the strip, Brown's 22 rooms are a fairly comfortable bunch even

if they're a little shabby looking. They fill up quickly and there's usually a pretty lively atmosphere, although we could do without the noise from the hostel next door.

CASTLE HOTEL Map pp102–3   Hotel €€
☎ 874 6949; www.castle-hotel.ie; 3-4 Great Denmark St; s/d from €70/100; 🚌 36 or 36A; Ⓟ ♿
In business since 1809, the Castle Hotel may be slightly rough around the edges but it's one of the most pleasant hotels this side of the Liffey. The fabulous palazzo-style grand staircase leads to the 50-odd bedrooms, whose furnishings are traditional and a tad antiquated, but perfectly good throughout – check out the original Georgian cornicing around the high ceilings.

JURY'S INN PARNELL ST
Map pp102–3   Hotel €€
☎ 878 4900; www.jurysinns.com; Moore St Plaza, Parnell St; r from €99; 🚌 36 or 36A; 📶 💻 ♿
Jury's hotels are nothing if not reliable, and this edition of Ireland's most popular hotel chain is no exception. What do you care that the furnishings were once mass-produced and flat-packed and that the décor was created to be as utterly inoffensive to everything save good taste? The location is terrific.

CLIFDEN GUESTHOUSE
Map pp102–3   Guesthouse €€
☎ 874 6364; www.clifdenhouse.com; 32 Gardiner Pl; s/d from €50/90; 🚌 36 or 36A; Ⓟ
A great place to stay in the area, the Clifden is a very nicely refurbished Georgian house with 14 tastefully decorated rooms. They all come with bathroom, are immaculately clean and extremely comfortable. A nice touch is the free parking, even after you've checked out!

ABBEY COURT HOSTEL Map pp102–3 Hostel €
☎ 878 0700; www.abbey-court.com; 29 Bachelor's Walk; dm/d from €22/84; 🚌 all cross-city
Spread over two buildings, this large, well-run hostel has 33 clean dorm beds with good storage. Its excellent facilities include a dining hall, conservatory and barbecue area. Doubles with bathroom are in the newer building where a light breakfast is provided in the adjacent café, Juice (p149). Not surprisingly, this is a popular option for travellers. Reservations are advised.

JACOB'S INN Map pp102–3 Hostel €

☎ 855 5660; www.isaacs.ie; 21-28 Talbot Pl; dm/d from €12/76; 🚊 Luas Red Line to Connolly; ♿
Sister hostel to Isaacs (below) around the corner, this clean and modern hostel offers spacious accommodation with private bathrooms and outstanding facilities, including some disabled-access rooms, a bureau de change, bike storage and a self-catering kitchen.

ANCHOR GUESTHOUSE

Map pp102–3 Guesthouse €
☎ 878 6913; www.anchorguesthouse.com; 49 Lower Gardiner St; s/d from €55/75; 🚊 Connolly Station; Ⓟ ♿
Most B&Bs round these parts offer pretty much the same stuff: TV, half-decent shower, clean linen and tea- and coffee-making facilities. The Anchor does all of that, but it just has an elegance you won't find in many of the other B&Bs along this stretch. This lovely Georgian guesthouse, with its delicious wholesome breakfasts, comes highly recommended by readers. They're dead right.

MOUNT ECCLES COURT Map pp102–3 Hostel €

☎ 873 0826; www.eccleshostel.com; 42 North Great George's St; dm/d from €16/72; 🚌 36 or 36A
A Georgian classic on one of Dublin's most beautiful streets, this popular hostel has a host of dorms and doubles, all with private bathroom. Facilities include a full kitchen, two lounges and a bureau de change.

GLOBETROTTERS TOURIST HOSTEL

Map pp102–3 Hostel €
☎ 878 8088; www.globetrottersdublin.com; 46-48 Lower Gardiner St; dm/d €22/64; 🚊 DART Connolly Station
This is a really friendly place with 94 beds in a variety of dorms, all with bathrooms and under-bed storage. The funky décor is due to the fact that it shares the same artistic ethos (and dining room) as the Townhouse (p206) next door. There's a little patio garden to the rear for that elusive sunny day.

ISAACS HOSTEL Map pp102–3 Hostel €

☎ 855 6215; www.isaacs.ie; 2-5 Frenchman's Lane; dm/d from €14/62; 🚊 Luas Red Line to Connolly; 🚌 ♿
The north-side's best hostel – hell, for atmosphere alone it's the best in town – is in a 200-year-old wine vault just around the corner from the main bus station. With Summer barbecues, live music in the lounge, internet access and colourful dorms, this terrific place generates consistently good reviews from backpackers and other travellers. There's also a disabled-access room.

CHARLES STEWART Map pp102–3 Guesthouse €

☎ 878 0350; www.charlesstewart.ie; 5-6 Parnell Sq; s/d from €47/60; 🚌 36 or 36A; Ⓟ
Just north of O'Connell St, Oliver St John Gogarty's birthplace has been converted into the Charles Stewart (as in Parnell), a large and functional guesthouse with 76 clean and unfussy rooms. The ceilings are very high, but the bathrooms are small. Rooms in the extension to the rear are bigger and quieter.

BEYOND THE ROYAL CANAL

About 30 minutes' walk (3km, five minutes by bus) east of Upper O'Connell St, along Dorset St on the way to the airport, is the leafy suburb of Drumcondra (Map pp102–3), a popular area for B&Bs. Most of the houses here are late-Victorian or Edwardian, and are generally extremely well-kept and comfortable. As they're on the airport road, they tend to be full virtually throughout the year, so advance booking is definitely recommended.

JURY'S CROKE PARK HOTEL

Map p118 Hotel €€
☎ 607 0000; www.jurys-dublin-hotels.com; Croke Park, Jones's Rd; r from €109; 🚌 3, 11, 11A, 16, 16A or 123 from O'Connell St
Ireland's most Irish hotel chain hit on a sure-fire winner when it opened a hotel at the most sacred cathedral of Gaelic sports (see p117). It makes perfect sense: as tens of thousands arrive in Dublin to support their county's efforts at Croker, the clever few hundred who booked in advance won't have far to go to sleep off their celebrations – or commiserations. If you're looking for full immersion into the joys of Gaelic sports, find out when a big game is on and book early.

TINODE HOUSE off Map p118 B&B €

☎ 837 2277; www.tinodehouse.com; 170 Upper Drumcondra Rd; s/d €55/80; 🚌 11A, 11B, 36 or 36A; Ⓟ
This comfortable Edwardian town house has four elegant bedrooms, all with bath-

rooms. A friendly welcome and excellent breakfast are part of the package.

GRIFFITH HOUSE off Map p118   B&B €

☎ 837 5030; www.griffithhouse.com; 125 Griffith Ave; s/d €50/80; 🚌 41, 41B or 16A; Ⓟ
Suburban elegance should never be underestimated, especially not if it comes in the shape of this handsome Victorian home with four elegant rooms, three of which are en suite. It's a simple, traditional place that puts the emphasis on a warm welcome, a good night's sleep and a filling breakfast.

DUBLIN CITY UNIVERSITY (DCU)
off Map p118   Campus Residence €

☎ 700 5736; www.summeraccommodation.dcu.ie; Larkfield Apartments, Campus Residences, Dublin City University, Glasnevin; r per person from €43; ⓧ mid-Jun–mid-Sep; 🚌 11, 11A, 11B, 13, 13A, 19 or 19A; Ⓟ 🅡
This accommodation is proof that students slum it in relative luxury. The modern rooms have plenty of amenities at hand, including a kitchen, common room and a fully equipped health centre. DCU's Glasnevin campus is only 15 minutes by bus or car from the city centre.

EXCURSIONS

Without even the smallest hint of irony Dubliners will happily tell you that one of the city's best features is how easy it is to get out of it. Whenever they get the chance – come sun, a Bank Holiday or a sneaky 'sick' day off work – Dubliners will stuff their families, picnic hampers, golf clubs or whatever else they need into their cars and head for the hills, the beach, the countryside or anywhere else not hemmed in by grey concrete. Ireland is pretty small, so you can get pretty much anywhere within four or five hours' drive, but you don't have to go to Kerry or Donegal to really get into the heart of the country. A short, non-rush-hour drive will literally transport you into the countryside.

Beachcombers can jump the bus or DART and within half an hour grey concrete gives way to seaside villages with cosy harbours and sandy beaches. If you want to dig a little into the country's remote and recent past, Dublin's neighbouring counties – Wicklow to the south, Kildare to the west and Meath to the north – have ruins, prehistoric sites and stately country piles that rank among the country's most important historical attractions. Or, if you just fancy a rugged walk or gentle gambol in the Irish countryside, then there are plenty of spots to indulge, from the taxing hikes around the mountains surrounding Glendalough in County Wicklow to the gorse-bracketed paths of Howth Head immediately north of Dublin Bay.

If you're on a short visit to Dublin, then obviously timing is all-important. Sure, there's plenty to keep you amused, entertained and interested within the confines of the city centre, but Dublin's environs are as much a part of the Dublin experience as a weekend in Temple Bar; to most Dubliners, in fact, even more so. All of the sights listed in this chapter are worthwhile destinations in their own right and deserving of any effort you make to get to them. But what makes them doubly attractive for the short-term visitor is that they're all a short distance from the city, and travel to and from them is generally hassle-free.

COASTAL BREAKS

You'd never think it while walking around the city centre, but Dublin is a mere stone's throw from a number of lovely seaside towns, most of which have been incorporated into the greater city but have managed to retain that quiet village feel. The traditional fishing village of Howth (p214) – that bulbous headland on the northern edge of Dublin Bay – is now one of Dublin's most prestigious addresses, primarily because the residents are fiercely protective of their unspoilt headland, dotted with fancy houses and rising above the beautiful harbour where many of them keep their pleasure boats. Further north along the coast is the ever-elegant village of Malahide (p216), fronted by a long, sandy coastal basin and an impressive marina full of shops, restaurants and – naturally – expensive boats.

To the south of Dublin Bay is Dalkey (p217), a compact village that is virtually attached to the southern suburbs. You can rent boats at the small harbour and explore the southern reaches of the bay, and after you've hit dry land there are a couple of great restaurants that alone make the journey worthwhile.

Visiting all three is pretty easy. All are connected to the city centre via the DART, which cuts travel time to under 45 minutes in any direction. The obvious itinerary is to visit Howth and Malahide in one day, but each is worth devoting a little more time to if you can. If golf is your thing, Howth's wonderful courses will take up the better part of half a day, leaving you the other half to explore the port and have a seafood dinner in one of the harbour's restaurants. If you feel like a good walk, then an amble across the top of Howth Head to the lighthouse is a thoroughly enjoyable experience, especially in good weather.

As Dalkey lies on the opposite end of Dublin Bay, it is really a trip in itself, but there's plenty to keep you amused for at least half a day. Besides renting a boat and exploring the nearby waters and offshore island, there are some lovely walks in the hills above the town and further south in Killiney (p218), which is also home to a fabulous beach.

THE DISTANT PAST

Dublin is old, but it ain't that old. If you really want to get stuck into Ireland's past, you need to get out of the city, but you don't have to go far. The obvious destination for fans of

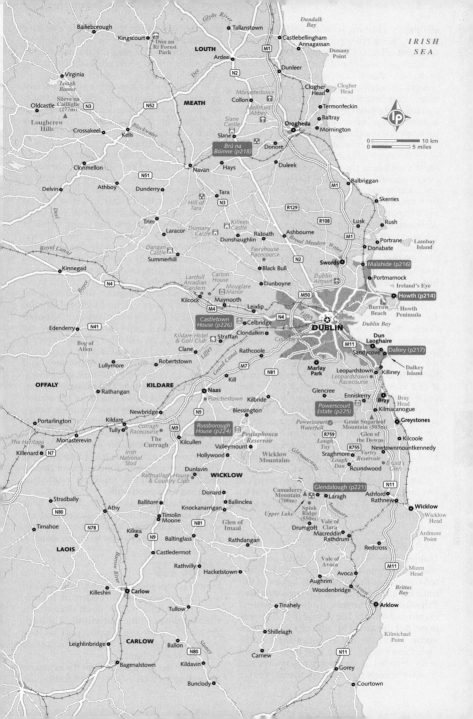

all things prehistoric is the magnificent Brú na Bóinne (p218), an extensive Neolithic graveyard northeast of Dublin in County Meath. This is, without question, one of the most important prehistoric sites in Europe, a testament to the genius and imagination of the pre-Celts. A fabulous interpretative centre explains the history and use of the passage tombs in a thoroughly satisfying way, but a tour of the two graves themselves (Newgrange and Knowth; a third, Dowth, is under excavation) is the real treat.

To the south of Dublin, and skipping forward a couple of thousand years, is the ancient monastic settlement of Glendalough (p221), once a contemplative paradise for Ireland's first monks and now one of the country's most important sets of early-Christian ruins. Although undoubtedly fascinating in themselves, it is their setting that makes this place so special, around two glacial lakes at the foot of a secluded valley in the middle of the Wicklow Mountains. There are plenty of walking opportunities here, including a couple of mountain hikes.

Although Brú na Bóinne and Glendalough are only 40km and 25km respectively from Dublin, they are not easily accessible by public transport. A private bus company runs buses to and from Glendalough twice a day from the city centre, but Brú na Bóinne is a little harder to get to if you don't have a car and is best visited by organised coach tour – the price of which includes transport and all admission fees. Aside from leaving the hassle of getting there in someone else's hands, tours provide the bonus of a guide, who has all the facts and will answer any questions you may have about the site. There are also organised tours to Glendalough, although the main advantage of joining one is that you can kill a few birds with one stone and get in a visit to Russborough House (p224) as well as a quickie tour of northern Wicklow.

STATELY HOMES

Dublin came of age in the 18th century, when the Protestant Ascendancy committed themselves to making the city one of the most beautiful in Europe. Up went stunning Palladian town houses around handsome, manicured squares and Georgian Dublin was born. But the actual breadth of the Palladian vision – and the full extent of the kind of cash these people had to play with – is only really revealed in the weekend getaways and country retreats they built for themselves far

from the city's madding crowds. Here we have included the three finest houses of all. Each is a breathtakingly magnificent example of what vainglorious power and oodles of money can produce.

In County Wicklow, to the south, are two examples of Georgian top-dog Richard Cassels' finest work: the wonderful Powerscourt Estate (p225), built for the Power family and embellished by one of the most beautiful gardens in Europe; and Russborough House (p224), home to an extraordinary art collection built up over the years by Sir Alfred Beit (despite a number of robberies, it remains one of the most important private collections in the world).

West of Dublin, County Kildare is not just home to the most important private stud farms in Ireland, but to the grandest Georgian pile of the lot, Castletown House (p226). The first complete example of the Palladian style that was all the rage between 1720 and 1820, Castletown is simply huge, without a doubt reflecting owner William Conolly's vast wealth (he was, in his day, Ireland's richest man). Not far from the house lies a relatively undiscovered delight, the Larchill Arcadian Gardens (see the boxed text, p227). Here, amid the wonderfully wild garden layout, are a number of follies, proof of the owners' oddities and eccentricities.

The actual houses at Russborough and Castletown are open to visitors, but Powerscourt House is not. Since a massive fire gutted the inside in 1974 a process of restoration has been going on that will eventually restore each room to its original splendour. However, a visit is still more than worthwhile, as the estate itself is a marvellous place to while away an afternoon, with its gardens the main draw. The nearby waterfall is the tallest in Britain and Ireland, and the surrounding countryside is perfect for a good walk.

All three houses are within about an hour and a half of Dublin's city centre, and are served by public bus. Organised tours to Glendalough also take in a visit to Powerscourt.

HOWTH

Howth is a popular excursion from Dublin and has developed as a residential suburb. It is a pretty little town built on steep streets running down to the waterfront. Although the harbour's role as a shipping port has long gone, Howth is now a major fishing centre and yachting harbour.

Most of the town backs onto the extensive grounds of Howth Castle (Map p215), originally built

HOWTH

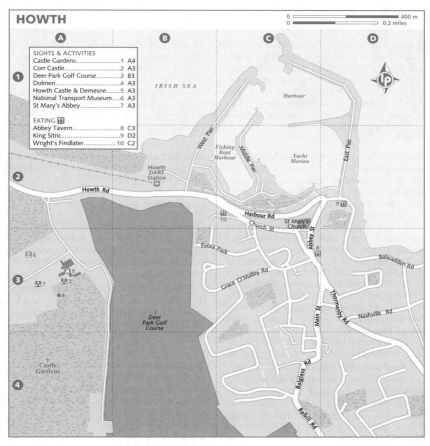

SIGHTS & ACTIVITIES
Castle Gardens...................1 A4
Corr Castle.........................2 A3
Deer Park Golf Course.....3 B3
Dolmen..............................4 A3
Howth Castle & Demesne.......5 A3
National Transport Museum...6 A3
St Mary's Abbey................7 A3

EATING 🍴
Abbey Tavern.....................8 C3
King Sitric...........................9 D2
Wright's Findlater..............10 C2

in 1564 but much changed over the years, most recently in 1910 when Sir Edwin Lutyens gave it a modernist makeover. Today the castle is divided into four separate – very posh and private – residences. The original estate was acquired in 1177 by the Norman noble Sir Almeric Tristram, who changed his surname to St Lawrence after winning a battle at the behest (or so he believed) of his favourite saint. The family has owned the land ever since, though the unbroken chain of male succession came to an end in 1909.

Also on the grounds are the ruins of the 16th-century Corr Castle and an ancient dolmen (a Neolithic grave memorial built of vertical stones and topped by a table stone) known as Aideen's Grave. Legend has it that Aideen died of a broken heart after her husband was killed at the Battle of Gavra near Tara in AD

184, but the legend is rubbish because the dolmen is at least 300 years older than that.

The Castle Gardens (Map p215; admission free; ⏰ 24hr) are worth visiting, however, as they're noted for their rhododendrons (which bloom in

TRANSPORT: HOWTH

Distance from Dublin 9km

Direction Northeast

Bus Dublin bus 31, 31A or 31B (€2.10, 45 minutes, every 30 minutes) from Lower Abbey St.

Car Northeast along Clontarf Rd; follow the northern bay shoreline.

Train DART (€2.10, 20 minutes, every 20 minutes) to Howth.

DETOUR: IRELAND'S EYE

A short distance offshore from Howth is Ireland's Eye, a rocky sea-bird sanctuary with the ruins of a 6th-century monastery. There's a Martello tower at the northwestern end of the island, where boats from Howth land, while the eastern end plummets into the sea in a spectacularly sheer rock face. As well as the sea birds overhead, you can see young birds on the ground during the nesting season. Seals can also be spotted around the island.

Doyle & Sons (☎ 01-831 4200; return €12) takes boats out to the island from the East Pier of Howth Harbour during summer, usually on weekend afternoons. Don't wear shorts if you're planning to visit the monastery ruins because they're surrounded by a thicket of stinging nettles. And bring your rubbish back with you – far too many island visitors don't.

May and June), for their azaleas and for the long, 10m-high beech St Mary's Abbey (Map p215; Abbey St, Howth Castle; admission free), originally founded in 1042 by the Viking King Sitric, who also founded the original church on the site of Christ Church Cathedral. In 1235 the abbey was amalgamated with the monastery on Ireland's Eye (a rocky island outcrop, just offshore from Howth, which is now home to a cacophony of sea birds). Some parts of the ruins date from that time, but most are from the 15th and 16th centuries. The tomb of Christopher St Lawrence (Lord Howth), in the southeastern corner, dates from around 1470. See the caretaker or read the instructions on the gate for entry.

A more recent addition is the rather ramshackle National Transport Museum (Map p215; ☎ 01-832 0427; Howth Castle; adult/child or student €3.50/2; ☑ 10am-5pm Mon-Sat Jun-Aug, 2-5pm Sat-Sun & bank holidays Sep-May), which has a range of exhibits including double-decker buses, a bakery van, fire engines and trams – most notably a Hill of Howth electric that operated from 1901 to 1959. To reach the museum, go through the castle gates and turn right just before the castle.

The allure of history and public transport aside, most visitors set foot in the demesne armed with golf clubs, as here you'll find Deer Park Golf Course (Map p215; ☎ 01-832 2624; Howth Castle; 18-holes Mon-Fri €17.50, Sat & Sun €25, club rental €16; ☑ 8am-dusk Mon-Fri, 6.30am-dusk Sat & Sun), a public facility attached to a hotel. An 18-hole course, two nine-hole courses and a par-three course, all with splendid views of Dublin Bay and the surrounding countryside, are the big draw.

Howth is essentially a very large hill surrounded by cliffs, and the peak (171m) has excellent views across Dublin Bay right down to Wicklow. From the summit you can walk to the top of the Ben of Howth, which has a cairn said to mark a 2000-year-old Celtic royal grave. The 1814 Baily Lighthouse, at the southeastern corner, is on the site of an old stone fort and can be reached by a dramatic cliff-top walk. There was an earlier hill-top beacon here in 1670.

SLEEPING & EATING

Abbey Tavern (Map p215; ☎ 01-839 0307; Abbey St; s/d €110/220; mains around €24, 3-course dinner €30) Enjoy better-than-average pub grub, with the emphasis on seafood and meat at this 16th-century tavern. Upstairs are eight lovely rooms.

King Sitric (Map p215; ☎ 01-832 5235; www.kingsitric.ie; East Pier; mains €35-48, 5-course dinner €55; ☑ lunch & dinner Mon-Fri, dinner only Sat) A well-established seafood spot with a big reputation that has been seriously challenged by new arrivals; the wine list, however, is still tops.

Wright's Findlater (Map p215; ☎ 01-832 4488; www.wrightsfindlaterhowth.com; Harbour Rd; mains €10-21) A modern all-in restaurant, bar and lounge, there's the Asian-influenced Lemongrass on the first floor, above a stylish bar that does terrific grub, with the emphasis mostly on fish.

MALAHIDE

Malahide (Mullach Ide) was once a small village with its own harbour, a long way from the urban jungle of Dublin, but the only thing protecting it from the northward expansion of Dublin's suburbs now is Malahide Demesne – 101 well-tended hectares of parkland domi-

TRANSPORT: MALAHIDE

Distance from Dublin 13km

Direction North

Bus Dublin bus 42 (€2, 45 minutes, every 30 minutes) from Lower Abbey St.

Car North along Malahide Rd.

Train DART (€2.35, 35 minutes, every 20 minutes) to Malahide.

nated by a castle once owned by the powerful Talbot family. The handsome village remains relatively intact, but the erstwhile quiet marina has been massively developed and is now a bustling centre with a pleasant promenade and plenty of restaurants and shops.

Despite the vicissitudes of Irish history, the Talbot family managed to keep Malahide Castle (☎ 01-846 2184; www.malahidecastle.com; adult/child/student/family €7/4.40/5.95/20, incl Fry Model Railway €12/7.40/10/34; ☺ 10am-5pm Mon-Sat, 11am-6pm Sun Apr-Oct, 11am-5pm Sat & Sun Nov-Mar) under its control from 1185 to 1976, apart from the time when Cromwell was in power (1649–60). The castle is now owned by the Dublin County Council. It displays the usual hotchpotch of additions and renovations. The oldest part is a three-storey, 12th-century tower house, and the façade is flanked by circular towers, which were tacked on in 1765.

The castle is packed with furniture and paintings. Highlights include a 16th-century oak room with decorative carvings and the medieval Great Hall with family portraits, a minstrel's gallery and a painting of the Battle of the Boyne. Puck, the Talbot family ghost, is said to have last appeared in 1975.

The country's biggest collection of toy trains is the Fry Model Railway (☎ 01-846 3779; Malahide Castle; adult/child/student/family €7/4.40/5.95/20; ☺ 10am-1pm & 2-5pm Mon-Sat, 2-6pm Sun Apr-Sep, 2-5pm Sat, Sun & holidays only rest of year), a 240-sq-metre model that authentically displays much of Ireland's rail and public transport system, including the DART line and Irish Sea ferry services, in O-gauge (32mm track width). There is also a separate room featuring model trains and other memorabilia. Unfortunately, the operators suffer from the overseriousness of some grown men with complicated toys. Rather than let you simply look and admire, they herd you into the control room in groups for demonstrations.

The parkland (admission free; ☺ 10am-9pm Apr-Oct, 10am-5pm Nov-Mar) around the castle is a good place for a picnic. If you fancy seeing a bit of Dublin from the sea, Sea Safaris (☎ 01-806 1626; www.seasafari.ie; Malahide Marina; per hr €25) runs speedboats from the marina as far south as Dalkey and back.

SLEEPING & EATING

Grand Hotel (☎ 01-845 0000; www.thegrand.ie; Main St; s/d €230/280; Ⓟ Ⓡ) A 19th-century hotel that is a Dublin classic, with beautifully furnished rooms and a tradition of excellent service.

Bon Appétit (☎ 01-845 0314; 9 St James' Tce; mains €23-36; ☺ 7-9.30pm Tue-Sat) The village's best restaurant features a superb menu of fish, meat and vegetarian options.

Gibney's (☎ 01-845 0863; New St; dishes €4-8; ☺ 10.30am-11.30pm Mon-Thu, 10.30am-12.30am Fri-Sat & noon-11pm Sun) Malahide's best and most popular pub does a roaring trade in sandwiches, burgers and salads.

Siam Thai Restaurant (☎ 01-845 4698; Gas Lane, the Marina; dishes €18-22; ☺ 6pm-midnight) Thai classics for local palates means that you can vary the spiciness and be assured no MSG is used.

DALKEY

Dublin's most important medieval port has long since settled into its role as an elegant dormitory village, but there are some revealing vestiges of its illustrious past, most notably the remains of three of the eight castles that once lorded over the area. Facing each other on Castle St are the 15th-century Archibold's Castle and Goat Castle. The latter (aka the Towerhouse), along with the adjoining St Begnet's Church, has been converted into the Dalkey Castle & Heritage Centre (☎ 01-285 8366; www.dalkeycastle.com; Castle St; adult/child/student €6/4/5; ☺ 9.30am-5pm Mon-Fri May-Oct, 11am-5pm Sat & Sun year-round), where models, displays and exhibitions form a pretty interesting demonstration of Dalkey's history and also give an insight into the area during medieval times.

Overlooking Bullock Harbour are the remains of Bulloch Castle, built by the monks of St Mary's Abbey in Dublin around 1150.

A few hundred metres offshore is Dalkey Island, home to St Begnet's Holy Well (admission free; boat from Coliemore Harbour per hr €25), the most important of Dalkey's so-called holy wells. This one is reputed to cure rheumatism, making the island a popular destination for tourists and the faithful alike. The island is easily accessible by boat from Coliemore Harbour; you can't book a boat, so just show up. The waters around the island are popular with scuba divers; qualified divers can rent gear in Dun Laoghaire, further north, from Ocean Divers (☎ 01-280 1083; www.oceandivers.ie; West Pier; half-day dive with full equipment & boat €49).

To the south there are good views from the small park at Sorrento Point and from Killiney Hill. Dalkey Quarry is a popular site for rock climbers, and originally provided most of the granite for the gigantic piers at Dun Laoghaire Harbour. A number of rocky swimming pools are also found along the Dalkey coast.

DETOUR: SANDYCOVE & JAMES JOYCE MUSEUM

About 1km north of Dalkey is Sandycove, with a pretty little beach and the Martello tower – built by British forces to keep an eye out for a Napoleonic invasion. It now houses the James Joyce Museum (☎ 01-280 9265; Sandycove; adult/child/student €6.70/4.20/5.70; ☺ 10am-1pm & 2-5pm Mon-Sat, 2-6pm Sun Apr-Oct, by arrangement only Nov-Mar). This is where the action begins in James Joyce's epic novel *Ulysses*. The museum was opened in 1962 by Sylvia Beach, the Paris-based publisher who first dared to put *Ulysses* into print, and has photographs, letters, documents, various editions of Joyce's work and two death masks of Joyce on display.

Below the Martello tower is the Forty Foot Pool, an open-air sea-water bathing pool that took its name from the army regiment, the Fortieth Foot, that was stationed at the tower until the regiment was disbanded in 1904. At the close of the 1st chapter of *Ulysses*, Buck Mulligan heads off to the Forty Foot Pool for a morning swim. A morning wake-up here is still a local tradition, winter or summer. In fact, a winter dip isn't much braver than a summer one since the water temperature varies by only about 5°C. Basically, it's always bloody cold.

Pressure from female bathers eventually opened this public stretch of water, originally nudist and for men only, to both sexes despite strong opposition from the 'forty foot gentlemen'. They eventually compromised with the ruling that a 'Togs Must Be Worn' sign would now apply after 9am. Prior to that time, nudity prevails and swimmers are still predominantly male.

About 1km south of Dalkey is the super-affluent seaside suburb of Killiney, home to some of Ireland's wealthiest people and a handful of celebrities, including Bono, Enya and film-maker Neil Jordan. The attraction is self-evident, from the long, curving sandy beach of Killiney Bay (which 19th-century residents felt resembled Naples' Sorrento Bay, hence the Italian names of all the local roads) to the gorse-covered hills behind it, which make for a great walk. Alas, for most of us, Killiney will always remain a place to visit; on the rare occasion that a house comes on the market, it would take a cool €5 million to get the seller to bite.

EATING

Guinea Pig (☎ 01-285 9055; 17 Railway Rd; mains €32-45) Despite the name, is this the best seafood restaurant in Dublin? Many a food critic seems to think so.

Caviston's Seafood Restaurant (☎ 01-280 9245; Glasthule Rd, Sandycove; mains €14-28) All self-respecting crustacean lovers should make the 1km trip to Caviston's for a seafood meal to remember.

TRANSPORT: DALKEY

Distance from Dublin 8km

Direction South

Bus Dublin bus 8 (€2, one hour, every 25 minutes) from Burgh Quay to Dalkey.

Car N11 south to Dalkey.

Train DART (€2.10, 20 minutes, every 10 to 20 minutes) south to Dalkey.

BRÚ NA BÓINNE

One of Ireland's genuine five-star attractions, the extensive Neolithic necropolis known as Brú na Bóinne (the Boyne Palace) is among the most extraordinary sites in Europe. A thousand years older than Stonehenge, this is a powerful and evocative testament to the mind-boggling achievements of prehistoric humans.

This necropolis was built to house the VIP corpses – no ordinary Joes or Janes here. Its tombs were the largest artificial structures in Ireland until the construction of Anglo-Norman castles 4000 years later. The area consists of many different sites, the three principal ones being Newgrange, Knowth and Dowth.

Over the centuries the tombs decayed, were covered by grass and trees, and were plundered by everybody from Vikings to Victorian treasure hunters, whose carved initials can be seen on the great stones of Newgrange. The countryside around them is littered with countless other ancient mounds (or tumuli) and standing stones.

To keep visitors from mucking up the ruins at random, all visits to Brú na Bóinne have to start at the Brú na Bóinne Visitor Centre (☎ 041-988 0300; www.heritageireland.ie; Donore; adult/child €2.90/1.60, visitor centre plus Newgrange & Knowth €10.30/4.50; ☺ 9am-7pm Jun-Sep, 9.30am-5pm Oct-Apr). Happily, this is a superb interpretive centre with an extraordinary series of interactive exhibits on the passage tombs and prehistoric Ireland in general. The building is a stunner, picking up the spiral design of Newgrange. It has regional tourism info, a good café and a bookstore. It's south of the River Boyne and 2km west of Donore.

Allow plenty of time to visit this unique centre. If you're only planning on taking the guided tour of the interpretative centre, give yourself about an hour. If you plan a visit to Newgrange or Knowth, allow at least two hours. If, however, you want to visit all three in one go, you should plan at least half a day. In summer, particularly at the weekend and during school holidays, the place gets very crowded, and you will not be guaranteed a visit to either of the passage tombs. Call ahead to book a tour and avoid disappointment. In summer, the best time to visit is midweek and/or early in the morning.

Brú na Bóinne is one of the most popular tourist attractions in Ireland, and there are oodles of organised tours transporting busloads of eager tourists to the visitor centre (everybody must access the sites through there) – especially from Dublin. Highly recommended are the Mary Gibbons Tours (☎ 01-283 9973; www.newgrangetours.com; tours €35), which depart from numerous Dublin hotels beginning at 9.30am Monday to Saturday, and take in the whole of the Boyne Valley. The expert guides offer a fascinating insight into Celtic and pre-Celtic life in Ireland and you'll get access to Newgrange even on days when all visiting slots are filled. Bus Éireann (☎ 01-836 6111; www.buseireann.ie; adult/child €29/18; Mon-Thu, Sat & Sun mid-Mar–Sep) runs Newgrange and the Boyne Valley tours, departing from Busáras in Dublin at 10am and returning at approximately 5.45pm.

NEWGRANGE

From the surface, Newgrange (Newgrange & Brú na Bóinne Visitor Centre adult/child €5.80/2.90; ☺ 9am-7pm Jun-Sep, 9.30am-5pm Oct-Apr) is a somewhat disappointing flattened, grass-covered mound, about 80m in diameter and 13m high. Underneath, however, lies the finest Stone Age passage tomb in Ireland and one of the most remarkable prehistoric sites in Europe. It dates from around 3200 BC, predating the great pyramids of Egypt by some six centuries. The purpose for which it was constructed remains uncertain. It may have been a burial place for kings or a centre for ritual – although the alignment with the sun at the time of the winter solstice also suggests it was designed to act as a calendar.

The name Newgrange derives from 'new granary' (the tomb did in fact serve as a repository for wheat and grain at one stage), although a belief more popular in the area

is that it comes from the Irish for 'Cave of Gráinne', a reference to a Celtic myth taught to every Irish schoolchild. The story of 'The Pursuit of Diarmuid and Gráinne' tells of the illicit love between Gráinne, the wife of Fionn McCumhaill (or Finn McCool), leader of the Fianna, and one of his most trusted lieutenants. When Diarmuid was fatally wounded, his body was brought to Newgrange by the god Aengus in a vain attempt to save him, and the despairing Gráinne followed him into the cave, where she remained long after he died. This suspiciously Arthurian legend (for Diarmuid and Gráinne read Lancelot and Guinevere) is undoubtedly untrue, but it's still a pretty good story. Newgrange also plays another role in Celtic mythology, serving as the site where the hero Cúchulainn was conceived.

Over the centuries, Newgrange, like Dowth and Knowth, deteriorated and was even quarried at one stage. There was a standing stone on the summit until the 17th century. The site was extensively restored in 1962 and again in 1975.

A superbly carved kerbstone, with double and triple spirals, guards the tomb's main entrance and the front façade has been reconstructed so that tourists don't have to clamber in over it. Above the entrance is a slit, or roof box, which lets light in. Another beautifully decorated kerbstone stands at the exact opposite side of the mound. Some experts say that a ring of standing stones once encircled the mound, forming a Great Circle about 100m in diameter, but only 12 of these stones remain – with traces of some others below ground level.

Holding the whole structure together are the 97 boulders of the kerb ring, designed to stop the mound from collapsing outwards. Eleven of these are decorated with motifs similar to those on the main entrance stone, although only three have extensive carvings.

The white quartzite stone was originally obtained from Wicklow, 70km to the south –

TRANSPORT: BRÚ NA BÓINNE

Distance from Dublin 40km

Direction Northeast

Bus Bus Éireann (return €12.20, 1½ hours, one daily) to the interpretative centre.

Car Take M1 north to Drogheda and then N51 west to Brú na Bóinne.

in an age before horse and wheel, it was transported by sea and then up the River Boyne – and there is also some granite from the Mourne Mountains in Northern Ireland. More than 200,000 tonnes of earth and stone also went into the mound.

You can walk down the narrow 19m passage, lined with 43 stone uprights – some of them engraved – which leads into the tomb chamber, about one-third of the way into the colossal mound. The chamber has three recesses, and in these are large basin stones that held cremated human bones. Along with the remains would have been funeral offerings of beads and pendants, but these must have been stolen long before the archaeologists arrived.

Above your head the massive stones support a 6m-high corbel-vaulted roof. A complex drainage system means that not a drop of water has penetrated the interior in 40 centuries.

At 8.20am during the winter solstice (19–23 December), the rising sun's rays shine through the slit above the entrance, creep slowly down the long passage and illuminate the tomb chamber for 17 minutes. There is little doubt that witnessing this is one of the country's most memorable, even mystical, experiences; be sure to add your name to the list that is drawn by lottery every 1 October. Even if you miss out, there is a simulated winter sunrise for every group taken into the mound.

KNOWTH

The burial mound of Knowth (Cnóbha; Knowth & Brú na Bóinne Visitor Centre adult/child €4.50/1.60; ☻ 9am-7pm Jun-Sep, 9.30am-5pm Oct-Apr), northwest of Newgrange, was built around the same time and seems set to surpass its better-known neighbour, both in the extent and the importance of the discoveries made here. It has been under excavation since 1962, and has the greatest collection of passage-grave art ever uncovered in Western Europe.

Modern excavations at Knowth soon cleared a 34m passage to the central chamber, much longer than the one at Newgrange. In 1968 a second 40m passage was unearthed on the opposite side of the mound. Although the chambers are separate, they're close enough for archaeologists to hear each other at work. Also in the mound are the remains of six early-Christian souterrains (underground chambers) built into the side. Some 300 carved slabs and 17 satellite graves surround the main mound.

Human activity at Knowth continued for thousands of years after its construction, which accounts for the site's complexity. The Beaker folk, so called because they buried their dead with drinking vessels, occupied the site in the Bronze Age (c 1800 BC), as did the Celts in the Iron Age (around 500 BC); remnants of bronze and iron workings from these periods have been discovered. Around AD 800 to 900 it was turned into a *ráth* (earthen ring fort), a stronghold of the very powerful Uí Néill (O'Neill) clan, and in 965 it was the seat of Cormac MacMaelmithic (aka Cormac mac Airt), later Ireland's high king for nine years. The Normans built a motte and bailey here in the 12th century, but around 1400 the site was finally abandoned. Further excavations are likely to continue at least for the next decade, and one of the thrills of visiting Knowth is being allowed to watch archaeologists at work (although given the cramped conditions inside, you won't be jealous).

DOWTH

The circular mound at Dowth (from the Irish 'Dubhadh', meaning 'dark') is a little smaller than Newgrange – about 63m in diameter – but is slightly taller at 14m high. It has suffered badly at the hands of everyone from road builders and treasure hunters to amateur archaeologists, who scooped out the centre of the tumulus in the 19th century. For

FIONN & THE SALMON OF KNOWLEDGE

One of the best-known stories in the Fenian Cycle is set around Newgrange and tells of the old druid Finnegan, who struggled for seven years to catch a very slippery salmon that, once consumed, would bestow enormous wisdom on the eater, including the gift of foresight. The young Fionn McCumhaill arrived at his riverside camp one day, looking for instruction, and no sooner did the young hero arrive than Finnegan managed to land the salmon. As befits the inevitable tragedy of all these stories, Finnegan set the fish to cook and went off for a bit, ordering Fionn to keep an eye on it without eating so much as the smallest part. You'd think that after all these years of labour Finnegan could have put off what he went off to do until after dinner, but it wasn't to be. As Fionn turned the fish on the spit a drop of hot oil landed on his thumb, which he quickly put in his mouth to soothe. Finnegan returned, saw what had happened and knew that it was too late: he bade Fionn eat the rest of the fish and so it was that Fionn acquired wisdom and foresight.

DETOUR: NEWGRANGE FARM

One for the kids. Situated a few hundred metres down the hill to the west of Newgrange tomb (or follow the signs on the N51) is a 135-hectare working farm (☎ 041-982 4119; www.newgrangefarm.com; Newgrange; adult €8, family €12-30; ☺ 10am-5pm Easter-Aug). The truly hands-on, family-run farm allows visitors to feed the ducks and lambs, and tour the exotic bird aviaries. Amiable Farmer Bill keeps things interesting and demonstrations of threshing, sheepdog work and shoeing a horse are absorbing. Sunday at 3pm is a very special time when the 'sheep derby' is run. Finding jockeys small enough wasn't easy, so teddy bears are tied to the animals' backs. Visiting children are made owners of individual sheep for the race.

a time, Dowth even had a teahouse ignobly perched on its summit. Relatively untouched by modern archaeologists, Dowth shows what Newgrange and Knowth looked like for most of their history. Because it's unsafe, Dowth is closed to visitors, though the mound can be viewed from the road. Excavations began in 1998 and will continue for years to come.

There are two entrance passages, which lead to separate chambers (both sealed), and a 24m early-Christian souterrain at either end, which connects up with the western passage. This 8m-long passage leads into a small cruciform chamber, in which a recess acts as an entrance to an additional series of small compartments, a feature unique to Dowth. To the southwest of the mound is the entrance to a shorter passage and another smaller chamber.

North of the tumulus are the ruins of Dowth Castle and Dowth House.

SLEEPING & EATING

Newgrange Lodge (☎ 041-988 2478; www.new grangelodge.com; dm/d €15/50; P ☐) A beautiful new place just east of the Brú na Bóinne Visitor Centre, the lodge has dorm beds and hotel-standard en-suite rooms with TVs. Reception is open 24 hours and there is a café, outdoor patios, bicycle hire and much more.

Glebe House (☎ 041-983 6101; www.theglebehouse.ie; Dowth; r €120; P) This charming 17th-century, wisteria-clad country house has views of Newgrange and Dowth. It has four gorgeous rooms with open, log fires and vibrant purple carpet. It is 7km west of Drogheda; children under 10 are not allowed.

Rossnaree (☎ 041-982 0975; rossnaree@eircom.net; Newgrange; s/d €100/160) A magnificent Palladian-style country house between Donore and Slane, just south of the visitor centre, with exquisite bedrooms and fabulous cuisine (dinner €45). The river at the bottom of the garden is the same one where your old pal Finnegan landed the Salmon of Knowledge (see the boxed text, opposite).

Boyle's Licensed Tea Rooms (☎ 041-982 4195; Main St, Slane) About 2km west of Knowth; a wonderful tea shop

and café, with a 1940s ambience. The menu, written in 12 languages, is strictly of the tea-and-scones type (around €3).

GLENDALOUGH

If you're looking for the epitome of rugged and romantic Ireland, you won't do much better than Glendalough (Gleann dá Loch, 'Valley of the Two Lakes'), truly one of Ireland's most beautiful corners and a highlight of any trip along the eastern seaboard.

The substantial remains of this important monastic settlement are certainly impressive, but the real draw is the splendid setting, two dark and mysterious lakes tucked into a deep valley covered in forest. It is, despite its immense popularity, a deeply tranquil and spiritual place, and you will have little difficulty in understanding why those solitude-seeking monks came here in the first place. Visit early or late in the day – or out of season – to avoid the big crowds. Remember that a visit here is all about walking, so wear comfortable shoes.

If you don't fancy doing Glendalough on your own steam, there are a couple of tours that will make it fairly effortless. The award-winning Wild Wicklow Tour (☎ 01-280 1899; www .discoverdublin.ie; adult/student & child €28/25; ☺ departs

TRANSPORT: GLENDALOUGH

Distance from Dublin 25km

Direction South

Bus St Kevin's Bus (☎ 01-281 8119, one way/return €9/15, 1½ hours) departs 11.30am and 6pm Monday to Saturday, and 11.30am and 7pm Sunday from outside the Royal College of Surgeons, St Stephen's Green West, returning at 7.15am and 4.15pm Monday to Friday, and 9.45am and 4.15pm Saturday and Sunday.

Car N11 south to Kilmacanogue, then R755 west through Roundwood, Annamoe and Laragh.

9.10am & returns 5.30pm) of Glendalough, Avoca and the Sally Gap never fails to generate rave reviews for atmosphere and all-round fun, but so much craic has made a casualty of informative depth. The first pick-up is at the Dublin Tourism office, but there are a variety of pick-up points throughout Dublin; check the point nearest you when booking. Alternatively, Bus Éireann (☎ 01-836 6111; www.buseireann.ie; Busáras; adult/child/student €28.80/18/25.20; ☯ 10am mid-Mar–Oct) runs good but slightly impersonal whole-day tours of Glendalough and the Powerscourt Estate, which return to Dublin at about 5.45pm.

At the valley entrance, before the Glendalough Hotel, is the Glendalough Visitor Centre (☎ 0404-45325; adult/child & student €5.30/2.10; ☯ 9.30am-6pm mid-Mar–Oct, 9.30am-5pm Nov–mid-Mar). The centre screens a high-quality 17-minute audiovisual presentation, *Ireland of the Monasteries*, which does exactly what it says on the tin.

The original site of St Kevin's settlement, Teampall na Skellig, is at the base of the cliffs towering over the southern side of the Upper Lake, and is accessible only by boat; unfortunately, there's no boat service to the site and you'll have to settle for looking at it across the lake. The terraced shelf has the reconstructed ruins of a church and early graveyard. Rough wattle huts once stood on the raised ground nearby. Scattered around are some early grave slabs and simple stone crosses.

Just east of the lake and 10m above its waters is the 2m-deep artificial cave called St Kevin's Bed, said to be where Kevin lived (for more on St Kevin, see the boxed text, below). The earliest human habitation of the cave was long before St Kevin's era – there's evidence that people lived in the valley for thousands of years before the monks arrived.

In the green area just south of the car park is a large circular wall thought to be the remains of an early-Christian *caher* (stone fort).

Follow the lakeshore path southwest of the car park until you find the considerable remains of Reefert Church above the tiny Poulanass River. This is a small, rather plain, 11th-century Romanesque nave-and-chancel church, with some reassembled arches and walls. Traditionally, Reefert (meaning King's Burial Place) was the burial site of the chiefs of the local O'Toole family. The surrounding graveyard contains a number of rough stone crosses and slabs, most made of shiny mica schist.

Climb the steps at the back of the churchyard and follow the path to the west and you'll find, at the top of a rise overlooking the lake, the scant remains of St Kevin's Cell, a small beehive hut.

While the Upper Lake has the best scenery, the most fascinating buildings lie in the lower part of the valley, east of the Lower Lake.

Around the bend from the Glendalough Hotel is the stone arch of the monastery gatehouse, the only surviving example of a monastic entranceway in the country. Just inside the entrance is a large slab with an incised cross.

Beyond that lies a graveyard, which is still in use. The 10th-century round tower is 33m tall and 16m in circumference at the base. The upper storeys and conical roof were reconstructed in 1876. Near the tower, to the southeast, is the Cathedral of St Peter and St Paul, with a 10th-century nave. The chancel and sacristy date from the 12th century.

At the centre of the graveyard, to the south of the round tower, is the Priest's House. This odd building dates from 1170 but has been heavily reconstructed. It may have been the location of shrines of St Kevin. Later, during the

ST KEVIN & GLENDALOUGH

In AD 498 a young monk named Kevin arrived in the valley looking for somewhere to kick back, meditate and be at one with nature. He pitched up in what had been a Bronze Age tomb on the southern side of the Upper Lake and for the next seven years slept on stones, wore animal skins, maintained a near-starvation diet and – according to the legend – became bosom buddies with the birds and animals. Kevin's eco-friendly lifestyle soon attracted a bunch of disciples, all seemingly unaware of the irony that they were flocking to hang out with a hermit who wanted to live as far away from other people as possible. Over the next couple of centuries his one-man operation mushroomed into a proper settlement and by the 9th century Glendalough rivalled Clonmacnoise as the island's premier monastic city. Thousands of students studied and lived in a thriving community that was spread over a considerable area.

Inevitably, Glendalough's success made it a key target of Viking raiders, who sacked the monastery at least four times between 775 and 1071. The final blow came in 1398, when English forces from Dublin almost completely destroyed it. Efforts were made to rebuild and some life lingered on here as late as the 17th century, when, under renewed repression, the monastery finally died.

WALKS AROUND GLENDALOUGH

The easiest and most popular walk is the gentle hour-long walk along the northern shore of the Upper Lake to the lead and zinc mine workings, which date from 1800. The better route is along the lakeshore rather than on the road, which runs 30m from the shore. Continue on up to the head of the valley if you wish.

Alternatively, you can walk the railway sleepers that form the path along the Spink (550m), the steep ridge with vertical cliffs running along the southern flanks of the Upper Lake. You can go part of the way and turn back, or complete a 5km circuit of the Upper Lake by following the top of the cliff, eventually coming down by the mine workings and going back along the northern shore.

The third option is the 7.5km hike up and down Camaderry Mountain (700m), hidden behind the hills that flank the northern side of the valley. The walk starts on the road 50m back towards Glendalough from the entrance to the Upper Lake car park. Head straight up the steep hill to the north and you come out on open mountains with sweeping views in all directions. You can then continue up Camaderry to the northwest, or just follow the ridge west looking over the Upper Lake.

18th century, it became a burial site for local priests – hence the name. The 10th-century St Mary's Church, 140m southwest of the round tower, probably originally stood outside the walls of the monastery and belonged to local nuns; it has a lovely western doorway. A little to the east are the scant remains of St Kieran's Church, the smallest at Glendalough.

Glendalough's trademark is St Kevin's Church – or Kitchen – at the southern edge of the enclosure. With its miniature round-tower-like belfry, protruding sacristy and steep stone roof, it's a masterpiece. How it came to be known as a kitchen is a mystery as there's no indication that it was ever anything other than a church. The oldest parts of the building date from the 11th century – the structure has been remodelled since but it's still a classic early Irish church.

At the junction with Green Rd, as you cross the river just south of these two churches, is the Deer Stone, in the middle of a group of rocks. Legend claims that when St Kevin needed milk for two orphaned babies, a doe stood here waiting to be milked. The stone is actually a *bullaun*, used as a grinding stone for medicines or food. Many are thought to be

prehistoric and they were widely regarded as having supernatural properties; women who bathed their faces with water from the hollow were supposed to keep their looks forever. The early churchmen brought them into their monasteries, perhaps hoping to inherit some of the stones' powers.

The road east leads to St Saviour's Church, with its detailed Romanesque carvings. To the west a nice woodland trail leads up the valley past the Lower Lake to the Upper Lake.

SLEEPING & EATING

Derrybawn Mountain Lodge (☎ 0404-45644; derrybawnlodge@eircom.net; Derrybawn; s/d €50/90; P) A handsome eight-room lodge on Derrybawn Mountain (474m), 4km south of Laragh, with spectacular views; the owners are avid hikers and are full of insider tips.

Glendalough Hotel (☎ 0404-45135; www.glendalough hotel.com; Glendalough; s/d €120/190; P) Forty-four luxurious bedrooms right next to the ruins.

Glendalough River House (☎ 0404-45577; www .glendaloughriverhouse.com; Laragh; s/d €58/82; P) A 200-year-old restored farmhouse with delightfully large rooms overlooking the river.

SPIRITUAL SLEEPS

Glendalough Cillíns (☎ 0404-45140, bookings ☎ 0404-45777; St Kevin's Parish Church, Glendalough; r per person €45) In an effort to re-create something of the contemplative spirit of Kevin's early years in the valley, St Kevin's Parish Church rents out six hermitages (or *cillíns*) to people looking to take time out from the bustle of daily life and reflect on more spiritual matters. In keeping with more modern needs, however, there are a few more facilities than were present in Kevin's cave. Each hermitage is a bungalow consisting of a bedroom, a bathroom, a small kitchen area and an open fire (supplemented by a storage heating facility). The whole venture is managed by the local parish, and while there is a strong spiritual emphasis here, it is not necessarily a Catholic one. Visitors of all denominations and creeds are welcome, so long as their intentions are reflective and meditative – backpackers looking for a cheap place to bed down are not. The hermitages are in a field next to St Kevin's Parish Church, about 1km east of Glendalough on the R756 to Laragh.

Glendalough Hotel (☎ 0404-45135; 3-course lunch €19, bar mains around €10; ☻ noon-6pm) The hotel's enormous restaurant serves a very good lunch of unsurprising dishes, usually involving some chicken, beef and fish. The bar menu – burgers, sandwiches, sausages and the like – is also quite filling.

Wicklow Heather Restaurant (☎ 0404-45157; Main St, Laragh; mains €12-18; ☻ noon-8.30pm) This is the best place for anything substantial. The trout (farmed locally) is excellent. During summer, villagers put out signs and serve tea and scones on the village green.

RUSSBOROUGH HOUSE

Magnificent Russborough House (Map p213; ☎ 045-865 239; Blessington; adult/child/student €6.50/3.50/5; ☻ 10am-5pm Mon-Sat May-Sep, 10.30am-5.30pm Sun & bank holidays Apr & Oct, closed rest of year) is one of Ireland's finest stately homes, a Palladian pleasure palace built for Joseph Leeson (1705–83), later the first earl of Milltown and, later still, Lord Russborough. It was built from 1741 to 1751 to the design of Richard Cassels, who was at the height of his fame as an architect. Poor old Richard didn't live to see it finished, but the job was well executed by Francis Bindon.

The house has always attracted unwelcome attention, beginning in 1798 when Irish rebels took hold of the place during the Rising (see p22); they were soon turfed out by the British Army who got so used to the comforts of the place that they didn't leave until 1801, and then only after a raging Lord Russborough challenged their commander, Lord Tyrawley, to a duel 'with blunderbusses and slugs in a sawpit'. Miaow.

The house remained in Leeson family hands until 1931. In 1952 it was sold to Sir Alfred Beit, the eponymous nephew of the cofounder of the de Beers diamond mining company. Uncle Alfred was an obsessive art collector, and when he died his impressive haul – which included works by Velázquez, Vermeer, Goya and Rubens – was passed on to his nephew, who brought it to Russborough House. The collection was to attract the interest of more than just art lovers.

The house has been the victim of four major robberies, beginning in 1974 when 19 paintings were stolen by the Irish Republican Army (IRA); all were eventually recovered. Ten years later, despite increased security, notorious Dublin gangster Martin Cahill masterminded another robbery, but this time the clients were Loyalist paramilitaries. Some paintings were recovered, though several were irreparably damaged – a good thief does not a gentle curator make (this series of events features in the film *The General*, see p43). Twice bitten but thrice shy, Beit decided to give the most valuable paintings to the National Gallery in 1988. In return, the National Gallery often lends paintings to the collection as temporary exhibits.

In 2001 a pair of thieves took the direct approach and drove a jeep through the front doors, making off with two paintings worth nearly €4 million, including a Gainsborough that had been stolen – and recovered – twice before. And then, to add abuse to the insult already added to injury, the house was broken into again in 2002, with the thieves taking five more paintings, including two by Rubens. Incredibly, however, both hauls were quickly recovered.

The admission price includes a 45-minute tour of the house and all the important paintings, which, given the history, is a monumental exercise in staying positive; whatever you do, make no sudden moves. You can take an additional 30-minute upstairs tour (adult/child €4/free) of the bedrooms, which contain more silver and furniture. The tour takes place at 2.15pm Monday to Saturday, and hourly on Sunday, when the house is open.

SLEEPING & EATING

Haylands House (☎ 045-865 183; haylands@eircom.net; Dublin Rd, Blessington; s/d €45/70; Ⓟ) Highly recommended B&B with a warm welcome and lovely rooms.

Rathsallagh House & Country Club (Map p213; ☎ 045-403 112; www.rathsallaghhousehotel.com; Dunlavin; s/d from €135/185) This fabulous country manor off the N81, converted from Queen Anne stables in 1798, has splendidly appointed rooms and a superb golf course. The restaurant offers a five-course meal (€65).

Grangecon Cafe (☎ 045-857 892; Tullow Rd, Blessington; mains €9-16; ☻ 10am-5pm Tue-Sat) Salads, homebaked dishes and a full menu of Irish cheeses are the staples at this tiny, terrific café located in a converted schoolhouse.

TRANSPORT: RUSSBOROUGH HOUSE

Distance from Dublin 35km

Direction Southwest

Bus Dublin bus 65 (€3.60, 1½ hours, 10 daily) from Eden Quay.

Car N81 southwest via Blessington.

POWERSCOURT ESTATE

About 500m south of the charming village of Enniskerry is the entrance to the 64-sq-km Powerscourt Estate (Map p213; ☎ 01-204 6000; www.powerscourt.ie; adult/child/student €7.50/4.50/6.50; 9.30am-5.30pm Feb-Oct, 9.30am-4.30pm Nov-Jan), Wicklow's grandest country pile. This is one of the most popular day trips from Dublin, and the village – built in 1760 by Richard Wingfield, Earl of Powerscourt, so that his labourers would have somewhere to live – is a terrific spot to while away an afternoon.

If getting there under your own steam is an issue, you can visit it and Glendalough together as part of a Bus Éireann Tour (☎ 01-836 6111; www.buseireann.ie; Busaras; adult/child/student €27/17.55/25.20; 10.30am-5.45pm daily mid-Mar–Oct), which departs from the Dublin Tourism office.

Powerscourt Estate has existed more or less since 1300 when the LePoer (later anglicised to Power) family built themselves a castle here. The property then changed Anglo-Norman hands a few times before coming into the possession of Richard Wingfield, newly appointed Marshall of Ireland, in 1603; his descendants were to live here for the next 350 years. In 1731 the Georgian wunderkind, Richard Cassels, turned his genius to building the stunning Palladian-style mansion, which he finished in 1743. An extra storey was added to the building in 1787 and other alterations were made in the 19th century. The house was restored after the Wingfields sold up in the 1950s, but the whole building was gutted by fire on the very eve of its reopening in 1974.

The estate has since come into the hands of the sporting goods giants the Slazengers, who have overseen a second restoration, as well as the addition of two golf courses, a café, a huge garden centre and a bunch of cutsey little retail outlets. Basically, it's all intended to draw in the punters and wring as many euros out of their pockets as possible, so as to finish the huge restoration job and make the estate a kind of profitable wonderland. If you can deal with the crowds (summer weekends are the worst) or, better still, avoid them and visit midweek, you're in for a real treat.

Easily the biggest draw is the simply magnificent 20-hectare formal gardens and the breathtaking views that accompany them. Originally laid out in the 1740s, they were redesigned in the 19th century by Daniel Robinson, who had as much a fondness for the booze as he did for horticultural pursuits (see the boxed text, above). Perhaps this influenced his largely informal style, which resulted in a magnificent blend of landscaped gardens, sweeping terraces, statuary, ornamental lakes, secret hollows, rambling walks and walled enclosures replete with over 200 types of trees and shrubs – all beneath the stunning natural backdrop of the Great Sugarloaf Mountain to the southeast. Tickets come with a map laying out 40-minute and hour-long tours of the gardens. Don't miss the exquisite Japanese Gardens or the Pepperpot Tower, modelled on a three-inch actual pepperpot owned by Lady Wingfield. Our own favourite, however, is the animal cemetery, final resting place of the Wingfield pets and even some of their favourite milking cows. Some of the epitaphs are astonishingly personal.

A 7km walk to a separate part of the estate takes you to the 130m Powerscourt Waterfall (☎ 01-204 6000; adult/child/student €5/3.50/4.50; 9.30am-7pm May-Aug, 10.30am-5.30pm Mar-Apr & Sep-Oct, to 4.30pm Nov-Jan). This is the highest waterfall in Britain and Ireland, and is most impressive

THE BOOZY GARDENER

Daniel Robertson was not your typical gardener. He supervised the construction of the gardens from a wheelbarrow, in which he would lay prostrate, armed only with a bottle of sherry. To his underlings he would bark orders that, as the day passed, grew more and more incoherent as his bottle became lighter. Work usually went on until 5pm, when the tanked-up Robertson would call an end to the day's work on account of bad light. A perfectly reasonable suggestion, you may think, but considering that the summer day doesn't end until at least 10pm...

TRANSPORT: POWERSCOURT ESTATE

Distance from Dublin 18km

Direction South

Bus Dublin bus 44 (€2.10, 1¼ hours, every 20 minutes) from Hawkins St.

Car Drive south on Ranelagh Rd (R117), right onto Milltown Rd, left onto Dundrum Rd and on through Kilternan and Enniskerry; alternatively, head south to Bray along N11 and west for 3km on R117.

Train DART to Bray (€2.50), bus 185 to Enniskerry (€1.40, 20 minutes, hourly) from station.

after heavy rain. You can also get to the falls by road, following the signs from the estate. A nature trail has been laid out around the base of the waterfall, which takes you past giant redwoods, ancient oaks, beech, birch and rowan trees. There are plenty of birds in the vicinity, including the chaffinch, cuckoo, chiffchaff, raven and willow warbler.

SLEEPING & EATING

Coolakay House (☎ 01-286 2423; www.coolakayhouse .com; Waterfall Rd, Coolakay; s/d €45/80; P) Four comfortable bedrooms and a terrific restaurant (mains around €12).

Summerhill House Hotel (☎ 01-286 7928; www .summerhillhousehotel.com; Enniskerry; s/d from €80/100; P) Enniskerry's best hotel is a fabulous country mansion set amid its own woodland and landscaped park. It's off the N11.

Organic Life/Marc Michel (☎ 01-201 1882; Tinna Parc, Kilpedder; mains around €16; ☟ 10am-5pm, restaurant noon-4pm) Situated just off the N11, past the turn-off for Glendalough, is the east coast's best-kept organic secret: a superb restaurant located in the middle of a lush forest.

Poppies Country Cooking (☎ 01-282 8869; The Square, Enniskerry; mains €9; ☟ 8.30am-6pm) A pokey little café serving wholesome salads, filling sandwiches and award-winning ice cream…even if the service can be slow.

Powerscourt Terrace Café (☎ 01-204 6070; Powerscourt House; mains €8-13; ☟ 10am-5pm) The folks at Avoca (p149) have applied all their know-how and turned what could have easily been just another run-of-the-mill tourist attraction café into something of a gourmet experience.

CASTLETOWN HOUSE

In a country full of elegant Palladian mansions, it is no mean feat to be considered the grandest of the lot, but Castletown House (Map p213; ☎ 01-628 8252; adult/child €3.70/1.30; ☟ 10am-6pm Mon-Fri, 1-6pm Sat & Sun Easter-Sep, 10am-5pm Mon-Fri, 1-5pm Sun Oct) simply has no peer. It is Ireland's largest and most imposing Georgian estate, and a testament to the vast wealth enjoyed by the Anglo-Irish gentry during the 18th century.

The house was built between the years 1722 and 1732 for William Conolly (1662–1729), speaker of the Irish House of Commons, and, at the time, Ireland's richest man. Born into relatively humble circumstances in Ballyshannon, County Donegal, Conolly made his fortune through land transactions in the uncertain aftermath of the Battle of the Boyne (1690).

The original design of the house was by the Italian architect Alessandro Galilei (1691–1737), who in 1718 designed the façade of the main block so as to resemble a 16th-century Italian *palazzo* (palace). Construction began in 1722 but Galilei didn't bother hanging around to supervise, having left Ireland in 1719. Instead, the project was entrusted to Sir Edward Lovett Pearce (1699–1733), who returned from his grand tour of Italy in 1724 (where he had become friends with Galilei).

Inspired by the work of Andrea Palladio, which he had studied during his visit to Italy, Pearce enlarged the original design of the house and added the colonnades and the terminating pavilions. The interior is as opulent as the exterior suggests, especially the Long Gallery, replete with family portraits and exquisite stucco work by the Francini brothers. Pearce's connection with Conolly was a fortuitous one, as he was commissioned in 1728 to design the House of Commons in Dublin. That building, now the Bank of Ireland (p73) on College Green, is one of the most elegant examples of the Georgian style in Dublin.

As always seems the way with these grand projects, Conolly didn't live to see the completion of his wonder-palace. His widow continued to live at the unfinished house after his death in 1729, instigating many of the improvements made to the house after the main structure was completed in 1732. Her main architectural contribution was the curious 42.6m Obelisk, known locally as the Conolly Folly. Designed to her specifications by Richard Cassels, and visible from both ends of the Long Gallery, it is 3.2km north of the house.

The house remained in the family's hands until 1965, when it was purchased by Desmond Guinness. He spent vast amounts of money on restoring the house to its original splendour, an investment that was continued from 1979 by the Castletown Foundation. In 1994 Castletown House was transferred

TRANSPORT: CASTLETOWN HOUSE

Distance from Dublin 21km

Direction West

Bus Dublin buses 67 and 67A (one way €1.60, about one hour, hourly) depart from D'Olier St for Celbridge and stop at the gates of Castletown House.

Car Take N4 to Celbridge.

to state care and today it is managed by the Heritage Service.

Immediately to the east of the grounds of Castletown House, and on private property that never belonged to the house, you will find the even more curious, conical Wonderful Barn (☎ 01-624 5448; Leixlip; ☻ closed to the public). Standing at 21m high, this extraordinary five-storey structure, which is wrapped by a 94-step winding staircase, was commissioned by Lady Conolly in 1743 to give employment to local tenants whose crops were ruined by the severe frosts in the winters of 1741 and 1742. The building was ostensibly a granary, but it was also used as a shooting tower – doves were considered a delicacy in Georgian times. Flanking the main building are two smaller towers, which were also used to store grain. Be warned however: the land surrounding the barn has been zoned for redevelopment and there is a scandalous plan to build 500-odd houses around it, so prepare to trundle through a building site.

SLEEPING & EATING

Kildare Hotel & Golf Club (Map p213; ☎ 01-601 7200; www.kclub.ie; Straffan; r from €250; Ⓟ 🖳 🐦) Better known for the superb golf course that hosted the 2006 Ryder Cup, the estate is home to a palatial Palladian villa that is one of the best hotels in Ireland. It is 6km southwest of Celbridge just off the R403.

DETOUR: LARCHILL ARCADIAN GARDENS

Green thumbs and shrubbery fanatics will not want to miss a detour to the Larchill Arcadian Gardens (Map p213; ☎ 01-628 7354; www.larchill.ie; Kilcock; adult/child €7.50/5.50; ☻ noon-6pm Tue-Sun Jun-Aug, noon-6pm Sat & Sun Sep), Europe's only example of a mid-18th-century *ferme ornée* (ornamental farm). A 40-minute walk takes you through beautiful landscaped parklands, passing eccentric follies (including a model of the Gibraltar fortress and a shell-decorated tower), gazebos and a lake. Children will be chuffed with the adventure playground, maze and rare-breed farm animals. The gardens are 12km northwest of Castletown House.

Carton House (Map p213; ☎ 01-505 2000; www.carton house.com; r from €140; Ⓟ 🖳 🐦) It really doesn't get any grander than this vast early-19th-century estate set on lavish grounds, including two outstanding golf courses.

Kehoe's (☎ 01-628 6533; Main St, Maynooth; meals €5-8; ☻ 8am-4pm Mon-Sat) The place for a classic Irish breakfast, Kehoe's offers a warm, trad welcome to its small and cosy quarters. There are numerous daily lunch specials.

Meghna (☎ 01-505 4868; Main St, Maynooth; meals €10-20; ☻ noon-2.30pm & 5-11pm) Several cuts above the usual curry joint, Meghna has a wide range of excellent South Asian dishes.

TRANSPORT

Ireland's capital and biggest city is the most important point of entry and departure for the country – the overwhelming majority of airlines fly in and out of Dublin Airport. The city has two ports that serve as the main points of sea transport with Britain; ferries from France arrive in the southern port of Rosslare. Dublin is also the nation's primary rail hub. Flights, tours and rail tickets can be booked online at www.lonelyplanet.com/travel_services.

AIR

There are direct flights to Dublin from all major European centres (including a dizzying array of options from the UK) and from Boston, Baltimore, Chicago, New York and Los Angeles in the USA. Flights from further afield (Australasia or Africa) are usually routed through London.

Airlines

No airline has a walk-in office in Dublin, but most have walk-up counters at Dublin airport. Those that don't have their ticketing handled by other airlines. The website of the Fáilte Ireland (Irish Tourist Board; www.ireland.ie) has information on getting to Dublin from a number of countries.

Airlines that serve Dublin:

Aer Árann (☎ 1890 462 726; www.aerarann.ie)

Aer Lingus (☎ 01-886 8888; www.aerlingus.com)

Aeroflot (☎ 01-844 6166; www.aeroflot.com)

Air Canada (☎ 1800 709 900; www.aircanada.ca)

Air France (☎ 01-605 0383; www.airfrance.com)

Air Malta (☎ 1800 397 400; www.airmalta.com)

ONLINE BOOKING AGENCIES

- www.bestfares.com
- www.cheapflights.com
- www.ebookers.com
- www.expedia.com
- www.flycheap.com
- www.opodo.com
- www.priceline.com
- www.statravel.com
- www.travelocity.com

THINGS CHANGE...

The information in this chapter is particularly vulnerable to change. Check directly with the airline or a travel agent to make sure you understand how a fare (and ticket you may buy) works and be aware of the security requirements for international travel. Shop carefully. The details given in this chapter should be regarded as pointers and are not a substitute for your own careful, up-to-date research.

Air Wales (☎ 1800 465 193; www.airwales.com)

Alitalia (☎ 01-844 6035; www.alitalia.com)

American Airlines (☎ 01-602 0550; www.aa.com)

BMI British Midland (☎ 01-407 3036; www.flybmi.com)

British Airways (☎ 1800 626 747; www.britishairways.com)

City Jet (☎ 01-8700 300; www.cityjet.com)

Continental (☎ 1890 925 252; www.continental.com)

CSA Czech Airlines (☎ 01-814 4626; www.csa.cz)

Delta Airlines (☎ 1800 768 080; www.delta.com)

Finnair (☎ 01-844 6565; www.finnair.com)

Iberia (☎ 01-407 3017; www.iberia.com)

KLM (☎ 01-663 6900; www.klm.com)

Lufthansa (☎ 01-844 5544; www.lufthansa.com)

Malev Hungarian Airlines (☎ 01-844 4303; www.malev.com)

Ryanair (☎ 01-609 7800; www.ryanair.com)

Scandinavian Airlines (☎ 01-844 5440; www.scandinavian.net)

Airport

Dublin's only airport (Map p213; DUB; ☎ 814 1111; www.dublinairport.com) is 13km north of the city centre. Along with pubs, restaurants, shops, ATMs and car-hire desks, there are several airport facilities in the one passenger terminal:

Aer Rianta Information Desk (Irish Airport Authority; ⏰ 24hr Jun-Sep, 6am-1am Oct-May)

Bank of Ireland (⏰ 10am-4pm Mon, Tue, Thu & Fri, 10am-5pm Wed, bureau de change 5.30am-9pm Mon-Fri, 5.30am-midnight Sat, 5.30am-10pm Sun)

Dublin Airport Pharmacy (☎ 814 4649; ⏰ 6.30am-6.30pm Mon-Thu, 9am-10.30pm Fri-Sun)

Dublin Tourism Office (🕑 8am-10pm)

Greencaps Left Luggage & Porterage Office (☎ 814 4633; left luggage per 24hr €5-11; 🕑 6am-11pm)

International Currency Exchange (🕑 5.30am-midnight)

Nursery (🕑 9am-10pm)

Post Office (🕑 9am-5pm Mon-Fri, 9am-12.30pm Sat)

BICYCLE

Rust-red cycle lanes throughout the city make cycling in Dublin easier than ever, although traffic congestion, motorised maniacs and seemingly permanent roadworks can make the city something of an obstacle course. Bike theft is a major problem, so be sure to park on busier streets, preferably at one of the myriad U-shaped parking bars, and lock it securely. Never leave your bike on the street overnight. The following shops may come in handy for pedal pushers.

Cycle-logical (Map pp102–3; ☎ 872 4635; 3 Bachelor's Walk) A shop for serious enthusiasts. It has all the best equipment and is a good source of information on upcoming cycling events. It does not, however, do repairs.

Square Wheel Cycleworks (Map p85; ☎ 679 0838; South Temple Lane) Does repairs, and will have your bike back to you within a day or so (barring serious damage).

Bicycles on Public Transport

Bikes are only allowed on suburban trains (not the DART), either stowed in the guard's van or in a special compartment at the opposite end of the train from the engine. There's a flat €4 charge for transporting a bicycle up to 56km.

Hire

Bike rental has become increasingly difficult to find because of crippling insurance costs. Typical rental for a mountain bike is between €12 and €30 a day, or up to €150 per week. Raleigh Rent-a-Bike agencies can be found through Eurotrek (☎ 456 8847; www.raleigh.ie).

Cycleways (Map pp102–3; ☎ 873 4748; www.cycleways .com; 185-186 Parnell St) Dublin's best bike shop, with expert staff who pepper their patter with all the technical lingo. Top-notch rentals.

MacDonalds Cycles (Map pp66–7; ☎ 475 2586; 38 Wexford St) Friendly and helpful, perfect for the amateur enthusiast.

BOAT

Dublin has two ferry ports. The Dun Laoghaire ferry terminal (Map p213; ☎ 280 1905; Dun Laoghaire), 13km southeast of the city, serves Holyhead in Wales; and the Dublin Port terminal (off Map pp62–3; ☎ 855 2222; Alexandra Rd), 3km northeast of the city centre, serves Holyhead and Mostyn in Wales, and Liverpool in England.

From Holyhead to Dublin and Dun Laoghaire, the ferry crossing takes just over three hours and costs around €35 for foot passengers or €185 for a medium-size car with two passengers. The fast-boat service from Holyhead to Dun Laoghaire takes a little over 1½ hours and costs €45 or €210 for the same.

CLIMATE CHANGE & TRAVEL

Climate change is a serious threat to the ecosystems that humans rely upon, and air travel is the fastest-growing contributor to the problem. Lonely Planet regards travel, overall, as a global benefit, but believes we all have a responsibility to limit our personal impact on global warming.

Flying & Climate Change

Pretty much every form of motor transport generates CO_2 (the main cause of human-induced climate change) but planes are far and away the worst offenders, not just because of the sheer distances they allow us to travel, but because they release greenhouse gases high into the atmosphere. The statistics are frightening: two people taking a return flight between Europe and the US will contribute as much to climate change as an average household's gas and electricity consumption over a whole year.

Carbon Offset Schemes

Climatecare.org and other websites use 'carbon calculators' that allow travellers to offset the greenhouse gases they are responsible for with contributions to energy-saving projects and other climate-friendly initiatives in the developing world – including projects in India, Honduras, Kazakhstan and Uganda.

Lonely Planet, together with Rough Guides and other concerned partners in the travel industry, supports the carbon offset scheme run by climatecare.org. Lonely Planet offsets all of its staff and author travel.

For more information check out our website: www.lonelyplanet.com.

GETTING INTO TOWN

There is no train service to and from the airport. It takes about 45 minutes to get there by bus or taxi. For details of car hire, see opposite. Transport options are as follows:

Bus

Aircoach (☎ 844 7118; www.aircoach.ie; one way/return €7/12) Private coach service with two routes from the airport to 18 destinations throughout the city, including the main streets of the city centre (check the website for stop details). Coaches run every 10 to 15 minutes between 6am and midnight, then hourly from midnight until 6am.

Airlink Express Coach (☎ 872 0000, 873 4222; www.dublinbus.ie; adult/child €5/2) Bus 747 runs every 10 to 20 minutes from 5.45am to 11.30pm between the airport, central bus station (Busáras) and Dublin Bus office on Upper O'Connell St; bus 748 runs every 15 to 30 minutes from 6.50am to 10.05pm between the airport and Heuston and Connolly Stations.

Dublin Bus (☎ 872 0000; www.dublinbus.ie; 59 Upper O'Connell St; adult/child €2/0.75) A number of buses serve the airport from various points in Dublin, including buses 16A (Rathfarnham), 746 (Dun Laoghaire) and 230 (Portmarnock); all cross the city centre on their way to the airport.

Taxi

There is a taxi rank directly outside the arrivals concourse. A taxi should cost about €20 from the airport to the city centre, including a supplementary charge of €2.50 (not applied when going to the airport). Make sure the meter is switched on.

Between Liverpool and Dublin the ferry service takes 8½ hours and costs €34 (foot passenger) or €240 (car with two passengers). Cabins on overnight sailings cost more. The fast-boat service takes four hours and costs up to €60 or €370 respectively.

There are several ferry companies that run services to and from Dublin:

Irish Ferries (Map pp78–9; ☎ 1890 313 131; www.irish ferries.com; 2-4 Merrion Row, Dublin 2) Ferry and fast-boat services from Holyhead to Dublin.

Isle of Man Steam Packet Company/Sea Cat (☎ 836 4019; www.steam-packet.com; Maritime House, North Wall, Dublin 1) Ferry and fast-boat services from Liverpool to Dublin via Douglas on the Isle of Man.

Norfolk Line (☎ 819 2999; www.norfolkline.com; Alexandra Rd Extension, Dublin Port) Ferry services from Liverpool to Dublin.

P&O Irish Sea (☎ 407 3434; www.poirishsea.com; Terminal 3, Dublin Port) Ferry services from Liverpool or Mostyn to Dublin.

Stena Line (☎ 204 7777; www.stenaline.com; Ferry Terminal, Dun Laoghaire) Ferry and fast-boat services from Holyhead to Dun Laoghaire.

To/From the Ferry Terminals

Buses from Busáras are timed to coincide with arrivals and departures from the Dublin Port terminal. For the 9.45am ferry departure from Dublin, buses leave Busáras at 8.30am; for the 9.45pm departure, buses depart from Busáras at 8.30pm. For the 1am sailing to Liverpool, the bus departs from Busáras at 11.45pm. All buses cost €2.

To travel between Dun Laoghaire ferry terminal and Dublin, take the DART to Pearse Station (for south Dublin) or Connolly Station (for north Dublin). Or take bus 46A to St Stephen's Green, or bus 7, 7A or 8 to Burgh Quay.

BUS
To/From the UK

Busáras (Map pp102–3; ☎ 836 6111; www.buseireann.ie; Store St) is just north of the river behind Custom House; it has a left-luggage facility costing €2.50 per item per day.

It's possible to combine bus and ferry tickets from major UK centres to Dublin on the bus network, but with the availability of cheap flights it's hardly worth the hassle. The journey between London and Dublin takes about 12 hours and costs around €34 return. For details in London, contact Eurolines (☎ 0870 514 3219; www.eurolines.com).

Around Dublin

The Dublin Bus Office (Map pp102–3; ☎ 872 0000; www .dublinbus.ie; 59 Upper O'Connell St; ☼ 9am-5.30pm Mon-Fri, 9am-2pm Sat) has free single-route timetables for all its services.

Buses run from around 6am (some start at 5.30am) to about 11.30pm. Fares are calculated according to stages:

1–3 stages €1

4–7 stages €1.40

8–13 stages €1.60

14–23 stages €1.90

More than 23 stages €1.90 (inside Citizone; outer suburban journeys cost €2.10, €3.10 or €4.10)

The city centre (Citizone) is within a 13-stage radius. You must tender exact change when boarding; anything more and you will be given a receipt for reimbursement, only possible at the Dublin Bus main office.

A range of fare-saver passes is on offer:

Adult (Bus & Rail) Short Hop (€8.80) Valid for unlimited one-day travel on Dublin Bus, DART and suburban rail travel, but not Nitelink or Airlink.

Bus/Luas Pass (adult/child €6.50/3.10) One-day unlimited travel on both bus and Luas.

Family Bus & Rail Short Hop (€13.50) Valid for travel for one day for a family of two adults and two children aged under 16 on all bus and rail services except for Nitelink, Airlink, ferry services and tours.

Rambler Pass (1/2/5/7 days €6/11/17.30/21) Valid for unlimited travel on all Dublin Bus and Airlink services, but not Nitelink.

NITELINK

Nitelink late-night buses run from the College, Westmoreland and D'Olier Sts triangle (Map p85). From Monday to Wednesday there are usually only two departures, at 12.30am and 2am. From Thursday to Saturday, departures are at 12.30am, then every 20 minutes until 4.30am on the more popular routes, and until 3.30am on the less frequented ones. Fares are €4 (€6 to the far suburbs). See www.dublinbus.ie for route details.

CAR & MOTORCYCLE
Driving

The Automobile Association of Ireland (AA; Map pp66–7; ☎ 617 9999, breakdown ☎ 1800 667 788; www.aaireland.ie; 56 Drury St, Dublin 2) is located in the city centre.

Traffic in Dublin is a nightmare and parking is an expensive headache. There are no free spots to park anywhere in the city centre during business hours (7am to 7pm Monday to Saturday), but there are plenty of parking meters, 'pay & display' spots (€3 to €5.20 per hour) and over a dozen sheltered and supervised car parks (around €6 per hour).

Clamping of illegally parked cars is thoroughly enforced, and there is a €80 charge for removal. Parking is free after 7pm Monday to Saturday, and all day Sunday, in all metered spots and on single yellow lines.

Car theft and break-ins are a problem, and the police advise visitors to park in a supervised car park. Cars with foreign number plates are prime targets; never leave your valuables behind. When you're booking accommodation, check on parking facilities.

Hire

Car rental in Dublin is expensive, so you're often better off making arrangements in your home country with some sort of package deal. In July and August it's wise to book well ahead. Most cars are manual; automatic cars are available but they're more expensive to hire. Motorbikes and mopeds are not available for rent.

Nova Car Hire (www.rentacar-ireland.com) acts as an agent for Alamo, Budget, European and National, and offers greatly discounted rates. Typical weekly high-season rental rates are around €150 for a small car, €185 for a medium car and €320 for a five-seater people carrier. People aged under 21 are not allowed to hire a car; for the majority of rental companies you have to be at least 23 and have had a valid driving licence for a minimum of one year. Many rental agencies will not rent to people over 70 or 75.

ROAD SAFETY RULES IN DUBLIN

- Drive on the left, overtake to the right.
- Safety belts must be worn by the driver and all passengers.
- Children aged under 12 aren't allowed to sit on the front seats.
- Motorcyclists and their passengers must wear helmets.
- When entering a roundabout, give way to the right.
- Speed limits are 50km/h or as signposted in the city, 100km/h on all roads outside city limits and 120km/h on motorways (marked in blue).
- The legal alcohol limit is 80mg of alcohol per 100mL of blood, or 35mg on the breath (roughly two units of alcohol for a man and one for a woman).

The main rental agencies, which also have offices at the airport (☻6am-11pm), include the following:

Avis Rent-a-Car (Map pp78–9; ☎ 1890 405 060; www .avis.com; 1 East Hanover St)

Budget Rent-a-Car (Map pp62–3; ☎ 837 9611, airport 844 5150; www.budget.ie; 151 Lower Drumcondra Rd, Dublin 7)

Dan Dooley Car Hire (Map pp78–9; ☎ 677 2723, airport 844 5156; www.dan-dooley.ie; 42-43 Westland Row, Dublin 2)

Europcar (Map pp78–9; ☎ 614 2800, airport 844 4179; www.europcar.com; Baggot St Bridge, Dublin 4)

Hertz Rent-a-Car (Map p99; ☎ 660 2255, airport 844 5466; www.hertz.com; 149 Upper Leeson St, Dublin 2)

Irish Car Rentals (off Map p118; ☎ 862 2715, airport 844 4199; www.irishcarrentals.ie; Old Airport Rd, Santry, Dublin 9)

Thrifty (Map pp90–1; ☎ 454 6600, airport 840 0800; www.thrifty.ie; 125 Herberton Bridge, South Circular Rd, Dublin 8)

TAXI

All taxi fares begin with a flag-fall fare of €3.80, followed by €1.50 per kilometre thereafter from 8am to 10pm. In addition there are a number of extra charges – €1 for each extra passenger and €2 for telephone bookings. There is no charge for luggage.

Taxis can be hailed on the street and found at taxi ranks around the city, including on the corner of Abbey and O'Connell Sts (Map pp102–3), College Green in front of Trinity College (Map pp66–7) and St Stephen's Green at the end of Grafton St (Map pp66–7). Numerous taxi companies dispatch taxis by radio. Some options:

City Cabs (☎ 872 2688)

National Radio Cabs (☎ 677 2222)

Phone the Garda Carriage Office (☎ 475 5888) if you have any complaints about taxis or queries regarding lost property.

TAXI TRAUMA

Taxi queues are frustratingly long late at night (when the bars and clubs close), ensuring waits of up to an hour or more. Calling one by phone is often met with a negative response during these busy hours, and you can't book one in advance (unless you're travelling to the airport). Try to avoid the busy period between 2am and 3.30am; otherwise we suggest learning tantric meditation to deal with the interminably long queues.

TRAIN
DART

The Dublin Area Rapid Transport (DART; ☎ 1850 366 222; www.irishrail.ie) provides quick train access to the coast as far north as Howth (about 30 minutes) and as far south as Greystones in County Wicklow. Pearse Station (Map pp78–9) is convenient for central Dublin south of the Liffey, and Connolly Station (Map pp102–3) for north of the Liffey. There are services every 10 to 20 minutes, sometimes even more frequently, from around 6.30am to midnight Monday to Saturday. Services are less frequent on Sunday. Dublin to Dun Laoghaire takes about 15 to 20 minutes. A one-way DART ticket from Dublin to Dun Laoghaire or Howth costs €2.20; to Bray it's €2.50.

There are also Suburban Rail services north as far as Dundalk, inland to Mullingar and south past Bray to Arklow.

DART passes include the following:

Adult Weekly Inner Rail Pass (€23) Valid on all DART and suburban train services between Bray to the south and Rush and Lusk to the north.

All Day Ticket (€7.20) One-day unlimited travel on DART and suburban rail services.

Irish Rail

All rail information, including timetables and ticket and pass sales, is available from the Rail Travel Centre (Iarnród Éireann; Map pp102–3; ☎ 836 6222; www.irishrail.ie; 34 Lower Abbey St). The city has two main train stations: Heuston Station (Map pp90–1), on the western side of town near the Liffey; and Connolly Station (Map pp102–3), a short walk northeast of Busáras, behind Custom House. Heuston Station has left-luggage lockers of three sizes, costing €2 to €6 for 24 hours. At Connolly Station the facility costs €3.

Luas

The Luas (www.luas.ie) light-rail system has two lines: the green line (running every five to 15 minutes) connects St Stephen's Green with Sandyford in south Dublin via Ranelagh and Dundrum; and the red line (every 20 minutes) runs from Lower Abbey St to Tallaght via the north quays and Heuston Station. There are ticket machines at every stop or you can buy a ticket from newsagents in the city centre; a typical short hop fare (around four stops) is €1.70. Services run from 5.30am to 12.30am Monday to Friday, from 6.30am to 12.30am Saturday and from 7am to 11.30pm Sunday.

DIRECTORY

BUSINESS HOURS

The standard business hours in relatively late-rising Dublin are as follows:

Banks 10am to 4pm Monday to Friday (to 5pm Thursday).

Offices 9am to 5pm Monday to Friday.

Post offices 9am to 6pm Monday to Friday, 9am to 1pm Saturday.

Pubs 10.30am to 11.30pm Monday to Thursday, 10.30am to 12.30am Friday and Saturday, noon to 11pm Sunday (30 minutes 'drinking up' time allowed). Pubs with bar extensions open to 2.30am Thursday to Saturday, pubs with theatre licences open to 3.30am; closed Christmas Day and Good Friday.

Restaurants Noon to 10.30pm; many close one day of the week.

Shops 9am to 5.30pm or 6pm Monday to Saturday (until 8pm on Thursday and sometimes Friday), noon to 6pm Sunday in bigger towns only.

CHILDREN

Dublin is a very child-friendly city. Hotels will provide cots at no extra charge and most restaurants have highchairs. Overall, restaurants and hotels go to great lengths to cater for children, although some restaurants lose their interest in kids after 6pm. Children are not allowed in pubs after 7pm. Children under five years of age travel free on all public transport.

Family tickets are available to most attractions; many tourist sites have made exhibitions more child-friendly, creating interactive spaces for kids to play (and learn) in.

Although breast-feeding in Dublin is not a common sight (Ireland has one of the lowest rates of it in the world), you can do so with impunity pretty much everywhere without getting so much as a stare. There are virtually no nappy-changing facilities in Dublin, so you'll have to make do with a public toilet. For more information and inspiration on how to make travelling with children as hassle-free as possible, check out Lonely Planet's *Travel with Children* by Cathy Lanigan. Two great websites are www.eumom.ie for pregnant women and parents with young children, and www.babygoes2.com, which is an excellent travel site about family-friendly accommodation worldwide.

Baby-sitting

Many hotels can provide baby-sitting on request (normally €8 to €13 per hour). There are agencies that provide professional nannies. It's up to you to negotiate a fee with the nanny but €15 per hour is the average, plus taxi fare if they aren't driving. You'll need to sign a form beforehand that the agency will fax to your hotel. Agencies include the following:

Belgrave Agency (☎ 280 9341; www.nanny.ie; 55 Mulgrave St, Dun Laoghaire; per hr €18 plus 21% VAT)

Executive Nannies (Map pp102–3; ☎ 873 1273; www .executivenannies.com; 43 Lower Dominick St; per hr €20)

CLIMATE

Dublin enjoys a milder climate than its northerly position might indicate, largely thanks to the influence of the North Atlantic Drift, or Gulf Stream. The warmest months of the year are July and August, when temperatures range from 15° to 20°C, while the coldest months – January and February – see the thermometer drop to between 4° and 8°C. It never gets too cold (major snowfalls are a rarity) but it never gets too hot either; even in summer you're better off carrying a sweater or a light jacket.

Dublin is one of the drier parts of Ireland, but in a typical year it still rains on 150 days (dropping a total yearly average of 75cm). Summers are a meteorological lottery: it's impossible to predict whether it'll be a wet one or not, making forecasting a favourite subject of amateurs throughout the city ('Well, it rained all of April, so that means we'll have a good June'). Bring an umbrella. What is a certainty, however, is the long summer day; in July and August there are about 18 hours of daylight and it's only truly dark after about 11pm. For weather forecasts, dial ☎ 1550 123 822.

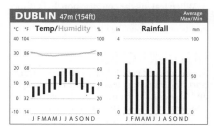

COURSES

Dublin is well known for its English-language schools. For a list of these and other courses, get a copy of the yearly *Dublin's Evening Classes* (Oisín Publications; €4.99), available at most bookshops (also check out www.eveningclasses.ie). Most courses run for extended periods, ranging from four or six weeks to a year and more.

CUSTOMS REGULATIONS

Duty-free sales are not available when travelling within the European Union (EU). Goods for personal consumption bought in, and exported within, the EU incur no additional taxes if duty has been paid somewhere in the EU. Over certain limits you may have to show they are for personal use. The amounts that officially constitute personal use are: 800 cigarettes, 400 cigarillos, 200 cigars or 1kg of tobacco; 10L of spirits, 20L of fortified wine, 60L of sparkling wine, 90L of still wine or 110L of beer.

Travellers coming from outside the EU are allowed to import, duty-free, 200 cigarettes, 1L of spirits or 2L of wine, 60mL of perfume and 250mL of toilet water.

It is illegal to bring into Ireland meat, meat products, plants and plant products (including seeds). Dogs and cats from anywhere outside Ireland and the UK are subject to strict quarantine laws. The EU Pet Travel Scheme, whereby animals from certain countries *might* be allowed into the country (as long as they're fitted with a microchip, vaccinated against rabies and blood-tested six months prior to entry), came into force in the Republic of Ireland in mid-2004. Otherwise animals arriving into Ireland are quarantined for six months unless they first pass through the UK and meet British criteria for entry. Do not just try and travel with your animals. Contact the Department of Agriculture, Food & Rural Development (☎ 607 2877; www.agriculture.gov.ie) for further details.

When leaving the country, non-EU visitors can take the equivalent of US$4000 worth of goods per person (see p130).

DISCOUNT CARDS

Senior citizens get discounts on public transport and museum fees (with proof of age), and students and under-26s are entitled to a variety of discounts, from admission fees to cinema tickets, so long as they have the appropriate card (International Student Identity Card, International Youth Travel Card or European Youth Card/Euro<26). A couple of local discount cards are worth checking out:

Dublin Pass (www.dublinpass.ie; adult/child 1-day €31/17, 2-day €49/29, 3-day €59/34, 6-day €89/44) Not only do you get free entry into 30 attractions, but you can skip whatever queue there is by presenting your card. The card is available from any of the Dublin Tourism offices.

Heritage Card (☎ 647 2461; www.heritageireland.com; Education & Visitor Service, 6 Upper Ely Pl, Dublin 2; adult/child or student €21/8) This card entitles you to free access to all Dúchas-managed sights in and around Dublin.

ELECTRICITY

The standard electricity supply in Dublin is 220 volts AC, and all sockets fit a three-pin plug. Pin converters are available in all electrical suppliers.

EMBASSIES

Countries with diplomatic offices in Dublin include the following:

Australia (Map pp78–9; ☎ 664 5300; www.australianembassy.ie; 2nd fl, Fitzwilton House, Wilton Terrace, Dublin 2)

Canada (Map pp78–9; ☎ 234 4000; 7-8 Wilton Tce, Dublin 2)

France (off Map pp62–3; ☎ 277 5000; chancellerie@ambafrance.ie; 36 Ailesbury Rd, Dublin 4)

Germany (off Map pp62–3; ☎ 269 3011; germany@indigo.ie; 31 Trimleston Ave, Booterstown, Blackrock, County Dublin)

Italy (Map p99; ☎ 660 1744; info@italianembassy.ie; 63-65 Northumberland Rd, Ballsbridge, Dublin 4)

Netherlands (off Map pp62–3; ☎ 269 3444; info@netherlandsembassy.ie; 160 Merrion Rd, Ballsbridge, Dublin 4)

UK (Map p99; ☎ 205 3700; www.britishembassy.ie; 29 Merrion Rd, Ballsbridge, Dublin 4)

USA (Map p99; ☎ 668 8777; webmasterireland@state.gov; 42 Elgin Rd, Ballsbridge, Dublin 4)

EMERGENCY

For emergency assistance, phone ☎ 999 or ☎ 112. This call is free and the operator will connect you with the type of assistance you specify: fire, police (gardaí), ambulance, boat or coastal rescue. There are garda stations at Fitzgibbon St (Map pp102–3; ☎ 836 3113), Harcourt Tce (Map pp78–9; ☎ 676 3481), Pearse St (Map pp78–9; ☎ 677 8141) and Store St (Map pp102–3; ☎ 874 2761).

A full list of all emergency numbers can be found in the front pages of the telephone book.

Alcoholics Anonymous (Map pp90–1; ☎ 453 8998, after hr ☎ 679 5967; 109 South Circular Rd, Dublin 8)

Confidential Line Freefone (☎ 1800 666 111) Garda confidential line to report crime.

Drugs Advisory & Treatment Centre (Map pp78–9; ☎ 677 1122; Trinity Ct, 30-31 Pearse St, Dublin 2)

Rape Crisis Centre (Map pp78–9; ☎ 1800 778 888, 661 4911; 70 Lower Leeson St)

Samaritans (Map pp102–3; ☎ 1850 609 090, 872 7700; 112 Marlborough St) For people who are lonely, depressed or suicidal.

Senior Helpline (☎ 1850 440 444) For senior citizens with any kind of problem.

Women's Emergency Hostel (Map pp102–3; ☎ 873 2279; Haven House, Morning Star Ave, Dublin 7)

GAY & LESBIAN TRAVELLERS

Dublin's not a bad place to be gay. Most people wouldn't bat an eyelid at public displays of affection between same-sex couples, or cross-dressing in the city centre, but discretion is advised in the suburbs. If you do encounter any sort of trouble or harassment call the Gay & Lesbian Garda Liaison Officer (☎ 666 9000) or the Sexual Assault Unit (☎ 666 000) at the Pearse St Garda station (Map pp78–9).

There are several useful organisations, publications and online resources:

Gaire (www.gaire.com) Online message board and resource centre.

Gay Community News (www.gcn.ie) A free news and issues-based monthly paper.

Gay Men's Health Project (☎ 660 2189) Practical advice on men's health issues.

Gay Switchboard Dublin (☎ 872 1055; www.gayswitch board.ie; ⏰ 7.30am-9.30pm Mon-Fri, 3.30-6pm Sat) A friendly and useful voluntary service that provides information such as legal issues and where to find accommodation.

Ireland's Pink Pages (www.pink-pages.org) A free directory of gay-centric and gay-friendly services.

Lesbian Line (☎ 872 9911; ⏰ 7-9pm Thu)

National Lesbian & Gay Federation (Map p85; NLGF; ☎ 671 9076; 2 Scarlett Row, Temple Bar, Dublin) Publishers of *Gay Community News*.

Outhouse (Map pp102–3; ☎ 873 4932; www.outhouse .ie; 105 Capel St) Gay, lesbian and bisexual resource centre. Great stop-off point to see what's on, check noticeboards and meet people. It also publishes *Ireland's Pink Pages*.

HOLIDAYS

The only public holidays that will impact on you are Good Friday and Christmas Day, the only two days in the year when all pubs close. Otherwise, the half-dozen or so bank holidays (all of which fall on a Monday) mean just that – the banks are closed, along with about half the shops.

Public Holidays

The following are national holidays:

New Year's Day 1 January

St Patrick's Day 17 March

Easter (Good Friday to Easter Monday inclusive) March/April

May Holiday 1 May

June Holiday First Monday in June

August Holiday First Monday in August

October Holiday Last Monday in October

Christmas Day 25 December

St Stephen's Day 26 December

St Patrick's Day, St Stephen's Day and May Day holidays are taken on the following Monday should they fall on a weekend.

School Holidays

Mid-term break 31 October to 4 November

Christmas/New Year 22 December to 9 January

Mid-term break 13 to 17 February (16 & 17 only for primary schools)

Easter 7 to 24 April

Summer July and August (June also for secondary schools)

INTERNET ACCESS

If your computer isn't equipped to handle 220 volts AC or a three-point socket, you'll need a universal AC adapter and a plug adapter, which will enable you to plug in anywhere.

WI-FI HOT SPOTS

Wi-fi (or wireless fidelity) is a handy mobile alternative to plugging into a local area network (LAN). Many public places offer access to wi-fi networks so that customers can use the internet on the move. Try the following hotspots for free access: Chester Beatty Library (p70), Solas (p164), Market Bar (p163), Ron Black's (p163), the Globe (p164) and Aya (p146).

All hotel rooms have phone lines and you can plug the phone lead into the back of your laptop; although most have direct-dial services, you'll most likely have to dial an outside line access number (usually 9) to get online. Provided you're dialling a local access number you'll be charged the price of a local call (which from a hotel is usually timed and 50% more than usual).

Major internet service providers (ISPs) such as AOL (www.aol.com), CompuServe (www.compuserve.com) and AT&T Business Internet Services (www.attbusiness.net) have dial-in nodes in Ireland. If you access your email account through a home-based ISP, your best option is to open an account with a local, global ISP provider: the most reliable ones are Eircom (☎ 702 0022; www.eircom.ie) or O2 (☎ 1800 924 924; www.o2.ie).

For hassle-free internet access, your best bet is to rely on internet cafés, which are everywhere in Dublin. Connections are usually quick, and should be no more than €5 per hour. The following city-centre internet cafés offer quick, reliable connections:

Central Cyber Café (Map pp66–7; ☎ 677 8298; 6 Grafton St; ⏰ 9am-9pm)

Global Internet Café (Map pp102–3; ☎ 878 0295; 8 Lower O'Connell St; ⏰ 8am-11pm)

Internet Exchange (Map p85; ☎ 670 3000; 1 Cecilia St; ⏰ 24hr)

LEGAL MATTERS

If you need legal assistance contact the Legal Aid Board (☎ 1890 615 200). It has eight offices spread throughout Dublin; the central operator will direct you to the one most convenient to you.

The possession of small quantities of hash or marijuana (deemed Class C drugs) attracts a fine or warning, but harder drugs are treated more seriously. Cocaine, ecstasy and heroin are considered Class A drugs; if you're caught

FOR THE RECORD
- The legal age to vote is 18.
- You can leave school when you're 16.
- The legal drinking age is 18.
- Smoking is legal at 16.
- The heterosexual and homosexual age of consent is 17.
- You can get married at 16, with consent of court.
- You can ride a moped when you're 16.
- You can drive a car when you're 17.

in possession you can count on being arrested and prosecuted. The consumption of alcohol on the street and public drunkenness are both illegal, but the police are usually pretty lenient and at worst will issue a verbal warning and confiscate your booze.

MAPS

Lonely Planet publishes a laminated pocket-size map of Dublin, which is widely available in bookshops around town. The free maps of Dublin are usually quite adequate, at least for the major sites in the city centre. The Dublin Tourism Centre has a basic map of the city centre (€1), which covers the major sights, but it also has fairly detailed maps for hotels and restaurants.

If you prefer an indexed street directory, the *Dublin Street Guide* (€13.99; scale 1:15,000, city centre 1:10,000), published by Ordnance Survey Ireland (OSI; see the boxed text, p116, for their retail outlet details), is the best. A handy pocket-size version of the same (€6.99; 1:10,000) is also available, but it does not include the outlying suburbs.

The OSI also publishes a *Map of Greater Dublin* (€8; scale 1:20,000), which includes a street index and details of bus routes. The *Collins Streetfinder Map* (€9.99; scale 1:15,000) is also pretty good, with easy-to-use laminates that won't get damaged in the (inevitable) rain.

You can buy a limited selection of maps in most bookshops and some newsagents, but the National Map Centre (Map pp66–7; ☎ 476 0471; www.mapcentre.ie; 34 Grafton Hall, Aungier St; ⏰ 10am-6pm Mon-Sat) has a comprehensive selection of all OSI maps and other geographic sundries.

MEDICAL SERVICES
Dentists

Dental care is a costly business in Dublin. Unless you have a medical card (only available to registered residents), you can expect to pay from €50 for a basic check, about €65 for a cleaning and €85 for a filling. There are several reliable city-centre dentists:

Anne's Lane Dental Centre (Map pp66–7; ☎ 671 8581; 2 Anne's Lane; ⏰ 9am-6pm Mon-Fri, by appointment Sat)

Dame House Dental Surgery (Map pp66–7; ☎ 670 9256; 24-26 Dame St; ⏰ 9am-6pm)

Gallagher & Associates (Map pp78–9; ☎ 670 3735; 38 Fenian St; ⏰ 9am-8pm Mon, 8am-8pm Tue & Wed, 9am-5pm Thu & Fri, 9am-4pm every 2nd Sat)

Doctors

If you don't have a medical card you'll have to pay for all visits to a doctor. Charges begin at €45 for even a cursory examination. You can request a doctor to call out to your accommodation at any time on the 24-hour private Doctors on Call (☎ 453 9333) service line.

The Eastern Regional Health Authority (ERHA; Map pp90–1; ☎ 679 0700, 1800 520 520; www.erha.ie; Dr Steevens' Hospital, Steevens' Lane, Dublin 8) has a Choice of Doctor Scheme, which can advise you on a suitable general practitioner (GP) from 9am to 5pm Monday to Friday. The ERHA also provides information services for those with physical and mental disabilities.

Your hotel or embassy can also suggest a doctor, but there are two good walk-in doctors' clinics in town:

Grafton Medical Practice (Map pp66–7; ☎ 671 2122; www.graftonmedical.ie; 34 Grafton St; ⏰ 9am-6pm Mon-Fri)

Mercer Medical Centre (Map pp66–7; ☎ 402 2300; Johnston Pl, Lower Stephen St; ⏰ 9am-6pm Mon-Thu, 9am-5pm Fri)

Hospitals

EU citizens are encouraged to obtain a European Health Insurance Card (EHIC; formerly the E111 form) before they leave home, which will cover hospital costs should they require hospitalisation. This card, which provides cover for a year, is easily obtained from a local health authority or, in the UK, the post office. The main city-centre hospitals are the following:

Baggot St Hospital (Map p99; ☎ 668 1577; 18 Upper Baggot St)

Mater Misericordiae Hospital (Map pp102–3; ☎ 830 1122; Eccles St) Off Lower Dorset St.

St James's Hospital (Map pp90–1; ☎ 453 7941; www .stjames.ie; James St)

Pharmacies

All pharmacies in Dublin are clearly designated by a green cross. There are branches of the English chain pharmacy, Boots, spread throughout the city centre. Most pharmacies stay open until 7pm or 8pm, but the following city-centre chemists stay open until 10pm:

City Pharmacy (Map pp66–7; ☎ 670 4523; 14 Dame St)

O'Connell's Late Night Pharmacy (Map pp102–3; ☎ 873 0427; 55-56 O'Connell St)

MONEY

Ireland's currency is the euro (€), which is divided into 100 cents. While the notes are all the same throughout the 12 countries of the euro zone, the Irish coins feature a harp on the reverse side – but all non-Irish euro coins are also legal tender. For information on Dublin's economy and costs, see p19.

See the Quick Reference on the inside front cover for a list of exchange rates.

ATMs

All banks have ATMs. We've noticed recently that machines in the city centre quickly run out of smaller denominations (€10 and €20) on Friday night, and the smallest denomination they'll dispense is €50. Some even run out of money altogether, and as cash deposits aren't replenished until Monday morning, the machine stays out of order until then. We strongly recommend that if you're staying in the city centre, you get your money out early on a Friday: not only will you avoid the problems described but you won't have to face the enormous queues that form behind after about 8pm.

Changing Money

You'll get the best exchange rates at banks. Bureaux de change and other exchange facilities usually open for more hours but the rate and/or commission will be worse. Many post offices have a currency-exchange facility and are open on Saturday morning. There's a cluster of banks located around College Green opposite Trinity College and all have exchange facilities.

Allied Irish Bank (Map p85; ☎ 679 9222; Westmoreland St; ⏰ 10am-4pm Mon-Wed & Fri, 10am-5pm Thu)

Amex (Map pp66–7; ☎ 605 7709; Dublin Tourism Centre, St Andrew's St; ⏰ 9am-5pm Mon-Sat)

Bank of Ireland (Map p85; ☎ 677 6801; 2 College Green; ⏰ 10am-4pm Mon-Wed & Fri, 10am-5pm Thu)

First Rate (Map p85; ☎ 671 3233; 1 Westmoreland St; ⏰ 8am-9pm Mon-Fri, 9am-9pm Sat, 10am-9pm Sun Jun-Sep, 9am-6pm Oct-May)

Thomas Cook (Map pp66–7; ☎ 677 1721, 677 1307; 118 Grafton St; ⏰ 9am-5.30pm Mon, Tue, Fri & Sat, 10am-5.30pm Wed, 9am-7pm Thu)

Credit Cards

Visa and MasterCard are more widely accepted in Dublin than Amex or Diners Club, which are often not accepted in smaller establishments. You can also use credit cards to withdraw cash, but be sure to obtain a PIN from your bank before you leave. This service usually carries an extra charge, so if you're withdrawing money, take out enough so that you don't have to keep going back.

If a card is lost or stolen, inform the police and the issuing company as soon as possible; otherwise you may have to bear the cost of the thief's purchases. Here are some 24-hour hotlines for cancelling your cards:

Amex (☎ 1800 282 728)

Diners Club (☎ 0818 300 026)

MasterCard (☎ 1800 557 378)

Visa (☎ 1800 558 002)

Travellers Cheques

Most major brands of travellers cheques are accepted in Ireland. We recommend that you carry them in euros, as you can use them in other euro zone countries and avoid costly exchange rates. Amex and Thomas Cook travellers cheques are widely recognised and branches don't charge commission for cashing their own cheques. Travellers cheques are rarely accepted for everyday transactions so you'll need to cash them beforehand.

Eurocheques can be cashed in Dublin, but special arrangements must be made with your home bank before you travel if you are thinking of using personal cheques.

NEWSPAPERS & MAGAZINES
Newspapers

Dubliners are avid consumers of the printed word. There are newspapers and magazines to suit virtually every taste and interest. All the main English newspapers are readily available. News Corp, the Rupert Murdoch–owned media group that publishes the *Times* and the *Sun*, has an Irish office that's responsible for an Irish edition of their papers – basically a section of Irish news and sport inserted into the English version.

DAILY NEWSPAPERS

The following are the main daily local newspapers:

Evening Herald (€1) Available from just after lunchtime, this tabloid is a bit of a scurrilous rag specialising in shock-horror headlines about government wastage, heartless killers and immigrant scams. No-one takes it all that seriously and it usually makes for good bus-journey reading on the way home. It is, however, the best newspaper for finding

a flat, and its Thursday entertainment listings pages are pretty thorough.

Irish Examiner (€1.70; www.examiner.ie) A solid national newspaper with more of a non-Dublin slant than others, probably because it used to be the *Cork Examiner*. Good features and well-written stories make for a dependable read.

Irish Independent (€1.70; www.independent.ie) Ireland's most widely read broadsheet is great for breaking domestic stories, as its journos usually have one-up on every other hack for stories of national importance. It has good features on all facets of Irish current affairs, but its foreign coverage is appalling: limited to the back page, the content is usually reliant on stories about Russian women who've given birth to eight children, the break-up of Hollywood marriages and other 'you'll never believe this' titbits.

Irish Times (€1.70; www.ireland.com) The country's oldest and most serious daily newspaper; the most liberal broadsheet published in Ireland. In recent years its reputation for excellent journalism has been somewhat tarnished by the fact that it picks up far too many of its stories from its liberal British counterparts (most notably the *Guardian*) and the news wires, with the result that it doesn't break as much news as it used to. Many non-Dubliners dismiss it as an Anglo-centric newspaper that devotes too much space to issues that aren't pertinent to the country; it is, however, still an excellent read. The online version is now a partly pay-and-view service; you can only read the breaking news and front page for free.

Star (€1.20; www.thestar.ie) Ireland's answer to the English *Sun*, this tabloid is pretty much what you'd expect: plenty of celebrity pictures and very little news. It prides itself, however, on its efforts to reveal the sordid underbelly of Irish affairs: politicians on the take and gangsters on the make are a big part of its news cycle. Most of the stories are blatant exaggerations and simplistic takes on what's really going on.

SUNDAY PAPERS

Most Dubliners buy English Sunday papers, as the Irish equivalents just can't match their size and content. Our list covers the Irish newspapers:

Ireland on Sunday (€2) Exaggeration and smear is just another routine week for Ireland's silliest Sunday broadsheet: Is that cellulite on Jordan's belly?

Star on Sunday (€2) The usual tabloid nonsense, with plenty of juice and very little news. If you want a salacious tabloid, buy the *Sunday Mirror*; at least the sports pages are better.

Sunday Business Post (€2) If you want to know what makes the Irish economy tick, then this superb financial paper is for you; if not, buy something else.

Sunday Independent (€2.30) A Sunday edition of the daily broadsheet, with similar news content but plenty more lifestyle sections, restaurant reviews and social gossip.

Sunday Tribune (€2.30) Although its content pales in comparison to its English rivals, this is the best Irish Sunday paper. It offers the best summary of the week's events, has good features and also breaks its fair share of pertinent stories.

Sunday World (€2) A fairly low-brow tabloid paper with the usual fare about celebrities and their misdoings, politicians and their backroom deals, and oodles of sport. The paper's crime correspondent, Paul Williams, is the country's foremost authority on the criminal underworld; his two books on the subject, *The General* and *Gangland,* are bestsellers.

Magazines

Generic international magazines aside, there are many local publications:

Dublin Event Guide (www.eventguide.ie; free) The best weekly listings magazine, it has film, theatre and music reviews, a feature or two and a comprehensive guide to what's on and where.

Dubliner (www.thedubliner.ie; €2.99) Glossy and gossipy, this monthly magazine takes a soft look at the issues concerning the city's groovy brigades. Its credo is Oscar Wilde's dictum that 'history is gossip, and scandal is gossip made boring by morality'. Such cleverness does not disguise the fact that the mainstay of its content is to tell us where and with whom we need to be seen having dinner, and what we should be wearing and discussing while eating it.

Hot Press (www.hotpress.com; €3.95) The first, and once the best, guide to the city's music scene, this fortnightly publication is a bit like the Rolling Stones: once a cutting-edge force that shaped musical minds, today it's stuck in the past and is reluctant to come to terms with modern times. Its reputation and prestige ensures that it is still the most widely read of the city's music mags.

Image (www.image.ie; €4.25) Ireland's version of the glossy woman's magazine. Aside from the usual focus on beauty tips and fashion hints, what we really love about this monthly mag is its vain attempt to turn the country's B-list celebs into international superstars. *Puh-lease.*

In Dublin (free) A monthly ad-rag disguised as a listings magazine, its over-reliance on ads means that the listings are hardly objective…but it is free.

Mongrel (www.mongrel.ie; free) The best of a new breed of publications, Mongrel mixes a hilarious irreverence with some top-class interviews and features that appeal to the X(Box) generation.

Phoenix (€2.25) A fortnightly magazine that specialises in clever political satire. The problem for non-nationals is that many of the references are strictly insider, so you'll have to know your current affairs to get the jokes.

Social & Personal (www.socialandpersonal.ie; €3.99) Utter nonsense really, but who doesn't get stuck into this stuff

while waiting in the dentist's anteroom? Lifestyles of the rich, and often unknown, make up the bulk of the content of this monthly publication; like most mags of its kind, it seeks to confirm that if only we plebs had what they had, then we'd be happy. Yeah right.

Village (www.village.ie; €3.50) Edited by veteran journalist Vincent Browne, this is a weekly hard stare at the major issues of the day, both local and international. The quality of the writing is good and the editorial line is uncompromising in its efforts to uncover the truth behind the issues, no matter how uncomfortable it may be. An excellent read.

For information on gay- and lesbian-specific publications, see p235.

ORGANISED TOURS

Dublin isn't that big, so a straightforward sightseeing tour is only really necessary if you're looking to cram in the sights or avoid blistered feet. What is worth considering, however, is a specialised guided tour, especially for those of a musical, historical or literary bent.

Boat

Liffey Voyage (Map pp102–3; ☎ 473 4082; www.liffey voyage.ie; Liffey Voyage kiosk, Liffey boardwalk, Bachelor's Walk; adult/child €11/6; ⏰ from 11am hourly Mar-Nov) Cruise up and down the Liffey in a comfy air-conditioned, all-weather vessel that accommodates up to 48 passengers. Gen up on Dublin's history as seen from the river, from the Viking raids to the recent dockland development.

Viking Splash Tours (Map pp90–1; ☎ 707 6000; www .vikingsplashtours.com; 64-65 Patrick St; adult/child/family from €15.50/8.50/50; ⏰ 10 tours daily 9am-5.30pm Mar-Oct, 10am-4pm Wed-Sun Feb, 10am-4pm Tue-Sun Nov) Go on, what's the big deal? You stick a plastic Viking's helmet on your head and yell 'yay' at the urging of your guide, but the upshot is you'll get a 1¼-hour semi-amphibious tour that ends up in the Grand Canal Dock. 'Strictly for tourists' seems so…superfluous.

Bus

Dublin Bus Tours (Map pp102–3; ☎ 872 0000; www.dublin bus.ie; 59 Upper O'Connell St), the city's bus company, runs a variety of tours, all of which can be booked at its office, or at the Bus Éireann counter at Dublin Tourism (Map pp66–7) in St Andrew's Church, Suffolk St.

The **Dublin City Tour** (adult/child/student €14/6/12.50; ⏰ tours every 15min 9.30am-4.30pm) is a 1½-hour hop-on-hop-off tour you can join at any of the 19 designated stops covering the city centre's major attractions; admission to the sights isn't included. The Ghost Bus Tour (adult €25; ☏ tours 8pm Mon-Fri, 7pm & 9.30pm Sat & Sun) is a popular 2¼-hour tour of graveyards and 'haunted' places, while Coast & Castles (adult/child €22/12; ☏ tours 10am & 2pm) takes in the Botanic Gardens in Glasnevin, the Casino at Marino, Malahide Castle and Howth, all in about three hours. The South Coast & Gardens Tour (adult/child €25/12; ☏ tours 11am) takes around 4½ hours and runs along the stretch of coastline between Dun Laoghaire and Killiney before turning inland into Wicklow and on to Powerscourt Estate (admission included). Other options inlcude the following:

City Sightseeing (Map pp102–3; www.citysightseeing .co.uk; Dublin Tourism, 14 Upper O'Connell St; adult/child/family €16/7/38; ☏ tours every 8-15min 9am-6pm) A typical tour should last around 1½ hours and lead you up and down O'Connell St, past Trinity College and St Stephen's Green, before heading up to the Guinness Storehouse and back around the north quays, via the main entrance to Phoenix Park.

Grayline Dublin Tour (Map pp102–3; ☏ 872 9010; www .irishcitytours.com; 33 Bachelor's Walk; adult/child/family €15/12.50/36; ☏ tours every 15min 9.30am-5pm Sep-Jun, 9.30am-5.30pm Jul & Aug) Another hop-on-hop-off tour of the city's greatest bits, with stops en route at Trinity College, the Guinness Storehouse, Dvblinia and Kilmainham Gaol. A straight-through tour without getting off takes about 1½ hours – but what's the point in that? You can also arrange tours from Dublin Tourism (Map pp66–7), Suffolk St.

Wild Wicklow Tour (☏ 280 1899; www.discoverdublin .ie; adult/child €28/25; ☏ tours 9.10am) Award-winning and lots of fun, this 8½-hour top tour does a quick spin of the city's main attractions before heading southwards along the coast to County Wicklow, bringing its high-energy buzz to Glendalough and the Sally Gap. Book at Dublin Tourism (Map pp66–7) in St Andrew's Church, Suffolk St.

Carriage

Is there anything more romantic than a horse-drawn carriage clippity-clopping around the city centre? Now add the groups of drunken stag weekenders shouting at passers-by as the carriage driver laughs resignedly at their terrible jokes…you get the picture. Half-hour tours cost up to €60, but different length trips can be negotiated: fix a price *before* the driver says giddy-up. Carriages take four or five people and are found primarily at the top of Grafton St, by St Stephen's Green.

Musical

Dublin Musical Pub Crawl (Map p85; ☏ 478 0193; www .discoverdublin.com; 58-59 Fleet St; adult/student €12/10; ☏ tours 7.30pm daily Apr-Oct, 7.30pm Thu-Sat Nov-Mar) The story of Irish traditional music and its influence on contemporary styles is explained and demonstrated by two expert musicians in a number of Temple Bar pubs over 2½ hours. Tours meet upstairs in the Oliver St John Gogarty pub and are highly recommended.

Private Tours

Accredited guides can be contacted via the tourist board (☏ 602 4000). They cost an average of €100 per day for an English-speaking guide and €125 for other languages. A reputable firm that hires out guides is Meridien Tour Guides (Map pp66–7; ☏ 677 6336; 26 South Frederick St).

Walking

1916 Rebellion Walking Tour (Map pp66–7; ☏ 676 2493; www.1916rising.com; adult/child €10/free; ☏ tours 11.30am & 2.30pm Thu-Sat, 11.30am Tue-Wed, 1pm Sun Mar-Oct) The Easter Rising was the seminal event in the struggle to establish a modern nation, and this absolutely superb 1½-hour tour – starting in the International Bar, Wicklow St – tells it exactly as it was, with a decent sprinkling of humour and irreverence to boot. After all, what good are heroes if you can't poke some fun at them? The guides – all Trinity graduates – are uniformly excellent and will not say no to the offer of a pint back in the International at tour's end.

Dublin Footsteps Walking Tours (Map pp66–7; ☏ 496 0641; 78 Grafton St; adult €10; ☏ tours 10.30am Mon, Wed, Fri & Sat Jun-Sep) Literature and Georgian architecture are woven together on this two-hour tour that departs from the Bewley's Building on Grafton St and finishes at the Powerscourt Townhouse (where you get a complimentary cup of decent Italian coffee). It covers the lives and works of the big guns: Joyce, Wilde, Shaw and Yeats, as well as a host of others.

IWALKS

If you fancy a go-it-alone guided walk, why not download one of Pat Liddy's excellent iWalks (to subscribe, go to www.visitdublin.com/iwalks/iwalks .xml), which you can play on your ipod or equivalent mp3 player. All you have to do is subscribe to the podcasts at the above address (or search for them on itunes). There are a bunch of walks, from tours of the city's different districts to walks tailored to historical, architectural and activities themes.

Dublin Literary Pub Crawl (Map pp66–7; ☎ 454 0228; www.dublinpubcrawl.com; adult/student €12/10; ☺ tours 7.30pm daily year-round, noon Sun Apr-Nov, Thu-Sun Dec-Mar) A tour of pubs associated with famous Dublin writers is a sure-fire recipe for success, and this 2½-hour tour/performance by two actors – which includes them acting out the funny bits – is a riotous laugh. There's plenty of drink taken, which makes it all the more popular. It leaves from the Duke on Duke St; get there by 7pm to reserve a spot for the evening tour.

James Joyce Walking Tour (Map pp102–3; ☎ 878 8547; 35 North Great George's St; adult/student €10/9; ☺ tours 2pm Tue, Thu & Sat) Joyce lived, was schooled and lost his virginity on the north side – and he put it all down on paper with cartographical precision from his self-imposed continental exile. You can explore all of the north-side attractions associated with the bespectacled one on a 1¼-hour tour run by the James Joyce Centre (p108).

Pat Liddy Walking Tours (☎ 831 1109; www.walking tours.ie; adult/child/student €12/5/10) We highly recommend these award-winning themed tours of the city by well-known Dublin historian Pat Liddy, which include Viking & Medieval Dublin (10.30am Tuesday, Thursday and Sunday, 2.30pm Saturday), the Historic Northside (10.30am Wednesday and Friday) and Georgian and Victorian Splendours (10.30am Monday, 2.30pm Friday). All tours depart from Dublin Tourism (Map pp66–7) on Suffolk St. He also has a bunch of podcast walks available for download (see iWalks boxed text, opposite).

Zozimus Ghostly Experience (Map pp66–7; ☎ 661 8646; www.zozimus.com; adult €10; ☺ tours 9pm May-Oct, 7pm Nov-Apr) Departing from the gates of Dublin Castle, this is a theatrical and highly entertaining exploration of the ghoulish side of medieval Dublin. The costumed guide recounts stories of murders, great escapes and mythical events over the 1½-hour experience. You'll need to book in advance.

POST

The Irish postal service, An Post, is reliable, efficient and usually on time. Post boxes in Dublin are usually green and have two slots: one for 'Dublin only', the other for 'All Other Places'. Postal rates (priority/first class) are as follows:

Type	Ireland	Britain	Europe	Other
letter/postcard	€0.55	€0.78	€0.78	€0.78 (up to 100g)
package	€1.30	€2.85	€2.85	€2.85 (250g)
package	€5.70	€7.25	€7.25	€10.40 (1kg)

First-class payment should ensure next-day delivery within Dublin, and following-day delivery to country areas. Economy (second-class) rates are slightly cheaper, but delivery is considerably slower.

Mail can be addressed to poste restante at any post office; it's officially held for two weeks only. If you write 'hold for collection' on the envelope it *may* be kept for a longer period.

All mail to Britain and Europe goes by air, so there is no need to use airmail envelopes or stickers.

Post Offices

There are a couple of post offices in the city centre:

An Post (Map pp66–7; ☎ 705 8206; St Andrew's St; ☺ 8.30am-5pm Mon-Fri)

General Post Office (GPO; Map pp102–3; ☎ 705 7000; O'Connell St; ☺ 8am-8pm Mon-Sat, 10am-6.30pm Sun & holidays)

Postal Codes

Postal codes in Dublin (presented as 'Dublin + number') are fairly straightforward. Their main feature is that all odd numbers refer to areas north of the Liffey and all even ones to areas south of the Liffey. They fan out numerically from the city centre, so the city centre to the north of the river is Dublin 1 and its southern equivalent is Dublin 2.

RADIO

Radio na Telefís Éireann (RTE; www.rte.ie) is Ireland's government-sponsored national broadcasting body and runs four radio stations. Licensed, independent broadcasters are gradually filling up the airwaves, replacing the old pirate stations that are being perpetually closed down. Most stations now have an online live stream, so you can listen in before you get here. The following are the big FM players:

98FM (98FM; www.98fm.ie) A commercial music station playing a predictable range of popular tunes.

FM 104 (104.4FM; www.fm104.ie) Commercial radio playing Top 40 tunes almost exclusively.

Newstalk 106-108 (106-108FM; www.newstalk.ie) National news, current affairs and sport talk radio.

Phantom FM (105.2FM; www.phantom.ie) New alternative rock music station.

Q 102 (102.2FM; www.q102.ie) Strictly middle-of-the-road easy listening.

Radio Na Gaeltachta (92.6-94.4FM; www.rte.ie) A state-sponsored Irish-language station; culture, music and current affairs.

RTE Radio 1 (88-94FM; www.rte.ie) Culture, current affairs and music.

RTE Radio 2 (90.2-92.4FM; www.rte.ie) Commercial radio with some evening alternative shows.

Spin 103.8 (103.8FM; www.spin1038.com) Chart music and chat for 18-24 year-olds.

Today FM (100-102FM; www.todayfm.com) The biggest independent radio station, with music and current affairs.

Other smaller stations include the following:

Anna Livia (103.2FM) A community radio station that plays mostly alternative music.

Beaumount Hospital Radio (107.6FM) A light programming schedule of talk and music.

Dublin's Country (106.8FM) Banjos, slide guitars and doleful lyrics about 'momma'.

Dublin South FM (104.9FM) Community radio, only on from 4pm to 9pm.

Lyric FM (96-99FM) State-sponsored classical music radio.

Mater Hospital Radio (107.4FM) Community-based hospital radio.

Premier (92.6FM) Playing mostly hits from the '70s and '80s.

Radio na Liffe (106.4FM) Irish-language radio with the best and most wide-ranging music programmes on the airwaves.

SAFETY

Dublin is a safe city by any standards, except maybe those set by the Swiss. Basically, act as you would at home. However, certain parts of the city are pretty dodgy due to the presence of drug addicts and other questionable types, including north and northeast of Gardiner St and along parts of Dorset St, on the north side, and west along Thomas St, on the south side.

TELEPHONE

You shouldn't have any problems making phone calls to anyone, anywhere.

Prices are lower in the evening, after 6pm, and weekends. Phone calls from hotel rooms cost twice the standard rate. You can send and receive faxes from post offices (or most hotels). Local telephone calls from a public phone in Dublin cost €0.30 for around three minutes (around €0.60 to a mobile), regardless of when you call.

The number for local and national directory enquiries is ☎ 11811. For international it's ☎ 11818.

Pre-paid phonecards by Eircom and private operators are available in newsagencies and post offices, and work from all payphones. For cheap international phone calls, try the following phone centres:

Talk Is Cheap (Map pp102–3; ☎ 872 2235; 87 Capel St; ⊙ 9am-midnight)

Talk Is Cheap (Map pp102–3; ☎ 874 6013; 55 Moore St; ⊙ 9am-midnight)

Talk Shop (Map p85; ☎ 672 7212; www.talkshop.ie; 20 Temple Lane; ⊙ 9am-11pm)

Talk Shop (Map pp102–3; ☎ 872 0200; www.talkshop .ie; 5 Upper O'Connell St; ⊙ 9am-11pm)

Direct Home Call Codes

Instead of placing reverse-charge calls through the Dublin operator, you can dial direct to your home-country operator and then reverse the charges or charge the call to a local phone credit card. To use the home-direct service dial the codes listed here, the area code and, in most cases, the number you want. Your home-country operator will come on the line before the call goes through.

Australia (☎ 1800 550 061 + number)

France (☎ 1800 551 033 + number)

Italy (☎ 1800 550 039 + number)

New Zealand (☎ 1800 550 064 + number)

Spain (☎ 1800 550 034 + number)

UK – BT (☎ 1800 550 044 + number)

USA – AT&T (☎ 1800 550 000 + number)

USA – MCI (☎ 1800 551 001 + number)

USA – Sprint (☎ 1800 552 001 + number)

Mobile Phones

Virtually everyone in Dublin has a mobile phone. Ireland uses the GSM 900/1800 cellular phone system, which is compatible with European and Australian, but not North American or Japanese, phones.

There are four Irish service providers: Vodafone (087), O2 (086), Meteor (085) and 3 (083). All have links with most international GSM providers, which allow you to 'roam' onto a local service on arrival. This means you can use your mobile phone to text and make local calls, but you will be charged at the highest possible rate. You can also purchase a pay-as-you-go package (for around €70) with a local provider with your own mobile phone.

Phone Codes

The area code for Dublin is 01. When calling Dublin from abroad, dial your international access code, followed by 353 and 1 (dropping the 0 that precedes it). To make international calls from Dublin, first dial 00, then the country code, followed by the local area code and number.

TIME

In winter, Dublin (and the rest of Ireland) is on GMT, also known as Universal Time Coordinated (UTC), the same as Britain. In summer, the clock shifts to GMT plus one hour. When it's noon in Dublin in summer, it's 3am in Los Angeles and Vancouver, 7am in New York and Toronto, 1pm in Paris, 8pm in Singapore, and 10pm in Sydney.

TOILETS

Forget about the few public facilities on the street: they're dirty and usually overrun with drug dealers and addicts. All shopping centres have public toilets; if you're stranded, go into any bar or hotel.

TOURIST INFORMATION

You'll find everything you need to kick-start your visit at Dublin Tourism Centre (Map pp66–7; ☎ 605 7700; www.visitdublin.com; St Andrew's Church, 2 Suffolk St; ☼ 9am-7pm Mon-Sat, 10.30am-3pm Sun Jul & Aug, 9am-5.30pm Mon-Sat Sep-Jun). Besides general visitor information on Dublin and Ireland, there's also an accommodation booking service, a book and gift shop, an Amex bureau de change, a branch of Ticketmaster (for tickets to all major events in the city, including concerts), local and national bus information, rail information, a car-hire desk, tour information and bookings, and a café.

There are several other tourism centre branches throughout the city:

14 Upper O'Connell St (Map pp102–3; ☼ 9am-5pm Mon-Sat)

Baggot St Bridge (Map pp78–9; foyer of Fáilte Ireland office, Wilton Tce; ☼ 9am-5.15pm Mon-Fri)

Dublin Airport (Arrivals Hall; ☼ 8am-10pm)

Dun Laoghaire (Ferryport; ☼ 10am-1pm & 2-6pm Mon-Sat)

None of these tourist information offices will provide information over the phone – they are exclusively walk-in services. All telephone bookings and reservations are operated by Gulliver Ireland (www.gulliver.ie), which is a computerised information and reservation service available at all walk-in offices or from anywhere in the world. The service provides up-to-date information on events, attractions and transport, and also allows you to book accommodation. To access the service in Ireland, call ☎ 1800 668 668; from Britain, call ☎ 00800 6686 6866; from the rest of the world, call ☎ 00 353 669 792083.

For information on the rest of the country, call into the head office of Fáilte Ireland (Map pp78–9; ☎ 1850 230 330; www.ireland.travel.com; Wilton Tce, Baggot St Bridge; ☼ 9am-5.15pm Mon-Fri). Web-based tourist information on Dublin is available at the following sites:

Daft.ie (www.daft.ie) The best website for all kinds of house and flat rentals, including short-term leases.

Dublinks (www.dublinks.com) A catch-all website with info on things like shopping, parking, hotels, restaurants and other necessary titbits.

DublinTourist.com (www.dublintourist.com) An excellent and thorough guide to virtually every aspect of the city, from booking a room to going for a drink.

Lunch.ie (www.lunch.ie) Sponsored by Newstalk 106 and Dubliner magazine, this offers you the chance to get to know the city by being taken to lunch by a local stranger and then returning the favour quid pro quo: a new slant on 'there's no such thing as a free lunch'.

Pigsback.com (www.pigsback.com) Offers all kinds of city-wide discounts, from cinema tickets to free lunches.

Temple Bar (www.templebar.ie) Website dedicated to Dublin's cultural quarter.

TRAVELLERS WITH DISABILITIES

Despite the fact that many of the city's hotels, restaurants and sights are increasingly being adapted for people with disabilities, there's still a long way to go – especially as there still exists an attitude that can best be summarised as: 'if a problem comes up, we'll find a solution somehow'. Fáilte Ireland's annual accommodation guide, Be Our Guest, indicates which places are accessible by wheelchair. Public transport can be a nightmare, although a limited number of buses are now equipped with electronic elevators for wheelchairs, and nearly all DART stations have ramps and/or elevators.

The Access Service (Map pp102–3; ☎ 8747503; www.com hairle.ie; 44 North Great George's St), which is part of the Social Service Board (Comhairle), provides plenty of helpful information regarding Dublin's accessibility to wheelchairs.

Another useful organisation is the Irish Wheelchair Association (☎ 818 6400; Áras Chúchulain, Blackheath Dr, Clontarf, Dublin 3).

VISAS

UK nationals don't need a passport to visit Dublin, but are advised to carry one (or some other form of photo identification) to prove that they are a UK national. It's also necessary to have a passport or photo ID when changing travellers cheques or hiring a car. EU nationals can enter Ireland with either a passport or a national ID card.

Visitors from outside the EU will need a passport, which should remain valid for at least six months after their intended arrival.

For citizens of EU states and most Western countries, including Australia, Canada, New Zealand and the USA, no visa is required to visit either the Republic or Northern Ireland. Citizens of India, China and many African countries do need a visa for the Republic. Full visa requirements for visiting the Republic are available online at www.gov.ie/iveagh/services/visas.

EU nationals are allowed to stay indefinitely, while other visitors can usually remain for three to six months. To stay longer in the Republic, contact the local garda station or the Department of Foreign Affairs (Map pp66–7; ☎ 478 0822; www.gov.ie/iveagh; Iveagh House, 80 St Stephen's Green, Dublin 2).

Although you don't need an onward or return ticket to enter Ireland, it could help if there's any doubt that you have sufficient funds to support yourself while in Dublin.

WOMEN TRAVELLERS

Women travellers will probably find Dublin a blissfully relaxing experience, with little risk of hassle on the street or anywhere else. Nonetheless, you still need to take elementary safety precautions. Walking alone at night, especially in less salubrious parts of the city, and hitching are probably unwise. Report serious problems to the garda.

There's little need to worry about what you wear in Dublin; the climate will probably dictate your choice of clothing anyway. Finding contraception is not the problem it once was, although anyone on the pill should bring adequate supplies. For female health issues, including contraceptives and the morning-after pill (€39), contact the Well Woman Clinic (Map pp102–3; ☎ 661 0083; 35 Lower Liffey St); there's another office at Pembroke Road (Map p99; ☎ 660 9860; 67 Pembroke Rd).

In the unlikely event of a sexual assault, get in touch with the police and the Rape Crisis Centre (Map pp78–9; ☎ 1800 778 888, 661 4911; 70 Lower Leeson St).

WORK

Citizens of other EU countries are able to work legally in Dublin without a visa. Non-EU citizens require a work permit or work visa, although there is plenty of black-market labour about, especially in low-paying seasonal jobs in the tourist industry. Visiting full-time US students aged 18 and over can get a four-month work permit for Ireland through CIEE (☎ 617 247 0350; www.ciee.org; 2nd fl, 3 Copley Pl, Boston, MA 02116). Contact your local Irish embassy for more information. Work-related information can be found at the following:

Department of Enterprise, Trade & Employment (Map pp78–9; ☎ 631 2121; www.entemp.ie; Davitt House, 65a Adelaide Rd, Dublin 2)

Nixers.com (www.nixers.com) An excellent online resource listing jobs in Dublin.

Working Ireland (Map p85; ☎ 677 0300; www.workingireland.ie; 26 Eustace St; ☷ noon-6pm Mon-Fri) An excellent resource is this one-stop, state-funded help centre which, for €35 a year, will lay out your CV, set up interviews, help find accommodation, recommend language courses and offer discounts on tours and phone calls.

A large number of recruitment agencies in Dublin will locate work for non-nationals, whether they be travelling backpackers or long-term residents in Dublin. These include the following:

Brightwater Selection (Map pp78–9; ☎ 662 1000; 36 North Merrion Sq, Dublin 2)

Careers Register (Map pp78–9; ☎ 679 8900; 26 Lower Baggot St, Dublin 2)

Global Partnerships (Map pp78–9; ☎ 661 8740; 95 Lower Baggot St, Dublin 2)

Planet Recruitment (Map pp102–3; ☎ 874 9901; 21 Eden Quay, Dublin 1)

Reed Recruitment Agency (Map pp66–7; ☎ 670 4466; www.reed.ie; 47 Dawson St, Dublin 2)

BEHIND THE SCENES

THIS BOOK

This guidebook was commissioned in Lonely Planet's London office, and produced by the following:

Commissioning Editors Fiona Buchan, Janine Eberle, Clifton Wilkinson

Coordinating Editors Susie Ashworth, David Carroll

Coordinating Cartographer Malisa Plesa

Coordinating Layout Designer David Kemp

Managing Editor Geoff Howard

Senior Editor Sasha Baskett

Managing Cartographer Mark Griffiths

Managing Layout Designer Celia Wood

Assisting Editors Andrea Dobbin, Susannah Farfor, Charlotte Orr, Louisa Syme

Cover Designer Marika Mercer

Indexer Susan Paterson

Project Manager Chris Love

Thanks to Helen Christinis, Jennifer Garrett, Jim Hsu, Yvonne Kirk, Wayne Murphy, Trent Paton, Wibowo Rusli

Cover photographs Façade on St Stephen's Green North, Martin Moos/Lonely Planet Images (top & back); Beer taps at the Voodoo Lounge, Olivier Cirendini/Lonely Planet Images (bottom).

Internal photographs p7 (#1) Darryl Webb/Alamy; p8 (#2) Dennis Gilbert/VIEW Pictures Ltd/Alamy; p10 (#3) Karl Johaentges/LOOK Die Bildagentur der Fotografen GmbH/Alamy; p10 (#1) Alzbeta Bajgartova/Profimedia International s.r.o./Alamy; p6 (#2) Julian Herbert/Getty Images; p7 (#3) Costume; p9 (#1) JJ Smyth's. All other photographs by Lonely Planet Images, and by Doug McKinlay p2, p7 (#2), p8 (#1), p9 (#2); Eoin Clarke p4 (#2), p5 (#2); Hannah Levy p6 (#3); Holger Leue p3, p11 (#1); Jonathan Smith p5 (#1); Martin Moos p4 (#3), p5 (#3), p10 (#2); Olivier Cirendini p4 (#1), p6 (#1), p9 (#3), p12 (#1 & 3); Richard Cummins p8 (#3), p11 (#2), p12 (#2); Tony Wheeler p11 (#3).

All images are the copyright of the photographers unless otherwise indicated. Many of the images in this guide are available for licensing from Lonely Planet Images: www.lonelyplanetimages.com.

THANKS
FIONN DAVENPORT

Thanks to all the usual suspects, without which this book just wouldn't have happened. Helen James, Ger Gilroy, Marc Bereem and Niamh Kiernan were helpful and gracious with it – thanks a lot for contributing your thoughts to the book. At Lonely Planet, thanks to Fiona Buchan, Janine Eberle and then Cliff Wilkinson, who have all handled this particular hot spud during the term of the update. Thanks to Mark Griffiths and his carto crowd for all their work on the mapping.

THE LONELY PLANET STORY

Fresh from an epic journey across Europe, Asia and Australia in 1972, Tony and Maureen Wheeler sat at their kitchen table stapling together notes. The first Lonely Planet guidebook, Across Asia on the Cheap, was born.

Travellers snapped up the guides. Inspired by their success, the Wheelers began publishing books to Southeast Asia, India and beyond. Demand was prodigious, and the Wheelers expanded the business rapidly to keep up. Over the years, Lonely Planet extended its coverage to every country and into the virtual world via lonelyplanet.com and the Thorn Tree message board.

As Lonely Planet became a globally loved brand, Tony and Maureen received several offers for the company. But it wasn't until 2007 that they found a partner whom they trusted to remain true to the company's principles of travelling widely, treading lightly and giving sustainably. In October of that year, BBC Worldwide acquired a 75% share in the company, pledging to uphold Lonely Planet's commitment to independent travel, trustworthy advice and editorial independence.

Today, Lonely Planet has offices in Melbourne, London and Oakland, with over 500 staff members and 300 authors. Tony and Maureen are still actively involved with Lonely Planet. They're travelling more often than ever, and they're devoting their spare time to charitable projects. And the company is still driven by the philosophy of Across Asia on the Cheap: 'All you've got to do is decide to go and the hardest part is over. So go!'

OUR READERS

Many thanks to the travellers who used the last edition and wrote to us with helpful hints, useful advice and interesting anecdotes:

Sarah Beamish, Ron Broadfoot, Lorcan Cawley, Marcello Farioli, Jane Jakeman, John Moratiel, Sam Owens, Karen Piotrowski, Olli Salonen, Dennis Schenkel, Leonard Scuderi, Colette Smith, Elisabeth Thijssen, Ben Wilkinson and Jean-nette Van Eekelen.

ACKNOWLEDGMENTS

Dublin Transit Map © Iarnród Éireann 2006

SEND US YOUR FEEDBACK

We love to hear from travellers — your comments keep us on our toes and help make our books better. Our well-travelled team reads every word on what you loved or loathed about this book. Although we cannot reply individually to postal submissions, we always guarantee that your feedback goes straight to the appropriate authors, in time for the next edition. Each person who sends us information is thanked in the next edition — and the most useful submissions are rewarded with a free book.

To send us your updates — and find out about Lonely Planet events, newsletters and travel news — visit our award-winning website: www.lonelyplanet.com/contact.

Note: We may edit, reproduce and incorporate your comments in Lonely Planet products such as guide-books, websites and digital products, so let us know if you don't want your comments reproduced or your name acknowledged. For a copy of our privacy policy visit www.lonelyplanet.com/privacy.

Notes

INDEX

A

Abbey Theatre 41
accommodation 195-210,
 see also Sleeping *index*
 booking services 197
 costs 197
 self-catering 199
activities 188-94, *see also*
 Sports & Activities *index*
 Christmas Dip at the
  Forty-Foot 17
 Dublin City Marathon 19
 golf 189, 224, 227
 Liffey Swim 17
 Women's Mini-
  Marathon 18
Act of Union 27, 74
Ahern, Bertie 54
Aideen's Grave 215
air travel 228-9
Alcoholics Anonymous 235
All-Ireland Finals 17
ambulance 234
Anglo-Irish Treaty 28
Anglo-Normans, the 24
Anti-Catholic laws 26, 27
archaeology 75, 80-1, 95
architecture 47-53
 Anglo-Dutch 48, 96
 contemporary develop-
  ment 51-3
 Georgian 48-9, 71, 73,
  76, 77, 83, 226-7
 institutes 77-9

000 map pages
000 photographs

 medieval 48
 modern 50-1
 Regency & Victorian 50
archives 81
Ardagh Chalice 80
area codes *see inside front
 cover*
arts 32-47, 174-86
 bookings 174
 cinema 42-4, 178-9
 comedy 47, 177-8
 dance 47
 literature 33-7
 music 37-41, 179-84
 television 44-5
 theatre 41-2, 184-6
 visual arts 45-6
Asgard 96
ATMs 237
*A Portrait of the Artist as a
 Young Man* 34, 111

B

B&Bs 196
Bacon, Francis 45, 104, 105
Baily lighthouse 216
Banville, John 35
Barnacle, Nora 34
bars 159-72
bathrooms 243
Battle of Clontarf 29
Battle of the Boyne 92
Beatty, Alfred Chester 70
Beaux Walk 71
Beckett, Samuel 30, 34,
 41, 109
beer 160-1
Behan, Brendan 35, 41,
 109, 126
Berkeley, George 70
Berkeley Library 70, **8**
Beyond the Grand Canal 58,
 98-100, 99, **11**
 accommodation 204-6
 drinking 169-70
 food 155-6
 shopping 138-9
Beyond the Royal Canal
 117-20, **118**
 accommodation 208-10
 drinking 172
 food 158

bicycle travel 229
Binchy, Maeve 36
bird sanctuary 216
Black James 92
blind travellers 72
Bloody Sunday 29, 77, 118
Bloom, Leopold 30, 163,
 see also Ulysses
Bloom, Molly 34, *see
 also Ulysses*
Bloomsday 17, 34
Boardwalk, the 51
boat travel 229-30
Boer War 71
Bono, *see* U2
books 25, 36, *see also*
 literature
bookshops, *see* Shopping
 index
Book of Kells 64, 69, 71
Brú na Bóinne 214, 218-21
Bud Rising 17
Bulmer's Comedy
 Festival 18
business hours 233, *see also
 inside front cover*
 pubs 162
 restaurants 144
 shops 130
bus travel 230-1
Byrne, John 46

C

cafés, *see* Eating *index*
Cahill, Martin 224
Camaderry 223
Camaderry Mountain 223
carbon offsetting 21, 229
Carmilla 30
Carson, Edward 73
car travel 231-2
Casement, Sir Roger 118
Cassels, Richard 49, 68, 72,
 73, 76, 82, 111, 224, 225
castles, *see* Sights *index*
Castletown House 214,
 226-7
cathedrals, *see* Sights *index*
Catholic Church 27-8
Catholic University of
 Ireland 73
Cavendish, Lord 114

Celtic Revival Movement
 41, 46
cemeteries, *see* Sights *index*
Chambers, Sir William 49,
 104, 119
Charlemont, Earl of 119
chemists 237
Chester Beatty Library
 70-1, 150
Chieftains, the 38
children, travel with 233
 accommodation 200
 activities 72, 86, 114,
  116, 185, 186, 227
 baby-sitting 233
Christmas Dip at the Forty-
 Foot 17
Christ Church Cathedral 48,
 93, 94-5, **94**
churches, *see* Sights *index*
cinema 42-4, 177, 178-9
City Hall 76
Clarke, Derry 152
climate 16, 233, **233**
clubbing 174-7
coastguard 234
coffee 150
Collins Barracks 105
Collins, Michael 74, 96,
 107, 118
comedy 47, 177-8
Connolly, James 22, 24,
 75, 95
Conolly, William 226
Convergence Festival 17
costs 19-20, 144
 accommodation 197
 cinema 179
 clubs 175
 discount cards 234
 live music 181
 sports 192
 theatre 184
courses 234
crafts, *see* Shopping *index*
credit cards 237-8
Croke Park 117-18, 192, **6**
Cúchulainn 219
culture 2-3, 28
Curragh Racecourse 193
Custom House 107-8
customs regulations 234
cycling 229

000 map pages
000 photographs

INDEX

000 map pages
000 photographs